JOSEPH BANKS AND THE ENGLISH ENLIGHTENMENT
Useful Knowledge and Polite Culture

JOHN GASCOIGNE

School of History, University of New South Wales

CAMBRIDGE
UNIVERSITY PRESS

PUBLISHED BY THE PRESS SYNDICATE OF THE UNIVERSITY OF CAMBRIDGE
The Pitt Building, Trumpington Street, Cambridge, United Kingdom

CAMBRIDGE UNIVERSITY PRESS

The Edinburgh Building, Cambridge CB2 2RU, UK
40 West 20th Street, New York NY 10011–4211, USA
477 Williamstown Road, Port Melbourne, VIC 3207, Australia
Ruiz de Alarcón 13, 28014 Madrid, Spain
Dock House, The Waterfront, Cape Town 8001, South Africa

http://www.cambridge.org

First published 1994
First paperback edition 2003

A catalogue record for this book is available from the British Library

Library of Congress cataloguing in publication data
Gascoigne, John, Ph.D.
Joseph Banks and the English Enlightenment: useful knowledge
and polite culture / John Gascoigne.
    p.   cm.
Includes bibliographical references and index.
1. Science - Great Britain - History - 18th century. 2. Banks,
Joseph, Sir, 1743-1820 - Views on science. 3. Enlightenment -
Great Britain. 4. Great Britain - Intellectual life - 18th century.
I. Title.
Q127.G7G37   1994
508′.092-dc20
[B]   93-31696
                                                         CIP

ISBN 0 521 45077 2 hardback
ISBN 0 521 54211 1 paperback

For Kate

Contents

Illustrations

Acknowledgements

In pursuing Banks and his scattered remains around the globe I have incurred many debts. I am grateful in the first place to my own institution, the University of New South Wales, for providing travel funds which made possible research trips to New Zealand, the United States and the United Kingdom as well as the purchase of photocopies of manuscripts housed in distant archives. The project would have taken even longer to complete without a grant from the Australian Research Council which made possible a semester's release from teaching. An invitation to participate in a conference on 'Visions of Empire', organised by John Brewer and Simon Schaffer and generously sponsored by the Andrew Clark Library at the University of California, Los Angeles, provided both an opportunity to share my Banksian interests with fellow specialists and a further opportunity to work in American libraries. I am also grateful to my colleague, David Miller, for his comments on Chapter Six.

This book has depended on the willing co-operation of librarians at the many different libraries noted in the List of Abbreviations, who either provided me with photocopies or personally assisted me in my attempts to piece together the scattered Banksian archive. I would like to thank all these libraries and their staff. In particular I am grateful to the staff of the Mitchell Library, Sydney, the British Library, the Royal Society, Mr Clyde Janes and the staff of the Sutro Library, San Francisco, and to Mr Rex Banks, Director of Library Services, and the staff of the General and Botany Libraries at the British Museum of Natural History. I am indebted, too, to Mr H.B. Carter for permitting me to consult material in the Banks Archive at the British Museum of Natural History and for making available to me a number of welcome typescript transcripts of Banks's often gout-ridden handwriting. To my editor, Jean Cooney, I am indebted for her meticulous attention to my text and I owe Alan Walker my thanks for compiling the index with such a careful eye to detail.

For their support during the long gestation of this book and for sharing with me its pains and privileges I would like to thank my family. I am grateful to my father for uncomplainingly acting as a reader and commentator. My wife, Kate, and my children, Robert and Catherine, have had to listen to interminable references to Banks and to follow me around the world in pursuit of his papers. For their companionship, both at home and abroad, on my voyage in search of Joseph Banks I owe them much thanks.

Introduction

In his will Joseph Banks decreed that 'my body shall be interrd in the most private manner in the Church' and exhorted his family to remember that 'I earnestly request that they will not erect any Monument to my Memory'.[1] Posterity has followed the spirit of these injunctions with inappropriate fidelity. For a man who once bestrode the wide world of the late eighteenth and early nineteenth-century British Empire like a colossus, monuments to his presence in the past are few. His name may have been scattered around the world's geography and the botanical lexicon but for most he remains merely a name, since the historical record of the period on which he left such a deep imprint has little to say about his manifold activities. The image of Banks the long-lived President of the Royal Society, the *de facto* director of the Royal Gardens at Kew, the Privy Counsellor, the confidant of the king and the adviser to government on a whole host of scientific and imperial issues (including the addition of Australia to Britain's imperial possessions), can generally only be fleetingly and fragmentarily discerned in the accounts of his age. It is ironic, for example, that a man who left such a documentary treasure trove should not have been the subject of a biography until 1911,[2] a work reluctantly accepted by Bodley Head, after drastic abridgement, following twelve rejections by other publishers, who were not persuaded that there was much public interest in Banks.[3] A fully-researched biography of Banks did not appear until 1988.[4]

A number of considerations help to explain why Banks has received such scant attention. In the first place, the sheer bulk of his papers deterred some of the early would-be biographers who might have been able to draw more fully on contemporary recollections of Banks. Secondly, some of his descendants regarded this carefully constructed and catalogued collection as little more than a source of spare cash, with the result that much

1

of it was scattered about the globe and, in all too many cases, lost to scholarly scrutiny.[5] Together with such practical considerations the vagaries of historiographical fashion have played a role in consigning Banks to the shadows of the past. Though a scientific statesman of enormous significance, Banks's contribution to the store of published scientific disciplinary knowledge was slight. It was a point that the great Cuvier conceded in his éloge on Banks: that he published only a 'few sheets' and that 'their importance is not greatly superior to their extent'. However, Cuvier, who had experienced Banks's determination not to let Anglo-French hostility stand in the way of scientific progress, hastened to add that, despite such meagre publications, 'his name will shine with lustre in the history of the sciences'.[6] For Cuvier could recognise that science depends not only on its practitioners but also on its organisers and entrepreneurs–roles that Banks pioneered, shaping institutions and practices which were to become part of the established terrain of British science. Historians of science have been slower subsequently to acknowledge this and Banks has languished at the outer portals of the scientific pantheon because he added little to the scientific publications of his day. Moreover, historians of science, like historians generally, are naturally attracted to periods of dramatic change. Banks, however, embodied the old unreformed order, particularly in the world of scientific institutions. Studies of the Royal Society, then, have tended to bypass Banks, either by going back to the stirring beginnings of the Society in the late seventeenth century, or by focusing on the early nineteenth-century reformers for whom Banks and his institutional legacy represented what they regarded as being in need of change and revitalisation.

Banks, however, is too large an historical presence to be comfortably ignored. Of his many different activities his role in the foundation and maintenance of Australia as a European settlement has done most to keep his memory alive. In a nation in need of founding fathers Banks has rather intermittently played such a part. The most active promoter of Banks in such a role was J.H.Maiden, Government Botanist in New South Wales and Director of the Sydney Botanic Gardens from 1896 to 1924. The title of his book, *Sir Joseph Banks: The 'Father of Australia'* (1909), aptly conveys his conception of the role that Banks should play in Australia's historical consciousness. Thanks to Maiden's efforts, too, a memorial fund was established which, after many delays and misadventures, eventually produced two durable documentary monuments to Banks in the form of Beaglehole's authoritative edition of Banks's *Endeavour* journal and Carter's meticulous edition of Banks's sheep and wool correspondence. This fund was also among the sponsors of Lysaght's splendid edition of Banks's journal of his trip to Newfoundland and Labrador in 1766.

The persistence of the Banksian legacy in Australia and particularly in the Mitchell Library in Sydney (the repository of many of the Banks papers sold off by his descendants) helped to awaken the interest of Carter in Banks's work. His efforts, together with those of Dawson in compiling his monumental calendar of Banks's correspondence in British archives, have done much to undo the prodigal scattering of Banks's papers. Thanks to such work, the full extent and wonder of Banks's multifarious activities have become more apparent, and it has become possible to follow the rich and detailed documentary trail left by Banks. With the documentary base thus established, the first task-which Carter has recently brought to a full and authoritative fruition-was to establish a biographical record of Banks's life. But the vast archive generated by Banks, and now being edited for publication in the British Museum of Natural History under Carter's direction, lends itself to many other uses. Banks was so much at the centre of the scientific, institutional and imperial concerns of his day that his voluminous correspondence provides a way of understanding not only Banks himself, but also the broader currents of his age. The aim of this study, then, is not to provide a biography of Banks-a task already completed by Carter-but rather to relate Banks and his circle to some of the major movements of the period. Thus only Chapter One, 'Joseph Banks: A Biographical Sketch', devotes itself explicitly to a short account of Banks's career and character in order to provide some background for the contextual studies that follow.

In the body of the work, the connecting fabric which is used to give shape and direction to Banks's bewildering array of activities is the Enlightenment in its English guise-subject to the limitations dictated by Banks's personality, social position and political concerns. For in England-in contrast to France-enlightened opinion was, at least until the dark shadow of the French Revolution passed over the land, generally seen as providing a defence for the constituted order in Church and State. For one such as Banks, anxious to promote the improvement of his country and of its empire through the rational use of the study of Nature, the currents of thought associated with enlightened opinion provided a way of understanding the world and society which gave scope to rational and improving goals without threatening the social order of which he, as a broad-acred gentleman, was a beneficiary. However, as Chapter Two, 'The Limits of Enlightenment', attempts to show, such enlightened sentiments could be in tension with other social imperatives such as the maintenance of hierarchy or the advancement of empire.

Chapters Three and Four explore the way in which the cultural ideal of the virtuoso collector-the origins of which stretch back to the Renaissance-fused with the Enlightenment belief that the study of Nature should form part of the polite culture of the age. As the title of Chapter Three, 'From Virtuoso to Botanist', suggests, however, the cultural ideal of the virtuoso did not readily lend itself to the specialisation and rigour of such emerging scientific disciplines as botany, a transformation encapsulated in Banks's own career. For, though Banks demanded both of himself and his scientific clients the attention to system and order which characterised the beginnings of botany as a scientific discipline, as distinct from the more generalised pursuit of natural history, he never entirely lost the breadth of interest and delight in collecting which were legacies of the culture of the virtuoso. Like the virtuoso, too, Banks naturally coupled together the study of the human settlement of an area with an investigation of its flora and fauna, an attitude of mind which helped to stimulate his interest in the infant discipline of anthropology–hence the title of Chapter Four, 'From Antiquarian to Anthropologist'. His interest in anthropology also owed much to the Enlightenment's quest to extend the study of Nature and Nature's laws to human society and its laws. And the detailed observations of Banks and other Pacific explorers–including a number of Banks's later protégés–was to do much to promote this quest for a 'Science of Man'.

For Banks, as for the Enlightenment generally, science was above all applied science–a source of knowledge which could transform society for the benefit of humankind, lifting it above the bleak Hobbesian reality of life being 'nasty, brutish and short'. Just as the French Encyclopedists enlisted science in the quest to achieve what their mentor, Francis Bacon, had termed 'the relief of man's estate' so, too, Banks attempted, wherever possible, to apply science to the cause of increasing the yield and diversity of the earth and the products that could be derived from it, both within Britain and its Empire. The primacy of agriculture in this quest for what, in eighteenth-century Britain, was known as 'improvement' is reflected in the title of Chapter Five, 'The Principles and Practice of Improvement'. For, as this chapter attempts to show, the faith in the possibilities of improvement was first nurtured by agriculture and then extended to manufacture and eventually to the improvement of society more generally.

The last chapter, 'The Waning of the English Enlightenment', aims to show how many of the familiar landmarks of Banks's Enlightenment-tinctured cultural terrain were subject to increasing pressure around the beginning of the nineteenth century. In the first place, the annexation of enlightened rhetoric by many of the leaders of revolutionary opinion, both in France and elsewhere, shook the confidence of the English Establishment in the natural consonance between enlightened opinion and a defence of the established order in Church and State. Secondly, the growth of scientific specialisation challenged the way in which Banks conceived of science as being primarily a civilising and improving influence. Science might continue to serve such ends, but increasingly scientists were demanding that science's own needs for disciplinary specialisation and detailed research for its own sake, rather than for some hoped-for direct application, should be addressed. Banks's role in maintaining the Royal Society as a clubbable institution in which gentlemen of greatly varying scientific competence could learn and profit from the findings of their fellow members came under increasing attack. The Enlightenment view that science should be part of the polite culture of the age became harder to maintain in the face of increasing specialisation, while the belief that science was chiefly an agent for social improvement did not combine readily with a research ethic that pursued scientific truth as an end in itself. The death of Banks in 1820, then, symbolised the eclipse of many of the features of the enlightened culture of the eighteenth-century elite, which had helped to sustain and promote an interest in science and its diffusion but which was something of an obstacle in meeting the different scientific demands of the nineteenth century.

The theme of the Enlightenment and its limitations, therefore, provides a thread through much of the labyrinth of Banks's activities although there are many aspects of Banks's life and work which a book of this size has had to ignore. In particular, as Mackay has shown in his *In the Wake of Cook. Exploration, Science and Empire, 1780–1801* (1985), Banks did much to intertwine his scientific interests with the activities of government and, in particular, with its imperial policies–a field that this book barely touches on (though I hope to address it in a subsequent study). This role as a scientific adviser to the British State was a role well in keeping with the Enlightenment's confidence in the possibilities of rational government to reshape society to realise more fully the fruits of science and enlightened opinion.

CHAPTER ONE

Joseph Banks (1743–1820): A Biographical Sketch

PUBLIC LIFE

Like Francis Bacon, Banks's importance lies not in his own scientific contributions–which were few and slight–but rather in his ability to publicise the possibilities of science when linked with sympathetic patrons, particularly government. For, to Banks, science above all meant useful learning which could, as Bacon had put it, contribute to 'the relief of man's estate'. The origins of Banks's belief in the possibilities of science as an agent for improving the wealth of nations and the welfare of humankind more generally lie in the cultural ambience of his age and class rather than in the influence of any specific institution or individual–though the long-term influence of the Baconian tradition was doubtless an important, if imponderable, factor. Banks received little systematic scientific training at Harrow (1752–6), Eton (1756–60) and Christ Church, Oxford (1760–3), where he was educated in a manner fitting his social status as the heir to a considerable landed estate. However, these institutions exposed him to the values of a society where science, and rational discourse generally, were accorded respect as natural allies of the cause of true religion and sound government. Moreover, at Oxford particularly, Banks's wealth and status enabled him to pursue his own interests, including his early enthusiasm for natural history. In time-honoured fashion, too, these educational bastions of the Establishment laid the foundation for life-time friendships with men who would later open many useful doors, among them Lords Mulgrave and Auckland who greatly assisted Banks in his later endeavours to link science with the workings of government.

When Banks left Oxford in 1763 (his social position sparing him the tiresome necessity of having to take a degree), he could enter London society as a man of fortune in his own right since his father had died in 1761. Thus he succeeded to the Revesby estates which had been built up over the century by a line of Bankses who had an eye both to the possibilities of agricultural improvement and advantageous marriages. Banks carried on both traditions; his whole career, both in his capacity as a private landowner and as a scientific statesman, was characterised by zeal for the promotion of improvement and he had the prudence to marry an heiress, who brought with her an estate in Kent worth three thousand pounds a year. By 1807 it was said that he was worth fourteen thousand pounds a year, with eight thousand coming from the Revesby estate, three thousand from the Overton estate in Derbyshire (which he had inherited from his uncle, Robert Banks-Hodgkinson, in 1792) and three thousand from his wife's estate.[1] By the time of his death in 1820, his income had risen to around thirty thousand pounds per annum.[2] Thus had the Banks family, which had begun its rise with an earlier Joseph Banks (1665–1727), an attorney with a good eye to a profitable investment in land, ensconced itself in the landed oligarchy that largely determined the nation's affairs.

The young Banks's wealth enabled him to indulge his scientific interests and to establish the beginnings of his vast collection which eventually became the nucleus of the British Museum of Natural History. London society, with its many convivial clubs and opportunities for those with similar interests to gather together, helped to stimulate Banks's interests in science, antiquities and other learned pursuits. London also provided him with some of his scientific collaborators of whom far and away the most important was the genial Daniel Solander, whom Fanny Burney described in 1780 as being 'very sociable, full of talk, information, and entertainment . . . a philosophical gossip'.[3] This Swedish botanist greatly strengthened Banks's links with the system and methods of Linnaeus, Solander's teacher, and it was Banks's confidence that Linnaeus's system offered a guiding thread through the labyrinths of nature which helped to give his earlier investigations into natural history direction and focus. His youthful interests were also given a disciplined and systematic form through his experience as a scientific observer on board HMS *Niger* on its expedition to Newfoundland and Labrador in 1766, a voyage prompted by Britain's recent victory over the French in Canada. Banks's presence on board was made possible by his long-standing friendship with Constantine Phipps (later Lord Mulgrave) who served on board the *Niger* under its commander, Sir Thomas Adams.

The experience thus acquired was in turn to serve Banks well when he undertook his epochal voyage on board the *Endeavour* from 1768 to 1771 – a voyage that catapulted him to prominence among natural historians both within Britain and in Europe more generally. The attention that the *Endeavour* voyage brought him also laid the foundation for his long friendship with George III, which was to do so much to enable Banks to incorporate his scientific projects into the fabric of government. Indeed, within two years of the return of the *Endeavour*, he was made virtual director of the Royal Gardens at Kew–an institution which, under Banks, began its long career as a forcing-house for turning the fruits of botanical exploration to imperial advantage.

However, the adulation that Banks received in the wake of the *Endeavour* voyage, which in some ways exceeded that accorded to Cook himself, appears to have given him rather too high an estimate of his importance. For in 1772 he was to discover that the Royal Navy–always suspicious of civilian involvement–drew the line at his attempt to reshape the character of Cook's second great Pacific voyage in order better to accommodate the needs of himself and his large party. Hence the complaint of the Navy Board to the First Lord of the Admiralty that 'Mr Banks seems throughout to consider the Ships as fitted out wholly for his use; the whole undertaking to depend on him and his people; and himself as the Director and Conductor of the whole; for which he is not qualified and if granted to him would have been the greatest Disgrace that could be put on His Majesty's Naval Officers'.[4] And on this occasion the First Lord of the Admiralty, the Earl of Sandwich, who had done so much to facilitate Banks's inclusion on the *Endeavour* voyage, sided with the Navy.

After withdrawing from the *Resolution* voyage in high dudgeon, Banks occupied the second half of 1772 with an expedition to Iceland. The trip was occasioned both by his desire to provide employment for his followers who had loyally stood by him during the *Resolution* fiasco, and by a wish to explore an island which (as he himself put it) 'had been visited but seldom & never at all by any good naturalist to my knowledge'.[5] It was a voyage that laid the foundation for Banks's continuing interest in the affairs of that island, which ultimately bore fruit in his successful intervention with government during the Napoleonic War to remove the naval blockade of the island (a dependency of Denmark which was allied to France), which threatened to result in the mass starvation of the Icelandic people. The voyage to Iceland was, however, a poor substitute for the great Pacific voyage which Banks had to forgo because of his lack of diplomacy in dealing with the Navy. His journal of the voyage reflects something of this disappointment with the last entry listlessly recording 'Idle Tird resolve to go away fair or foul'.[6] And, despite various plans that Banks entertained for other scientific voyages, the Iceland voyage was to prove his last. It was, indeed, his last trip outside England apart from a brief visit to Holland in the following year.

The three overseas voyages–to Newfoundland, to the Pacific and to Iceland–together with a number of excursions within Britain, ensured for Banks a position as one of the country's foremost naturalists. The hoped-for scientific publications from these voyages, and above all from the *Endeavour* voyage, did not materialise in Banks's lifetime, though the riches he had accumulated were available to the scientific world in his home-cum-research institute at Soho Square. The voyages also created a tradition of linking scientific research with naval exploration which Banks did much to perpetuate–thus laying the groundwork for such nineteenth-century expeditions as the *Beagle*, the *Rattlesnake* and the *Commander*. More and more, however, the hitherto itinerant Banks redirected the focus of his scientific energies away from collecting in the field to promoting the public uses of science.

The most obvious institution for such ends was the Royal Society of which Banks had become a fellow in 1766 having earned his early scientific spurs with the voyage to Newfoundland. After his return from Iceland in 1772 Banks devoted himself more actively to the affairs of the Society, becoming a member of the Council in 1774. When Sir John Pringle resigned as President in 1778 Banks was a natural successor, largely because of his good relations with the king, with whom his predecessor had clashed politically in the heated atmosphere generated by the war with the American colonies.[7] During the election there were some indications of the split between the followers of the natural and the physical sciences which was to mar Banks's early presidency, for Pringle made it apparent that he favoured Alexander Aubert, governor of the London Assurance Company and a keen astronomer, as his successor.[8] However, in the absence of a suitable nobleman Banks was, as the naturalist, the Reverend Sir John Cullum, put it, 'elected unanimously to appearance by 220 votes'.[9] Along with his election as President another indication that Banks's travelling days were behind him was that in the following year finally, at the age of thirty-six, he bowed to social convention by marrying a suitably broad-acred bride.

Banks's position as President of the Royal Society was the hub around which his other public functions revolved and it gave him a distinction which lifted him out of the ranks of other country squires to the position of a confidant of the king and his ministers. Accordingly its duties received the first claim among Banks's multifarious activities: despite the gout that blighted his later life Banks presided at 417 of the 450 Council meetings held while he was in office.[10] But, although he was to be the Society's longest-serving president, he faced much opposition in the years soon after he took up office.

Such opposition derived from a number of sources. Firstly, Banks was young and therefore, no doubt, in the eyes of his opponents inexperienced– whereas previous presidents had usually been aged between forty-five and sixty-five, Banks was a mere thirty-five when he was elected.[11] Secondly, and more significantly, he was a naturalist in a Society the presiding deity of which was Newton, the greatest of mathematical scientists. Moreover, Banks had published nothing at the time of his election and added little to the *Philosophical Transactions* or, indeed, any other scientific journal thereafter. Such considerations had not prevented his election by an overwhelming margin but they exacerbated the ill-feeling generated by his early attempts to exert his authority over the Society and its affairs. In particular, Banks incurred the enmity of the existing office-holders when he attempted to curb their authority and to reshape the Society's administration. The Secretaries, for example, had hitherto enjoyed the right to nominate new fellows with the expectation that they would be elected unopposed–Banks, however, let it be known that any such candidates he considered unsuitable would be opposed.[12] It was later alleged, too, that Banks judged candidates not only on their scientific worth but also on their social standing, and that some candidates nominated for their abilities in the mathematical sciences were rejected because they were of humble birth. Since its foundation the Royal Society had been at pains to seek the support of well-born patrons who could provide it with both financial and political support and Banks appears to have seen himself as carrying on this tradition. Thus Kippis, in his *Observations on the Late Contests in the Royal Society* (1784), described the Society as consisting of three categories: 'the real philosophers', 'the men of general literature' and 'the nobility, and gentlemen of rank and fortune'. Writing of this last group, Kippis defended their 'numerous introduction . . . into the Society' under Banks on the grounds that 'They give as well as receive honour; and their contributions serve to carry on the valuable purposes of the Society. They stand forth as the patrons of philosophical knowledge, and have means of promoting it, which do not fall to the lot of common individuals'.[13]

These underlying tensions began to surface in 1783 as Banks became more assertive in his dealings with the Society's Secretaries, Paul Maty and Joseph Planta, and also its Foreign Secretary (or, as the office was then officially termed, the Assistant to the Secretaries), Charles Hutton.[14] In April 1783 Banks's attempt to persuade Planta, Secretary of the Society, of the need to revise the rules governing publication of papers presented to the Society resulted in an acrimonious exchange. This culminated in Banks's refusal to enter into any more correspondence with Planta, leaving it to the Council to 'answer the charge of arbitrary injustice'.[15] As a Secretary to the Society since 1776 and Assistant Librarian at the British Museum since 1773, Planta was not without allies. By September Blagden, who was to act as Banks's eyes and ears in the Royal Society disputes of 1783–4, reported to Banks 'that Mr. Planta has been going about this summer among his friends, especially of the Society, complaining of the ill treatment he received from you & the Council, & shewing his correspondence with you as a proof'.[16]

Banks, however, was not to be deterred in his quest to reform the Society's internal administration, his next target being the office of Foreign Secretary which, since January 1779, had been filled by Dr Charles Hutton, Professor of Mathematics at the Royal Military Academy at Woolwich. Banks's discontent with Hutton had been evident as early as January 1782 when the Council established a committee 'to determine accurately the duties of the Foreign Secretary' on the grounds that it had 'been represented to the Council that the Foreign Correspondence was not carried on with sufficient punctuality'. Hutton swallowed his pride sufficiently to accept the recommendations of the committee when it reported in April 1782 but plainly Banks and the Council were determined to oust him: for, on 20 November 1783, the Council resolved 'that it would be for the benefit of the Society, that the business of the Foreign Secretary be done by a person constantly residing in London'[17]–an impossible condition for Hutton with his post at Woolwich. Not surprisingly, this rather high-handed way of depriving Hutton of the post caused much disquiet within the Society and, despite Banks's opposition, a motion of thanks to Hutton for his services to the Society was carried in December 1783.

Scenting weakness–since this motion of thanks had been carried in the face of Banks's attempts to prevent it–a number of Fellows, led by that great exemplar of the Church militant, the Reverend Samuel Horsley, staged a more thoroughgoing attack on Banks's administration of the Society. In the pamphlet war that followed Banks was accused of neglecting the mathematical sciences, of being a scientific non-entity, of favouring well-born candidates, of stacking the Council with his supporters and generally 'of taking away the privilege of the body at large, and making himself the sole master of the admissions, in other words, the *Monarch* of the Society'.[18] Banks dealt with such charges with Olympian disdain– so much so that the politically more acute Blagden reproved him, writing in late December 1783 that 'Several have said that you neglect this business too much, by remaining out of the way, whilst your opponents are stirring so actively in town'.[19] Banks, however, maintained his aloofness replying with some *hauteur* to Blagden that 'it is a matter of glory to me to be President of the Royal Society but I am too independent even for a Salary to accept the place of Chairman among debaters'.[20] Meanwhile, Banks's enemies were mobilising under the leadership of Horsley who, as editor of Newton's scientific works, saw himself as the leader of the Society's ill-used mathematicians. 'Horsley', wrote Blagden on 30 December, 'pretends to have received information that you are to move for his expulsion at the next meeting of the Society, and gives it as a motive for his friends to come down'.[21]

In the event, however, Banks's opponents found themselves greatly outnumbered. When, in January 1784, a motion of confidence in Banks was moved, it was passed by 119 to 42. An attempt to reinstate Hutton was also defeated, albeit by the slimmer margin of 85 to 47. In the following month two motions reflecting discontent with Banks's style of presidency were also defeated. Both attempted to rule it out as 'highly indecent and improper' for the President 'to avail himself of his situation to influence the vote of any officer of the Society' or to 'solicit votes either for or against any person, duly recommended by certificate as qualified to be made a Fellow of the Royal Society'.[22] Yet another sally at Banks in March resulted in the resignation of another Secretary, Paul Maty, a long-standing supporter of Hutton. In the following month he was replaced by Blagden, despite Horsley's characteristically rebarbative attempt to have Hutton elected. Indeed, Horsley's incendiary style probably did much to alienate support from the dissenting cause and thus ironically may have helped Banks. Kippis, who claimed to be neutral in the dispute, wrote of Horsley as adopting a 'high tone ... [which] went beyond the usual custom of public debates'.[23]

The election of Blagden in the place of Maty greatly strengthened Banks's position and largely brought to an end the public attacks on his presidency.[24] By June news of Banks's victory in the Royal Society disputes had even reached Brussels, with the Abbé Mann writing to congratulate Banks on the fact 'that the late troubles in the Royal Society are nearly quelled'. Mann added that 'They have made a good deal of noise on the Continent' and commented on 'the extraordinary animosity' of Banks's opponents.[25] Despite the fact that Benjamin Franklin had been among the most prominent of the American rebels, Banks also shared with him his relief at the suspension of hostilities within the Royal Society. In November 1784 he expressed the hope to Franklin 'that the dissensions of the Royal Society are at an end at least that the opposition will at last give way to the decided & continual majorities which have appeard against them'. Hutton he dismissed as a man who 'did not like to lose twenty pounds a year which he used to receive without any trouble whatever'. More plausibly he characterised Horsley as being 'glad to make himself President which I am convinced he thought to[o] easy & considered as a good step towards a Bishoprick'.[26] Two years later, Banks again wrote to Franklin to rejoice at the fact 'that the most perfect harmony has now taken place of the dissention with which the Royal Society was for a short time disturbd'.[27]

Part of the credit for the restoration of order lay with Banks himself for, though he had fanned the flames of the dispute with his maladroit treatment of Hutton, he acted with greater delicacy in preventing any semblance of a vendetta against the losing party after Horsley quit the Society following his defeat. Thereafter Banks never again faced such open opposition despite continued murmuring from the followers of the mathematical sciences that the Society was too much dominated by genteel practitioners of natural history. Banks continued to claim the right to a close personal scrutiny of intending Fellows but this appears to have become accepted as standard practice. When, in 1805, Bishop Goodenough, the Vice-President of the Linnean Society, explained to a friend 'The usual steps taken to be introduced into the Royal Society', he began by emphasising the necessity of being 'introduced to Sir Joseph Banks-this must be done either personally or through some common friends who can personally communicate with Sir Joseph, explain to him from their own knowledge all particulars relating to him-his *profession*-his *demeanour*-his *abilities*-It is in vain to make the attempt, unless Sir Joseph be first satisfied about him. Sir Joseph's thumb will be heavier than it will be in his power to remove'. Among the enquiries that Goodenough listed as customary on Banks's part was whether the candidate was 'by no means troublesome or factious'-a concern which may well have derived from Banks's unhappy experiences in 1783-4. 'When Sir Joseph is satisfied', added Goodenough, 'nothing but mere form remains afterwards'.[28]

Plainly, Banks was undisputed master of the Royal Society but the accusation levelled by his critics during the disputes of 1783-4 and, after his death, by Humphry Davy that he stacked the Council with his supporters–or, as Davy wrote, that 'In his relations to the Royal Society he was too personal and made his circle too like a court'[29]–has been disposed of by Lyons through a careful examination of the Council minutes.[30] For Banks's continual re-election to the Presidency can only be explained by the good will and respect of a substantial majority of the fellows most of whom were, like him, largely independent gentlemen not easily browbeaten into submission or dragooned into supporting an individual they disliked. When Banks, weighed down by years and gout, attempted in May 1820, the month before his death, to lay down the office he had held for so long the Society's Council paid him a last and unanimous tribute by refusing his resignation and 'with one voice express[ing] their most ardent wishes that the president should not withdraw from the Chair of the Society which he has filled so ably and honourably during a period of forty two years'.[31] Even allowing for the natural hyperbole of such an occasion and the Council's knowledge that Banks would soon vacate the post through death, if not resignation, it is a tribute that he earned through his many years of tireless devotion to what he considered were the best interests of the Society–even if, as Chapter Six argues, his longevity had the effect of postponing the Society's reform to meet the changed needs of the nineteenth century.

Banks's position as President of the Royal Society made him a natural source of advice to government on matters related to science. The problems of agriculture and the need to foster new crops, both at home and abroad, led to his being consulted by a number of government agencies– and, in particular, the committee of the Privy Council concerned with trade–together with institutions such as the East India Company that were more and more being absorbed into the apparatus of government. Banks's role as an adviser to government was eventually given formal recognition in 1797 with his elevation to the Privy Council, where he served both as a member of the committee on trade and the committee on coin. Like Newton before him, then, Banks combined direction of the Royal Society with scrutiny of the affairs of the Mint and, at the Board of Trade, he attempted to add to the nation's wealth and security by fostering the growth of basic materials in areas of the globe which were under British control. As Banks's standing in government circles grew his advice was also sought on matters only tangentially related to his scientific competence. His role in the promotion and maintenance of Australia as a European settlement began in 1779, when he urged the suitability of Botany Bay as a dumping-ground for convicts before a committee of the House of Commons. Thereafter Banks continued to act as the infant colony's main advocate within the British government and played a major role in choosing its governors, in promoting voyages of exploration to determine its nature and extent, and in shaping its overall destiny.

Along with the Royal Society, Banks was also involved in a number of other scientific bodies which impinged on the affairs of government. His position as President of the Royal Society brought with it the responsibility of helping to oversee the affairs of the Board of Longitude and the Royal Greenwich Observatory. He was actively involved, too, in aiding the Board of Agriculture which was founded in 1793 with a constitution based on that of the Royal Society, though with more direct links with government. Banks was also prominent among those who, in 1788, established the African Association which sponsored a series of generally ill-fated expeditions which, nonetheless, greatly enhanced British interest in Africa and helped pave the way for eventual British colonial involvement in West Africa.

Banks's role as a member of the Privy Council began to fade after 1804 with the eclipse of his old colleague, the first Earl of Liverpool. He had served under Liverpool since the latter had become the first President of the Privy Council Committee on Trade in 1786 and maintained cordial relations with him until his death in 1808. But Banks remained at home in the world of Westminster and Whitehall: in 1819, a year before his death, he was appointed chairman to two committees established by the House of Commons, the first to enquire into ways of preventing the forgery of banknotes and the second to consider systems of weights and measures. Until his death in 1820, too, he kept a firm hand on the Royal Society's tiller and continued to steer the Royal Gardens at Kew along channels which were likely to enhance Britain's scientific and commercial standing.

PERSONALITY AND PRIVATE LIFE

So much, then, by way of a very brief summary of the diverse and multifarious public career of Banks. If, however, we want to enquire what manner of man he was, we are confronted by the irony that, for all the great mound of correspondence and memoranda that Banks bequeathed to posterity, we have few records of his private life. For Banks's vast correspondence–with inward and outward letters probably totalling between fifty and one hundred thousand items[32] (though many of these are no longer extant)–is very largely that of a public man, almost at times that of a virtual department of government, and so is nearly devoid of personal allusions. We come closest to Banks as an individual in the journals of his early travels, written before the cares of public office descended upon him–though even in these there is little account of his emotions. These journals are the record of a young man of great curiosity with a zest for discovering and recording the new and the curious. Not only did he delight in the hitherto unrecorded flora and fauna which he encountered in his travels but he also sought out as much information as possible about the human societies he encountered in his travels. This was particularly true in Tahiti where the *Endeavour*'s long stay enabled him to get to know both the people and their language. His account in his *Endeavour* journal displays a remarkable eagerness to learn from the native people and, with it, a lack of Eurocentric superiority or condescension. His thirst for new encounters and impressions even extended to the painful experience of having himself tattooed in the Tahitian manner.

The young Banks was, however, a man very used to having his own way, who had to learn by bitter experience the necessity of winning over allies and moderating his demands. This comes out most clearly in the behaviour which resulted in his withdrawal from the *Resolution* expedition in 1772. Here he overreached himself both by demanding that his own needs and those of his scientific party determine the type of vessel employed, and by attempting to outface the First Lord of the Admiralty in public controversy. Something of this youthful wilfulness and even petulance comes out in the account of John Elliott, a midshipman on the *Resolution*, of Banks's reaction when it became evident that it was impossible to combine seaworthiness with the changes he had demanded to the shape and capacity of the *Resolution*. 'Mr. Banks', he wrote, 'came to Sheerness, and when he saw the Ship, and the Alterations that were made, He *swore* & *stamp'd* upon the *Wharf*, like a *Mad Man*; and instantly order'd his Servants, and all his things out of the Ship'. But, concluded Elliott,

> it has always been thought, that it was a most fortunate circumstance for the purposes of the voyage, that Mr. Banks did not go with us; for a more proud, haught[y], Man could not well be, and all his plans seem'd directed to shew his own greatness; which would have accorded very Ill, with the *discipline* of a *Man of War*, and been the means of causing many quarrels in all parts of the Ship.[33]

In more muted language even one of Banks's fellow naturalists delivered a similar judgement on his behaviour in the *Resolution* affair. When writing to Gilbert White, William Sheffield expressed both his disappointment as a naturalist that Banks and Solander had not been included on the voyage and his conviction that 'I fear they have been high & peremptory in their demands'.[34]

In his private life, too, the young Banks appears to have been impatient of interference, which probably accounts for the fact that he did not marry until 1779 at the age of thirty-six. His early letters to his old school friend, William Perrin, display a wariness of matrimony and its commitments. In November 1767 he spoke cautiously of marriage as a 'State from whence I may sometime enjoy true happiness tho not I can assure you till I am unhappy without it'. Banks added that 'as well as I love experiment' he did not do so sufficiently to imperil 'my own happiness'.[35] A few months later he was still cautious of the married state, telling Perrin in February 1768 that 'Matrimony never would have come under my dispraise but from its uncertain consequences. [H]ow many instances both you & I know of the happiness of the state lasting for weeks months nay years in uninterrupted pleasures but how few have lasted lives'.[36] They are unlikely sentiments for a young man who, around this time, was linked romantically with one Harriet Blosset (whose parents were friends of Solander and James Lee of the Vineyard Nursery at Hammersmith)[37] and help to explain why the attachment did not lead to marriage. Whether there was a formal engagement between Banks and Blosset is doubtful but there is evidence that there was some sort of understanding between them. The Swiss geologist, Horace de Saussure, records that while in London in August 1768 at the time when Banks was getting ready to depart on the *Endeavour* expedition, he 'Saw for the first time Miss Harriet Blosset, with Mr. Banks, her betrothed'. He writes of Miss Blosset as being 'desperately in love with Mr. Banks, from whom she was to part next day–hitherto a prudent coquette, but now only intent on pleasing her lover, and resolved to spend in the country all the time he is away'. And, indeed, according to the society gossips of the time, Harriet Blosset spent the three years that Banks was away in seclusion whiling away the time making 'worked waistcoats' for her absent beau.[38]

On his return Banks broke off the attachment on the grounds that 'he was of too volatile a temper to marry' even though, according to the naturalist, Daines Barrington, 'he admits he gave Miss Bl[osset] the strongest reason to expect he would return her husband'.[39] In due course, however, Blosset, having received a large settlement from Banks, was 'extremely well married to a virtuous clergyman'[40]–a very considerable change from the young Banks who, for all his other good qualities, was neither very virtuous nor religious. Much of the Blosset family's wrath was directed at Solander since he appears to have played a role not only in bringing the two together, but also in persuading Banks to break off the attachment.[41] Perhaps the bachelor, Solander, regarded such a marriage as an intrusion into their scientific partnership or perhaps over the long voyage he had come to know Banks sufficiently to realise that he was unsuited to Miss Blosset, or even possibly, at that stage, to the married state in general. In any event Banks found female companionship in a series of liaisons which–to the best of our knowledge–were terminated after he eventually dutifully accepted his social responsibilities and married a broad-acred heiress, Dorothea Hugessen, whom he met through relatives of his aunt, Bridget Banks-Hodgkinson.[42]

Banks's marriage in 1779 and his election the previous year as President of the Royal Society mark the watershed in his life between the youthful adventurer and the public man, shouldering the responsibilities that fell to him because of his social position and scientific standing. This increasing prominence on the public stage led in time to an appreciation of the need to conciliate others, though Banks always retained a strong will and was not lightly diverted from what he felt was the proper course of action. It took time, however, for him to learn the need for tact and diplomacy, and the dissensions of 1783-4 in the Royal Society appear to have been inflamed by his rather heavy-handed style. Hence the accusations that 'The president is incurably sick with the lust of domination' and that 'he imagines himself born to rule'.[43] But Banks appears to have learnt from such experiences and his ability to work with so many different men and institutions is an indication that he learnt the skills of compromise and persuasion. His letters, which largely date from the 1780s onwards, are those of a man with definite views but they are almost uniformly courteous; it took a very high degree of impertinence or obstinacy to provoke Banks into anger.[44] Generally, too, they seek to win over the reader by argument rather than by assertion, though Banks could adopt a firm tone, especially when dealing with inferiors.

Banks could be friends with men of all sorts and conditions, but still he had a strong sense of social rank. In particular, though his own family had crossed the divide from the professional classes to the Elysian fields of the landed gentry at the beginning of the eighteenth century, Banks was a strong defender of the dignity and importance of the landed classes. The attempt, for example, by a banker to have himself elected as a Member of Parliament for Lincolnshire in 1807 moved Banks to contrast in verse the ancient virtues of the landed interest as opposed to those who lived by trade. In his 'Questions for a Lincoln Candidate' he proclaimed that

> A Shire should send Knights of respect
> Knights girded with Sword & with Rapier
> & not like a Borough, elect
> A dealer & chapman in paper.

In an accompanying set of verses (one hesitates to call it a poem) entitled 'The Beam', Banks described the world of commerce in even more derogatory tones:

> Who can expand a narrow mind
> While toiling after wordly pelf,
> To generous views it must be blind,
> Else it can nere enrich itself.[45]

The attempt by Sir John Sinclair, the founder of the Board of Agriculture, to raise a subscription in his own favour offended Banks's sense of the proper conduct of members of the landed classes, prompting him to write that he thought it 'a disparagement for a Gentleman of Blood & Coatarmour to ask money for himself on any terms but that of a loan'.[46]

But along with Banks's views about the high dignity of the landed estate went an equally strong sense of the duty of its members to put their leisure and wealth at the service of the public. Banks conveyed something of this sense of duty when explaining why he adopted the figure of a lizard as part of his crest: 'I have taken the Lizard, an Animal said to be Endowed by nature with an instinctive Love of mankind, as my Device, & have causd it to be Engraved as my Seal, as a Perpetual Remembrance, that a man is never so well employd, as when he is Laboring for the advantage of the Public; without the Expectation, the hope or Even a wish to Derive advantage of any kind, from the Result of his Exertions'.[47] Those who put security or self before what he conceived of as their public or scientific duty received the full blast of Banksian contempt. When the young Hooker expressed reservations about the wisdom of conducting a botanical expedition to Java because of the high death-rate of Europeans there,

Banks retorted that he seemed to wish 'to adopt Sardinopolis's advice to his citizens to Eat drink & propagate ... I was about 23 when I began my Peregrinations you are somewhat older but you may be assured that if I had Listend to a multitude of voices that were Raisd up to dissuade me from my Enterprise I should have been now a Quiet countrey Gentleman ignorant of a multitude of matters I am now acquainted with & probably have attained to no higher rank in Life than that of a countrey Justice of the Peace'.[48]

With this sense of duty went a sort of stoicism about the pains that he or others might have to bear in the pursuit of public duty. The mounting anguish felt by Flinders and his wife at Banks's vain efforts to secure Flinders' release as a French prisoner of war was answered by Banks with cold philosophy. '[H]is Present Misfortune', he wrote to Mrs Flinders in 1804, 'is one of the calamities of war which you & I must bear with as much patience as we can muster'.[49] In the previous year, when others had objected that Mungo Park's proposed second expedition to Africa would be too dangerous, Banks responded in Roman fashion by placing duty to one's country before the safety of the individual:

> I am aware that Mr Park's expedition is one of the most hazardous a man can undertake; but I cannot agree with those who think it too hazardous to be attempted: it is by similar hazards of human life alone that we can hope to penetrate the obscurity of the internal face of Africa.[50]

Park duly died in the service of the British Empire. More personal misfortunes Banks also regarded as no excuse for shirking one's duty. In a letter of condolence to a relative who had lost his wife, Banks combined sympathy with a call to duty by asserting his confidence that 'your Efforts against useless & unavailing melancholy will be vigorous & unceasing: that there is a pleasure in the indulgence of Sorrow I am ready to admit, but like the forbidden fruit of Paradise it is a kind of Pleasure which no man who wishes well to himself his Family, or his Countrey, can be justified in indulging'.[51] Banks followed his own precepts by, for example, not letting the agonies of gout-which blighted his life from 1787 onwards[52]-stand in the way of his performance of a multitude of public duties. As George Suttor, an early Australian settler and one of Banks's clients, wrote: though Banks was a sufferer from the gout 'he was thought to possess some of the store of philosophy, and bore his troubles with admirable patience'.[53]

Not surprisingly, then, Banks was a strident critic of what he saw as oversentimentality or squeamishness in the course of duty-even in cases which some of his contemporaries regarded as requiring mercy and humanity. Governor King of New South Wales was rebuked by Banks in 1804 for his 'frequent reprieves' of convicts condemned to death. 'I would have justice,' wrote Banks sternly,

in the case of those under your command who have already forfeited their lives and
been once admitted to a commutation of punishment, to be certain and inflexible,
and no-one case on record where mere mercy, which is a deceiving sentiment, should
be permitted to move your mind from the inexorable decree of blind justice.
Circumstances may often make mercy necessary–I mean those of suspected error in
conviction–but mere whimpering soft-heartedness never should be heard.[54]

Both Banks's influence over Australian affairs and his belief that the
colony needed stronger discipline are illustrated by his letter to Bligh
virtually offering him the post of successor to King. Among Bligh's
qualities that Banks praised was the fact that he was 'firm in discipline,
civil in deportment and not subject to whimper and wine when severity
of discipline is wanted'.[55] Bligh duly enforced 'severity of discipline'
though with the unfortunate result that his term of office as Governor
of New South Wales was effectively brought to an end by the Rum
Rebellion of 1808.

Banks displayed a similar robustness, not to say callousness, when
discussing the practice of animal vivisection in the cause of scientific
experimentation. Thus in 1816 he advised Thomas Knight against the
submission of scientific papers involving 'the dissections of living
animals' since within the Society 'the tender hearted & ever human part
of the body who are not the wisest are at this moment evidently in possession of the elective power & thus object to it'–a remark that underlines
the fact that he did not always have things his own way within the Royal
Society. Banks indeed went so far as to link opposition to vivisection with
hostility to the slave trade as instances of the increasing squeamishness
and sentimentality of society, writing in this same letter that the issue
'of the Slave trade is one in which the tender hearted nonsense of the
community has & will ever triumph over the firm hearted & more rational
part'.[56] In the following year, however, he could express his satisfaction
that the paper based on vivisection experiments had been approved for
publication since it showed 'that the little ferment which had risen in
minds deeply tinctured by overweening humanity which is the curse
of the age & will be the ruin of the country has materially softened &
abated'.[57]

But Banks could also exhibit some other rather more endearing traits.
In the first place he was evidently a man whose company others generally
enjoyed, which explains why he was prevailed upon to become a member
of so many clubs and to take an active role in their affairs. That other
great late eighteenth-century clubman, Dr Johnson, was among those
who valued Banks's company, writing in February 1772 to 'return thanks
to you and to Dr Solander for the pleasure which I received in yesterday's
conversation' and to send on a playful Latin epigram about a goat that
had accompanied them on their voyage.[58] Boswell shared the master's
opinion when he met Banks around the same time, describing him as
'a genteel young man . . . of an agreeable countenance, easy and communi-
cative, without any affection or appearance of assuming'.[59] Along with
this affability went a genius for friendship which could transcend political

divisions. Despite Banks's political conservatism, radicals like Wilkes and Charles James Fox were on good terms with him. Fox, for example, wrote to him in 1802-a time when political opinion was highly polarised-to praise him as 'a true friend to science' and to express 'that respect which I always bore to your Character'.[60]

Banks was, then, a generally amiable man with a wide acquaintance-something which helps to explain why he had such a ready entrée into so many institutions and agencies of government. But his friendships extended well beyond the range of useful 'contacts' and he did not restrict his affections to his social equals. As he himself wrote in 1811: 'my wish in Life has been to enjoy the utmost Familiarity with those whom I can trust. I rejoice therefore in every opportunity of letting the public know that I am not of an aristocratic disposition'.[61] On the *Endeavour* voyage he formed a life-time friendship with Charles Clerke, then a master's mate, who plainly deeply regretted the fact that Banks withdrew from Cook's second great Pacific voyage, since he declared in May 1772 that he would 'go to sea in a Grog Tub' with Banks if he wished it.[62] When Clerke was dying in 1779, having assumed command of the *Resolution* following Cook's murder in Hawaii, it was to Banks that he addressed a poignant letter of farewell, bequeathing to him his collection of specimens and commending various friends to him before concluding with 'a final adieu' from 'your devoted affectionate departing Servant' and with the hope that Banks would 'attain that fame your indefatigable industry so richly deserves'.[63] As the example of Clerke suggests, Banks could inspire strong loyalty. Another of his travelling companions, Dr James Lind, refused in 1775 to take part in a proposed voyage 'for making discoveries on the N.W. side of America beyond California' unless Banks was also involved-for 'to serve and attend on Mr. Banks, on whatever Expedition he shall undertake, I shall esteem my Duty, as well as my greatest Pleasure for the real regard I have for so noble and excellent a man'. Lind remained grateful for the way in which Banks had provided him with scientific employment on the voyage to Iceland after his position as a member of Banks's scientific entourage on board Cook's second voyage failed to eventuate. At the time, wrote Lind to Maskelyne, the Astronomer Royal, in response to the invitation to participate in the American expedition, Banks told him that 'his estate he looked on as belonging to his friends as well as himself'.[64]

Once Banks had elevated someone to the position of a friend or even a client, he was prepared to tolerate much wayward behaviour rather than break off the connection. He was, as Kippis noted in his defence during the Royal Society disputes of 1783-4, 'very persevering in his friendship'.[65] When, in 1789, Blagden, his lieutenant in dealing with the Royal Society, turned against him with accusations that Banks had neglected to advance his interests, claiming 'That your general conduct has been for some time past that of a Friend I cannot think'[66] Banks responded with quiet dignity leaving the door open for the friendship to be renewed. Blagden's accusations he dismissed with the observation that 'I have hitherto conducted myself according to that strait rule of right which in my opinion it is every mans duty to Follow', while he charitably attributed Blagden's outburst to 'some bodily infirmity'.[67] And, indeed, this incident proved to be but a passing squall in the life-time correspondence and good relations between the two men. Banks also generally stood by his clients so long as he considered they were properly performing their duties. Though George Caley, the botanical collector Banks sent to New South Wales in 1798, alienated all around him Banks continued to use his influence with the colony's governors on Caley's behalf. Eventually, too, in 1816 he interceded with the War Office to obtain for Caley the position of superintendent of the Botanical Garden at St Vincent where, once again, he rapidly made enemies.[68] Banks also continued to support Bligh throughout his career despite his very accident-prone record.

Nor was Banks one to bear grudges. The contretemps over the *Resolution* voyage did not lessen his regard for Cook or his determination to advance Cook's interests where possible. When news of his death reached England, Banks sent Mrs Cook a letter of condolence expressing regret, 'As his friend', at the 'Loss this nation has suffered in the death of so invaluable a man'.[69] Banks could even overlook the erratic behaviour of that learned but difficult man, Johann Reinhold Forster, who took Banks's place as naturalist on board the *Resolution*. With more charity than accuracy he indulgently wrote of his relations with Forster from the safe distance of 1794 that 'I lived in habits of Friendship with Mr. Forster & had an excellent opinion of his Talents & still higher of the indefatigable nature of his curiosity'.[70] Banks made a number of attempts to reclaim money which Forster owed to him but when, in 1798, Forster died he overlooked the debt because of the exiguous financial condition of the long-suffering Frau Forster.[71]

Banks appears to have been much more at ease in male than in female society. This partly reflects the fact that intellectual life in Georgian England was largely conducted in the very male world of the clubs rather than in the fashionable salons with their gracious hostesses which were such a feature of eighteenth-century French culture. In the few instances where we have a description of Banks in a setting resembling a salon, he does not appear to have shone. Fanny Burney (the future Madame d'Arblay) observed that, on a visit to Windsor, in 1788 'Sir Joseph was so exceedingly shy that we made no sort of acquaintance at all. If instead of going round the world he had only fallen from the moon, he could not appear less versed in the usual modes of a tea-drinking party'.[72] Though Banks was very much at home in a London club or at a bibulous male dinner, he appears to have lacked the social niceties that would readily recommend him to female society. The diarist, Farington, wrote in 1796 that 'his manners are rather coarse and heavy'[73] and Lord Glenbervie echoed the same opinion–albeit more charitably–writing of Banks in 1816 that 'He is awkward in his person, but extremely well bred, in the best mode of English breeding, where

Mrs William Banks (née Sarah Bate) (1719–1804). Pastel drawing by John Russell. Courtesy of the Knatchbull Portrait Collection; photograph Courtauld Institute of Art

Sarah Sophia Banks (1744–1818) aged 44. Pastel drawing by John Russell, 1788. Courtesy of the Knatchbull Portrait Collection; photograph Courtauld Institute of Art

good breeding may be fairly pronounced the highest of all countries. In short he is one of the many instances to prove that personal graces are far from essential to politeness'.[74]

Yet, in his domestic setting, Banks owed much to the women of his family. He was obviously deeply attached to his mother who died at his Soho Square residence in 1804. She also may have played some part in encouraging his interest in natural history: as a woman 'devoid of all imaginary fear' (as Banks described her) she allowed him to conduct his youthful investigations among toads and other local fauna and perhaps it was no accident that Banks found his first botanical text, Gerard's *Herbal*, in his mother's dressing room.[75] His sister, Sarah Sophia, manifestly shared Banks's love of collecting and, in a society that offered few outlets for women of an intellectual bent, submerged her own energies in advancing her brother's career and interests. Sarah was not, however, one to do much to refine Banks's manners or to make him a more fitting companion for female society. She herself seems to have had little time for such graces. Her style of dress was, for example, designed for utility rather than elegance with a 'quilted petticoat' which 'had a hole on either side for the convenience of rummaging two immense pockets, stuffed with books of all sizes'. On one occasion she disconcerted her hosts by appearing in riding-habit throughout her visit–an indication of her abilities as a horse-woman since 'she was in the prime of life a fashionable whip, and drove four-in-hand'.[76] Both her style and her interests owed much to the influence of her brother on whom she plainly doted and with whom she lived for most of her life.

Ironically, it was Banks's marriage that appears to have smoothed the way for Sarah's permanent residence in Banks's Soho Square residence and for a more harmonious relationship with her brother. Previously, Banks's bachelor style of life, complete with various liaisons, appears to have clouded their amity. Sarah's anxiety at being excluded from her bachelor brother's life is reflected in a rather pathetic letter that she wrote to him around August 1777, when he was moving into his Soho Square residence. Sarah pleaded with him to be allowed to contribute to the cost of furniture perhaps because such an outlay brought with it something of a right to be a part of the new household. Hence her anxiety that Banks was reluctant to accept her offer:

> I realy was not comfortably happy yesterday, as I feared by answer you did not seriously think of complying with my request ... if you do not I shall think it very hard, that *you only* are to indulge yourself, & not let me have *a little share* of the pleasure ... pray do not be angry with your Sophy, but humour her & grant her request; she flatters herself you will not refuse her, as she has so often experienced your kindness & indulgence.[77]

But such slight shadows in their close lifelong friendship faded from view when Banks reported her death in October 1818. 'I have indeed been severely afflicted by the Loss of my Sister', he wrote to Lady Somerset, 'She [lived] in my house for nearly 50 years & we never had, during that Long period, a single debate on any Subject; I was wholly unprepard for the Loss having always confided in her being younger than I am & in the habitual temperance of her sex for her outliving me'.[78]

For all her obeisance to her brother, Sarah was a determined woman who shared her brother's strong will as well as his delight in collecting. Banks, for example, described her affectionately to Boulton in 1791 as being 'a great pusher'–particularly when it came to augmenting her collection of coins, tokens, playbills and other curiosities.[79] After her death the *Gentleman's Magazine* praised her as one who 'Like her venerable brother ... was strongly animated with a zeal for science and the study of natural history, of whom she had made a valuable collection'. The obituarist also praised her 'moral worth' which 'rendered her the object of esteem and regard to all who had the pleasure of being acquainted with her, and who from the rank and character of her brother, in addition to her own merits, constituted a very large circle of friends'. It was a tribute which underlined the extent to which her life became very much an extension of her brother's, a reflection of the fact that English society at the time offered little opportunity for one with her obvious talents to make a mark in her own right as she loyally served her illustrious brother as a companion, hostess and amanuensis.

Lady Banks (née Dorothea Hugessen) (1758–1828), aged 30. Pastel drawing by John Russell, 1788. Courtesy of the Knatchbull Portrait Collection; photograph Courtauld Institute of Art

Indeed, sister Sarah looms far larger in the records of Banks's life than his wife, Dorothea, née Hugessen. This may have been partly due to the difference in ages. The fact that Sarah was a mere two years younger than Banks –in contrast to the sixteen years that separated him and his wife– may help to explain why Sarah appears to have been more his intellectual equal. Nonetheless, both these female satellites of Banks appear to have co-existed in harmony while living together in the same house. Sarah's will provided–along with the provision that she not be buried 'till I change sufficiently that there may be no doubt of my being dead'–that her collections should go to both her brother and Lady Banks. For, she added, 'no two people ever contributed more to the happiness of others than they both have to mine [. T]hey are every thing to me'.[80]

Lady Dorothea appears to have been an amiable woman who tolerated Banks's absorption in a multiplicity of outside interests, a constant stream of visitors and the transformation of much of their London residence into a virtual scientific research institute. In contrast to the ill-used Harriet Blosset, she appears to have gained the approval of Solander as an appropriate spouse for his scientific comrade-in-arms. In June 1779, a month after the wedding, Solander described her with rather measured praise as being 'rather handsome, very agreable, chatty & laughs a good deal, of course our family is much enlivened'; he also enumerated in great detail the property settlement that had added to her charms.[81] The main testimony that Banks left of his affection for her is a set of verses which do seem to indicate some genuine emotion along with the customary compliment. Banks addressed verses to her on both the first anniversary of their wedding day and in 1807; appropriately, it is the latter, based on twenty-eight years' co-habitation, which have the greater ring of sincerity:

> Now my Dorothy we're steering
> Down the Gentle stream of years,
> Youthfull Transports disappearing
> Cause no Sorrows, lost no Tears
>
> If Loves Rapturous Flights are leaving
> Milder Joys their Place supply,
> Friendships Calmer Bliss increasing,
> Fills the Place of Ecstasy.[82]

Another poem addressed to her about the same time also suggests that their union was a reasonably happy one, for he praises her as one who

> have studied nought so much, as how
> best to fulfill your marriage vow
> in ways most kind to me.[83]

Inevitably, in a house such as the Banks's, Lady Dorothea was also a collector, though she confined herself to the genteel and ladylike area of Chinese porcelain–Banks affectionately describing her as being 'a little old-china mad'.[84]

Not surprisingly, we receive no hint as to why the marriage was childless even though Banks had had at least one child by a pre-marital liaison. This may or may not have been the daughter who is casually but fleetingly referred to in a letter of 1788.[85] The want of an heir–or, at least, of a legitimate heir–was doubtless a disappointment to Banks with his strong

Revesby Abbey, Lincolnshire, Banks's country seat. Woodcut from the *Gentleman's Magazine* (December 1821). Courtesy of Cambridge University Library

sense of family and his close connection with the estates on which the family's fortunes were based.

Running throughout Banks's life is the thread of the annual migrations from town to country whereby he, along with others of his class, maintained the amphibious skill of being a part of the way of life of both their rural and urban habitats. Virtually every year of his married life, until a year before his death, Banks, together with his wife, sister and accompanying servants, would set off for the family seat at Revesby around mid-August.[86] From time to time such journeys were combined with a visit to his Derbyshire estates, which he inherited from his uncle in 1792. By the beginning of November, the Banks family was generally once again ensconced in Soho Square, with Banks the Lincolnshire squire and active participant in local affairs giving place to Banks, the President of the Royal Society and the confidant of the king and his ministers. But even while in London Banks still maintained a vicarious involvement in the management of his estates and local affairs generally, thanks to the regular correspondence of his capable and long-serving Revesby stewards, Benjamin Stephenson (1744–95) and John Parkinson (1795–1820). Conversely, while in Revesby, Banks was able to maintain contact with the busy world of London, thanks to the services of a series of lieutenants at Soho Square: Solander, who was followed after his death in 1782 by his fellow Swede, Dryander, who, in turn, was replaced after he died in 1810 by Robert Brown. The work of both his rural and urban deputies was assisted by an efficient filing system in both his town and country residences. For Banks brought to bear on his own multifarious concerns something of the same order and system that Linnaeus and his admirers had brought to the world of Nature. At Revesby, for example, a contemporary recorded that

> Nests of drawers numbered consecutively lined the walls; and it was Sir Joseph's custom to have two catalogues, descriptive of their contents; one of which always accompanied him, the other remained at Revesby. Thus, if when in London, he required any paper contained in the drawers, he had merely to refer to his catalogue, and sending the number to his steward at Revesby, the latter was enabled, by means of the Catalogue in the office, to put his hand in a moment upon the desired document, and forward it to his master.[87]

Whether in town or country, his origins as the offspring of a family of squires drawing their wealth from shrewd investment in agriculture was always a part of him. Homely agricultural similes came naturally to him even when dealing with matters far removed from the land. His unsatisfactory experiences in dealing with government, when arranging the gift of an array of plants to the Empress Catherine II, prompted him to exclaim in earthy style that 'if I am to do all to write all to direct all & to pay all & no human being feel inclind to thank me I shall I fear in due time feel as sulky as a measly Sow who has lost her scrubbing Post'.[88] With Revesby Abbey so distant, Banks maintained some contact with the rhythms of agriculture while in London by leasing throughout his married life a fifty acre estate at Spring Grove, just across the river from Kew. As well as being a retreat from the city it also served as the site for a number of Banks's agricultural experiments.

Banks, then, was able to combine effectively the roles of Lincolnshire squire and London man of affairs thanks to his indefatigable industry as a correspondent, together with his ability to choose able lieutenants. It was a balancing act that many of his contemporaries also managed to perform, enabling England's landowning oligarchy to dominate the political arena both in the capital and in the provinces. Banks, however, went further than most by extending his circle of contacts and correspondents to embrace not only England but virtually all parts of the world where English or indeed European settlement could be found. As one of his Lincolnshire neighbours wrote to him when apologising for not being able to meet him at the Sheriff's ball at Lincoln since he had been appointed Governor of Madras: 'wide as the world is, traces of you are to be found in every corner of it'.[89] It is the purpose of the following chapters, then, to trace the ways in which the Georgian elite culture that Banks embodied served to encourage and promote such a wide reach and to delineate the values and attitudes which gave Banks's multifarious activities coherence and direction.

CHAPTER TWO

The Limits of Enlightenment

THE CHARACTER OF THE ENGLISH ENLIGHTENMENT

To the late nineteenth-century editors of the *Oxford English Dictionary* the word 'Enlightenment' was a new-fangled, foreign-sounding word for a horrid, foreign thing–'Something used to designate the spirit and aims of the French philosophers of the eighteenth century, or of others whom it is intended to associate with them in the implied charge of shallow and pretentious intellectualism, unreasonable contempt for tradition and authority, etc'.[1]

The elite of eighteenth-century England, however, generally rejoiced in the belief that they lived in an enlightened society and in an enlightened age. Where else but in England could one find liberty and order so dextrously balanced with the powers of king and Parliament ordered– or so the theory went–with the harmony of the Newtonian universe? Where else was commerce allowed to flourish with so little intervention from the dead hand of the State? Where else was the Established Church so committed to illustrating the consonance between reason and religion and its powers to persecute so firmly kept in check by an enlightened legislature? To reply that such things could be found in Scotland was likely only to elicit the complacent anglocentric response that such were the benefits of the fruitful legislative marriage of England and Scotland under the terms of the Act of Union of 1707.

Indeed, enlightened values became part of the ideological armoury of the apologists for the Hanoverian constitution who looked back on the Revolution of 1688 as the victory of rational government over the forces of mysticism and reaction. Such an outlook was strengthened still further by the continual wars against absolutism in the form of the French State. Ironically, however, after 1789 the French State began to proclaim itself as the embodiment of enlightened values, thus engendering within Britain an increasingly ambivalent attitude towards the Enlightenment, the more negative aspects of which are epitomised in the *Oxford English Dictionary*'s caustic definition of 'Enlightenment'. Such a transformation was to be made manifest in the attempt by Thomas Paine in his *Rights of Man* to use the enlightened values which had been appropriated by the French revolutionaries as weapons against the English Establishment.

In the long term, then, the values of the Enlightenment were to prove rather uncertain supports for the eighteenth-century British constitution. However, for many of those members of the elite–such as Sir Joseph Banks (1743–1820)–whose minds were formed in the more tranquil decades of the mid-eighteenth century before the Augustan calm became more and more ruffled by the American and, still more, the French Revolutions, 'enlightened' was a word which captured all that they saw as being of value about their own society and their age. Such a faith in the power of enlightenment rested, as May points out, on a belief in two propositions: first, 'that the present age is more enlightened than the past' and, second, 'that we understand nature and man best through the use of our natural faculties'.[2] For Banks, the favoured child of a family that had, over the course of the century, made the transition from country attorneys to broad-acred members of the gentry and had provided the young Joseph with an education in those bastions of Establishment values, Eton and Christ Church, the term 'enlightened' conveyed just such a confidence in both the possibilities of progress and the capabilities of our natural faculties: a set of values which animated his life and gave direction and purpose to the bewildering array of his activities.

Banks shared the view of William Worthington (whose *Essay on the Scheme and Conduct ... of Man's Redemption* was published in the year of Banks's birth) that his own age was 'enlighten'd beyond the hopes and imaginations of former times'.[3] When, in his capacity as a Privy Counsellor, Banks addressed an issue as practical as the recoinage of silver money in the late 1790s he, as was his custom, preceded what was, in effect, a policy document with an historical preamble which concluded by praising the move from a monetary standard based on both silver and gold to one based exclusively on gold as something which 'it was reserved for the Enlightened Policy of the Eighteenth Century to do'.[4] The objections of the Scottish clergy to the appointment of Sir John Leslie (who was suspected of heterodoxy) to a chair at the University of Edinburgh in 1805, prompted Banks to decry such clerical fulminations as running contrary to the fact of human progress in theology as in other areas of thought: thus he viewed earlier credal statements as the work of 'our half-informed predecessors ... left behind as a legacy, to their more enlightened successors'.[5] For Banks, as for the Enlightenment generally, the battle between the Ancients and the Moderns had been decisively settled in favour of the Moderns. His work on the nation's coinage prompted the avowal that late eighteenth-century Britain could surpass the numismatic skills of the Romans since 'the three last centuries hav[e] opened to her view a mass of human knowledge utterly unknown to the Ancients'. 'With this advantage', he continued, 'can we doubt that the intellects of the present generation are more expanded & their energies more effective than those of our remote predecessors were two thousand years ago, when their minds were clouded by ignorance & oppressed by abundant prejudices, which the splendid discoveries of their distant successors have now utterly & effectually done away'.[6]

The equally mundane subject of the care of the king's sheep elicited yet another affirmation of that belief in progress which was a cornerstone of the Enlightenment: 'that the deep-rooted prejudice ... that Spanish wool degenerates in this climate, will now be finally lodged in that catalogue of vulgar errors, which the increase of human knowledge daily enlarges'.[7] In Banks's view not only was his own age the beneficiary of a vastly increased store of knowledge but it was also more humane. The account of punishments inflicted at his *alma mater*, Eton, in the mid-sixteenth century, which he found in an Elizabethan work on agriculture, moved him to remark that 'The duties of Humanity, to which Society at present owes so large a Share of the Comforts we enjoy, appear to have been scarce known among us [then] nor in Fact till the Restoration or possibly the Revolution [of 1688]'. The evidence of this text also led him to conclude that 'the age we live in is far more Comfortable as well as more Polishd than the 16th Century'.[8]

Not that Banks was entirely complacent about his own times and his own society. Though things had generally improved, he acknowledged that there were areas where further improvement was necessary. One such area was England's system of criminal law which, as he acknowledged to a correspondent at the Imperial Academy of Sciences of St Petersburg around 1804, was 'too severe', thus encouraging judges to permit too many criminals to be acquitted. '[T]ho the Laws of his [Banks's] Country', he continued, 'have been for many Centuries in a state of progressive improvement they are yet far from perfection'. He was, however, inclined to recommend 'The Maxims of our Civil Code' as being 'worthy the Perusal of Enlightened Men'.[9] On the whole, then, Banks was disposed to agree with his friend, the naturalist and antiquarian, Sir John Cullum, who regarded his scholarly labours on the history of Suffolk (published in 1784) as encouraging his reader 'to set a proper value upon his being born in the eighteenth century, distinguished above all that preceded it by equal and well-executed laws, by civil and religious liberty, and a general civilization and philanthropy'.[10]

The belief in progress was, then, one premise of the Enlightenment; another was the belief that we best understand ourselves and the world of nature through the use of our natural faculties, what the eighteenth century called 'reason'. By reason, however, it understood something different from the rationalism which pervaded the work of such great seventeenth-century metaphysicians as Descartes or Leibniz with their elaborate systems constructed through the patient application of reason to philosophical first principles. For the French *philosophe*, Baron

D'Holbach, reason was 'truth discovered by experience, meditated upon by reflection, and applied to the conduct of life'[11]–a definition which reflects the all-pervading influence of John Locke's *Essay Concerning Human Understanding* (1690) on the thought of the Enlightenment. The roles of experience and utility, then, were of primary importance in the Enlightenment's conception of the proper place of reason. Knowledge was to be derived as far as possible from first-hand observation and then utilised for the public good, or, as Francis Bacon, one of the Encyclopedists' patron saints, had put it, applied 'for the relief of man's estate'.

For Banks, too, true enlightenment meant the dispelling of ignorance through observation and its application for the benefit of humankind or, more particularly, for that of his native land. On such a view exploration and discovery were particularly enlightened activities, since they both made available often dearly-bought first-hand observations to the general public and the possibility of greater wealth and comfort from new products and new lands; more pragmatically, such voyages of discovery frequently offered further avenues for British commerce. Thus in 1818 Banks praised Governor Macquarie of New South Wales for 'your enlightened activity in causing the Country beyond the blue mountains to be explored'–thus allowing European settlement to extend inland.[12] More programmatically the first statement of the goals of the African Association on 9 June 1788–an organisation which was largely founded and maintained through Banks's initiative–urged the need for the exploration of Africa in order to strengthen the enlightened credentials of both the age and of Britain. As its founders themselves put it, they were 'desirous of rescuing the age from a charge of ignorance, which, in other respects, so little belongs to its character'; they were also 'strongly impressed with a conviction of the practicability and utility of thus enlarging the fund of human knowledge'.[13]

Banks saw his own great voyage of discovery on the *Endeavour* as pioneering the tradition of linking naval exploration with scientific discovery. Though Banks adopted a rather anglocentric view in overlooking the work of the Dutch and the French in promoting such scientific discovery, nonetheless there is substance in his claim that his work helped to make such voyages a source of national prestige as an instance of British promotion of enlightened goals. As Banks himself wrote: 'I may flatter myself that being the first man of scientific education who undertook a voyage of discovery and that voyage of discovery being the first which turned out satisfactorily in this enlightened age, I was in some measure the first who gave that turn to such voyages'.[14] The émigré German, Johann Reinhold Forster, was to pay tribute to British success in promoting such goals by referring to the *Resolution* (on which Forster performed a role similar to that which Banks had created for himself on the *Endeavour*) as belonging to 'the most enlightened nation in the world'.[15] This association between Enlightenment and discovery was carried still further by Georg, Forster's son and fellow traveller on Cook's second voyage. His essay, 'Cook the Discoverer: Attempts at a Memorial'

(1786) was based on the premise that 'Enlightenment advances to infinity from experience to experience', while Cook was singled out for praise as one who had 'led his century in knowledge and Enlightenment'.[16]

Such an enlightened pursuit of useful knowledge embraced the collection of living plants and their cultivation in familiar environments. Thus the domestication of the new and useful through the establishment of botanical gardens, either in England itself or within the British Empire at large, was an appropriate activity for an enlightened age. The principal agency for promoting such goals was the Royal Botanic Gardens at Kew, of which Banks acted as *de facto* director. Thus the great catalogue of these gardens, the *Hortus Kewensis* (1810-3) compiled by William Aiton, the head gardener, was prefaced by a dedication to George III conveying 'the heartfelt gratitude of an enlightened nation' not only for his support of the botanical activities at the Gardens but also for the way in which Kew had become a centre for an archetypal source of useful knowledge, the breeding of improved (and more profitable) sheep under the supervision of Banks.[17] In distant Jamaica Thomas Dancer urged the need to maintain a botanical garden as one of the amenities of an enlightened community. 'A Botanical Garden', he wrote, 'is not now, as formerly, considered merely as an appendage to a college or an university, but is become an object of general concern with enlightened men of every description, even the mercantile class, in maritime and manufacturing towns, &c'.[18] Banks's work in promoting such institutions and advancing natural history more generally led to one correspondent describing him as 'The Liberal Patron of Science, and the Enlightened Cultivator of Natural Knowledge'.[19] Such epithets as 'liberal' and 'enlightened' could be applied not only to those who discovered and applied useful knowledge in the natural world but also to those who utilised such methods in dealing with the problems of human society. Thus in 1818, two years before his death, Banks praised Sheffield for his recent pamphlet on the Poor Laws, viewing its advocacy of 'employing so large a number of labourers' as a 'liberal and enlightened policy'.[20]

The pervasiveness of such an appeal to enlightened values in such a quintessential embodiment of the English Establishment as Sir Joseph Banks–Baronet, President of the Royal Society and, for many years, confidant of the king–underlines the extent to which the Enlightenment formed part of the mental world of the eighteenth-century English elite and the validity of the term 'English Enlightenment'. True, as Venturi and Palmer have emphasised in their attempt to question the usefulness of such a phrase, the Enlightenment in England lacked the self-consciousness and the crusading zeal of other countries, such as France, where a small band of thinkers and writers saw themselves as engaging in battle against the forces of obscurantism and reaction.[21] But this, as Porter has emphasised,[22] is to confine the Enlightenment's importance as a movement for change and the reshaping of traditional institutions to the work of a relatively small group of intellectuals, rather than to a large mass of intellectually less eminent figures (like Banks or William Paley or Josiah Tucker) who nonetheless played a major part in diffusing

Enlightenment values and making them a part of the cultural self-image of their age. Because they did so in a manner which helped to make such values so much a part of the fabric of their own society and its modes of thought, their work generally attracted little controversy and hence less historical notice than that of the continental *philosophes*. Because, too, the Enlightenment in England became part of the everyday currency of intellectual and social life it lost the distinctiveness of its continental counterparts and thus could be easily overlooked and even dismissed by later historians. In short, one must distinguish between the Enlightenment as a body of ideas, defined in conscious opposition to the prevailing order in Church and State (as was most conspicuously the case in France), and the Enlightenment as a set of often barely conscious social attitudes which coloured the values and actions of society. As Plumb writes: 'Too much attention, it seems to me, is paid to the monopoly of ideas amongst the intellectual giants, too little to their social acceptance. Ideas acquire dynamism when they become social attitudes, and this was happening in England.'[23]

That England was a major centre for the ideas and attitudes to which we give the name 'The Enlightenment' is borne out by the frequency with which continental visitors used the English example as a yardstick with which to measure the lack of enlightenment in their own society–a genre of which the most celebrated example was Voltaire's *Letters on the English*. In 1779, for example, the Abbé Mann, a correspondent of Banks from the Austrian Netherlands, bemoaned his fate in having to 'live in a Country where good Philosophy is still in its leading-strings, where every thing that is new, is suspected of Heresy, of Atheism, &c &c'.[24] Mann's response was to propose the publication of his work in London. Subsequently, in 1790, he expressed to Banks his envy of the success of another foreigner, William Herschel, 'in being wholly occupied in the pursuits of science under the protection of an enlightened and beneficent Sovereign'–thanks to Banks's intervention on his behalf with George III. In the same letter Mann once again contrasted English Enlightenment with the situation that prevailed in his native land where 'Our late Government, having only arbitrary power in view, declared itself openly against the Sciences for several years past. The great plan was to reduce the body of the people to two classes, *Peasants and Soldiers*'. Mann closed his letter by congratulating Banks on 'the inestimable blessing of being in a free country'.[25]

It was appropriate that Mann's correspondence with Banks and his praise for England should have arisen out of the literary exchange between the Royal Society and its newly-founded Belgian analogue, the Académie Impériale et Royale des Sciences et Belles Lettres de Bruxelles (founded 1772). Both within England and on the Continent such learned academies and societies were the natural centres for the dissemination and promotion of enlightened values. After all, it was a central impulse of the Enlightenment to attempt to bring to bear on society's problems that order and harmony which the achievements of Newton and his predecessors had

revealed in the natural world. One of the major points in the correspondence between Banks and Mann was the attempt to bring some degree
of scientific system to society's affairs by instituting a rationally-based
system of weights and measures which Mann hoped would transcend
national boundaries.[26] It was, of course, to be one of the lasting achievements of the French Revolution (and one of its most tangible links with
the goals of the French Enlightenment) to institute such a reform in the
form of the metric system. Throughout his career Banks took a close
interest in this area culminating in his appointment, a year before his
death, as chairman of a committee established by Parliament to investigate
England's system of weights and measures. It was an appropriate way
for Banks to end his work as an adviser to government on scientific
matters, since weights and measures was an area where the rationalising
impulse of the Enlightenment impinged directly on the concerns of
everyday life. However, it is also an indication of the extent to which such
an impulse was kept in check by tradition that neither Banks nor
Parliament recommended any wholesale reform of the imperial system.[27]

At the international level the interchange between scientific academies
(such as that between Banks and Mann) helped to provide a common
European culture based on Enlightenment values. At the local level, too,
the growing number of provincial bodies which promoted science and
Enlightenment culture more generally–what, in the eighteenth century,
was frequently called 'rational amusement'–served to integrate the values
of the Enlightenment into the mentality of the English elite.[28] One of
the first such provincial bodies was the Spalding Gentlemen's Society
(founded 1712) which promoted the study of the natural world and the
application of such knowledge to the improvement of the locality
(together with other elite amusements, such as the study of antiquities).[29]
Like his grandfather before him, Banks was a member and took an active
interest in the Society's affairs.[30] As President of the Royal Society, he also
promoted other more recently-founded provincial societies. On the foundation of the Literary and Philosophical Society of Newcastle-upon-Tyne
in 1793, for example, he accepted honorary membership of the Society
and six years later arranged for zoological specimens sent by Governor
John Hunter from New South Wales to be delivered to it, concluding
his letter with 'his best respects to the members' and his assurance that
'I shall at all times be ready to obey any commands [they] may honor
me with'.[31] As Jacob points out, such societies provided a fertile environment for the spread of Enlightenment culture since they offered a 'milieu
created by secular fraternising for the purpose of personal improvement
and social intercourse' free from the restraints of more traditional
gatherings based around the Church or the family.[32]

But this clubbable world of which Banks, the member and active
supporter of a myriad of societies, was so much a part (being at least as
eligible for the title of 'The Great Clubman' as his contemporary, Dr
Johnson), was also well suited to the social world of a landed elite. For
membership of a club naturally carried with it the notion of social as

well as intellectual respectability and it offered many an opportunity for enforcing canons of social or intellectual conformity through the gentle art of blackballing. Attempts to push enlightened values beyond the point where they no longer served the established order were naturally discouraged by the ethos of a club which promoted consensus and civility. There also always remained the ultimate sanction of exclusion, or what was often of greater practical significance, the exclusion of one's nominees. Moreover, generally the publications of such clubs were first delivered verbally, a procedure which acted as a brake on too overt an attack on the cherished beliefs of the general membership. For, although the elite of eighteenth-century England may have absorbed many of the values of the Enlightenment, such a process of intellectual and social digestion was often partial and subject to some dyspepsia. After all, on what was the power and position of the landed elite of England based?– primarily on inherited privilege and wealth justified by tradition. True, the governing classes had exhibited an ability to adapt themselves to change by diversifying their financial interests to embrace not only land, but commercial and even (by the late eighteenth century) industrial wealth. Banks, for example, supplemented his considerable landed income by investing in the East India Company[33] and by the development of a mine on one of his estates using the latest steam-driven technology available from his friends, Boulton and Watt.

The governing elite had also diversified the ideological justification for their position: to the traditional religious sanction of a divinely-ordained social hierarchy with its rich man in his castle and the poor man at his gate, other modes of asserting rights to social pre-eminence became more manifest in the eighteenth century: the need for a balanced constitution with the landed classes as a counterweight to the power of the king, or the justification in terms of social utility through their activities as Justices of the Peace, as Members of Parliament or, as in the case of Banks, as government advisers and servants. Nonetheless, there did remain some tension between an enlightened ideology which was critical and, potentially at least, corrosive of tradition and a social order where tradition overshadowed all, from the haphazard distribution of parliamentary seats to the arcane activities of the Exchequer, which maintained into the nineteenth century the medieval practice of keeping financial records by cutting notches on tally-sticks. Such tensions were generally overlooked or kept in check for much of the century but the impact of the French Revolution was to prompt a more critical appraisal of such beliefs and, with it, a reaction against many of the values of the Enlightenment.

The youthful Joseph Banks could comment critically in his *Endeavour* journal about the Tahitians' excessive veneration for tradition–what he called 'the Customs which they have learnt from their forefathers'–adding, with an eye to his own society, that this was 'a fault which is too frequent even among the politest nations'.[34] By contrast, the Banks of the early 1800s was to be much more cautious about dismissing the fruits of tradition: the attempt by John Rickman to institute a reform of the division of the country into more manageable and practical units of local government provoked the reply that he could not support the scheme, since 'I am so much alive to the dread of Reform & so convinced that we are often unable to discover all the advantages we derive from an Established Custom till they are pointed out to us by their Loss ... Plausible as your Project for a new Territorial division certainly is'.[35] Perhaps Banks had in mind the unfortunate parallel with the work of the French Revolution in implementing a major reform of its local government system by replacing the traditional provinces with departments, the organisation of which, in Enlightenment fashion, was based on utility, order and an attempt at uniformity: all of which entailed a clean break with tradition. Five years before, Banks had been moved to pen another paean to tradition apropos of the problem of maintaining the ancient system of controls on the price of bread at a time of grain shortage: 'I am always inclind to tread in the footsteps of our ancestors in all matters that require consideration having repeatedly observd, that as they had more time for thinking than their descendants now have ... they thought much more profoundly than their successors now do'.[36]

ENLIGHTENMENT AND HUMAN EQUALITY

One of the most obvious respects in which the values of the Enlightenment could clash with those of a landed elite was in the degree of respect accorded to traditional conceptions of social hierarchy. Though rarely made explicit by the *philosophes* (apart from such outsiders as Rousseau), the thought of the Enlightenment could tend to promote notions of human equality. If, in the manner of Locke and other political theorists of the Enlightenment, one cast a critical eye on traditional religious sanctions for paternalistic conceptions of monarchy it was difficult to avoid also calling into question the social hierarchies which had for so long been associated with them. Even Locke, a stalwart defender of the position of the governing elite of post-revolutionary England, envisaged a sort of primitive democracy in the early state of nature before hastily erecting a justification for the development of a social hierarchy which, in Enlightenment fashion, he based not on tradition or religious sanction but on the accumulation of property. From the safety of the grave Lord Chesterfield could acknowledge that there was no real foundation in natural law for the hierarchical order of which he had been such a beneficiary. When stipulating the distribution of generous legacies to his old servants, he described such retainers as 'unfortunate friends, my equals by Nature, and my inferiors only by the difference of our fortunes'.[37] Banks, too, on occasions could acknowledge that human equality was, at least, a theoretical possibility. When writing to his protégé, George Caley, a stablehand turned botanical collector, Banks graciously overlooked Caley's earlier intemperate language since 'I have been for many years of opinion that all mankind are really equal, notwithstanding the artificial distinctions which custom has placed amongst them, and deem us to treat them so, as far as the usages of the country I live in will permit'.[38]

But the qualification that Banks expressed in the last sentence was important–in practice any such conception of equality had to be tempered by deference to the normal practices of social intercourse which had been moulded by tradition and respect for a hierarchical ordering of society. Perhaps more characteristic, and certainly more socially instinctive, was Banks's remark about Caley's well-developed ability to make enemies. In a letter to Governor King of New South Wales–someone who, compared with Caley, approached Banks's social position and values–he wrote of his wayward botanist that 'Had he been born a gentleman, he would have been shot long ago in a duel'.[39] And an English gentleman in Banks's social lexicon was a being worthy of respect and (when it came to lesser mortals) obedience. The imperious manner of Captain Vancouver prompted Banks to remark that his 'conduct towards me ... was not such as I am used to receive from persons in his situation'.[40] The attempt by the Viceroy of Brazil to impede the botanising of Banks and his entourage when the *Endeavour* called at Rio de Janeiro resulted in Banks's declaration that he was every inch an English gentleman and hence (by implication) at least the equal of a Portuguese grandee: 'Disagreable as it is for any man to declare his own rank and consequence my situation makes it necessary: I am a gentleman, and one of fortune sufficient to have (at my own expense) fitted out that part of this expedition under my direction'.[41]

When, in 1792, Banks recommended Dr James Lind to the aristocrat, Lord Macartney, as a useful member of the embassy to the Emperor of China, Banks sought to strengthen Lind's cause by remarking that 'he is a man accustomed to Obedience & well acquainted with the Station of an inferior'.[42] Lind was a close friend of Banks, who had travelled with him to Iceland, an FRS, an Edinburgh MD and a physician to the royal household and yet such accomplishments had still, in the aristocratic world of eighteenth-century England, to be combined with the ability to know one's place–the Enlightenment ideal of a career open to talents could only find a very partial realisation in such a society.

By the 1790s, too, the spectre of the French Revolution had further weakened the always attenuated conception of human equality within the English Establishment: thus Banks described the closing decade of the eighteenth century as 'times like ours teeming with the monstrous Birth of Equality'.[43] Such attitudes help to explain the increasingly socially elevated character of the Royal Society under Banks's presidency, this being one among the various grievances which led to the Royal Society disputes of 1783. As Banks's lieutenant, Blagden, commented: 'One of the great articles of complaint against you is keeping out deserving men because they are not of a certain mark'.[44] But the gentrification of the Royal Society continued with aristocrats and landed gentry making up forty per cent of the Council during the last two decades of Banks's presidency from 1800-1820 (a figure that dropped to ten per cent in the two decades that followed Banks's death).[45] So, too, did the criticism and satire: the poem, 'Peter's Prophecy' by 'Peter Pindar' refers both to Banks's alleged bias against the mathematical and to his social aspirations in the lines:

> Poh! poh! my friend, I've stargazers enough
> I now look round for different kind of stuff:
> Besides-untitled members are mere swine:
> I wish for princes on my list to shine . . .[46]

One area where the ideals of the Enlightenment about the essential equality of humankind clashed most overtly with the needs of empire was over the issue of slavery. The whole logic of Enlightenment thought ran contrary to the institution of slavery-though this did not prevent the American and French revolutionaries combining their espousal of the 'rights of man' with a justification, or, at least a recognition, of the necessity of slavery as an integral part of the plantation economies from which their countries drew much of their wealth. Enlightenment critiques of slavery centred firstly on its basic inhumanity-as in Montesquieu's acid aside in his *Spirit of the Laws* (1748) that 'Sugar would be too expensive if the plant that produces it were not cultivated by slaves, or if one treated them with some humanity'[47]-but also, increasingly, British critics pointed to its inutility and poor economics. The pioneering sociologists of the Scottish Enlightenment argued that the advance of society, and especially of commerce, had rendered slavery increasingly economically unsound, as well as unjust. John Millar concluded from his historical survey of slavery that the advance of civilisation should mean that society would be 'influenced by more extensive considerations of utility' and recognise that unskilled, reluctant labour was a brake on technological progress. Invoking his contemporaries' self-image of themselves as belonging to an enlightened civilisation-or, as he put it, 'an age distinguished for humanity and politeness'- he also reaffirmed the more basic objection that slavery was 'inconsistent with the rights of humanity'.[48] Adam Smith in his *The Wealth of Nations* also took up the issue of the inutility of slavery as part of his general theme of the economic benefits of 'the liberal reward of labour' arguing that 'the work done by slaves, though it appears to cost only their maintenance, is in the end the dearest of any'.[49]

Banks, too, could discourse on the way in which the advance of civilisation was more and more rendering slavery uneconomic, but he was by no means sure that this desirable state of affairs had been fully realised within the British Empire and especially not in its lucrative possessions in the West Indies. In a long and revealing letter written to Thomas Coltman, a fellow Lincolnshire squire, in March 1792, Banks began by criticising, in the manner of Adam Smith, the institution of slavery on the basis of its inutility. He wrote:

> I have no doubt it is impolitic & inexpedient to imploy slaves when free men can be procurd & am fully convinced that the Labor of Slaves is in every instance dearer than that of free men deprivd of all hope of improving their circumstances by successful efforts . . . the ambition of a slave is to do as little labor as possible.

But such a line of argument was soon qualified by an appeal to the experience of the West Indian planters with their plantation economy based on slavery; these Banks had attempted to serve by introducing breadfruit from Tahiti as a cheap food for the slaves, a delicacy the slaves generally declined. If slavery were in such conditions less efficient than free labour why was it that the plantation owners had not abandoned slavery out of self-interest? Was it, he ruminated, the result of the fact that generally speaking black people would only work under compulsion since they are 'endowed with a much less proportion of mental vigor than the whites'? Banks did, however, qualify this assertion of racial superiority with the acknowledgement that there were many exceptions to this general rule. Moreover, Banks argued, slavery could be supported by arguments based on tradition, biblical texts and the assertion that 'a slave well provided for & humanly treated is certainly happier than a free man who has a choice only of bad masters or none'. Though Banks differed in his conclusions from John Millar about the need to hasten the end of slavery, he nonetheless adopted a similar historically-based approach in arguing that the institution of slavery should be left to die a natural death as society developed:

> The state of servitude adopted in this & other european nations is a complex system which in the end naturely arises out of slavery. We had slaves & no servants in England 1700 years ago & 1700 years hence the West Indies will be cultivated by free men . . . The motion of it from worse to better is slow but it is sure . . . let us be contented that we are free here without insisting that all mankind shall be made free.[50]

In taking such an apologist stance for the institution of slavery Banks was falling in line with his close friend, Lord Sheffield, a vigilant defender of the position of the landed interest and of the interests of British trade (including that of the West Indian plantation owners). In 1790 Sheffield set out to counter the rising tide of abolitionist opinion with his pamphlet, *Observations on the Project for Abolishing the Slave Trade*, which he sent to Banks for his comments.[51] In this work, Sheffield castigated 'the inconsiderable and impracticable manner in which a great proportion of the community possess a disposition to relieve Negroes from slavery'. It was his duty, wrote Sheffield, as 'a well-wisher to the empire to endeavour to check a prevailing rage'. He was particularly outraged that the abolitionists had 'not scrupled to make appeals to the people, as if their judgement was fit to decide on a matter so important and so complicated'.[52] However, he noted with satisfaction in a letter to Lord North apropos of this pamphlet that increasing awareness of the consequences of abolition for the 'welfare of the Africans, & the danger of it with respect to the commerce & Navigation of Great Britain' was undermining support for abolition within Parliament. Sheffield also took heart from the fact that 'the late determination of the National Assembly in France upon this proposition seems in a great measure to have given it its coup de grace'. Sheffield did, however, acknowledge the need for 'such regulations as are required by humanity' provided these were 'not inconsistent with the interests of commerce'.[53] When the abolitionist crusade again gathered political momentum in 1807, Sheffield was once more enlisted to defend the interests of the West Indian planters; he was perceived as someone whose 'voice will always be heard in support of the Commerce, and Navigation Laws of the United Kingdom'.[54] But, of course, Sheffield acted in vain and the Abolition Bill was duly passed in May 1807; even the slave-owners' attempt to alter the introductory clause, stating that slavery was 'contrary to expediency' rather than 'contrary to justice and humanity', was defeated.[55]

Banks, however, appears to have been far less committed to the anti-abolitionist cause than Sheffield. Even in the late 1790s he had become more and more persuaded of the inutility of slavery and the consequent need to phase it out. In 1799 the threat of competition to West Indian sugar interests from the newly-founded French sugar beet industry prompted him to observe that if the West Indies was to continue to compete it must use 'the Labor of Freemen'; 'in the mean time', he continued, 'a struggle almost equal to an Earthquake must take place & Slavery must be abolishd not on moral principles which are in my opinion incapable of being maintaind in argument, but on Commercial ones which weigh equaly in moral & in immoral minds'.[56] Nor was Banks always quite as hard-boiled about the moral objections to slavery as this passage suggests. By 1815 he had become an admirer of the newly-liberated people of Haiti and, in a letter to Wilberforce, enthusiastically remarked,

> Was I Five and Twenty, as I was when I embarked with Capt Cooke, I am very sure I should not Lose a day in Embarking for Hayti. [T]o see a sort of Human beings emerging from Slavery & making most Rapid Strides towards the perfection of Civilisation, must I think be the most delightfull of all Food for Contemplation.[57]

Slavery, then, was an issue about which Banks was rather ambivalent, oscillating between his Enlightenment (and perhaps, too, residual Christian) faith in the ultimate equality of humankind and the imperatives of Empire. Perhaps part of the appeal for Banks of arguments based on utility or inutility was that they offered an Enlightenment figleaf for concealing the more fundamental moral issues raised by slavery as well as offering a means of reconciling the abolitionist cause with the commercial interests of the British Empire.

BANKS'S STANCE TOWARDS THE ESTABLISHED CHURCH AND ITS BELIEFS AND VALUES

One of Banks's primary objections to the anti-slavery movement was the extent to which it led to clerical meddling in political affairs–one instance of a more widely-diffused anti-clericalism that is apparent in much of

Banks's career. Anti-clericalism was, of course, one of the most distinctive features of the French Enlightenment, as instanced by Voltaire's battle cry of 'Crush the infamy'. In England, the Church was much less powerful and therefore much less under attack but there, too, as the example of Banks indicates, the First Estate was frequently regarded with ambivalence, and even some hostility, by lay brethren within the Establishment. It was not only the small but well-organised band of Evangelical clergy but also many of the clergy of the Established Church as well as of the dissenting churches who took an active part in promoting the anti-slavery campaign[58]-something which Banks regarded as theologically unjustified and a departure from their proper social role. In the letter of 1792 to Thomas Coltman he devoted most of his vitriol to the clerical opponents of slavery: 'The part of the Question I most abhor is when those who study divinity in order to instruct the people take upon them to arrai[g]n divine providence by asserting that it is wicked in the eyes of God to deal in slaves'. It was blasphemous, he continued, to suppose that if slavery was so contrary to God's intentions 'that the Creator has suffered this trade to be carried on from the earliest period of which we have records'.

Banks's relations with the Evangelicals seem to have been particularly ambivalent-perhaps in part because of their active involvement in the opposition to the slave trade. He worked closely with Wilberforce over the establishment of a colony for freed slaves in Sierra Leone and regarded him as 'a Man of kind and gentle manners, as well as possessed of a mind regulated by views of religious propriety'.[59] He also greatly facilitated the work of Thomas Haweis and the embryonic London Missionary Society in its establishment of a mission in Tahiti[60]-though his motives for doing so owed more to the imperial advantages that he hoped would accrue from such a settlement than to any religious commitment. For elsewhere he made his lack of any real sympathy for missionary endeavour apparent: 'I am a Sincere Friend to religion as Establishd,' he wrote to George Staunton in 1806 about a Christian missionary in China, '& little inclined to Conversions. The will of God will, no doubt, put & keep all mankind on the right way; & his mercy will most assuredly despise all Ceremonial & all mistaken Faith.'[61]

But despite such harmonious dealings with leading Evangelicals, Banks was moved around 1809 to write a long tirade against 'those noxious vermins calld Saints' the term often applied to Evangelicals (though he subsequently thought better of it and crossed it out). Banks objected to the way in which they regarded 'Faith alone to be acceptable in the Eyes of the Benevolent Creator of the universe, & believe, if we may Judge by their Actions, that works are not carried to account in the System under which the Rewards & Punishments of a future State are distributed'. With a caustic description of their political skills Banks objected to 'The Dirty & Crooked paths they pursue in the accomplishment of their abominable Object'.[62] These remarks suggest that Banks objected not only to the success with which the Evangelicals pursued their political objectives, such as the abolition of slavery, but also the whole tone of their theology, which departed so markedly from the amalgam of Christian and Enlightenment values which had gained such wide currency within the English Establishment. Wilberforce had entitled his most important religious tract *A Practical View of the Prevailing Religious System of Professed Christians in the Higher and Middle Classes in this Country Contrasted with Real Christianity* (1797) and in it had decried the prevalence of the form of latitudinarian Christianity which sought 'to inculcate the moral and practical precepts of Christianity ... without justly laying the grand foundation of a sinner's acceptance with God'.[63] What residual Christianity Banks still professed was quite opposed to such a view of religion with its rejection of a form of enlightened Christianity which emphasised ethics rather than doctrine and reason rather than revelation. Banks himself hinted at this in a letter to Haweis over the proposed mission to Tahiti in which he affirmed his commitment to a form of enlightened Christianity, based almost entirely on the performance of good works, in implied contrast to the Evangelicals' doctrine of justification by faith alone:

> Tho you and I certainly differ in opinion respecting the things we both deem necessary for salvation, yet under a firm belief in the boundless mercy of God I have no doubt that all men who strive to their utmost according to their consciences to do what they think good in his sight will find favour in his Judgements.[64]

Along with Banks's objections to clerical meddling in such political issues as the abolition of the slave trade, his anti-clericalism was greatly heightened by his activities as an active proponent of agricultural improvement which led to frequent disputes with the Established Church in its role as a landowner and collector of tithes. As a large landowner, Banks himself clashed frequently with the Church. Plans for the draining of the fens near his seat at Revesby Abbey in Lincolnshire in 1799 led to a dispute with the bishop over the erection of new chapels. Banks reported with satisfaction to Arthur Young that a meeting of those involved had decided that 'as the Clergy would derive great benefit from the whole undertaking at the expense of the Laity we thought it their duty to make all proper provision for the Celebration of divine worship out of their share'.[65] However, this dispute was still festering in 1807 when Banks told Lady Dryden that the clergy were 'very unwilling also to give up such a Portion of their advantage to be derivd from the Fen for the Purpose of Endowing & erecting chapels upon it, as seems to the graver part of the Laity proper & Right'.[66] On occasions Banks would take the fight into the enemy's camp by laying claim to jurisdiction over ecclesiastical premises. By right of the ancient monastic privileges attached to Revesby Abbey Banks 'claim[ed] a right to the [local] church & churchyard free from all ecclesiastical jurisdiction' and he looked back with satisfaction to the occasion when 'My ancestors once turnd a parson off who preachd in their opinion seditiously'.[67] The ill-will generated by such battles is apparent in Banks's reported remark that 'It has been the study of my life to make myself a match for the parsons',[68] or in his curt response to a request to support a clerical charity: that he was 'of opinion that the clergy monopolise a larger share of Public Benevolence than their order, endowd as it is by the Public, ought to accept'.[69]

Banks clashed with the Church not only as a private landowner but also in his official capacities, particularly as a member of the Board of Agriculture, the activities of which in promoting large-scale improvement and enclosure inevitably led to disputes over tithes and other ecclesiastical rights to the land. Indeed, at the Board's foundation the Archbishop of Canterbury blocked the appointment of the Reverend Richard Shepherd (the son of Banks's childhood tutor) because of fears that the details of clerical tithes would be included in the statistical researches commissioned by the Board. To assuage such opposition the Board resorted to the more expensive device of issuing county rather than parochial reports.[70] In the event the position of Secretary to the Board went to Arthur Young, a trenchant critic of the system of tithes which he saw as a brake on agricultural improvement. But Young had to acknowledge that change would be slow in coming in an age when reform of all sorts had become tinged with the radicalism of the French Revolution. As he wrote in the *Annals of Agriculture* for 1791: 'we are to be left groaning under the slavery of tythes, after they have ceased through half Europe, because any change in the constitution of parliament, or the church, would be dangerous'.[71]

Together with such immediate and particular sources of anti-clericalism as the anti-slavery campaign and the battle over tithes, Banks also displayed some signs of sharing something of the French *philosophes'* hostility to clerical power on the grounds of a more fundamental aversion to the invoking of sacerdotal or mystical powers. Much of the occasion for this form of anti-clericalism had been drained away in England by the increasing subjection of the Church to the laity. Nonetheless, something of it remained, fanned by memories of the clergy's original reluctance to embrace the Revolutionary Settlement and the Hanoverian succession and their lingering nostalgia for divine right monarchy and a confessional state. This generalised aversion to priestcraft comes through in his remarks in his *Endeavour* journal about the religious practices of the Tahitians: 'Religion has been in all ages, is still in all countreys Cloak'd in mysteries inexplicable to human understanding'.[72] Nor was Banks unusual among Establishment figures in holding such views; as Langford remarks of eighteenth-century Britain: 'Anticlericalism was fashionable in politically influential circles'.[73] The reaction of Banks's friend, Sir John Barrow, to popular Chinese Confucianism was very similar to that of Banks to the Tahitians and again prompted a generalised attack on clerical power in all times and places: 'But the priests, who, in all ages, and in most nations, have been crafty enough to turn to their own account the credulity and superstitions of the people'.[74] Protestantism and Enlightenment anti-clericalism merged in Banks's account of medieval monastic sites which he described as 'formerly dedicated to the Evil Policy of Constraind Celibacy, & the Foolish project of compensating Sins by Gifts to Religious Persons'.[75]

Banks's latent anti-clericalism was also aroused by any instance of what he regarded as clerical meddling in intellectual matters. In his comments on Tahitian religion he remarked caustically that 'even here the Preists [sic] Monopolize the greatest part of the learning of the Countrey in much the same manner as they formerly did in Europe'.[76] Even the Royal Society dispute of 1783-4 appears to have included a faint element of anti-clericalism since Banks's main opponent was that very model of the church militant, Samuel Horsley (the future bishop). Thus Banks's admirer, Patrick Russell, wrote to congratulate him on his victory in the Royal Society fracas adding that 'Independent of other conditions I am always pleased to see clerical pride mortified'.[77] The attempt by the Presbyterian clergy to prevent the appointment of his friend, Sir John Leslie, as professor of mathematics at the University of Edinburgh prompted Banks to discourse at unusual length on the proper role of the Church and to castigate attempts at persecution on doctrinal grounds. The Church, in Banks's view, should not have any coercive powers:

> No Church surely has ever increased its influence over the minds of Men by unwholesome severity, mildness of demeanor carries or rather forces Religion into the hearts of Men & it soon finds its way from their hearts to their souls, while the opposite extreme renders its teachers odious in the eyes of all Mankind & puts Religion itself in continual risk of being abandoned.

Not only should the church be stripped of the power to impose doctrine but it should also recognise that a fair measure of theological pluralism was inevitable. In his letter to Leslie, Banks defended a qualified form of free thinking, arguing that 'unprejudiced & strong headed men have always thought for themselves & will continue to do in spite of all the Bishops Priests & Deacons that ever have or ever will be ordaind'. Interestingly, however, he added the prudential aside–which, no doubt, was partly autobiographical–that such independent thinkers 'may conscientiously abstain from commenting & Enlarging upon them, lest weaker brethren should be bewildered'.[78] For Banks the social conservative, freedom of thought needed to be balanced by the maintenance of religious and, with it, social order.

Not surprisingly, Banks's wariness and suspicion of the power and privileges of the clerical order was accompanied by a fair degree of scepticism, or, at least, indifference about the religious doctrines it professed. Banks himself kept his religious opinions largely to himself–one of his Lincolnshire clerical neighbours commented that 'he could never discover what his religious notions were'.[79] The little attention accorded to religious topics in the vast corpus of Banks's papers indicates that it was not a subject in which he took a great deal of interest but, as the remarks cited above suggest, if one were to locate Banks on the religious map of his times it would be somewhere between deism and a form of ultra-latitudinarian enlightened Christianity. At least one of Banks's obituarists seemed to have been aware of Banks's rather tenuous attachment to traditional Christianity, since the *Asiatic Observer* commented in 1823 that 'We fear, however, that he was too much linked in with disciples of the new school of philosophy, to have known as much as we could wish him to have known of vital Christianity'.[80] Banks's correspondence does include stray remarks which, particularly as he got older and became conscious of his own mortality, indicate some sort of belief in God and the next life. However, it is significant that such religious sentiments were expressed in language which made no reference to any specifically Christian doctrines–an indication of the secularising tendency of the Enlightenment. At the age of sixty-seven, for example, he commented in a letter of 1810 to his old friend, William Marsden, that 'I am not far distant from the haven of Rests, which I look to with hope rather than apprehensions ... I must & will say that Divine mercy has endowd me with a Plentifull Portion of Patience'.[81] The peaceful death of his mother in 1804 prompted him to remark to another old friend, Matthew Boulton: 'that we may all go to a better world with the same ease is a Consummation devoutly to be wished'.[82] In letters of condolence Banks invoked religious language though this may simply reflect the conventions of the time. Banks responded to a bereavement in the family of Lady Somerset with a letter which is as much a recommendation for stoicism as of Christian patience: 'May the Gracious & divine Bounty which sustains us all, Grant to your grace the inestimable Gift of Patience which alone can blunt the arrows of Pain, & deprive Fortune of its Sting'.[83]

Banks appears to have had a distaste for elaborate religious ceremonial and, though of the Establishment, he seems to have had sympathy with the simpler forms of worship associated with sects like the Quakers. One of the few occasions when there is a hint of religious emotion in his writing is in his diary of a journey to Holland in 1773, when he described his visit to a community of Moravians on 3 March: 'we attended their Service, & a decency was observed in it seldom to be met with in other Religions ... At 8 this Service, by which I confess I was much Edified'.[84]

Generally, however, his church attendance appears to have been dictated largely by social convention. Certainly his remark in his Iceland journal, that 'It being Sunday we resolvd to go to church in order to give the people a good impression in favour of us strangers', indicates more pragmatism than piety.[85] Overall, then, Banks wore his religion lightly–much to the regret of his doting and devout sister. For in a memorandum written after his return from the *Endeavour* expedition she gave thanks to the 'Merciful god who has not only daily preserv'd my Dear Brother from the perils & very great ones of the Sea' and concluded with the hope that those 'who are not enlightened with the Bright Sunshine of the Gospel, or who differ in points of faith; but who (according to their Faith) use their best Endeavours, far as in their power they can, to do the Will of the SUPREME BEING: will be accepted at the THRONE of GRACE'[86]–an obvious reference to her erring brother.

Quite plainly Banks regarded theological discussion with considerable distaste. The attempt by the Reverend Richard Shepherd to interest Banks in a pamphlet on the gospel of St John resulted in the work being returned with the comment (in the third person): 'He feels no doubt that his faith is sufficient, if his actions prove acceptable, to conduct him to his home hereafter, but believing that the Strait Path pointed out by the other Evangelists will lead him as safely to his object as the intricate one of St John'.[87] Banks's lack of interest in theology is evident, too, in the almost total lack of any attempt to link his scientific work with religious apologetic despite the very strong tradition of scientifically-based natural theology which was closely associated with the Royal Society of which he was President. From time to time, on official occasions, Banks would refer, in a manner which was almost *de rigueur* for a President of the Royal Society, to the way in which science and religion were natural allies. In 1781, for example, when presenting the Copley Medal to William Herschel, Banks did discourse on the way in which astronomy served to extend 'our Ideas of the immensity of Space, & of the Power Goodness & Wisdom of the Great Creator who has created & put into motion so many & such vast bodies'.[88] It is significant, however, that such an allusion is made in relation to astronomy, a subject well removed from the main focus of his own scientific interests. Ever since Ray's *The Wisdom of God Manifested in the Works of the Creation* (1691), Banks's 'favourite pursuit' of botany had been closely linked with natural theology and such an association was becoming more prominent in the late eighteenth century with the growing interest in natural history.[89] The Reverend William Jones, for example, in a work dedicated to Banks in 1784, entitled *The Religious Use of Botanical Philosophy,* underscored the potential of botany as an aid to devotion by urging that 'The flowers of the earth can raise our thoughts up to the Creator of the world as effectually as the stars of heaven'.[90] But Banks himself does not appear to have encouraged such uses for botany despite the fervent hope of his devoted sister, Sarah. 'May the Rational Study He takes so much delight in', she wrote, 'constantly remind Him of the wonderfull Order, Harmony, Mercy, and Goodness of God in the Creation'.[91] On one occasion Banks does refer to botany as 'that most engaging occupation of glorifying the Creator by observing & pointing out the wonders of his works'.[92] But this rare invocation of physico-theology occurs in a memorial of 1782 to the devout naturalist, George III; it is, then, more of a tribute to Banks's political skills than his piety.

Like most scientists of his age he assumed that the universe had been made by a purposeful Creator and thus that every aspect was designed for a purpose. But he took this teleological premise almost for granted so that he felt little need to defend it or to enlarge on its theological significance. There are, then, occasional references in his writings to the role of a designer in the natural world but they amount to little more than fleeting remarks which he never felt the need to develop into any more systematic form. When describing the flora of Tierra del Fuego in 1769, he made the conventional assumption that individual species had been specifically designed for their particular habitat: thus he admired 'the infinite care with which Providence has multiplied her productions, suiting them no doubt to the various climates for which they were designed'.[93] In a passage on the spread of fungus in one of his few substantive publications–*A Short Account of the Disease in Corn Called by Farmers the Blight, the Mildew and the Rust* (1805)–Banks did refer to the way in which 'Providence, however, careful of the creatures it has created, has benevolently provided against the too extensive multiplication of any species of being'.[94] Even more overtly teleological in tone is his comment to Blagden about the polar expedition of 1818: 'we may if we please conjecture that it is not likely that Providence should place land under the Pole for the mere Purpose of supporting the annually increasing Land of Snow & Ice till it Reaches above the regions of the Clouds'. However, as if embarrassed by this rare excursion into the realm of physico-theology, he concluded by remarking that 'the ways of Providence are inscrutable by the Limited Reason of Mankind'.[95] On occasion, too, Banks could refer to such teleological assumptions solely in terms of the laws of nature without any reference to a controlling Providence. When writing to Thomas Knight on issues related to plant physiology, for example, he spoke of the way in which 'nature seems in organic bodies to have followed one uniform plan; that is, she has arranged a certain number of parts necessary for the structure of the most perfect work of creation, and varied her works'.[96]

The fact that Banks–in common with his scientific contemporaries–viewed Nature as being ultimately the work of a purposeful designer did raise an issue on which Banks continued to ponder: if everything in Creation was part of a conscious design, why was it that some species seemed to have disappeared with the passage of time? Banks never abandoned the basic assumption of his age that species had been created *ex nihilo*, but his ruminations on the subject did prompt him to stray close to, and maybe beyond, the borders of the accepted interpretation of the scriptural account of Creation. Banks first appears to have given serious thought to the subject as a result of the discovery by Thomas Percy, bishop of Dromore (Ireland), of the fossil remains of a giant deer in 1783. Such a find, wrote Banks to Percy in November 1783, raised the question of whether such a species still existed; if not, he continued, it was 'a disquisition of no small Curiosity as the real abolition of a species of animal once created & in course necessary to the works of Creation is a matter which I hesitate most considerably to believe but concerning which I am curious in no inconsiderable degree'.[97] A month later Banks again wrote to the bishop with some speculations on the way in which the Creator might continue to maintain 'the duration of a species, while the individuals of it moulder into decay' for he still could not 'bring myself to Credit the Idea of a species being extinguished'; indeed, he concluded with the exclamation 'how can I admit the Loss of a species into my Creed!'.[98] By February 1784 he was able to give Bishop Percy the comforting news that the fossil appeared to be similar to the giant elk thus concluding that the fossil was a species 'hitherto unknown to our Naturalists'.[99]

But this was by no means the end of Banks's speculations on the subject. A few months later, in June 1784, he wrote to the German palaeontologist,

Johann Heinrich Merck, complimenting him on his dissertation on German fossils.[100] Such a study of 'The Antiquities of Creation' appeared to confirm the puzzling observation 'that at some distant period of remote antiquity many animals were to be met with on its surface whose species are now extinct'. The true cause of this, Banks remarked, with a conventional bow to religious doctrine, 'we must not enquire after till a new life opens our Faculties for the reception of more knowledge than in our present state of existence we are capable of'.

Nonetheless, he was prompted to suggest that the appearance and disappearance of species could be related to 'the increase of human knowledge': that as human beings developed better methods of hunting and agriculture so, too, the types of animals most suited to their needs also changed–an ingenious theory which, from an anthropocentric point of view, still retained the basic teleological assumption that all species were created for a purpose. Such a view did, however, imply a departure from the generally received view that Scripture had revealed that all species had been created together in a single once and for all act of Creation. This Banks acknowledged when he again returned to this subject in a letter to the great German physiologist and physical anthropologist, Johann Blumenbach, in 1806. Again he expressed his puzzlement that he had 'not yet been able to match any kind of Fossil Vegetable Remains with Vegetables now in Existence'. This made him speculate that in effect there had been at least two Creations: 'that the Whole of existing beings have been once if not oftener swept from the Face of the Earth & a new set of beings created in their steed'.[101] It was a view that Blumenbach himself advanced in his own writings drawing on the work of the prominent London physicians, John and William Hunter (who possibly may also have played a part in shaping Banks's own conception of this problem). Blumenbach drew out the full implications of such a position: that the traditional understanding of a Great Chain of Being linking all created things in an ascending hierarchy was no longer valid.[102] Banks was less given to pursuing the full theoretical implications of his insights and it is doubtful whether he altogether abandoned a belief in what he called in 1795 'the chain of animated beings'.[103] Just how deeply engrained such a concept was in Banks's thought (and that of his age) is evident in his eloquent description in his *Endeavour* journal of 'the admirable chain of nature in which Man, alone endowd with reason, justly claims the highest rank'.[104] Nonetheless, he appears to have sensed in later life that the existing framework of ideas about the way in which Creation was ordered was beginning to need revision.

Banks's anti-clericalism and apparent religious scepticism or, at least, indifference were, in the case of the youthful Banks, accompanied by a mode of life which indicated a more overt rejection of traditional Christian sanctions. In England, as in France, free living and free thinking were closely associated–thus the pedlars of radical Enlightenment tracts often mixed this trade with the sale of pornography. Banks's youthful mentor, the Earl of Sandwich, was well known for what a contemporary journal referred to as 'impropriety of conduct in his private life' and 'debauchery and libertinism'–though adding that 'being naturally of a social and convivial disposition . . . it is not astonishing that he should indulge in a species of dissipation, as agreeable to others as himself'.[105]

Banks's association with Sandwich (or 'Jemmy Twitcher' as he was called by the satirists) was well known: in August 1776, for example, the *Morning Post* coyly noted that he had been seen with 'J...y Twitcher who is almost the only surviving member of that club (formerly called the Hell-fire Club)'[106]–a notorious gathering place for libertines. Earlier that year David Hume reported that Sandwich and Banks, together with their mutual friend Lord Mulgrave, had been on a fishing expedition with 'two or three Ladies of pleasure'.[107] Under Sandwich's guidance Banks was introduced to some of London's more raffish characters. Among those he came to know was the arch-libertine, John Wilkes, for whom Banks (despite his political conservatism) appears to have retained a lasting affection. Thus he thanked him in 1788 for the gift of a de luxe edition of Catullus 'as a testimony of his Friendship which tho he has had but few opportunities of deserving he shall ever cherish with respect for superior abilities & gratitude For the Enjoyment of Brilliant Conversation'.[108]

Banks's own private life, and especially his *amours* in Tahiti, became the butt of the Grub Street satirists.[109] The *Town and Country Magazine* regaled its readers with accounts of Banks's undergraduate romantic exploits, his 'critical inspection' of 'the females of most countries that he has visited' and his liaison with a young lady of good birth but poor fortune.[110] A poem entitled *Mimosa or, the sensitive plant dedicated to Mr Banks* also linked him with aristocratic sexual intrigue.[111] How accurate this all was it is hard to know but Banks does appear to have had an ex-nuptial child in 1773[112] and reportedly he later boasted that 'he had tasted Womans flesh in almost every part of the Known habitable World'.[113]

His most public liaison was his co-habitation with Sarah Wells, a figure who flits through his papers a few years before he was married in 1779. Presumably the connection followed after the break with Harriet Blosset in 1771, following his return from the *Endeavour* voyage after–as Daines Barrington salaciously noted in a letter of 1771 to his fellow naturalist, Thomas Pennant–an interview which lasted 'from ten o'clock at night to ten the next morning'.[114] Whether Sarah Wells was the same woman whom Banks attempted to smuggle on board the *Resolution* in 1772 under the pseudonym 'Mr Burnett',[115] or whether this was yet another lady in his life we do not know. She was obviously regarded with affection by many of his friends and enjoyed a recognised position in Banks's bachelor establishment: in September 1777, for example, Banks's close friend, the Earl of Seaforth, acknowledged the receipt by his mistress of a letter from Mrs Wells and sent 'my kindest Comp[limen]ts to Sally [Wells] and all Friends'.[116] In the following month the visiting Swede, Johann Alstromer, wrote home that he had dined at Banks's 'and *Soupé* at his *Maitress* Mistress

Wells, with only Banks and Solander'.[117] The parting between Banks and Mrs Wells when he was duly married off to the inevitable heiress appears to have been amicable with, no doubt, some appropriate financial settlement having been made. Solander, who delighted in gossip, reported to the Welsh naturalist, John Lloyd, in June 1779 that they 'parted on very good terms–She had sense enough to find that he acted right, and of course she behaved very well. All her old friends visit her as formerly'.[118]

Banks's escapades were, of course, by no means unusual in his class and particularly not in the *demi-monde* of Lord Sandwich and his circle. The Grand Tour, for example, was often regarded as an episode which might include sexual as well as cultural initiation for the gilded youth of the landed classes.[119] Thus Banks in a youthful letter of 1767 to his Eton schoolmate, William Perrin, on Perrin's return from France, expressed the hope that 'you have no reason to repent of any Connection you may have made with the Filles d'Opera as I imagine every man who goes to see a people chuses to make Experiments upon the women before he gives his opinion of them',[120] a remark that appears to have been a guide to Banks's own practice in Tahiti.[121] But as well as the virtual *droit de seigneur* of his class, Banks's practice in these matters may have reflected a more fundamental rejection of Christian sexual ethics. Such a position formed a strand of French Enlightenment thought, most notably in Diderot's *Supplement to the Voyages of Bougainville* (written in 1772 but published posthumously) in which the exploration of the Pacific is linked with a rediscovery of a sort of sexual Eden and Enlightenment extended to a dismantling of many of the conventions governing the relations between the sexes. There are some hints that Banks regarded his experiences in Tahiti in a similar light. His account of Tahitian society in the *Endeavour* journal includes an anti-clerical aside on the association in Europe regarding relations between the sexes and religious guilt: 'If our preists excelld theirs in persuading us that the Sexes can not come lawfully together without having bought their benediction, they have done it by intermingling it so far with religion that the fear of punishment from above secures their power over us'.[122] In his letter of 1773 to the Dutch Count William Bentinck on the 'Manners of Otaheite', Banks praised the Tahitians for the fact that there 'the want of Chastity does not preclude a woman from the esteem of those who have it, no more than the want of Charity in this countrey ... yet are there women there as inviolable in their attachments as here'.[123]

By contrast, Banks on a number of occasions took issue with the accepted morality of his own country that rendered a woman whose chastity was questioned a social outcast. In a long letter written by Banks in reply to an enquiry from one, Mary Ann Radcliffe, about the need for more female employment and about the possibility of women attending the lectures of the Royal Institution, Banks began by praising her for being 'an able advocate for the natural rights of your sex'. He also argued (in an aside that again indicates his lukewarm attitude to the anti-slavery campaign) that 'the oppressed portion of [the female sex] ... have a far better claim to the interference of Parliament in their favor then either the free negroes of the various nations of Africa or the enslaved cultivators of our sugar colonies'. But, he continued, the 'greater part of the Evils to which your sex are liable under our present Customs of Society originate in the decisions of Women'. He singled out particularly the way in which women rigorously enforced traditional conceptions of morality-or, as he put it: 'The Penalty by which women uniformly permit the smallest deviation of a Female character from the Rigid Paths of virtue is more severe than Death & more afflicting than the Tortures of the Dungeons'.[124] Later in life Banks echoed these sentiments even more forcefully in a letter to Lady Somerset of September 1814, chiding her for her comments on another woman's lack of virtue:

> Tremendous is the punishment inflicted by the Class of Virtuous women on those who err & stray from the Paths of Propriety. To have the whole Bonds of Society broken asunder in an instant, to be compelled to shun all those who the day before were dear Friends ... to be in short a Criminal Banishd from all intercourse with the Society in the midst of which she lives & must continue to live is surely a more severe destiny than that of immediate death.[125]

Possibly, then, Banks in his characteristically cautious way, favoured some fundamental change in the accepted code of ethics and he does seem to have felt some compunction about the traditional double standard which consigned women who indulged in pre-marital relations to social outer darkness, while allowing gentlemen like himself to go on to become pillars of the Establishment despite a colourful past. But, whatever his views, Banks's free-living ways seem to have been discarded on marriage. Indeed the near conjunction of his election as President of the Royal Society in 1778 and his marriage in 1779 signalled an end to any such irregularities and the start of a devotion to a life of such intense activity in so many different fields of public endeavour that little time was left for any other private *divertissements*.

But whatever his reservations about the accepted interpretation of Christian ethics or doctrines and despite his anti-clericalism, Banks was too much a child of the Establishment to challenge the constituted order in Church and State. Again the limits of the Enlightenment in England are apparent: a figure such as Banks may have shared some of the anti-clerical assumptions of the French *philosophes* and even some of their intellectual questioning of aspects of Christian doctrine and morality, but ultimately the Church of England as by law established was too much a part of the fabric of the social and political order for Banks to challenge it in any fundamental or overt manner. Even the possibility of reform of the Church's organisation or simplification of its doctrine was regarded by Banks with indifference-as the Reverend Richard Shepherd found when he attempted to interest him in such schemes in 1798. Shepherd's plea that the superiors of the Church had set their faces against 'Reform in Doctrines for fear it should lead to a Reform in Temporals'[126] probably only strengthened Banks's determination not to become involved since, he, too, like most of his class in the aftermath of the French Revolution, was fearful of the contagion of reform spreading.

Though Banks regarded himself as being 'Tolerant in religious matters to the highest degree'[127] he remained a supporter of the privileged position of the Established Church. In response to Priestley's accusation that one of his scientific protégés had been rejected by Banks as a fellow of the Royal Society because of his dissenting religious beliefs, Banks responded by disclaiming any such prejudice on the part of the Royal Society. Nonetheless, his letter went on to offer a defence of the Test and Corporation Acts which denied full civil rights to non-Anglicans: 'I am convinced that the majority governed have a right to insist that the magistrates who govern them do profess the religious tenets which they beleive to be the only true [sic] and conform to the rites by which the sincerity of their religious profession can alone be put to the test'.[128] In a letter written a mere two months previously Banks had been very much less respectful of the Test Acts and of the Established Church, commenting of the dissenters' campaign to have these measures repealed that 'the Church of England have rallied & it does not appear that one clergyman among them has any conscientious scruples on the subject of prostituting the Elements to secular purposes'.[129] But in the latter case Banks was writing in a private capacity and so could indulge himself in a little anti-clericalism; in the former, however, he was writing *qua* President of the Royal Society, an office that carried with it the duty of defending the established order in Church and State.

Predictably, Banks's wariness about the political and social dangers that might accompany a weakening in the position of the Established Church became more pronounced after the French Revolution made apparent the fragility of the English old regime. By 1806 he was sufficiently solicitous about maintaining the Church's privileges to decline supporting the scheme of Joseph Lancaster to provide cheap, mass education for the lower orders, until he was assured that religious instruction under the auspices of the Church of England would be included. Banks declared himself 'tolerant in the extreme' of other religions but added that he nonetheless maintained that 'in all well-ordered Governments' the earliest religious instruction to young children should be such as to impart 'a bias in favor of the Established Religion of their Country'.[130] In the following year Banks, in his capacity as a Privy Counsellor, sprang to the defence of the Established Church as a bond between the Mother Country and the Empire. In his notes on Newfoundland he warned of the rapid growth in the number of Roman Catholics there, something which he saw as 'demand[ing] the immediate attention & instant counter-action by the Friends of the Established Church'.[131]

Like others of his class Banks recognised how closely intertwined were Church and State in the maintenance of the established order. As Pitt had put it when opposing the repeal of the Test Acts: 'It was impossible to separate the ecclesiastical and political liberties of this country; the church and state were united upon principles of mutual expediency and by indissoluble ties'.[132] Not only was it politically expedient to maintain the Church's administrative structures but it was also socially expedient to maintain an established church to instil public morality. Banks appears to have been largely indifferent as to the form of such an established church but saw it as important that the Church be given the support of the secular arm. Whatever his private doubts he was reluctant to disseminate ideas which might undermine the Church as a guardian of social order and, like Voltaire, thought the belief in the threat of divine retribution in the next life was essential to a well-ordered society.

In his correspondence with the plant physiologist, Richard Knight, Banks was resistant to the possibility of explaining human generation solely in material terms both because of his own lingering belief in the possibility of an afterlife and because of the social consequences of such a view gaining currency. Of beliefs in the existence of a soul he wrote:

> I am unwilling to disbelieve them & still more unwilling to give any human being any intimation of doubt. A portion of mankind are rendered virtuous by the fear of being damned a lesser portion by the fear of being hanged [.W]as it not for the fear of damnation our magistrates would have far more business than they now have.[133]

Like Napoleon, then, Banks saw in religion not so much the mystery of the Incarnation but that of social order–something which was too important to be weakened by an intemperate public utterance of any Enlightenment-induced doubts about the place of Christian Revelation or of the role of the clerical estate.

This is not to say, however, that Banks wished to leave the masses immersed in ignorance and superstition. Indeed, Banks was far more active than Voltaire and some of the French *philosophes* in promoting mass education.[134] His efforts in doing so largely came in the early nineteenth century when the fear of popular unrest was strong. Thus his motives, like those of the English Establishment generally, were mixed, combining both an Enlightenment (and, to some degree, Christian) faith in the utility and moral worth of education and a determination to counter the spread of subversive ideas by instructing the masses in their social and religious duties.

Banks was an active supporter of Joseph Lancaster's schemes for providing large-scale cheap elementary education 'on mechanical principles'. In this area, as in many others, Banks operated at a number of different levels. Firstly, in his local setting as a prominent Lincolnshire squire he both donated money to Lancaster and (in 1810) became first president of the National School of Boston. At the national level he could use his position as President of the Royal Society and as an adviser to government to disseminate such schemes for mass education; he also advised Lancaster on the best tactics to win over the good will of the elite (especially by avoiding any clash with the Established Church).[135] At the international level Banks's contacts with foreign (and especially French) learned societies enabled him to exchange information about other schemes of elementary education. The correspondence between Banks and the French educationalist, Edmé Jomard, culminated in 1816 in Jomard's sending via the visiting scientist, Gay-Lussac, a short account of the methods employed in French elementary schools.[136] In the same year Banks also received news of the progress of a Lancaster school in Haiti from the island's foreign minister;[137] two years later, Banks had a cordial letter from the king of Haiti informing him that six more schools had been established on the English (Lancastrian) model and thanking him for being one of 'the greatest friends' of the new State.[138] In a letter to Lady Somerset in 1815, Banks commented with satisfaction on the spread of such schools throughout England and on the way in which 'The Squires of the country who used to be the most idle class take Pains in superintending these schools'. It is a letter that also brings out Banks's ambivalent motives for promoting such schemes. With an Enlightenment respect for the improving effects of knowledge he wrote of the way in which 'the mass of People are I think improvd in their minds of Late'. However, in his Establishment guise, he also commented on the beneficial effects of education as a means of social control: that such schools 'improve the manners of the youth & teach them the valuable lesson of Subordination'.[139]

Banks, then, acts as a useful guide to the limits of the English Enlightenment. On the one hand, the Enlightenment promoted within the English Establishment a willingness to approach political and social problems in a secular spirit, to promote science–or, more broadly, useful knowledge–and to question tradition where it conflicted with observation and reason. But the hold of the English Enlightenment was not strong enough to weaken other, more traditional, beliefs of the English elite, above all their self-confidence in themselves as a class, the privilege and destiny of which it was to direct the affairs of the nation. The Enlightenment, too, might help to promote a common European culture among the elite and to weaken the force of such traditional justifications for mass blood-letting as dynastic and religious conflict but it was not strong enough to diminish greatly the strength of national rivalries. Banks and his class looked to such conflicts to advance the interests of an increasingly powerful commercial Empire which served to benefit the interests of both a growing number of the middling orders and the landed elite to whom such social inferiors generally continued to look for leadership and government. In advancing such an Empire science was, where possible, to play its part and no one was of more importance in harnessing it to the chariot-wheels of British imperial power than Sir Joseph Banks. Nonetheless when such issues of national interest were not at stake, he was also eager to promote science as an instrument of international co-operation. Though the Enlightenment was a central impulse in Banks's life and work it was, then, subject to the limits imposed by his social position and his support for the traditional order in Church and State.

CHAPTER THREE

From Virtuoso to Botanist

THE VIRTUOSO TRADITION

From the perspective of the twentieth century it seems only natural that educated men (and even a few women) of the seventeenth and eighteenth centuries should take an increasing interest in what came to be known as 'science'. But, of course, such an assumption overlooks just how marginal a role the study of nature occupied in a society where intellectual life had so long been based not on recourse to the first-hand observation of nature or of experiment but rather on the close scrutiny of the two main sources of authority: Scripture and the classics. One of the major features of both the Scientific Revolution and of the Enlightenment was to convince many of the elite that the store of human knowledge could indeed be expanded beyond the frontiers established by the Ancients–that, as Bacon graphically depicted it in his frontispiece of *The Advancement of Learning*, European society could venture beyond the Pillars of Hercules (Gibraltar), the effective limits of the ancient world. The scientific achievements of the seventeenth century–and particularly the crowning glory of Newton's *Principia* (1687)–helped to provide the foundation for that intellectual self-confidence and belief in the possibility of progress which characterised the Enlightenment–a movement which, as Kant put it, took as its motto, *Sapere aude* ('Dare to know'). The traditional authorities of Scripture and the classics were by no means discarded–though there were some, at least, who wished to dispense with the former–but increasingly they came to be seen as providing a guide to only a limited part of the total map of human knowledge which it was the privilege and the delight of the eighteenth century and subsequent ages to supplement and expand.

In a society so long accustomed to living in the shadow of classical and biblical antiquity one of the ways in which the possibilities of such

intellectual progress slowly took root was through the activities associated
with a cultural type known as a 'virtuoso'. The meaning of the term was
by no means clear-cut and was to change over time and, eventually, by
the nineteenth century, to die out as the professionalisation of science
rendered both the word and the reality it reflected obsolete. However, the
primary characteristic of the 'virtuoso' was that he (and even in a few
cases–such as Banks's sister, Sarah–she) was a collector. Such an activity
was a sign of social position–generally what was collected was rare and
expensive and the very fact that one had the leisure to engage in such
an avocation was, like the long fingernails of a Chinese mandarin, an
indication that one was a gentleman who did not have to trouble oneself
about earning a living. It also indicated the civilising effects of Renaissance
discourses on the ideal of a gentleman such as Castiglione's *The Courtier:*
no longer was social status measured simply by success in feats of arms
or by the number of retainers, since the size and value of an individual's
collection of rarities had become a way of establishing gentlemanly status.
The kind of rarities collected varied with time and fashion but when the
ideal of a virtuoso was first established there was a natural tendency to
concentrate on the self-evidently valuable remains of the ancient world.
Hence, Henry Peacham, in the first recorded English use of the term
'virtuoso' in 1634, wrote of classical antiquities in a passage which underlines the original association between the activities of a virtuoso and those
of a courtier: 'The possession of such rarities, by reason of their dead
costlinesse, doth properly belong to Princes, or rather to princely minds
. . . Such as are skilled in them, are by the Italians termed *Virtuosi*'.[1]

The activities of a virtuoso, like those of a bower-bird, could, and often
did, degenerate into a rather mindless collecting for collecting's sake. As
late as 1711 Lord Shaftesbury deplored the way in which 'the inferior
Virtuosi' seek 'so earnestly for Raritys, [that] they fall in love with Rarity
for Rareness-sake'. Nonetheless, the very act of collecting and closely
observing material objects did do something to weaken one of the major
obstacles to the Scientific Revolution: the traditional reliance on the
authority of texts rather than evidence gained by observation and experience, a battle reflected in the choice of the Royal Society's motto, *Nullius
in verba* ('on the word–or the text–of no one'). This may help to explain
why the term 'virtuoso' and the practices it reflected expanded beyond
its original connotations of collector to encompass one who also occupied
himself in experiments. By 1660 Boyle in his *New Experiments Physico-
Mechanical* could write, 'Perceiving by letters from . . . Paris, that several
of the Virtuosi there were very intent upon the examination of the interest
of the Ayr . . .'.[2]

A virtuoso, then, was someone who had the time and leisure to advance
knowledge either by collecting rarities or by promoting experiments. But
such practices still remained something of a badge of gentility which–
together with sheer ignorance of the nature and possibilities of the
emerging scientific movement–helps to explain why Restoration satirists
depicted the virtuosi as entirely unconcerned with the practical uses of
their discoveries or collections. Gimcrack, the main character in Shadwell's

Title page of Francis Bacon's *Instauratio Magna*. The ship is sailing beyond the traditional limits of the ancient world ('The Pillars of Hercules', i.e. Gibraltar) to the uncharted seas beyond, just as Bacon's book advocates a new method which will open up oceans of truth unknown to the Ancients. Courtesy of Cambridge University Library

play *The Virtuosi*, proclaims proudly: 'I seldom bring any thing to use, 'tis not my way, Knowledge is my ultimate end'. In her *Character of a Virtuoso* (1696), Mary Astell later echoed the same judgement: 'He Trafficks to all places, and has his Correspondents in every part of the World; yet his Merchandizes serve not to promote our Luxury, nor encrease our Trade, and neither enrich the Nation, nor himself'.[3]

Astell's remarks also point to another characteristic of the virtuoso–that he was frequently a traveller. This again underlies the gentlemanly status of a virtuoso–for who else could afford to travel widely or to purchase and ship home the expensive souvenirs which augmented the cabinets of the virtuosi? Naturally enough, many such travellers largely devoted themselves to inspecting and, where possible, collecting at the historical and archaeological sites of Roman antiquity which were the natural attractions for an elite raised on the classics. Increasingly, however, they took a wider view of a traveller's lot: not only should the compleat traveller bring back an account and, preferably, samples of the antiquities he had observed but also a record of the social and natural environment. A study of the flora, fauna and social customs of different lands became part of the staples of travellers' accounts. Nor did such a virtuoso-traveller necessarily need to cross the Channel: there was ample scope for such travel accounts of the antiquities and natural curiosities within Britain itself. The ultimate extension of the genre was to be Gilbert White's classic *Natural History and Antiquities of Selborne* (1789), a detailed account in the manner of a traveller's account of the total environment of one particular region by a man who virtually never left home. As Maddox writes what was 'new about *Selborne* is its successful appropriation of the general assumptions and strategies of the travel account to its own local interests, and consequently of its appropriation of an existing audience'.[4]

The natural association between the study of antiquities and of natural history which was reflected in the title of White's book and which was a feature of so many travel accounts helps to explain why it was that a virtuoso might be either an antiquarian or a student of the natural sciences or, very frequently, both. An institutional reflection of this was the frequency with which gentlemen combined membership of both the Royal Society and the Society of Antiquaries–Gibbon, for example, wrote in 1789 of having had 'the expensive honour of being elected a fellow of the Royal and Antiquarian Societies'.[5] Indeed, so frequent was this practice in the late eighteenth century that the abbreviation, FRASS, was often employed to denote membership of both societies[6]–an indication of the extent to which study of the natural and of the historical worlds continued to be regarded as complementary parts of the map of knowledge of gentlemanly society.

Thus travel and the ideal of the virtuoso naturally went together and the eighteenth century was the great age of English gentlemanly travel which became institutionalised in the practice of the Grand Tour as the culmination of a young gentleman's education. Much of the seventeenth century had been beset by long and murderous wars, by heightened religious conflict and by a consequent strengthening of the long and deeply-engrained tradition of English insularity. But the eighteenth century was relatively peaceful, religious divisions were less deeply felt and the growth of England as a major commercial and naval power helped to stimulate an interest in the world across the Channel. The growing wealth of many of the landed elite also enabled them to support the enormous cost of a Grand Tour, 'the most expensive form of education ever devised by European society'.[7] The extent of travel, then, suggests the need for some modification of Houghton's argument in his pioneering (and still unsurpassed) study of the phenomenon of the virtuoso; for he contends that the significance of the virtuoso as a cultural type had largely faded by the early eighteenth century. Both the term 'virtuoso' and the social and cultural values it represented were alive and well for much of the eighteenth century stimulated by the extent of travel not only within Europe but, thanks to England's growing commercial and naval power, also increasingly to remote quarters of the globe. Indeed, Banks regarded his *Endeavour* voyage as a variant of the Grand Tour traditionally spent in Europe; to an enquiry as to why he was not proceeding to the Continent he is supposed to have replied: 'Every blockhead does that; my Grand Tour shall be one round the whole globe'.[8] In a similar vein, one of Banks's obituarists wrote of him: 'To go the narrow round of the common fashionable tour, could appear but miserable trifling to a young man whose mind glowed with a love of ingenuous enterprize, and the knowledge of nature'; by contrast, the exploration of sciences and lands unknown 'was a plan of travel worthy of the desire and the contrivance of virtue and genius'.[9]

Moreover, in the eighteenth century the fashionableness of the activities of a virtuoso, which had first derived from the Renaissance ideal of the courtier, was strengthened by another European-wide cultural upheaval: the Enlightenment. The cosmopolitanism which travel brought was itself a sign of an enlightened break with provincialism even though such a transformation often took the trivial form of a self-conscious adoption of continental fashions and manners. The exaggeratedly European airs of many young recent graduates of the Grand Tour was a favourite butt of contemporary satirists: in 1764 Horace Walpole wrote dismissively of the activities of the Macaroni Club 'which is composed of all the travelled young men who wear long curls and spying glasses'.[10] The Macaroni Club continued deliberately to defy English insularity[11] and so the term 'macaroni' came to be used as a term of ridicule for those enamoured of European rather than English culture and fashions. Robert Hitchcock in his play, *The Macaroni* (1773), wrote scathingly of one who instead of being 'a man of spirit' had become 'a first-rate Macaroni ... fully qualified, and determined, I see, to shew the world what a contemptible creature an Englishman dwindles into, when he adopts the folly and vices of other nations'.[12]

Significantly, however, the term came to be used not only to describe the foppish graduate of the European Grand Tour (and, indeed, any person whose defiance of current fashion or manners was thought to make him an object of ridicule) but also as a virtual synonym for a 'virtuoso'. Around 1771-2, at much the same period as Hitchcock's play, a series of cartoons was published depicting variants of the species 'macaroni'. Some simply portrayed foppish dandies[13] but others were directed at the natural history activities of Banks and Solander recently made famous by the *Endeavour* expedition. In 'The Fly Catching Macaroni'[14] Banks is shown with one foot on each of two globes endeavouring to catch a butterfly. The picture mixes caricature of Banks's scientific pursuits with ridicule of macaronis more generally: true to the image of the macaroni as a fop, Banks is depicted as having an elaborate hair style and as wearing an ostrich feather. Other satirical prints of macaronis were also plainly directed at Banks and his circle. Banks figures in both 'The Botanic Macaroni' and 'The Polite Maccaroni presenting a Nosegay to Miss Blossom' (perhaps a play on Banks's romance with Miss Blosset); Solander in 'The Simpling Macaroni' and the Earl of Sandwich, Banks's patron, in 'The Macaroni Courtship Rejected' and 'The Grub Street Macaroni'.[15]

The term 'macaroni' again surfaced in the bitter faction-fighting within the Royal Society in 1783-4. Blagden, Banks's main lieutenant in dealing with this dispute, reported to him that his opponents were describing it as 'a struggle of the men of science against the Macaronis of the Society, dignifying your friends by the latter title'.[16] In the eyes of his opponents, then, Banks and his allies were men who shared the same leisured background as the dandified products of the Grand Tour and who looked on science as a source of gentlemanly amusement. In short, they were seen as virtuosi, that is as preoccupied with activities such as natural history and antiquities which gave them ample scope for collecting and display rather than with the mathematical sciences which required a degree of rigour and professional commitment quite foreign to the essentially amateur status of a virtuoso. Banks's chief opponent, Samuel Horsley, the editor of Newton's works, summed up the hostility to the virtuosi with the remark that 'science herself had never been more signally insulted, than by the elevation of a mere *amateur* to occupy the chair once filled by Newton';[17] elsewhere he spoke slightingly of Banks as one who tried 'to amuse the Fellows with frogs, flees and grasshopers'.[18] The mathematician and military engineer, James Glenie, another of Banks's opponents, deplored the way in which the Society was giving less attention to the mathematical sciences and thus exposing itself to the risk of being no longer 'the resort of philosophers' but becoming instead 'a cabinet of trifling curiosities' and of 'degenerat[ing] into a virtuoso's closet decorated with plants and shells'.[19] More damning still was the satirical *Philosophical Puppet Show* published in 1785 and addressed to Banks as 'A Celebrated Connoisseur in Chickweed, Caterpillars, Black Beetles, Butterflies, and Cockle-Shells' in the course of which botany was described as 'a study to be preferred above all others, as it furnishes the whole human race with amusement delicious, without either wasting the spirits, or hurting the brain'.[20]

But though mathematicians like Horsley or Glenie might sneer at the scientific worth of natural history the eighteenth-century virtuoso was increasingly able to claim for natural history the dignity of a science. Like the achievements of Newton the ordering of Nature's diverse products became associated with a belief in progress and in the capabilities of human reason to produce order and harmony: in short, with Enlightenment. In the first place, the natural historian had to produce the evidence of systematic observation rather than simply reproduce untested belief: as the naturalist, Peter Collinson, remarked in a letter to Linnaeus about the migration of swallows, 'This enlightened age will not be imposed upon and belief must be established on undeniable and uncontestable proofs'.[21] Botanical hypotheses also had to be examined with the close scrutiny that became a science. Banks's early botanical associate, James Lee, one of Linnaeus's first English popularisers, wrote approvingly in his *An Introduction to Botany* ... (1762) that 'the sexual Hypothesis ... was received with all that Caution that becomes an enlightened Age, and Nature was traced experimentally through all her variations, before it was universally assented to'.[22] Botany, claimed its practitioners, also contributed to the general progress of knowledge which was the hall-mark of their own age. As William Curtis put it, after enumerating the manifold uses of botany in his proposals for a London Botanic Garden: 'In this enlightened age, when arts and sciences are carried to a pitch unthought of in former times, it was not likely that this branch should be neglected'.[23] When Linnaeus died in 1778 his mantle as a promoter of the enlightened study of natural history was assumed by his disciples throughout Europe, among whom Banks and Solander were numbered. As Johann Forster wrote: 'Great as the loss of Linnaeus must certainly be to science, it will not be severely felt whilst we have so enlightened botanists, as Mr Banks and Dr Solander'.[24]

Though the virtuoso frequently saw himself as assisting the advancement of science through the patient accumulation of yet more specimens and data, others regarded such a pursuit as being too devoid of theory and of generalisation to be regarded as being truly scientific. This was an accusation frequently levelled against the early eighteenth-century virtuoso. In the *Tatler* of 1710 Addison lauded the enlightened credentials of science writing that 'There is no study more becoming a rational creature than that of natural philosophy but', he continued, 'as several of our modern virtuosi manage it, their speculations do not so much tend to open and enlarge the mind, as to contract and fix it upon trifles'.[25]

Later in the century Dr Johnson was of the same mind. 'The virtuoso', he wrote, damning the kind with faint praise, 'therefore cannot be said to be wholly useless; but perhaps he may be sometimes culpable for confining himself to business below his genius, and losing in petty speculations, those hours by which if he had spent them in nobler studies, he might have given new light to the intellectual world ... Collections of this kind are of use to the learned, as heaps of stones and piles of timber are necessary to the architect'.[26] The difficulty was that for much of the

The Fly Catching Macaroni (1772), a parody of Banks. Courtesy of the Trustees of the British Museum

The Simpling Macaroni (1772), a parody of Solander. Courtesy of the Trustees of the British Museum

eighteenth century natural history lacked any very well-developed system of classification–or, at least, lacked one that commanded widespread allegiance–and so languished in the shadow of the mathematical sciences with their highly developed theoretical structures. Hence the cutting remark of another of Banks's critics in the Royal Society disputes of 1783–4 that he had done nothing 'but what might have been given by one of the humblest of the votaries of the humblest of the sciences'.[27] Ardent botanists like John Hill protested at the confusion between their scientific pursuits and the activities of the virtuosi bemoaning the fact that 'The frivolous pursuits in which some have engaged, under the name of Enquiries into NATURAL KNOWLEDGE ... have brought that useful science to disgrace: the VIRTUOSO has been considered as a NATURALIST, and the FLORIST has been honoured with a name derived from BOTANY'.[28] Such insults help to explain why, despite many misgivings about its artificial nature, Linnaeus's classificatory system came to be seized upon with such enthusiasm by so many eighteenth-century naturalists. At last there was a commonly agreed means of filing the products of the natural world into an orderly and rational system and thus of investing the interests of the naturalist and virtuoso with the dignity of a true science. But in the process the virtuoso was slowly to give way to his scientifically more respectable descendant, the botanist or geologist, just as another sphere of the virtuoso's activities–the study of antiquities–was to be transformed into the disciplines of archaeology, history and even anthropology. As these disciplines proliferated and waxed in strength, however, there was a consequent waning in the virtuoso's traditional assumption that the study of all aspects of the human and natural environment were somehow integrally related–even though the virtuoso lacked any clearly developed theoretical basis for such a belief.

Such a metamorphosis from virtuoso to botanist is well reflected in the work and career of Banks. From his upbringing and education as the heir to a landed fortune he naturally acquired a taste for the virtuoso activities which were characteristic of his class. Though he deliberately chose to eschew the traditional Grand Tour he was nonetheless the well-travelled man *par excellence*. Moreover, his celebrated overseas journeys to Labrador, the South Seas, Iceland and Holland were preceded and interspersed with travel within Britain during which his journals indicate the extent to which he indulged the virtuoso's characteristic delight in collecting both historical and natural rarities. They also indicate, however, an interest in industrial processes and the practical uses of the earth and its products which sets Banks apart from the archetypal virtuoso interested in rarities only for their own sake without regard to their potential uses; indeed, these early travel journals prefigure Banks's subsequent career as the *de facto* scientific adviser to government in the age of the nascent Industrial Revolution.

Banks's enthusiasm for gathering the rare and the curious was shared by his sister, Sarah. Largely thanks to her brother's good offices, she continued throughout her life to amass a vast array of historical artefacts such as medals, coins, newspaper clippings, cards and playbills in the traditional manner of the virtuoso. Her collection of printed and engraved ephemera alone constituted some nineteen thousand items, while her broadsheets and newspaper cuttings now form nine bulky volumes in the British Library.[29] Appropriately, her collection of engravings included a section devoted to caricatures of the macaroni.[30] Brother and sister, then, were to reflect different aspects of the changing role of the virtuoso: the latter continuing to embody its most traditional and least scientific form, while the former more and more brought scientific order and system to his collection without ever losing that curiosity and delight in the novel and the rare which was the well-spring of a virtuoso's activities.

Among Banks's correspondents there were naturally many of his class and interests who assumed that he, like them, was a virtuoso of the traditional kind interested in collecting for its own sake. John Strange, for example, who inherited a fortune and devoted himself to the study of antiquities and natural history chiefly in Italy (where from 1773 he served as official English resident), could remark that Banks's comments on art 'made me smile, though the truth of it is rather humiliating to us virtuosi'.[31] A year before Banks's death he was sent as 'a Justly Celebrated Virtuoso' an account of that ultimate rarity, a five-legged kitten.[32] Predictably, the satirist, 'Peter Pindar' (alias John Wolcot), portrayed Banks as an archetypal virtuoso and his long poem 'Sir Joseph Banks and the Emperor of Morocco', a mock heroic account of Banks's pursuit of a rare butterfly, includes a section entitled 'the Virtuoso's Prayer' and the line 'the virtuoso did his prey pursue'.[33] Even some of Banks's paid collectors appear to have regarded him as yet another wealthy virtuoso who sought more rarities for his collections. In 1795 Anton Hove apologised to Banks for the fact that he had not had an 'opportunity of adding to your extensive collection of curiositys anything worth notice'.[34] Others also naturally tended to class Banks with the virtuosi in the more extended sense of one interested in science: thus in 1779 Jeremy Bentham described the physiologist, Jan Ingenhousz, as being 'on good terms with Banks, Priestly, Ld. Shelburne, etc., in short all the literati and amateurs'[35]–terms which were synonymous with 'virtuosi'.

But Banks himself does not appear to have used the term 'virtuoso' as a term of self-description and from quite early in his career sought to distinguish himself as a man of science rather than as the type of virtuoso who simply collected rarities. Banks, no doubt, looked favourably on the description of himself given in *Public Characters of 1800-1* as someone who was not 'merely a naturalist and a virtuoso' but rather one whose 'knowledge is not that of facts merely ... but of science in its elementary principles, and of Nature in her happiest forms'.[36] Even as a young man Banks referred to himself as a 'man of science', a phrase he employed when writing in 1768 about his proposed role on board the *Endeavour*. '[T]he south sea at least', he commented to his old school friend, William Perrin, 'has never been visited by any man of science'–though he added 'in any

Branch of Literature',[37] an indication of the extent to which science was still regarded as part of the fruits of polite culture more generally. In January of the same year, in the course of his trip through the Midlands, Banks called on a number of virtuosi of the most traditional kind but wrote dismissively of one such virtuoso's 'Collection of Curiosities' with its 'Very Bad Collection of Shells [and] a worse of Fossils'. Another collection amassed by a gentleman who had made his fortune in the East Indies he described as consisting 'of heaps of Shells' and added that 'as a punishment for the small Pleasure I had received from the Echinus [shells] I was oblig'd to admire drawers full of' miscellaneous objects ranging from Indian weapons to 'Closets full of China'.[38] By contrast, Banks's voyage to Iceland, as his servant, James Roberts, emphasised in the introduction to his journal, was prompted by philosophical enquiry rather than simply the quest for more curiosities since 'The enterprising Genius of Mr Banks is not confined to trifling remarks or useless discoveries, his Philosophical researches were intended to improve the mind, and as far as possible, become a universal Benefit by observing and explaining the wonderful works of nature in all her various Elements'.[39]

Predictably, as Banks's public and scientific stature grew he became more insistent on the need to distinguish between collecting for its own sake in the manner of the traditional virtuoso and collecting which was properly informed by scientific principles. In 1795 Banks was consulted by the Earl of Liverpool as to whether or not the British Museum ought to purchase the natural history collection of the French statesman, de Calonne, which, as Liverpool reported, had been sought after by 'the Virtuosi of several Foreign Countries'.[40] But Banks was lukewarm about the idea, essentially because de Calonne's collection was the work of a virtuoso rather than one of a man of science–or, as Banks himself put it: 'it has been collected by a man who though justly admird for his Political sagacity can only be considered as superficially versd in the study of nature'. 'Had it been collected', he continued, 'by a man who studied natural history professionally & had the specimens contained in it been illustrated by Printed Observations well Received by the Public' then he might have recommended purchase. In particular, Banks objected to the fact that the collection was largely devoted to shells, a favourite with virtuosi because of their rarity and appearance but of little use to the naturalist who looked to natural history collections to provide a coherent and systematic depiction of a basic scientific principle, 'the chain of animated beings'.[41] A similar judgement probably helps to explain Banks's controversial decision to reject the purchase of Sir Ashton Lever's vast collection of natural history and anthropological specimens for the British Museum in 1806. When writing to Banks in 1777 Blagden commented that Lever wanted anything 'that he happens not to have in his Museum, whether it tends to illustrate Science or not; on the contrary nothing can be an object to you but what will conduce to the improvement of natural History as a branch of Philosophy'.[42] This unfavourable view of Lever's collection as embodying the virtuoso's yearning for variety and show rather than system was shared by John Walker, professor of natural history at the University of Edinburgh from 1779 to 1803. In a letter to Lord Bute, Walker commented on a visit to Lever's museum in 1773 that 'I could not but regret, that such a man should be devoid of Science, in the Study he so eagerly pursues'.[43]

However, as Farington reported in his *Diary* for 9 July 1806, when Lever's vast and miscellaneous collection was put up for public auction, 'it has sold very wel ... Lord Ossery, Lord Stanley & others *Birds*;–Lord Tankerville *Shells*–Hoges is collecting *minerals*'[44]–a reminder that the species of virtuoso collector was by no means extinct by the end of the eighteenth century. And Banks was both too much a member of his own landowning class (from which such virtuosi were chiefly drawn) and too conscious of the political importance of enlisting elite support for science to exclude such virtuosi from the Royal Society. Quite consciously Banks maintained a policy of keeping the Royal Society open to both gentlemen and players–or, as Sir Benjamin Brocke (President of the Royal Society, 1858-61) put it in a letter to Weld, the historian of the Royal Society, in 1848: 'The view which Sir Joseph Banks took of the construction of the Royal Society was, that it shall consist of two classes: the working men of science, and those who, from their position in society or fortune, it might be desirable to retain as patrons of science'.[45]

Though such a policy caused some dissension within the Royal Society and was a major source of the faction-fighting which boiled over publicly in 1783-4 it was in keeping with the traditions of the Royal Society. The Society had appointed an aristocrat, Lord Brouckner, as its first President (1662-77) and, in the absence of government support, had long relied on its gentlemen amateurs for financial survival. Banks's ability to harness both constituencies–the 'working scientists' and the virtuosi–in a single institution was seen by some of his contemporaries as one of his main contributions as President. His obituarist in the *Gentleman's Magazine* wrote approvingly that after his election in 1778 'The new President formed a link between the scientific, and the enobled and wealthy, which no deep and abstracted scholar, no man of professional eminence could have supplied'. And, the obituarist continued, despite his critics within the Royal Society–those that had termed Banks and his supporters 'macaronis'–he 'lived to behold that intimate union which ought ever to exist between the patrons and the votaries of learning'. The great advantage of such a union was that it not only helped to pay the Royal Society's bills but it also helped to integrate science into the public and political culture of the times giving the scientific cause allies in the corridors of power or, as the *Gentleman's Magazine* more elegantly put it, it gave 'science a home in the courts of greatness'.[46]

Whereas in the seventeenth century the characteristic focus for virtuosi activity had been the gentleman withdrawn from the world in his private collection of cabinets, the virtuosi of the eighteenth century were of a more sociable disposition and their characteristic meeting-place was the London club. Stone suggests that the solitary nature of the mid-seventeenth-century virtuoso may have been a response to the exclusion of many of the elite from positions at court.[47] By the mid-eighteenth century, however, England's governing elite was relatively united and self-confident and glad of opportunities to gather together in London, the centre of politics, culture and, not least, fashion. Few participated in this clubbable world with more enthusiasm than Banks–it was no accident that many of his strongest supporters within the Royal Society were drawn from the break-away Royal Society Club, a highly convivial body of which Banks was 'Perpetual Dictator' from 1777 until it was disbanded in 1784.

The scientifically-inclined clubs of London included, in effect, Banks's home-cum-research institute at Soho Square. There Banks regularly held gatherings which were widely known as a means of keeping *au courant* with scientific developments or simply gossip. As Banks's protégé, William Marsden, put it, it was there that one 'met a variety of persons, and acquired information of what was going forward in the world of literature and science'.[48] The visiting Swede, Carl Thunberg, who was granted 'free and uncontrolled access to his [Banks's] incomparable collections' when he visited London in 1778, aptly summed up the function of these gatherings as making Banks's house seem 'an Academy of Natural History'. Six years later, another traveller, Faujas de St Fond, remarked on the club-like atmosphere of such occasions at which 'A friendly breakfast of tea or coffee maintains that tone of ease and fraternity which ought universally to prevail among men of science and letters'.[49]

The wide range of clubs to which Banks belonged was indicative of the wide and varied cultural life available to the late eighteenth-century gentleman. The world of the clubs was still closely attuned to the culture of the virtuosi who were interested in learning and discovery for their civilising and sociable uses but who did not generally regard such activities as full-time occupations. It was, then, an ambience which tended to discourage scientific or scholarly specialisation.[50] And Banks's active participation in such a world indicates, too, that, though *qua* naturalist, he saw himself as 'a man of science' he still felt the attraction of the varied and unprofessional culture of the virtuosi which the clubs continued to sustain. Along with his active involvement in supporting the two mainstays of the virtuosi–the Royal Society and the Society of Antiquaries–we find Banks serving as an active member of other clubs such as the Society of Dilettanti (a virtual synonym for virtuosi), the Royal Academy and the Athenian Club (before he left this since he felt that it failed to support him in the dissensions within the Royal Society).[51] Such was his reputation as a clubman that in 1791 when that most august of clubs, The [Literary] Club (which numbered among its members Johnson, Burke, Boswell, Reynolds, Fox, Gibbon, and Garrick), found that its accounts were muddled it called for Banks to act as treasurer to straighten things out[52]–Banks having served as treasurer of the Turk's Head Club and the African Association. The Club itself was an epitome of the wide and undifferentiated learning that the London clubs helped to sustain–Johnson is reported to have boasted of it that 'there is no branch of human knowledge, concerning which we could not collectively give the world good information'.[53]

The south-west corner of Soho Square, c1811. Banks's residence (no. 32) is on the extreme left facing. Engraving from *Hermann's Repository of Arts* (October 1812). Courtesy of Cambridge University Library

One characteristic of a virtuoso had long been an interest in collecting works of art, a natural association with the Grand Tour, one of the frequent goals of which was to augment the family's holdings of Great Masters. Such an interest was primarily another manifestation of the collecting mentality of the virtuosi though, among the scientifically-inclined, art was also valued for its utility in recording remote landscapes and rare specimens.[54] Like Banks, a number of virtuosi employed artists as the eighteenth-century equivalent of photographers–hence Farington's comment that 'Accuracy of drawing seems to be a principal recommendation to Sir Joseph'.[55] Though his own patronage of the arts may have been limited, the world of the arts–and particularly the clubs which supported them–was another part of the world of the London virtuosi in which Banks played a role. Thus we find him supporting the candidature of Charles Burney for the Royal Academy as 'one of the most learned men we have among us'.[56] He actively sought to enlist the support of William Smith, the Foxite politician and patron of the arts, for a new cultural body, the 'British Institution of the Arts' which would promote a British school of painting rather than continuing to patronise foreign artists. This was a characteristic Banksian initiative–whether in commerce, science, exploration or art one basic thread that runs through Banks's activities was the promotion of British self-sufficiency. With an historical perspective reminiscent of the Scottish social theorists he argued that artistic efflorescence and commercial prosperity had generally gone together–hence the prominence of the Venetian, the Flemish and the papal Roman schools of art. '[I]n this Point of view', he continued, 'the time is come when England has the means, through her Commercial prosperity to Foster a fourth school & has every prospect of excelling France'.[57] As he commented to the virtuoso collector, Sir Richard Worsley, in the previous year, he was further encouraged in his hopes of England surpassing France in the artistic realm because of the improvement in English taste prompted by 'the number of fine specimens of Sculpture & Painting which the oppressive Politics of France have driven into this Country'.[58] The interest in such issues is yet another indication of Banks's own wide-ranging interests which in turn reflected the diversity of cultural life supported by the world of the London clubs–an ambience largely created by that characteristic expression of eighteenth-century gentlemanly culture: the virtuoso.

In his efforts to enlist the support of fellow members of the landed classes Banks was prepared to take a very wide view of what constituted science and, with it, an indulgent attitude towards those of gentle birth seeking membership of the Royal Society. Nonetheless, Banks remained determined, as he phrased it in a letter of 1794 about the Botanic Gardens at Calcutta, to 'give considerable advancement to the Science of Botany here, which has always been my favourite pursuit'.[59] Thus he sought to establish it as a scientifically respectable discipline which could be clearly distinguished from the bower-bird activities of some of the virtuosi in whose company he lived and moved in the world of the London clubs. Why was it, then, that Banks from very early in his career was so attracted to such a study and remained so determined to establish and defend its scientific respectability? Such a question involves a detailed consideration of the nature and condition of natural history around the mid-eighteenth century (the time of Banks's early intellectual formation) and, subsequently, an examination of the way in which natural history was to develop in the later eighteenth and early nineteenth centuries up to Banks's death in 1820.

THE STATE OF NATURAL HISTORY IN THE MID-EIGHTEENTH CENTURY

Thanks to the activities of John Ray and his circle, British botany–and natural history more generally–had achieved an international reputation in the late seventeenth century which, however, was to dwindle away in the course of the first half of the eighteenth century. This decline was probably largely due to the immense prestige that the physical sciences achieved thanks to Newton's monumental work. This had the effect of overshadowing natural history even in one of its most popular and durable forms–as an apologetic aid in the defence of the argument from design–as astronomical data became more prominent as an adjunct to natural theology.[60] Under Newton's presidency, from 1703 to his death in 1727, the Royal Society naturally came more and more to focus its activities and prestige on the sciences most closely associated with its illustrious head. Thus in 1719 the naturalist, Walter Moyle, was moved to complain that 'I find there is no room in Gresham College [the Royal Society] for Natural History, Mathematics have engrossed all'.[61]

Despite the subsequent presidencies of physicians such as Sir Hans Sloane (1727–40) and Sir John Pringle (1772–8) or virtuosi like Martin Folkes (1741–52) and James West (1768–72), this was a heritage that remained deeply rooted in the Royal Society when Banks assumed its headship in 1778. True science for many FRSs meant the mathematical sciences. In an effort to prevent the election of Sir John Pringle as President in 1772 his fellow physician, but nonetheless determined opponent, Sir William Browne, reminded the Society of Newton's view (as interpreted by his acolyte, John Jurin) 'that something more than knowing the name, the shape, and obvious qualities of an insect, a plant, or a shell, was requisite to form a philosopher, even of the lowest rank, much more to qualify one to sit at the head of so great and learned a body'. 'The eighteenth century', Browne insisted, '. . . most justly deserves the distinguishing appellation of the Mathematical Age; from whence it may reasonably be expected, that no person, who is not a Mathematician, will now either judge himself, or be judged by others, qualified to take the chair of Natural Knowledge'.[62] Such conflicts between the devotees of the mathematical sciences and those of natural history were again to boil over in the dissensions within the Royal Society of 1783–4 with Banks at their epicentre as one who (as his opponent Hutton put it) showed his 'preference for the disciples of Linnaeus over those of Newton'.[63]

The increasing prevalence of such disputes in the latter part of the eighteenth century probably can be attributed to the fact that the supporters of natural history were less and less prepared to accept the lowly status to which they had been relegated in the first half of the century in the aftermath of Newton's great achievement. For in the first half of the century natural history appears to have lost the status it had enjoyed in the time of Ray and was frequently regarded with mild ridicule. In 1710 Addison remarked that it was 'the Mark of a little Genius to be wholly conversant among Insects, Reptiles, Animalcules, and those trifling Rarities that furnish out the Apartment of a Virtuoso'.[64] Thomas Martyn (professor of botany at Cambridge, 1762–1825) in a letter to the virtuoso, John Strange, looked back on their days as undergraduates at Cambridge in the 1750s as a time when

we were looked upon as no better than cockle-shell pickers; butterfly hunters, and weed gatherers; and I can remember very well that when I walked forth now & then, with a little hammer concealed under my coat, I looked carefully round me, lest I should be detected in the ridiculous act of knocking a poor stone to pieces.[65]

In his *History of English Thought in the Eighteenth Century,* Stephen comments, too, on the way in which in the early eighteenth century natural history 'had been regarded with good-humoured contempt as a pursuit of bugs, beetles, and mummies; and the "virtuoso" was one of the established topics for ... ridicule'; in the late eighteenth century, by contrast, 'it was beginning to be recognized that such pursuits might be a creditable investment of human energy'.[66]

But even in the stony soil of the first half of the eighteenth century there were a few signs of growth in the area of natural history. The heritage of Ray was kept alive, ironically, by a German immigrant, John Dillenius, who, in 1724, produced a widely-used compendium of English plants in the form of a third edition of Ray's *Synopsis Stirpium Britannicarum* (Synopsis of British plants). Subsequently, he became Oxford's foundation professor of botany (from 1728 to 1747) in which capacity he produced his exhaustively researched *Historia Muscorum* (History of Mosses) (1741). In a letter to Banks of 1768 his old school friend, the virtuoso, William Perrin, looked back on Dillenius's 1724 edition as marking the end of a long period of British supremacy in botany:

In regard to Botany From this Time last Century till at least the Death of Ray Eng[lan]d had certainly the lead in Europe & she preserved too this Superiority perhaps until 1724 the Time of the publication of the 3rd Edition of Ray's Synopsis which Linnaeus prefers to every Book of its Kind in the world, but for this Superiority she was in a great Degree indebted to Dillenius, a Stranger, tho' a naturalised one.[67]

But after the death of Dillenius in 1747, continued Perrin, Britain clearly lost its botanical pre-eminence and 'about that Time Linnaeus & his Followers transferred the Palm from us to Sweden'.

In this unpromising mid-eighteenth-century period some institutional

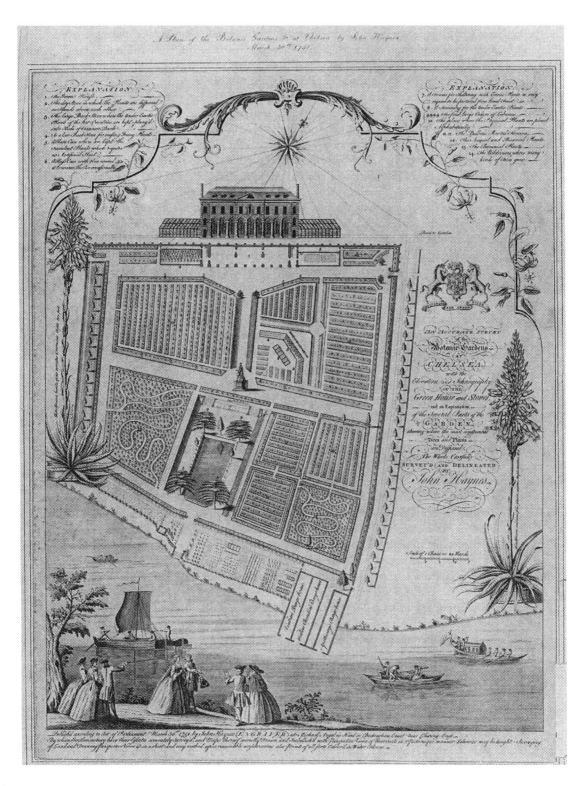

Plan of Chelsea Physic Garden. John Haynes, 1763. Courtesy of the British Library

support for botany was provided by the Society of Apothecaries which had an obvious professional interest in plants and their products. Its main contribution was its continued support for the Physic Garden at Chelsea[68] which had been founded in 1673 but was considerably augmented in 1721 by the gift of the manor of Chelsea from Sir Hans Sloane. Throughout the eighteenth century this garden continued to act as a centre for the introduction of new species and the exchange of specimens both within England and Europe at large–a particularly important function in the decades before the 1770s when Kew Gardens, under Banks's direction, assumed the task of acting as the British Empire's botanical clearing house. We find, for example, in 1728 the illustrious Dutch scientist, Herman Boerhaave, thanking Philip Miller (Chelsea's chief gardener from 1722 to 1771) for sending botanical specimens and undertaking to reciprocate in kind.[69] By 1771 when Miller died, after having been dismissed (as Ellis reported) 'for his impertinence to the Apothecaries Company, his masters', Chelsea was increasingly being eclipsed by Kew where 'every thing curious' was now being sent.[70] But before the late eighteenth century when naturalists began to reassert themselves in the Royal Society, the Chelsea Garden also helped to keep alight the sometimes flickering flame of natural history within the Society since, under the terms of Sloane's endowment, the Garden sent fifty specimens of dried plants with scientific descriptions to the Society annually.[71]

Naturally, the young Banks turned to the Chelsea Garden to foster his early, and still not quite fashionable, interest in botany particularly since, from 1761, Chelsea was the home of his mother.[72] There Banks benefited from the tuition of Miller whose herbarium Banks purchased after his death in 1771. It may well have been from Miller that Banks acquired that preoccupation with the acclimatisation of foreign plants which was to be a characteristic of the Kew Gardens, as it had been of the Chelsea Garden under Miller's direction.[73] Like Banks, too, Miller used his gardens not only to introduce new plants to Britain but also as a means of promoting useful products throughout the Empire. It was Miller, for example, who played an active part in promoting the planting of cotton in Georgia.[74] One mark of Banks's gratitude for the botanical instruction he received at Chelsea was his presentation to the Garden in 1781 of five hundred different kinds of seeds collected on his *Endeavour* voyage.[75] Along with Miller, another of Banks's early botanical tutors at Chelsea was William Hudson ('*praefectus horti*' at Chelsea from 1765 to 1771), who was Banks's travelling companion on a natural history expedition to Wales in 1767. Some fifty years later, in a letter to Sir James Smith (founder of the Linnean Society), Banks paid testimony to the importance of Hudson's *Flora Anglica* (1762), the earliest attempt to provide a systematic survey of British flora along Linnaean lines: 'I well remember the publication of Hudson, which was the first effort at well-directed science, and the eagerness with which I adopted its use'.[76]

A second source of support for natural history in the mid-eighteenth century was focused around two London merchants, Peter Collinson and

John Ellis, who, because of their trading links–especially with the American colonies–had regular access to new botanical specimens. Closely linked with them was the physician, John Fothergill (MD Edinburgh, 1736), who, like Collinson and a disproportionate number of British naturalists, was a Quaker–the apologetic uses of botany making it one of the few recreational outlets permitted to those of that denomination.

Collinson's early interest in botany was encouraged by Sir Hans Sloane and in 1728, the year after Sloane became President of the Royal Society, he was made an FRS. Collinson was also among the founders of the Society of Antiquaries,[77] another instance of the way in which an interest in natural history and antiquities were commonly linked. Collinson's work in helping to establish the early British Museum (which was largely the creation of his patron, Sloane) also helped to bring together both these two aspects of virtuoso culture. Appropriately, in 1741 Fothergill described Collinson as being 'very well known amongst the Virtuosi here [in London]'.[78] Through the trading networks established by his family drapery business he built up a close association with a number of American collectors and natural philosophers. Among them was Benjamin Franklin whose pioneering electrical experiments were, as Franklin himself put it in a letter to Collinson's son, 'encouraged by the friendly Reception he gave to the Letters I wrote to him upon it'.[79] Collinson worked to promote the introduction of new botanically-based products such as flax, hemp, silk and wine to the colonists of British North America as 'alike beneficial to themselves and to their mother country'[80]–an instance of that concern for the imperial uses of botany which was later to be so central to Banks's activities. His trading and botanical networks also extended beyond British dominions to Russia and even China.[81] The specimens that Collinson thus acquired, together with the fruits of his own collecting within Britain, resulted in his establishing a private botanical garden at Mill Hill which helped to raise the standards of English horticulture.

Collinson was a regular correspondent of Linnaeus and introduced him to Fothergill. In a letter to Linnaeus of 1774 Fothergill paid tribute to 'Our Collinson' as one who had 'taught me to love flowers, and who that shared his comradeship could do other than to cultivate plants?'.[82] Like Collinson, Fothergill sought to establish new crops of economic significance in America–among them coffee, tea and bamboo–though with even less success than his co-religionary. He also emulated Collinson in establishing a private botanical garden from which Banks received specimens.[83] Banks was later to write of these collections: 'At an expense seldom undertaken by an individual, and with an ardour that was visible in the whole of his conduct, he procured from all parts of the world a great number of the rarest plants, and protected them in the amplest buildings which this or any other country had seen'.[84] In effect, what both Collinson and Fothergill were doing in establishing such gardens at their own expense was providing the stimulus for the development of public botanical gardens which were to be established in many parts of the British world, frequently as a result of Banks's support. Dr Walker, the founder of the Cambridge Botanical Garden, acknowledged the role of Collinson in promoting such public establishments by writing to him that 'You were the first author of the design and it had not been undertaken without your encouragement'.[85]

In a number of other ways Collinson's and Fothergill's private activities were to intersect with those which Banks was later to promote himself, frequently with royal or government support. Fothergill employed a number of botanical artists to record his collections and this, together with the fact that the Parkinson family were Quakers, helps to account for his friendship with Sydney Parkinson, Banks's chief artist on the *Endeavour* expedition. When Banks and Fothergill met after Banks's return from this expedition they jointly helped to sponsor a botanical collecting expedition to Africa[86]–the beginnings of a tradition of imperial botany which Banks was to do so much to foster. We find, too, Fothergill enlisting the services of John Bartram–another Quaker who was one of Collinson's chief collectors in British America–on behalf 'of my Friend Jos Banks Esq'.[87] It was Fothergill, too, who helped to initiate the proposals for the introduction of the breadfruit to the West Indies[88] which Banks later brought to fruition. Most fundamentally of all, Fothergill (and Collinson and Ellis) shared with Banks a common commitment to promoting the gospel of improvement and a similar sense of public duty in placing the practical benefits of natural history at the disposal of the nation. For Fothergill's credo, that 'The great business of man as a member of society is to be as useful to it as possible in whatsoever department he may be stationed',[89] was one with which Banks emphatically agreed.

Like Collinson, Ellis also strove to introduce new botanical products to North America (particularly tea and rhubarb), using the good offices of the Society for the Encouragement of the Arts to promote these endeavours.[90] Again his trading interests in America enabled him to import a wide range of seeds and other natural history specimens and his investigations on these and other materials prompted Stephen Hales to describe him in 1757 as 'the great promoter of vegetable researchers'.[91] He was also an indefatigable correspondent and, like other industrious scientific letter-writers, such as Mersenne, did much to promote his discipline by keeping those of similar interests in touch with each other at a time when the institutional supports for the discipline–societies, journals and the like–were still underdeveloped. Such activities help account for Linnaeus's warm tribute to him in 1772:

> You are still the main support of Natural History in England, for your attention is ever given to all that serves to increase or promote this study. Without your aid, the rest of the world would know little of the acquisitions made by your intelligent countrymen, in all parts of the world. You are the portal through which the lovers of Nature are conducted to these discoveries. For my own part, I acknowledge myself to have derived more information, through your various assistance, than from any other person.[92]

Fittingly, Ellis's major work, the posthumously published *Natural History of Many Curious and Uncommon Zoophytes, ... Collected From*

Various Parts of the Globe ... (1786), was produced as a result of the collective endeavours of a number of the major figures of that British natural history community which Ellis had done so much to foster. Linnaeus's disciple, Daniel Solander, helped to arrange and describe his materials along systematically Linnaean lines while Fothergill provided many of the specimens on which the work was based.[93] Fothergill also acted as patron for the venture, a role which, after his death in 1780, was taken over by Banks–hence the dedication of the work to Banks by Ellis's daughter as 'The liberal patron of science, and the enlightened cultivator of natural knowledge'.[94]

Along with the Chelsea Physic Garden of the Society of Apothecaries and the activities of Collinson, Fothergill and Ellis, a third–though scientifically least important–source of light in the grey skies of mid-eighteenth-century natural history was the patronage dispensed by a number of aristocrats with interests in natural history. Thus we find Collinson in 1751 assuring Bartram that, despite the death of the Prince of Wales, the 'best friend and encourager' of 'Gardening and planting' nonetheless 'there is such a spirit and love of it, amongst the nobility and gentry'.[95] Such a genteel interest in matters botanical reflected the continuing vitality of the virtuoso tradition which had helped to integrate support for scientific activities into elite culture. And in a society where the values and interests of the landed class exerted such a hold over the literate population, such developments help to explain why those outside the gilded circle of the landed classes–like the merchants, Collinson and Ellis–also turned to natural history for leisure, pleasure and improvement. The far-flung collecting networks built up as a result of Ellis's and Collinson's trading interests also helped to provide aristocratic patrons with the novel specimens which were ever a virtuoso's delight. Collinson, for example, provided his indefatigable American collector, John Bartram, with such customers as Lord Petre and the Dukes of Norfolk, Bedford, Richmond and Argyll.[96] The Duke of Bedford also employed Philip Miller, the head gardener at Chelsea, to arrange his specimens and to tend his garden[97]–of which the prize exhibit was a plantation of American trees acquired through Collinson's good offices. Such a co-operative venture between merchant and peer provides a minor cameo illustration of the ability of eighteenth-century aristocratic society to absorb and to benefit from the activities of the trading classes whose general deference to their social superiors made them appear a source of wealth and national prestige rather than a challenge to the political dominance of the landed classes.

Aristocratic support for botany was frequently combined with patronage of other branches of natural history or of other aspects of virtuoso culture, such as the study of antiquities. One of Bartram's customers, Charles Lennox, the second Duke of Richmond, was praised by Martin Folkes to Emanuel Da Costa (respectively the President and Secretary of the Royal Society) in 1747 as one who 'as he cultivates and loves all sorts of natural knowledge, has just founded a wild receptacle for fossils in his garden'.[98] Characteristically, this virtuoso duke combined an interest in natural history and antiquities–a combination encapsulated in the fact that in 1750, a year after he took out a Cambridge MD, he was elected President of the Society of Antiquaries. Lennox had been a strong supporter of Walpole's government which fell in 1742 and his learned activities were, no doubt, partly prompted by his eclipse as an active politician. On the other hand, the Roman Catholic Lord Robert Petre was, by virtue of his religion, excluded from political life altogether and devoted himself energetically to the promotion of natural history. When he died in 1742, Collinson praised him for his character, for his wealth of 'fruitful and Experimental knowledge' and, as a tribute to his activities as a botanical importer, for the fact that 'If he had lived, all round Him would have been America in England'.[99] Collinson had to report to Bartram (of whom Petre had been his first aristocratic patron[100]) that 'he that gave motion, is motionless–all is at an end'; five years later another of Bartram's correspondents, the botanist, Dr John Mitchell, bemoaned the fact that 'Botany is at a very low ebb in England, since the death of Lord Petre. Dr Dillenius is likewise dead'.[101]

Natural history was not only suited to the virtuoso culture of the eighteenth-century male elite but it was also considered an appropriate pursuit for women, and *a fortiori*, aristocratic women. The most popular work of Thomas Martyn, professor of botany at Cambridge, was his translation of Rousseau's *Letters on the Elements of Botany Addressed to a Lady* (1785). The fashion for a genteel female interest in natural history was to become even more pronounced in the nineteenth century–hence Thackeray's remark in *Vanity Fair* that 'a ladylike knowledge of botany and geology' were among the appropriate accomplishments for a young lady of fashion.[102]

The most prominent eighteenth-century female aristocratic patron of natural history, the Duchess of Portland (Margaret Cavendish Bentinck), was by birth a member of the Cavendish family which both in the eighteenth and nineteenth centuries did so much to promote British science. At the Portland family seat at Bulstrode in Buckinghamshire she built up an enormous natural history collection though, in characteristic virtuoso fashion, her private museum also included other rarities such as a magnificent collection of porcelain. However, the Duchess was aware of the need to organise her collection in a systematic and scientific fashion and in doing so she provided a number of mid- and late-eighteenth-century naturalists with much needed employment. Most prominent among her protégés was the Reverend John Lightfoot (1735-88), who combined the office of domestic chaplain with that of a *de facto* curator.[103] He also acted as Banks's companion on a botanising expedition to Wales in 1773 which began as an attempt to retrace some of Ray's journeys. In an effusive letter of thanks to Banks in the same year he wrote that 'I believe it may without vanity be said, that few, if any Botanical Excursions in Great Britain have exceeded our Collection, either in Number or Rarity of Plants or Places'.[104] In the preface to his *magnum opus* the *Flora Scotica*

(1778)-a work arranged along Linnaean lines as 'the most ingenious and convenient . . . hitherto invented'-Lightfoot also acknowledged the help received from those 'respectable and celebrated names of Joseph Banks Esq. and Dr Solander, the two great philosophical luminaries of this nation'.[105] Soon after Solander arrived in England in 1760 he was employed by the Duchess to help to classify her collections. To judge by a letter of the Duchess to Banks soon after Solander's death in 1782 where she speaks of 'the sincere friendship & esteem I bear to Dr Solander's memory'[106] it was a successful partnership. Other naturalists who benefited from the Duchess's patronage were Richard Pulteney (who helped to organise and provide scientific names for her collection of shells) and Thomas Yeats (who was employed to organise her insect collection).

Like most aristocratic patrons, the Duchess of Portland was content to leave to others the task of arriving at and publishing the scientific conclusions suggested by the vast and expensive collections she amassed. By contrast, John Stuart, the third Earl of Bute-the most important of natural history's aristocratic patrons-took an active interest himself in promoting botany, not only through collecting and the use of patronage, but also by publishing his own botanical compendium, *Botanical Tables, Containing the different Familys of British Plants, Distinguished by a Few Obvious Parts of Fructification Rang'd in a Synoptical Method* [?1785]. The book was dedicated to the queen and it sought to promote the study of botany among 'the Fair Sex' both as a cure for boredom and, more compellingly, since 'the contemplation of Nature's works gradually leads to the omnipotent architect, to Nature's God'.[107] As the title suggests, it was a work which sought not only to collect and collate his botanical findings but also to establish a method of classifying such plants in a systematic and scientific manner. Bute hoped that his method would remedy what he considered was Linnaeus's vain attempt to marry systems of classification based on both artificial and natural criteria. Indeed, Bute thought any attempt at a natural system not only to be 'nugatory' but also 'subversive of the sole and proper use of systematical arrangements'- a view for which he claimed the support of 'the most enlightened naturalists this age can boast of-amongst whom the Count de Buffon holds the first station'.[108] Nonetheless, he acknowledged that before 'the celebrated LINNAEUS' 'the descriptions of the Genera were very imperfect; and those of the species quite unintelligible'.[109] The work, however, had little impact (which is not altogether surprising since only twelve copies were published) and it was succinctly dismissed by Jonas Dryander as being 'more splendid than useful'.[110] But the fact that an earl devoted himself so passionately to the study of botany helped to raise the prestige and public recognition of an area of knowledge which had been frequently dismissed as being of little or no scientific importance. This helps to explain why it was that when, in 1755, Collinson provided Linnaeus with a thumbnail sketch of the state of British natural history he began with Bute who had encouraged him when he had first taken up botany. Bute, he wrote, was 'The first in rank' and 'a perfect master of your

method'; he also added, with a remark which again underlines the extent
to which Bute differed from most of his fellow aristocratic patrons of
natural history, that 'we have great numbers of Nobility and Gentry that
know plants very well, but yet do not make botanic science their peculiar
study'.[111] Bute's more professional approach to natural history no doubt
owed much to his study of medicine and botany at Leyden in the early
1730s under Boerhaave and Van Royen. Among those he came to know
there was the British army physician, Isaac Lawson, who was to be one
of the first to promote the Linnaean system within Britain.

Bute's chief contribution to botany was not, however, his vain attempt
to improve on the Linnaean system of classification, but rather his success
in interesting his young pupil, the future George III, in botany and, with
royal support, in establishing the royal pleasure gardens at Kew as a major
centre of botanical enquiry–hence Collinson's tribute that 'From his
Lordship's great knowledge in the science of botany the gardens at Kew
have been furnished with all the rare exotick trees and flowers that could
be procured'.[112] In 1761, a year after the accession of George III when Bute
was at the height of his shortlived political influence, Collinson also
warmly thanked him for ensuring a 'very Gracious reception' by the king
and queen of him and his fellow botanists, which resulted in a royal
invitation to view Kew Gardens in Collinson's company.[113] The task of
building up Kew Gardens was later to be carried on by Banks after the
king was obliged to distance himself from Bute once he became a political
liability.[114] It was not only the king but also some naturalists who became
increasingly reluctant to be publicly associated with Bute after his political
eclipse. When the Linnean Society was founded in 1788 Bishop Goodenough, one of its major instigators, ruled out the possibility of nominating
Bute as an honorary member (an honour accorded to Banks) on the
grounds of his 'dubious politics'.[115] But despite the fact that Banks displaced
Bute as *de facto* director at Kew Gardens after 1773 the two men remained
on good terms. In 1777 Bute thanked Banks 'for procuring him so valuable
a collection of seeds' and urged him, as 'the first Patron of Botany' to visit
the Bute estate so that he (Bute) might profit from Banks and Solander's
'superior knowledge in his favourite Science'.[116] In his botanical *magnum
opus* Bute also paid tribute to 'The generous ardour' of Banks which had
'enriched our herbals with many new discoverd beauties'.[117]

Bute was also important as a botanical patron, his chief protégé being
that stormy petrel of mid-eighteenth-century scientific politics, the former
apothecary, John Hill (or Sir John Hill as he liked to style himself on
the strength of an honour from the King of Sweden), who began his
botanical career arranging the gardens and herbaria of Lord Petre and the
Duke of Richmond. Bute encouraged the publication of Hill's *The
Vegetable System* (1755) which, like Bute's own work, attempted to stem
the tide of the rapidly-spreading Linnaean system. He also secured for Hill
the post of superintendent of the Kew Gardens in which capacity he
published the first catalogue of its holdings, the *Hortus Kewensis* in 1768.

Among Bute's political allies in the early years of George III's reign was
Hugh Percy, the second Duke of Northumberland–indeed, the political

alliance between the two was sealed by a marriage between their respective daughter and son. The two aristocrats also shared an interest in botany, though Northumberland adopted the more normal aristocratic role of an interested amateur and patron. Among his early clients was Hill and it was probably Northumberland who first brought Hill to Bute's notice. His services as patron were warmly acknowledged by William Hudson in his dedication to Northumberland of the important *Flora Anglica* of 1762 (a work which also records the author's gratitude to Banks). Another botanist, Colin Milne, refers, in the dedication to his *A Botanical Dictionary* . . . (1770), to the way in which his interest in botany largely derived from the time he acted as tutor to Northumberland's son, who was later to carry on the family's interest in botany and science generally.[118] When the Society of Apothecaries needed a gardener to replace the dismissed Miller in 1771 it was to one Forsyth, a former gardener of the Duke, that they turned.[119] Northumberland is, then, another instance of the way in which the traditional aristocratic preoccupation with gardens and landscaping helped to keep alive an interest in botany.

BOTANY AND THE YOUNG BANKS

Banks's own early interest in botany at first probably owed most to this linkage between natural history and aristocratic culture. However, as his preoccupation with botany was transformed from a polite avocation to a virtual career (in so far as a gentleman could be said to have such a thing), he soon made contact with the other two major influences in keeping alive an interest in natural history in the mid-eighteenth century: the Society of Apothecaries and its Physic Garden at Chelsea and the circle of London botanists centred around Collinson, Fothergill and Ellis. Banks's own autobiographical account (which we have received via Sir Everard Home, one of his confidants in his old age) has it that his first interest in botany was entirely the result of his own untutored enthusiasm. At the age of fourteen (that is in 1757), while a student at Eton, he

> was walking leisurely along a lane, the sides of which were richly enamelled with flowers; he stopped and looked round, involuntarily exclaimed, How beautiful! After some reflection, he said to himself, it is surely more natural that I should be taught to know all these productions of Nature, in preference to Greek and Latin . . . He began immediately to teach himself Botany; and, for want of more able tutors, submitted to be instructed by the women, employed in culling simples, as it is termed, to supply the Druggists and Apothecaries shops, paying sixpence for every material piece of information.[120]

But this delightful anecdote continues by detailing the way in which Banks made use of a copy of Gerard's *Herbal* which he found in his mother's dressing room—a reminder of the fact that an interest in natural history was part of the genteel cultural ambience in which Banks lived and moved and from which he may well have first acquired an interest in botany by osmosis as it were. Significantly, his mother was to be an

active supporter of his botanical studies, not least by moving to Chelsea within easy reach of the Physic Garden when Banks was about eighteen. And possibly, too, Eton may not have been quite the botanical desert Banks's anecdote makes it appear: two decades earlier when the poet, Thomas Gray, was a pupil there his interest in natural history (which was to be his prevailing occupation in later life) had been stimulated by his tutor (and uncle), Robert Antrobus.[121]

When Banks matriculated at Christ Church in 1760 it was as a gentleman commoner, which meant that he was largely exempt from the academic exercises required of less socially-elevated undergraduates, particularly since, like most of his class, Banks did not take a degree. Nonetheless, the basic framework of his studies would continue to have been, as it had been at Eton, the classics supplemented with an Oxford speciality, logic based chiefly on Aristotelian thought (though also subsuming some forms of mathematics which were regarded as an aid to a training in logic).[122] Dillenius's successor as Sherardian professor of botany, Humphrey Sibthorp, a correspondent of Linnaeus, had long ago abandoned the task of interesting undergraduates in a subject which–apart from the handful of medical students–was of no immediate relevance to their prescribed syllabus. Nor did the enthusiasm of Banks and some of his contemporaries for botany persuade him to change his ways, though he did consent to allow Banks to import Israel Lyons from Cambridge for a summer course in botany in July 1764.

The connections of the Jewish Lyons with the staunchly Anglican Cambridge had been rather tenuous. While a resident in the town his interest in mathematics had been encouraged by Robert Smith, Master of Trinity and one of Newton's popularisers. He also worked with members of the university–such as Michael Tyson, a fellow of Corpus, and Thomas Martyn, professor of botany–in exploring the botany of the Cambridge region.[123] His investigations formed the basis of his *Fasciculus Plantarum circa Cantabrigiam* (A handbook of plants around Cambridge) which sought to supplement Ray's earlier findings, a work which appeared in 1763, the year before Banks prevailed upon him to come to Oxford. Later in life Banks was to reward Lyons by obtaining for him from the Board of Longitude a position on the expedition of Captain Constantine Phipps to the North Pole in 1773.[124] On this voyage Lyons was required to draw on both his mathematical and botanical skills since it was his function (as the antiquary, William Cole, reported) 'to make Observations in astronomy & natural history & to try experiments on the state of the atmosphere in the frigid zone ... in which undertaking he gave great satisfaction to his Employers'.[125]

(Left) Banks as a boy at Eton aged about fifteen, by an unknown artist (oil on canvas). Banks is depicted as examining a botanical text, an indication of his early interest in natural history (though the work was probably painted retrospectively when Banks was middle-aged). Courtesy of the Hon. Clive Gibson

Lyons's botanical lectures at Oxford attracted as many as sixty pupils who received his teaching with 'great applause',[126] an indication of the reviving interest in botany after the doldrums of the mid-century. We find, for example, the *Critical Review* proclaiming in 1763-perhaps more with hope than accuracy-that 'Natural History is now, by a kind of natural establishment, become the favourite study of the time'.[127] In the same year the Keeper of the Oxford Ashmolean Museum-who in 1760 had lamented that 'Every Science is dead at present especially Nat[ural] H[istory]'-rejoiced in the fact that 'a Spirit of Botanical Enquiries reigns here' in which 'Numbers of all ages employ themselves in Simpling'.[128] Such remarks, together with Lyons's relative success in attracting students, were indications that at Oxford Banks was by no means alone in his botanical interests and, indeed, some of his lifelong companions in this area were among his contemporaries at Christ Church. Among these were Samuel Goodenough, who was one of the founders of the Linnean Society (as well as being a vice-president of the Royal Society and an active member of the Society of Antiquaries), and John Parsons, who went on to study medicine at Edinburgh. There, as John Lightfoot put it, as 'a necessary concomitant to the knowledge of physic, [he] made *botany* one of his principal pursuits, and greatly excelled in it'.[129] In 1766 Parsons was made foundation professor of anatomy at Christ Church, then, two years later, university reader in the same discipline-posts he used to help revive the flagging Oxford medical school which from about this time underwent 'an institutional revival'.[130] After Banks left Oxford in 1763 Parsons continued to correspond with him, advising him in 1768, for example, of the zoological collecting activities of a common acquaintance at Jesus College and the anticlimax that ensued when an 'arrant cheat' of an Egyptian mummy was opened before 'half ye DDs in Oxford'.[131]

Of less scientific importance, but nonetheless representative of the interest in natural history among the landed elite, was Banks's friendship with William Perrin, a contemporary of his at both Eton and Christ Church. In 1765, two years after Banks left Oxford, Perrin accompanied him on his first botanising expedition exploring the Weald of Kent. Perrin, how_ver, remained a virtuoso-or, as Banks termed him, a 'philomath' (a 'lover of learning')-content to take a genteel interest in natural history (and antiquities) without feeling any compulsion to place his studies on a more systematic and scientific foundation. Thus, in 1767, we find Banks accompanying his letters of introduction for Perrin to the great French naturalists, Buffon and du Hamel, with some gentle satire: 'I beg Sr you will make good use of them[.S]ome of your friends have insinuated that you was but a kind of a Philomat & they would not risque their Credit in sending you Letters. I was forc'd to say much of your good intentions of becoming a true genuine naturalist altho I had not much hopes'.[132] Banks's expectations were realised: though he and Perrin maintained their friendship, Perrin-in the manner of many of his class-continued to dabble in natural history without becoming a naturalist of whom the scientific world had to take note. Nonetheless, Banks was among those who nominated him as an FRS in 1772 as 'a Gentleman well versd in Polite Literature & Natural history'.[133] In true virtuoso style Perrin also became a member of the Society of Antiquaries in the same year.

Overall, then, while Oxford's formal teaching may have contributed little to Banks's development as a botanist the university nonetheless appears to have stimulated his interest in more informal ways-particularly since it offered an opportunity for fellow members of the elite with similar interests to gather together and to form lasting ties. We find, for example, the formation around 1762 of three undergraduate associations in which Banks very possibly played a part: the Antiquaries' Club, the Botanical Club and the Fossil Club.[134] It was, no doubt, to the activities of the last of these to which Banks referred when, on 28 January 1768, while on an excursion through Wales and the Midlands, he 'Went this Morn to view my old Fossil haunts to see if I could meet with any thing worth notice Particularly Concerning the Oxford stone'.[135]

In later years Banks did regret that Oxford did not do more to cultivate the sciences, commenting rather waspishly in a letter of 1793 to John Sibthorp (Sherardian professor of botany 1784 to 1796) about the cost of shipping botanical specimens from New South Wales to the Oxford Botanical Gardens, that 'to send them in Pots will I fear be too costly for our University whose liberality in matters of science I have often deplord when I saw it less in degree than I thought it ought to have been'.[136] Five days previously Sibthorp had written to Banks requesting specimens from Kew and bemoaning the decline in the standing of the Oxford Botanical Garden because its maintenance grant had not been increased since 1726.[137] However, in conspicuous contrast to his friend, Gibbon, Banks later looked back on his undergraduate days with some affection-in 1819, the year before he died, he supported the idea of placing his portrait in Christ Church where he could be remembered by those 'who in Future Receive intellectual nourishment from the milk of the alma mater by whom I was Fed'.[138] It is a comment that suggests that Banks himself may have given some currency to the rather roseate role accorded to Oxford in his obituary in the *Gentleman's Magazine*, that 'it was in the retirement of collegiate studies that he acquired his taste for natural history, and resolved to devote himself to its advancement, with all the resources of his mind and his fortune'.[139]

When Banks came down from Oxford to London in 1763 to assume his place as an heir in fashionable society (for his father had died in 1761), he did so at a time when natural history was beginning to attract a growing number of active devotees. As the *Philosophical Magazine* put it: 'At the time when Sir Joseph Banks began to cultivate the study of natural history, it was beginning to emerge from the neglect into which the exclusive pursuit of natural philosophy had, for the last hundred years, thrown it'.[140] Indeed, an informal society for those sharing such interests sprang up in the early 1760s and Banks-along with Daniel Solander, James Cook and the anatomist, John Hunter-was among those who attended its weekly meetings at a Soho coffee house.[141] Banks's standing in such circles helped to ensure his twin election as an FRS and FSA in 1766 at the tender age of twenty-three. Even his connection with Harriet Blosset derived from his natural history connections. Both while at Oxford and subsequently 'The gardens of Lee, and Kennedy, at Hammersmith, offered him abundant specimens of plants and flowers'[142]–particularly as they specialised in exotic plants not native to Europe.[143] As the botanist, Robert Thornton, put it: 'Mr Lee was guardian to a young lady, Miss Blosset, who possessed extraordinary beauty, and every accomplishment, with a fortune of ten thousand pounds. Mr Banks had often seen her, when visiting the rare plants of Lee's, and thought her the fairest among the flowers'.[144] Lee also introduced Banks to Sydney Parkinson, a fellow Scottish Quaker, the chief botanical illustrator on the *Endeavour* voyage.[145]

Thanks to the stimulus of his London natural history associates, Banks became more and more determined to move beyond the status of a virtuoso to that of a fully-fledged naturalist. One indication of his growing interest in making natural history his career (in so far as a gentleman could be said to have such a thing) was his decision in 1766 to join his lifelong friend, Captain Constantine Phipps, on an expedition to Labrador and Newfoundland which provided a virtual dress-rehearsal for his scientific activities on the *Endeavour* expedition. Soon after his return John Hope, professor of botany at Edinburgh and a major influence in promoting its scientific study in Britain, greeted Banks as a scientific equal requesting that he would 'favour the Botanical world with an account of what you found at Labrador' or, at least, would provide him with any spare seeds from the expedition.[146] By this time Banks's own family was recognising that natural history had become for him a vocation rather than simply a gentlemanly hobby. In July 1767 his uncle, Robert Banks-Hodgkinson (who, because of the death of Banks's own father, acted as a sort of guardian), gave his blessing to Banks's plans for a trip to Sweden to visit Linnaeus and, more generally, his approval for Banks's preoccupation with botany:

> You are extremely kind in wishing my approbation, far be it from me to throw the least impediment in a Scheme that I dare say will be satisfactory hereafter & will forward the pursuit of natural History in which Vineyard you now place your principal Labor & which I hope will produce fruits of honor and happiness both to your self, [and] all your Friends.[147]

Along with Solander–whose lifelong collaboration with Banks was forged during this period–the other major figure who played a part in launching Banks on the national scientific stage was the Welsh gentleman naturalist and antiquarian, Thomas Pennant, whom Banks appears to have come to know through his old friend, William Perrin.[148] Pennant was best known for his numerous accounts of his travels, works which were praised by Dr Johnson, who described him as 'the best traveller I ever read; he observes more things than anyone else does'.[149] He was an archetypal instance both of the link between natural history and travel and of the way in which natural history and antiquities were seen as complementary activities, since he used his travels at home and abroad to advance both these areas. In his *British Zoology* (first published 1766), for example, he drew on both the study of antiquities and natural history in passages such as the following: 'Beavers, which are also amphibious animals, were formerly found in Great Britain; but the breed has been extirpated many years ago; the latest accounts we have of them, is in Giraldus Cambrensis, who travelled through Wales in 1188'.[150] In addition to the data that Pennant accumulated from his own travels he also drew on that obtained from questionnaires sent out to clergy and gentry around the country. It was appropriate, then, that much of Gilbert White's classic work of natural history and antiquities should take the form of letters addressed to Pennant and his close associate, Daines Barrington.

Pennant maintained contact with naturalists both at home and abroad which helped to lessen the hitherto rather parochial character of British natural history. From 1755 he corresponded with Linnaeus at whose instigation he was elected a member of the Royal Society of Uppsala in 1757. On his trip to the Continent in 1765 he came to know Buffon, with whom he continued to correspond, sending him later that year, for example, an advance copy of his *British Zoology*, which Buffon received with gratitude.[151] Buffon continued to draw on Pennant's work despite his chagrin at Pennant's unflattering comparison between Buffon's free thinking and the religious beliefs of Ray.[152] Pennant, in turn, saw himself (as he told the virtuoso, George Ashby) as 'bring[ing] de Buffon & Linnaeus together in all my works'–though he remained sceptical of Buffon's classificatory methods, writing that 'Buffon is systematic & will right or wrong make everything bend to his system'.[153] Another of Pennant's continental correspondents was Dr Pallas whom he met in The Hague in 1765. After Pallas settled in St Petersburg he was to become part of Banks's vast international network of suppliers of natural history specimens and information, a contact that Banks probably owed originally to Pennant who continued to correspond copiously with Pallas.[154]

In the preface to his *British Zoology*, Pennant commented both on the revival of interest in natural history and on his fear that Britain would lag behind in this European-wide movement. 'At a time', he wrote, 'when the study of natural history seems to revive in *Europe*; and the pens of several illustrious foreigners have been employed in enumerating the productions of their respective countries, we are unwilling that our own island should remain insensible to its particular advantages'.[155] Among these particular advantages which Pennant saw Britain as enjoying was its growing commercial power which, as naturalists like Ellis and Collinson had demonstrated, gave it access to a vastly increased number of natural history specimens–a development which, of course, Banks was later to exploit more fully and systematically with the aid of British imperial power. Thus in the preface to his widely-used *Synopsis of Quadrupeds* (1771), for example, Pennant paid his customary deference to John Ray, whose work and whose pious conviction that natural history was one of the best means of demonstrating what Ray called *The Wisdom of God Manifested in the Works of the Creation* Pennant saw himself as continuing. But, Pennant went on, Ray's work now needed to be revised and supplemented because Ray was 'living at a period when the study of Natural History was but beginning to dawn in these kingdoms, and when our contracted Commerce deprived him of many lights we now enjoy'.[156] Where possible, then, Pennant tried to use trading interests for the advantage of natural history. As a member of the Royal Society he established a long-lasting association between it and the Hudson's Bay Company in order to obtain specimens of North American natural history and scientific information more generally.[157] His *Indian Zoology* (1790) (published with Banks's financial assistance) reflected the growing commercial power of Britain in India though the original catalyst for the project came from a gift to Pennant of some natural history illustrations from a former governor of some 'of the *Dutch* islands in the *Indian* Ocean'.[158] Pennant's *Arctic Zoology* (1784-7) included 'a condensed view of the progress of discovery' along the northern coasts of Europe, Asia and America. Here, as he acknowledged,[159] he was much indebted to Banks's record of his natural history observations from his trip to Newfoundland, which had been made possible by his links with the British navy in the person of his old school friend, Constantine Phipps. The publication of the work in 1785 helped to strengthen Pennant's scientific ties with the newly independent United States of America, still a major trading partner as well as being a rich source of new specimens for British naturalists. Thus the work was honoured by Pennant's election in 1791 to the American Philosophical Society at Philadelphia prompting Pennant to write with a certain pride about Britain's former North American colonies, 'There science of every kind begins to flourish; among others, that of natural history'.[160] Earlier, in 1781, Pennant had communicated to the Royal Society, via Banks, the fruits of his study of one branch of American natural history, the nature and habits of the turkey.[161]

At a time when Banks was just beginning to build up his network of fellow natural historians Pennant provided an entrée into such circles. This was particularly important in widening Banks's associations beyond the London scientific world to some of the naturalists based in the provinces as well as to some of Pennant's European correspondents. Pennant and Banks met in March 1766[162] and it was presumably then that Pennant gave Banks a questionnaire about the natural history of Newfoundland, which Banks duly completed and returned.[163] And, for around the next seven years, Banks was prepared to accept this rather subordinate role of supplying Pennant with data. June 1767 brought two letters requesting information both from Banks's Newfoundland trip and from his excursion to the west of Britain.[164] No doubt, Pennant also hoped for more botanical and zoological riches from the abortive trip to Scandinavia to visit Linnaeus which Banks outlined in a letter to Pennant of late June 1767.[165] On the eve of Banks's departure on the *Endeavour* expedition Pennant sent a request for Banks to leave him his journal from the Newfoundland expedition (though also offering to help look after Banks's affairs while he was away).[166] Pennant was later rewarded with copious information on Banks's return from his Iceland trip in 1772, Pennant writing the following year to thank Banks 'for the liberal communication from the fruits of y[ou]r last voyage'.[167] Much of this material from the Newfoundland and Iceland voyages was in due course incorporated into Pennant's *Arctic Zoology* (1784).

But Banks, too, benefited from the association, particularly in his early years as a naturalist. In return for Banks's data from his voyages and the news he could provide of the London scientific world, Pennant sent Banks natural history specimens and scientific gossip drawn from his network of contacts based in his native Wales and in the west of England. While at Oxford in April 1768, for example, Pennant arranged for a fellow of Jesus College, 'the only virtuoso on the spot at present', to send Banks specimens of 'some rare plants'.[168] Three months later Pennant exchanged a cask and a box of fossils for the loan of Banks's drawings of penguins from Labrador.[169] On the international stage Pennant could offer Banks letters of introduction to various naturalists in Scandinavia–such as his friend, Fleischer, at Copenhagen–for his proposed (though abortive) pilgrimage to Linnaeus.[170]

Pennant's west country network was strengthened by the fact that he frequently spent time in Chester, the home of Thomas Falconer, his kinsman by marriage, a gentleman student of both antiquities and natural history. No doubt it was through Pennant that Banks came to know Falconer and thus became the recipient of his long and rather sermonising letters on the scientific possibilities of Banks's expeditions. Banks's projected 'Northern Journey' prompted a disquisition in February 1768 from Falconer on the importance of Banks's paying special attention to mineralogy both because 'Minerals indeed are the objects in w[hi]ch Sweden particularly excells' and because 'Metals are the only irregular branch in Nature'.[171] News of the proposed *Endeavour* expedition, and Banks's part in it, prompted Falconer to send Banks in April 1768 a discourse on the extent to which 'The present ardour of discovery (however doubtful its advantage may be in a political light)' would nonetheless be 'certainly of great use to Natural History' adding the flattering aside 'especially as it is accompanied by one so well qualified by art & Nature for observations in that branch of Science'. Falconer did, however, show considerable foresight in recommending that Banks pay particular attention to the breadfruit tree while in the South Seas–the future occasion for the ill-fated *Bounty* expedition which Banks largely initiated. Appropriately, Falconer closed the letter by announcing the arrival of 'Our Fr[ien]d Mr Pennant'.[172] Banks took such advice in good part and continued to keep Falconer informed of his travel plans: in April 1773, for example, he sent him word that he was lending Pennant the journal of his Iceland expedition of 1772 and raised the possibility (which was never realised) of joining Phipps on his expedition to the North Pole.[173] This, in turn, prompted another set of suggestions from Falconer about the possible scientific uses for such an expedition-in particular the testing of the specific gravity of salt water at the North Pole both in order to contrast it with that at the Equator (and thus to test the hypothesis that the salinity of the sea was lower at the poles) and because such findings 'may be usefull to the Naturalist, in accounting for the varieties of Fish in the Northern seas'. Falconer also suggested that if Banks proceeded with yet another proposed but abortive voyage-this time to the Mediterranean-that he should attempt to complete a catalogue of the plants of Africa. Again Falconer showed some foresight into Banks's future activities in suggesting that through such a project Banks might promote the exploration of Africa. Falconer even recommended particular attention to the Niger-the future focus of the activities of the African Association (of which Banks was a moving force)-since, as he noted in a letter later that same year (the last extant piece of correspondence between them): 'So large a body of water must naturally fertilize a large tract, & probably furnish ample materials for nat[ural] Hist[ory]'.[174]

After 1773 Falconer fades from Banks's ever more multifarious activities, but the correspondence indicates the increasing awareness within the British natural history community of the scientific uses to which the growing number of voyages of discovery might be put. It also suggests how elastic the boundaries of natural history still remained. Falconer urged that Banks should not only collect botanical, zoological, mineralogical and anthropological specimens but also conduct chemical experiments on sea water and observations of the Northern electrical lights. In a letter of February 1772, written at a time when Banks was planning for his ill-fated part in Cook's second great Pacific expedition, Falconer indeed went so far as to define natural history in the following generous terms: 'If we consider natural history in an enlarged view, it includes Astronomy & Geography, the knowledge of Climates, & every material object in the known world. A voyage like yours unattempted before will doubtless embrace every possible object'.[175] And, indeed, Banks's *Endeavour* journal reflects such an interest and delight in all aspects of the natural (and human) world. Johann Forster, who was to take Banks's place as naturalist on Cook's second voyage, also saw it as his brief to study 'nature in its greatest extent; the Earth, the Sea, the Air, the Organic and Animated Creation, and more particularly that class of beings to which we ourselves belong'.[176] Nor was such a conception of natural history at variance with that mapped out by the Royal Society's mentor, Francis Bacon, for whom natural history had involved 'the most comprehensive collection of experiments and observations gathered over the whole field of nature'.[177] Though Banks was to attempt to advance botany as a systematic discipline he, and many of his contemporaries, still looked on the natural historian and 'the man of science' more generally as someone whose quest for 'useful knowledge' should be unrestricted by disciplinary boundaries-a view of science which owed something to the wide cultural range of the virtuoso tradition.

Like Falconer, Daines Barrington, another close acquaintance of Pennant, combined his activities as naturalist with an enthusiasm for promoting scientific expeditions. Indeed, it was Barrington who was the instigator of Phipps's Arctic expedition of 1773.[178] As an active member of the Royal Society, Barrington persuaded the Society to write to Lord Sandwich, the First Lord of the Admiralty, proposing such an expedition. The Society had the tactical sense to emphasise the navigational advantages of a possible new route to the East Indies via the illusory Northwest Passage, though it made no secret of its hopes that such a voyage 'might be of service to the promotion of Natural knowledge, the proper object of their institution'.[179] When this expedition failed to find such a passage Barrington in February 1774 again mobilised Royal Society support for an appeal to Lord Sandwich to mount a voyage to the northern Pacific Ocean, the basis of Cook's third and fateful Pacific expedition.[180]

Such a concern with the unexplored portions of the globe was reflected in microcosm in Barrington's loving exploration of his more immediate natural environment. This gave rise, in true virtuoso fashion, to both a series of antiquarian publications (for as well as his active service in the Royal Society as a council member he was also a vice-president of the Society of Antiquaries) and to such works of natural history as his *Naturalist's Calendar* (1767) or the 'Experiments and Observations on the Singing of Birds' (published in the *Philosophical Transactions* and as an appendix to Pennant's *British Zoology*). As Gilbert White acknowledged in a letter to Pennant it was also Barrington who helped to prompt him to 'quicken [his] Industry, & sharpen [his] attention' in order to produce his loving and minute study of the natural world of Selborne.[181] It was Barrington who, in effect, provided the format for White's systematic observations by providing him with a copy of his *Naturalist's Calendar* in 1768 as well as contributing detailed commentaries on the data thus accumulated. White's links with Barrington and his close friend, Pennant, led naturally to contact with Banks to whom White wrote in April 1768, wishing him well for his 'voyage of discovery' (which White had heard about from Pennant). He also invited him for a visit since the district- as White had cause to know-was a good one for the natural historian.[182] The connection between the two naturalists continued: in December 1772 White visited Banks's Burlington Street home at his invitation describing it as 'a perfect museum, every room contains an inestimable treasure'.[183]

Barrington also played an active part in promoting the career of another of Pennant's naturalist protégés, that stormy petrel of late eighteenth-century scientific exploration, Johann Forster. Pennant came to know Forster in 1768 when the German émigré served-with a characteristically short and tempestuous term of office-as a lecturer at the Warrington Dissenting Academy near Birmingham from 1767 (when he arrived in England) to 1769. Through Pennant Forster soon came to know other naturalists such as Falconer[184] and Barrington. Barrington was, from Forster's point of view, a particularly useful contact not only for his abilities as a naturalist but also because of his family connections, Barrington being the fourth son of the first Viscount Barrington and brother both of William

Barrington, second Viscount and Secretary at War (1765–78) and Shute Barrington, from 1769 to his death in 1826 bishop successively of Llandaff, Salisbury and Durham. Both brothers also shared Daines's enthusiasm for natural history: Shute frequently accompanied Benjamin Stillingfleet, Linnaeus's first major populariser in Britain, on his botanising expeditions while William acted as Stillingfleet's patron, obtaining for him a sinecure. Forster had hopes of also enlisting the good offices of Daines Barrington's powerful eldest brother: we find, for example, Forster suggesting to Pennant in November 1768 that he might obtain a position as a naturalist and interpreter with the British army in Poland, since 'Mr Barrington could do something to this by influencing Lord Barrington his brother'.[185]

Nor were Forster's hopes in Barrington misplaced, for it was he who largely prompted Lord Sandwich to appoint Forster as the naturalist on board Cook's second voyage. Forster acknowledged his debt to Barrington in a letter to Pennant of June 1772, writing that 'Mr Barrington has done more in this affair than a father could have done'.[186] In this same letter, Forster informed Pennant that his French translation of Pennant's *Indian Zoology* was 'in the hands of Mr Barrington', an instance of the way in which Forster reciprocated for such patronage by assisting both Pennant and Barrington in their natural historical and antiquarian investigations. Similarly, in the preface to his translation of King Alfred's *Orosius* (1773), Barrington acknowledged the help of 'the very learned Mr. John Reinhold Forster, who hath made the northern geography of Europe his particular study'.[187] In the long wrangle after the voyage about Forster's entitlement to financial reward from the publication of the journal of the expedition, Forster's admiration for Barrington was extinguished by his close association with Lord Sandwich whom Forster had come to regard as his arch-enemy–a transformation reflected in his bitter remark in a letter of December 1778 that before setting out 'I relied on Mr Barrington's declaration, as I supposed him to be a friend'.[188] However, Pennant continued to correspond cordially with both Forster and his son long after their return to Germany in 1780.[189] In a letter to Pennant from his scholarly exile in Vilna in 1787 Georg Forster thanked Pennant for acting as 'a gentleman, to whom my father and his family owe the warmest gratitude for repeated obligations conferred in the most generous as well as engaging manner'.[190]

Forster was among those whom Pennant thanked for help with revisions for the second (1768) edition of his *British Zoology* along with a virtual roll-call of other prominent naturalists of the age including Falconer, Barrington, White, 'the late Peter Collinson', Stillingfleet, the Reverend Sir John Cullum and 'that Father of British Ornithologists, the late Mr George Edwards'; completing the list were Solander and Banks–an indication of the extent to which Banks had become part of the landscape of British natural history in the five years since he left Oxford. As this litany of names suggests, too, Pennant's network of naturalists extended beyond Falconer, Barrington, and Forster to other figures who played a part in Banks's early career. Pennant, like other prominent

naturalists of the period, benefited from the patronage of the Duchess of
Portland to whom he dedicated his *Crustacea Mollusca Testacea* 'as a grateful acknowledgement of the many favors conferred by her grace'. While
Banks was on the *Endeavour* expedition, Pennant arranged with Sarah
Banks (with whom he kept in touch about the progress of the voyage)
to have some of her brother's natural history material sent to the Duchess.[191]
Naturally, Pennant was closely acquainted with the Duchess's resident
naturalist, the Reverend John Lightfoot, with whom Pennant travelled
on his expedition to Scotland in 1772 when both men sent back specimens
for the Duchess's collections.[192] Subsequently, Pennant helped to finance
the publication of his *Flora Scotica* (1777),[193] the second (1789) edition of
this work including a *Fauna Scotica* and a brief life of Lightfoot by Pennant.

It was symptomatic of the changing relations between Banks and
Pennant, as Banks became more and more of a major naturalist and
scientific patron in his own right, that it was Banks who introduced
Pennant to the antiquarian and naturalist, George Low, minister of Birsa
in the Orkney Islands. Banks and Low met in 1772 when Banks stopped
off in Orkney on his way back from Iceland.[194] This meeting Low
followed up with a letter to Banks offering to do what he could for 'the
Advancement of Science' and, in particular, to assist 'Your Friend Mr
Pennant'.[195] Low undertook extensive surveys on Pennant's behalf and
provided Pennant 'with a most instructive journal, and several drawings'
much of the data from which Pennant incorporated into his *Arctic
Zoology*.[196] At Pennant's instigation, too, Low undertook a systematic
study of the natural history of Orkney with a view to producing a *Fauna
Orcadensis* and a *Flora Orcadensis*.[197] This latter work appeared belatedly
and posthumously in 1805 with a dedication to Banks, the delay in its
appearance being due, according to an anonymous correspondent of
Banks, to Pennant who 'after keeping the manuscript in his possession
for a considerable time, and inserting large Excerpts out of it into his
own Tour; returned it back to Mr Low, without interesting himself farther
in ye Business'.[198] Like Banks, Pennant took a close interest in the practical
application of knowledge that he encountered in his travels–his continental tour, for example, includes accounts of such objects as the Gobelin
tapestries or the water-works of Marly.[199] Hence Pennant valued Low's
work not only for its 'good account of the natural history and antiquities
of the several islands' but also for the fact that it 'enters deeply into their
fisheries and commercial concerns'.[200]

Banks contributed generously to Pennant from the store of knowledge
and specimens he accumulated while on his Iceland voyage. Nonetheless,
after Banks's return from this trip in April 1772 there were indications
that the now internationally-connected botanist, who had been lavishly
praised by Linnaeus after his return from the *Endeavour* voyage,[201] was
becoming rather restive in the role of a client of Pennant. In a letter to
Linnaeus in 1772 Pennant reported that 'I am sorry to say that Mr Banks
has conceived a jealousy of every old friend he had & is quite averse to
encourage merit in others'.[202] This *contretemps* was, however, overcome

Carl von Linné (1707–78), otherwise known as Linnaeus. Engraving by Pasch from a portrait by Roslin. By permission of the Linnean Society of London

and Pennant could report to Linnaeus in the following year that 'I dare say it will give you great satisfaction to hear that Mr Banks & I are reconciled: He lately passed two days at my house & very generously communicated several discoveries he made last year among the Hebrides, which I shall publish in my [Scottish] travels of 1772'.[203] Pennant greeted Banks's election as President of the Royal Society with a mixture of a sort of paternal pride in the achievements of his young protégé and delight that natural history had at last been accorded such recognition. He pressed on Banks his 'wishes that something like natural history may appear under your auspices in the annual productions of the Society. A true naturalist

Thomas Pennant (1726–98). Engraving from a portrait by Thomas Gainsborough.
Courtesy of the National Library of Wales

is so very rare a being among us, that I am sure you will rejoice in the
probability of my having contributed to add one to the number.'[204]

But, despite such outward amity, in 1783 the two men again clashed
and this time the rupture was to be much more long-lasting. Banks objected
to the fact that some of the drawings he had commissioned while on his
Iceland voyage had been sold to Pennant without his consent. Pennant's
reply, however, inflamed the situation for he argued that to withdraw such
plates would involve an extensive revision of the *Arctic Zoology* on which
he had lavished much time. Such labours, wrote Pennant, 'make me consider

myself as a public man meriting the assistance of his friends'.[205] The choice
of the phrase 'a public man' was a revealing one which indicates the extent
to which Pennant saw himself as the public face of a network ranging
from the humble Low to the well-born Banks whose data it was Pennant's
function to put in a form accessible to the community of those interested
in natural history and polite society generally. And indeed, without
Pennant's intervention, it is doubtful whether the data collected by Banks
on his Newfoundland or Iceland voyages would have been published in
any form. Banks responded severely–so severely indeed as to suggest that
his resentment against Pennant's demands had been building up for some
time. The claim that Pennant was a 'public man' he dismissed as
something which 'does not entitle you to expect from me the use of
another's property till you have obtained the consent of the owner' while
of Pennant's reluctance to revise his work he retorted: 'You say that your
Preface must not be suppressed: words to me unintelligible, unless they
mean a threat'.[206] Though Pennant hastily responded in conciliatory
terms–'You are a friend to whom I lie under obligation, therefore nothing
intentional would escape me which could savor of a threat'[207]–thereafter
the old relationship was never resumed. One indication of the strain in
the relations between the two men after this episode is the fact that
Pennant's acknowledgement to Banks in his *Arctic Zoology* was made in
very restrained terms. By contrast, in his *Tour in Scotland* (1774)–in which
Pennant incorporated Banks's account of the geology of the isle of Staffa–
Banks is placed in the same naturalists' pantheon as Raleigh and Wil-
loughby.[208] A long silence ensued in the correspondence between the two
men until a reconciliation was effected in 1790, eight years before Pennant's
death. But, though Banks may have outwardly forgiven Pennant, he
evidently never completely forgot Pennant's rather proprietorial attitude
to Banks's own findings. In a letter to the French naturalist, the Comte
de Lacépède, in 1803 Banks caustically described Pennant as having been
'an indefatigable searcher after other men's Observations'.[209] At the time
of 'the unhappy interruption of our friendship' in 1783 (as Pennant put
it[210]), however, Banks had well outgrown the need for Pennant and his
natural history connections. For, by then, he had become firmly established
at the centre of his own network of British and European naturalists and
no longer really needed Pennant's services. Pennant had helped to open
up the community of natural historians to the young Banks but, by 1783,
Sir Joseph Banks, President of the Royal Society and confidant to the king,
had moved into a well-established orbit of his own far beyond the position
of a satellite in Pennant's constellation of naturalists.

THE IMPACT OF LINNAEUS IN BRITAIN

The contrast between the natural history doldrums of the mid-century and
the increasingly effervescent community of natural historians that Banks
entered–partly with Pennant's assistance–after leaving Oxford in 1763 owed

much to the impact of the work of Linnaeus. Though Linnaeus had his critics–and particularly in England where devotion to John Ray and his system of classification remained strong–his classificatory methods helped to provide botany and zoology with the scientific standing which those who had dismissed natural historians as mere collectors and virtuosi claimed that it lacked. For all the inadequacies of Linnaeus's system of sexual classification (first set out in the *System Naturae* (1735)), which artificially yoked together disparate species, it nonetheless brought to botany and zoology a degree of order; it thus helped to make accessible and comprehensible the ever-mounting number of specimens that European (and especially British) commercial and naval power was steadily augmenting throughout the century. With the existing stock of specimens tidily filed away along Linnaean lines there was a greater incentive to add to their number in the confidence that such new specimens could be added to the store of knowledge made manageable by the Linnaean system. Hence the praise of John Sibthorp in his Oxford botany lectures for

the Cold but systematick Genius of Linnaeus [who] forged as it were a Chain which encompassed the whole of Nature. The Animal the Vegetable & the Fossil Kingdoms marched in a new but regular Order into his System, and he supported it by Laws so well contrived & devised that the Appearance of a new Plant or a new Animal occasioned neither Confusion nor Disorder. The One, or the Other, readily found its Place The Number of Links were increased, but the Chain was not disturbed–it was lengthened only, & that with Advantage.[211]

One of the great attractions of his system was a feature which to Linnaeus had been at first of minor significance: the binomial system of genus and species. This greatly facilitated the task of neatly docketing away new species[212] and thus of strengthening confidence in the belief that, like Adam and Eve of old, the human race was more and more the ruler of the natural world. Linnaeus himself combined the binomial description with the more elaborate system of polynomials (descriptive phrases), but such descriptions became ever more elaborate and the system eventually collapsed under its own weight,[213] leaving the binomial system to act as the naturalist's guiding thread through the labyrinths of nature. It was a system of nomenclature which, as the late eighteenth-century naturalist, Richard Pulteney, put it, 'much promoted the knowledge of plants and must be considered as a capital improvement'.[214]

Linnaeus's own links with Britain had been established early in his career though his system only began to gain adherents there in the 1750s and 1760s and there were still English critics of it when he died in 1778. Among his early contacts with Britain was Lord Bute's contemporary at Leyden, Dr Isaac Lawson, who helped to fund the publication of Linnaeus's first major work, the *Systema Naturae* (System of Nature) (1735), and, subsequently, while Physician General to the British Army, actively promoted the Linnaean system.[215] Among Linnaeus's hosts when he visited England in 1736–attracted chiefly by the fame of the Chelsea Garden[216]–was John Dillenius, the foundation professor of botany at

Oxford. In August 1736 he reported excitedly that 'A new Botanist is arisen in the North' though adding that 'I am afraid his method will not hold'.[217] Despite the continued fidelity of British naturalists to the system of classi-fication developed by John Ray (whose *Synopsis* Dillenius had edited), Linnaeus built up a network of correspondents within England. Predict-ably, chief among them were the London merchants and naturalists Ellis and Collinson; the latter organised the election of Linnaeus as an FRS in 1754. However, Collinson, as he candidly remarked to Linnaeus, was doubtful of the benefits of a system which was likely to make natural history the preserve of specialists rather than interested amateurs such as himself: 'Thus Botany, which was a pleasant study, and attainable by Most Men, is now become by alterations & New Names the Study of a Mans Life & none now but real Professors can pretend to attain it'.[218] It was a remark that suggests both how Linnaeus's work helped to stimulate the transition from virtuoso to botanist and the accompanying sense of loss as natural history became less accessible to a wider public.

By the time of his election as an FRS, however, Linnaeus's work was beginning to attract more attention within Britain. His *Species Plantarum* (1753) was reviewed enthusiastically in the *Gentleman's Magazine* for 1754 by the physician, naturalist and pioneering electrical experimenter, Sir William Watson, who described it as 'the masterpiece of the most compleat naturalist the world had seen'.[219] But the most influential of Linnaeus's early British advocates appears to have been the naturalist, Benjamin Stillingfleet, a client of the Barrington family who 'was intimately acquainted with the celebrated naturalist, Mr Pennant'.[220] In 1759 he published under the unprepossessing title of *Miscellaneous Tracts on Natural History* six essays by Linnaeus's pupils with an introduction which provided a convenient and widely read introduction to the Linnaean system. Indeed, it was a work that earned for him the rather ambivalent title of being 'one of the body-guards of Linnaeus'.[221] As Stillingfleet himself put it, it was his goal to remedy a situation where Linnaeus's name was increasingly well known 'but his works, I imagine, are little known, except to a few virtuosi who have a more than ordinary curiosity ... and ardour to look into the minutest parts of nature'[222]–a passage which suggests how few in Britain were really familiar with Linnaeus's work at the beginning of the 1760s.

Stillingfleet's remark also draws attention to the still ambivalent nature of the word 'virtuoso'. For Stillingfleet a virtuoso was plainly a serious student. Around the same time, however, the naturalist, Da Costa, could write dismissively of the collector and artist, Arthur Pond, that 'Pond was only a virtuoso, but Neilson [a musician] a scientific man'.[223]

Stillingfleet also encouraged the London apothecary, William Hudson, to organise his *Flora Anglica* (1762) along Linnaean lines[224] thus produc-ing a manual which Sir James Smith was to describe as 'mark[ing] the establishment of Linnean (sic) principles of botany in England, and their application to practical use'.[225] This widely used book–which was the first in England to use both the Linnaean nomenclature and system of classification–was to be the young Banks's constant companion on his early natural history expeditions and served to introduce him and many of his contemporaries to Linnaeus's work. The nurseryman, James Lee, who variously contributed to Banks's development by providing botanical specimens and advice and by introducing him to Harriet Blosset, also produced in 1760 an *Introduction to Botany* which was largely based on a translation of Linnaeus's *Philosophia Botanica*. The preface of this work again underlines the growing popularity of botany in Britain, a pursuit he describes as having 'in late years become a very general Amusement in this Country'. For Lee, as for many other naturalists, Linnaeus conferred on their subject the coherence and method which gave it the status of a true science–hence his preface also included high praise for Linnaeus as one who 'introduced truth, order, precision, and perfection, into Natural History'.[226] Another of Banks's early botanical tutors, the venerable Philip Miller of the Chelsea Garden, also assisted the spread of Linnaean principles by using binomial nomenclature in the eighth (1768) edition of his widely used *Gardener's Dictionary*.[227]

From 1760 Linnaeus had his own emissary in Britain in the person of his former pupil, Daniel Solander, who was sent with a letter from the master urging John Ellis to extend to him 'your protection, as I would my own son'. Ellis evidently respected this plea, for in August 1760 Linnaeus sent his thanks 'for the peculiar kindness with which you have received my friend Solander' and for 'recommending him also to your friends'.[228] Thanks to such connections Solander soon became an integral part of the London natural history world.[229] After assisting in the Duchess of Portland's museum he gained a post at the British Museum on Collinson's recommendation. Once ensconced there he was in a position actively to promote Linnaeus's classificatory system. As the naturalist, Pulteney, wrote,

his perfect acquaintance with the whole scheme enabled him to explain its minutest parts, and elucidate all those obscurities with which, on a superficial view, it was thought to be enveloped. I add to this, that the urbanity of his manners, and his readiness to afford every assistance in his power, joined to that clearness and energy with which he effected it, not only brought conviction of its excellence in those who were inclined to receive it, but conciliated the minds, and dispelled the prejudices, of many who had been averse to it.[230]

Among those who benefited from his tuition was his future patron and lifelong companion, Joseph Banks, who, as he himself wrote after Solander's death, first came to know Solander around 'the year 1764, when I was studying at Oxford'. 'From then on', continued Banks, 'our acquaintanceship grew until it developed into a friendship [the end of] which now has given me much grief'.[231] Banks echoed the same sentiments in a letter to the Welsh naturalist, John Lloyd, 'that few men howsoever exalted their pursuits were ever more feelingly miss'd either in the paths of Science or of Friendship'.[232]

Daniel Carl Solander (1736–82). Painting by John Zoffany. By permission of the
Linnean Society of London

Another émigré proselytiser for the Linnaean system was Johann
Forster who affirmed in a letter to Pennant of 1768 that 'Although I am
not a pupil of Linnaeus, however I know his method, & reckon myself
to be a kind of Linnaen (sic) being'.[233] True to such principles, Forster
included in his lectures at the Warrington Academy a defence of the
Linnaean system:

We look upon this with Impartiality, see the Faults & Imperfections of Linnaeus's System, but they are not so much faults peculiar to his Book, but Imperfections which are general to the whole Science. Let us study Nature & improve these Imperfections: but certainly let us look upon Linnaeus's System as the most perfect of them all upon the whole [and] follow this great Man in the Animal & Vegetable kingdoms.[234]

Linnaeus's system had earlier begun to penetrate other institutions of learning more closely linked with the Establishment. At Cambridge Thomas Martyn (the son of John, Cambridge's first professor of botany who had been a correspondent of Linnaeus as early as 1737) incorporated the Linnaean system into his lectures of 1763.[235] What finally won Thomas Martyn over to the Linnaean system was the binomial system which was to do much to account for the rapid advance of the Linnaean tide after this system of nomenclature was clearly presented in the *Species Plantarum* of 1753. As Martyn himself wrote:

About the year 1750 I was a pupil of the school of our great countryman Ray; but the rich vein of knowledge, the profoundness and precision, which I remarked everywhere in the *Philosophia Botanica* [of Linnaeus, published in 1751], withdrew me from my first master, and I became a decided convert to that system of botany which has since been generally received. In 1753, the *Species Plantarum* which first introduced the specific names, made me a Linnaean completely.[236]

In Edinburgh, Banks's indefatigable correspondent, John Hope, professor of botany and *materia medica* from 1761 to 1786, was introducing his students to the Linnaean system about the same time[237] even though Hope had studied in Paris under one of Linnaeus's main rivals, Bernard de Jussieu, of the Jardin du Roi. One testimony to the popularity both of Hope's lectures and their Linnaean content is a letter from John Balfour, an Edinburgh bookseller, to Linnaeus asking him to send more copies of his works since 'The study of botany had become very general in this City, and your books in great Reputation, being much recommended by our new Professor Dr John Hope'.[238]

This steady advance of the Linnaean system was not, however, without its critics. The most socially elevated of these anti-Linnaeans was the Earl of Bute who, as we have seen, attempted to resist its introduction on the grounds that it was an unsuccessful amalgam of natural and artificial methods of classification. In doing so he was aided by his botanical protégé, Sir John Hill, who, in 1761, wrote scathingly to Ellis that 'Linnaeus's method has pleased by its novelty; but it is false in the principles, and erroneous in his conduct of it. His discoveries have scarce done more service, than his method hurt to the science'.[239] Nonetheless, Hill came to recognise the utility of the Linnaean binomial nomenclature when he came to prepare his vast *The Vegetable System* (26 vols., 1759–75) and employed it in the second (1761) and subsequent volumes.[240] The physician and naturalist, Richard Brookes, in the preface to his six-volume *A New and Accurate System of Natural History ...* (1763), also castigated the Linnaean system for 'multiplying divisions, instead of impressing the mind with distinct ideas' thereby 'confound[ing] it, making the language of the science more difficult than even the science itself'.[241] But, at the end of the 1760s, the naturalist, John Berkenhout, could sum up Linnaeus's reception in England by remarking that, although 'the Linnaean System hath met with some opponents, and many objections have been been made to particular parts of it', nonetheless, 'this opposition, and their objections, were insufficient to prevent its being universally received and adopted'.[242]

Brookes and other English critics of Linnaeus saw themselves as defending the classificatory system of their countryman, Ray, a motive which also helps to explain the opposition of Thomas Pennant. For, despite his correspondence with Linnaeus and his friendship with such eager Linnaean popularisers as Stillingfleet, Solander or Forster, Pennant saw himself as loyally protecting the heritage of John Ray as improved by himself. Banks's plans for a visit to Linnaeus in 1767 attracted a scornful reply from Pennant which also emphasised Pennant's preference for zoology over botany. Pennant wrote that he was not 'greatly smitten with the charms of Linnaeus ... as in ornithology he is too superficial to be thought of ... [and] in fossils abler judges than myself think him incompetent. His fort[e] is Botany; & in that you may perhaps edify from his instructions'.[243] In his *British Zoology*, published the following year, Pennant more tactfully dismissed the Linnaean system by writing that he wished 'to avoid the perplexity arising from a new system, and that he therefore would continue to rely on 'that of the inestimable Ray, who advanced the study of nature far beyond all that went before him' though supplemented by 'the method of M. Brisson; whose merit, as a systematic writer is not yet known; or at least, not sufficiently acknowledged among us'.[244] By the time of the publication of his *Synopsis of Quadrupeds* (1771), Pennant had mellowed somewhat in his attitude to Linnaeus. He still had reservations about his system and was particularly critical of the way in which Linnaeus classified Man with the primates of the animal world, but he acknowledged the benefits of the binomial system, one aspect of the Linnaean system which Pennant did adopt. Linnaeus, wrote Pennant, 'hath, in all his classes, given philosophy a new language, hath invented apt names, and taught the world a brevity, yet a fullness of description, unknown to past ages'.[245] Nonetheless, Pennant continued to defy the general trend towards the Linnaean system by continuing to use a modified version of that of Ray. This homegrown English classificatory system continued to find some adherents for a few decades–in 1791 the *Critical Review* wrote of an anonymous work of natural history that 'the arrangement is that of Mr Pennant, improved from Ray; and it is, on the whole, the best that we have seen ... If our author had possessed a little of the modern affectation of arrangement, he might under each class have formed orders frequently natural'.[246]

But even among Pennant's circle of naturalists his attempt to stave off the Linnaean tide had limited success. In 1775, Thomas Martyn in his opening dedication of his *Elements of Natural History* to Thomas Pennant (in which he also paid tribute to Banks), apologetically explained that he had decided to follow Linnaeus's system rather than that of Pennant 'not so much from any objection which I found to it' but rather from 'a desire of explaining and familiarising a system, which has excited the general curiosity, and yet had been not understood at all, or misunderstood by many'.[247]

As the friend and patron of Solander, Banks was naturally seen as being among the defenders of the Linnaean system. Indeed, Banks's scientific exploration could be seen as an extension of that scientifically-informed travel that Linnaeus had pioneered both through his own travels in Lapland and by encouraging the global wanderings of his pupils.[248] Thus, when in August 1768 Ellis wrote to Linnaeus describing Banks's preparation for the study of natural history on the *Endeavour* expedition, he added that 'All this is owing to you and your writings'.[249]

Appropriately, Solander, Linnaeus's 'much-loved pupil', was among the most enthusiastic promoters of Banks's *Endeavour* voyage–as Banks wrote to Perrin in August 1768: 'I was much encouragd in this Scheme by our Freind Solander who so heartily agreed in the excellence of it that he promis'd to make application to the trustees of the Museum & if Possible get Leave to accompany me which he has done'.[250] The link with Linnaeus was strengthened not only by the presence of Solander on the *Endeavour* but also another of Linnaeus's pupils, Herman Sporing, who closely annotated the copy of Linnaeus's *Species Plantarum* which, along with Linnaeus's *Systema Naturae Regnum Animale* ('System of Nature, the Animal Kingdom'), formed part of the *Endeavour* library of the Banks entourage.[251] On his return to England, Banks entrusted the cataloguing of his insect collection to another pupil of Linnaeus, Johann Christian Fabricius.[252] On Solander's death in 1782, his place as Banks's resident librarian and naturalist was taken by Jonas Dryander who had attended Linnaeus's lectures at Uppsala just before his death in 1778. Though Banks's hopes of travelling to Sweden and sitting at the feet of the master were never realised, Banks corresponded both with Linnaeus and his son. In a letter to the latter, written after Linnaeus's death in 1778, Banks paid tribute to Linnaeus for whom 'I always had the highest respect' and to his intellectual legacy since 'I have invariably studied by the Rules of his System, under your learned Friend Dr Solander; so that the plants in my intended publication [the *Endeavour* florilegium] will be arranged according to his strictest rules'.[253] Appropriately, Banks was the dedicatee of a new English translation of Linnaeus's *Species Plantarum*, undertaken by Erasmus Darwin and the members of 'a botanical society at Lichfield' in 1781, one of the aims of which was 'to induce ladies & other unemploy'd scholars to study Botany'. (Consequently Darwin declared that 'The greatest care shall be observed to avoid any ridiculous terms, particularly in those bordering on obscenity'.[254]) However, Darwin was anxious to ascertain that Banks 'approved the design'[255]–a testimony both to the growing popularity of the Linnaean system in England and of Banks's position as one of its patrons and protectors.

But though Banks continued to heap extravagant praise on Linnaeus himself–describing him in 1792, for example, as 'that god of my adoration'[256]–Banks's loyalty to the Linnaean system was, like that of many others of the age, based simply on the belief that the Linnaean system offered the best means of bringing more order to bear on the ever-mounting collections of natural history specimens. Given the largely artificial nature of Linnaeus's system it was difficult to claim for it the status of a map of Nature's fundamental order or to view it, like the mighty system of Newton, as revealing to a dazzled humanity the secrets of 'Nature and Nature's laws'. Thus if there were other seemingly better ways of filing away Nature's products in an orderly fashion then Banks and some of his contemporaries were open to exploring their usefulness or eclectically melding together features of the Linnaean system with those of other classificatory systems.

Banks encouraged the work of Robert Brown, his protégé as a scientific explorer and, subsequently, his librarian (1810–20), in using the system of Antoine Laurent de Jussieu which was less artificial than that of Linnaeus in assigning different species to the same 'natural orders'. It was this system which Brown largely used to bring order to bear on the large number of specimens he collected as the naturalist on the *Investigator* expedition which circumnavigated Australia under Flinders' command–the botanical fruits of this voyage being set out in Brown's *Prodromus Florae Novae Hollandiae* ('An introduction to the Flora of New Holland') (1810). In the preface to this work Brown obliquely referred to what he saw as the inadequacies of the Linnaean system writing that in preparing his *magnum opus* 'it was absolutely necessary to adopt a natural system of classification, for only in this way could I hope to avoid the more serious errors, particularly in forming those new genera for which New Holland is preeminent'. Consequently, he continued, 'I have followed Jussieu's system in which the orders are for the most part truly natural' though even Jussieu on occasions did propose 'grouping into classes' which seemed 'artificial' and based 'upon doubtful principles'.[257] Such a quali-fication suggests that Brown's commitment to Jussieu's system, like that of Linnaeus's before it, was based on the pragmatic assumption that it was at present the best available but would, in turn, be superseded if another more convincingly natural system were to present itself. Such pragmatism was evident in the way in which Brown had earlier, while collecting in Australia, combined features of both the systems of Linnaeus and Jussieu, commenting to Banks in a letter of 3 August 1803 that 'In arranging the collection I at first follow'd Jussieu's Ord's Naturalis; but I soon found the plants of doubtful affinity so numerous that I judg'd it better to use the Linnaean method'.[258] Nonetheless, Brown's ultimate advocacy of the system of Jussieu as the best currently on offer was to do much to promote it within Britain as an alternative to the by then well-entrenched Linnaean system.

Appropriately, the chief defender of the Linnaean system in Britain was Sir James Smith, first president and founder of the Linnean Society and custodian of the Linnaean collections (which he bought at Banks's suggestion). Nonetheless, Smith permitted Brown to combine the office

of librarian to the Linnean Society with his work in weakening the hold
of the Linnaean system. Smith also continued to correspond cordially
with Banks even though the two men increasingly diverged in their
botanical loyalties. At Christmas 1817, Banks wrote to Smith to express
his admiration of 'your defence of Linnaeus's natural classes. It is ingenious and entertaining, and it evinces a deep skill in the mysteries of
classification'. However, continued Banks, such systems must 'continue
to wear a mysterious shape, till a larger portion of the vegetables of the
whole earth shall have been discovered and described'–a remark that
underlined the fact that he regarded all such systems of classification as
remaining provisional and partial. But, even given such qualifications,
Banks did not draw back from declaring·to Smith that Jussieu's system
offered the most useful means of bringing order to bear on the study of
the natural world–particularly since in many ways Jussieu had subsumed
many of the best features of Linnaeus's work:

> I fear you will differ from me in opinion when I fancy Jussieu's natural orders to
> be superior to those of Linnaeus. I do not however mean to allege that he had even
> an equal degree of merit in having compiled them–he has taken all Linnaeus had
> done as his own; and having thus possessed himself of an elegant and substantial
> fabric, has done much towards increasing its beauty, but far less towards any
> improvement in its stability.[259]

THE PURSUIT OF NATURAL HISTORY
IN THE LATE EIGHTEENTH CENTURY

Significantly, Banks rounded off this letter to Smith-written three years
before his death-with a brief summation of the progress of natural history
over the course of his lifetime. It was a natural association of ideas since
the Linnaean system had been the chief stimulus in placing natural history
on a scientific footing and in promoting its rapid growth within Britain
in the late eighteenth and early nineteenth centuries. The Linnaean system
helped to stimulate the production of a whole series of compendia of
British plants, among them the sixteen-volume *English Botany* (1790-
1803), produced by Smith and the botanical artist, James Sowerby, which
referred in its preface to 'The prevailing taste for botanical pursuits, and
the encouragement afforded in this country to every work which tends
to advance them'.[260] It was to this work that Banks paid tribute in the
conclusion of his letter to Smith, when he remarked: 'How immense has
been the improvement of botany since I attached myself to the study, and
what immense facilities are now offered to students, that had not an
existence till lately!' Harking back to his early botanical activities, he
contrasted such works as those produced by Smith and Sowerby which
'would have saved me years of labour, had they then existed' with the
paucity of such guides when he had first begun to take an interest in
botany in the 1760s. So relatively uncharted had been the world of British
botany that, despite the passage of fifty-five years, Banks still remembered

the excitement with which he had greeted the appearance of William Hudson's Linnaean-based *Flora Anglica* (1762) and the 'eagerness with which I adopted its use'.

Towards the end of the century, however, Banks had become much more confident about the popularity of botany. In a letter to the Spanish ambassador of 1796 he remarked that botany had become a pursuit 'not of men only but also of a large number of the handsomest & most amiable of the English Ladies who have of late years taken this amusing Study under their immediate Protection'.[261] Later that same year Banks echoed these remarks in a letter to Linnaeus's Swedish disciple, Carl Thunberg: 'Botany is much in Fashion & some very expensive [botanical] Works are in the Press'.[262]

Banks's impressions about the enormous expansion of natural history between the time of the publication of Hudson's work and the end of the century are confirmed by the labours of Henrey which show that there were about two and a half times as many floras published in Britain between 1762 and 1800 as there had been over the entire course of the earlier part of the century. The steady growth in interest in natural history in the late eighteenth century is also underlined by the accompanying table (Table 1) constructed by Emerson on the basis of Henrey's data.[263]

But this mushrooming of interest in natural history cannot be explained solely in terms of the growing dominance of the Linnaean classificatory system–important though it was in helping to give direction and order to the hitherto often disparate and miscellaneous activities of British naturalists. The Linnaean system gained currency in Britain at a time when British naval supremacy brought with it increasing dominance in the world of exploration and discovery–particularly in that hitherto largely unexploited realm, the Pacific including Australia where, as Smith put it, 'all is new and wonderful to the botanist'.[264] It also came at a time when the adulation for Newton's vast achievement was beginning to abate sufficiently for the physical and mathematical sciences no longer to enjoy quite the same degree of prestige that they had in the wake of the *Principia*. While Newton and his work continued to be admired as the ultimate example of the possibilities of human reason, the view that mathematical and experimental evidence, rather than the techniques of observation and collection, alone constituted the basis of true science was increasingly under challenge. The extent to which science had now to accommodate the claims of two such disparate sets of practitioners was reflected in Banks's acceptance speech as President of the Royal Society on 12 December 1778, when he had pledged 'attention to your interests & welfare & to an equal encouragement given to all branches of science without any undue preference to my Favourite Study'.[265] Though Banks largely appears to have lived up to this promise (as Carter's quantitative study of the papers printed under his presidency suggests[266]) the tensions between the two groups helped to produce the noisy altercations within the Royal Society in 1783-4. The increasing self-confidence of natural historians and their conviction of the worth and utility of their

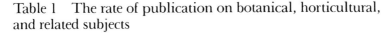

Table 1   The rate of publication on botanical, horticultural, and related subjects

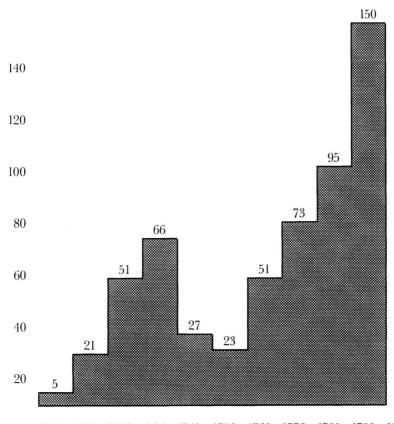

discipline was reflected in the foundation of the Linnean Society in 1788 with the approval and support of Banks, who saw it as complementing rather than competing with the activities of the Royal Society. Banks also commented to the Swedish naturalist, Olaf Swartz, in February 1788 about the new society that 'I incline to think it will Flourish as great care is taken in the institution to keep out improper people'.[267] Such hopes for its future were well founded and in 1814 Smith could report to his fellow naturalist, Sir Thomas Cullum, that 'the Linnean Society flourishes more & more every year'.[268]

Nor was the increasing tendency for natural historians to assert their scientific respectability solely a British phenomenon. In France, too, there was a reaction against the physical sciences. When d'Alembert resigned as editor of the great *Encyclopédie* in 1758, Diderot remarked to Voltaire that: 'The reign of mathematics is over. Tastes have changed. Natural history and letters are now dominant. D'Alembert at his age will not throw himself into the study of natural history'.[269] By 1775 Diderot was even more definite about the shift in taste away from the mathematical to the observational and experimental sciences: as he wrote in the *Encyclopédie* in that year, 'Men's minds seem caught in a general movement towards natural history, anatomy, chemistry, and experimental physics'.[270] As a keen student of the biological sciences, Diderot's comments naturally partly reflected his own interests but the general tenor of his remarks is borne out by the increasing prevalence of natural history publications (such as guides, almanacs and journals) in France in the second half of the eighteenth century.[271] Indeed, in many ways it was Britain that was catching up to the Continent (and especially France) in the promotion of natural history after the long lull that had followed the work of John Ray which, as the naturalist Daines Barrington wrote, 'may partly be attributed to the Newtonian Philosophy's affording a more interesting subject for discussion, till by the force of truth it was thoroughly established'.[272]

This contrast between the state of natural history at home and abroad in the 1760s was emphasised by Thomas Martyn in the course of his lectures at Cambridge in 1764: 'Whilst the Works of Nature are so much studied in most Countries of *Europe*; it is to be lamented that the Progress of Natural history has been but slow in *Great Britain*'[273]. In Martyn's view such a state of affairs was particularly lamentable given 'The great Enlargement of the *British* Dominions in *America* [which] has opened a wide Field for new Discoveries and Improvements in Natural History'-an instance of that linkage between the growth of British imperial power and British science which Banks was to do so much to promote. It was an association which was to survive, and indeed flourish, despite the loss of the British American colonies to which Martyn referred. The growing popularity of natural history meant, too, that voyages of discovery made possible by British imperial expansion not only continued the tradition forged by Banks of carrying naturalists but also that greater priority was given to the work of such peripatetic scientists. This was a transformation on which Banks remarked in a letter to Robert Brown in 1803 when he contrasted the scope given to himself on Cook's *Endeavour* with that accorded to Brown on Flinders' *Investigator*-a change Banks attributed to the fact that in the days of the *Endeavour* expedition

> the bias of the public mind had not so decidedly mark'd natural history for a favorite pursuit as it now has. Cook might have met with reproof for sacrificing a day's fair wind to the accommodation of the naturalists. Capt. Flinders will meet with thanks and praise for every sacrifice he makes to the improvement of natural knowledge which is compatible with the execution of his orders.[274]

Scientific exploration, then, became more and more an area where the goals of empire and enlightenment could meet in happy accord.

For Banks and for many of his contemporaries natural history meant first and foremost botany-a point well appreciated by Banks's Australian

collector, George Caley, who prudently wrote to assure Banks in 1800 that
while he would undertake to explore 'the three kingdoms of nature . . .
and also to the improvement of other arts that originate from the
advancement of natural history; but botany I shall make the principal
pursuit'.[275] Interest in zoology lagged behind botany though it, too, had
benefited from the stimulating effects of Linnaean order and from the
fruits of empire. In 1788 Banks had to discourage the naturalist, Robert
Ferryman, from embarking on a text outlining the different species of
British birds and mammals on the grounds that, while it might enhance
the author's reputation, it would not provide a means of livelihood since
'the Science of Zoology is not at present sufficiently in vogue to allow
[financial support for] any professor of it'.[276] In contrast to botany, zoology
lacked the institutional support of specialised university chairs or of the
royally supported Kew Gardens. However, like botany, it was regarded
as forming part of the province of the faculty of medicine–thus John
Hunter, for example, was a student of comparative anatomy, his researches
being aided by the fact that he had the right to dissect any animals that
died in the royal menagerie in The Tower of London.[277] Banks's work
in helping to establish the Royal Institution also provided some support
for zoology since, in 1806-7, it sponsored a series of zoological lectures
given by George Shaw, a keeper of the natural history sections of the
British Museum. Shaw commented favourably on the extent to which 'the
study of Natural History at large, in all its branches, has, of late been
so much cultivated'–something which sagely he attributed largely to the
fact that 'it has the peculiar advantage of uniting amusement with
instruction'.[278]

   The third kingdom of the natural world–that of minerals–largely fell
outside the Linnaean system though the study of it, too, was stimulated
by the classificatory urge that the success of Linnaeus's work did so much
to promote. In 1771, for example, John Hill lamented in his *Fossils
Arranged According to their Obvious Characters* that 'the Student in Fossils
has yet to work upon a chaos'.[279] This was a situation he attempted to
remedy with his classificatory system which employed such familiar
natural history classifications as 'genus'. In the following year Hill's
patron, Lord Bute, was moved to write to the virtuoso, John Strange,
about the need for greater classificatory rigour in the study of minerals:
'I am deeper in Minerals than I ever was, but the more I look into authors
that have treated on this Reign of Nature, the more I perceive confusion
& uncertainty, in short this beautiful branch of nat: History is still in the
Cradle'.[280] As the case of Bute suggests, those interested in collecting new
botanical and zoological specimens whether at home or abroad often cast
their net a little wider in order also to include new minerals and rocks.
Banks's trip to Scotland and Iceland, for example, led not only to the
collection of new plant and animal specimens but also drew attention
'to the columnar stratification of the rocks surrounding the caves of Staffa
[Scotland]; a phenomenon till then unobserved by Naturalists'.[281] As an
adjunct to his botanical studies Robert Brown built up a large collection

of fossils which he bequeathed to the British Museum. Banks's far-flung network of natural history collectors provided further specimens to test the classificatory systems and techniques which the infant science of geology was developing. The specimen of 'Terra Australis' which Banks provided for Wedgwood and Charles Hatchett led to a number of scientific papers about its properties,[282] culminating in one by Hatchett in 1799 refuting Wedgwood's claims that it possessed a 'primitive earth'. '[C]onsequently', concluded Hatchett, employing terminology drawn from Linnaean classification, 'the Sydneian genus must be omitted in the mineral system'.[283]

In 1792 John Hailstone, the Woodwardian professor of geology at Cambridge, had to acknowledge that 'Till within these few years the general attention of mankind was directed in Natural History to the departments of Botany and Zoology. The sister branch of Minerals seems to have been almost totally overlooked. It consisted of a few scattered unconnected facts, incapable of being digested into a system. And what is incapable of being reduced to system cannot be made the subject of public instruction.' But, he continued, 'The rapid progress which has since been made in Mineralogical knowledge has however made ample amends for the neglect with which it was first treated'.[284] As Hailstone's comments suggest, around the end of the eighteenth century geology began to emerge from its position as the Cinderella of natural history. This owed much to the work of German mineralogists of whom the most notable was Abraham Werner (1749–1817). Appropriately, Werner received his early training at the Mining Academy at Freiburg, for the development of German mineralogy was related to the extensive German mining industry. Such a linking of science with economic advantage naturally appealed to Banks who, through his extensive correspondence with the naturalist Johann Blumenbach of Göttingen and other Germans with geological interests, helped to assimilate such work into the British world. These contacts were promoted by Banks's supply of mineral specimens to Blumenbach and other Germans, such as Wilhelm Haidinger, the Counsellor of Mines, who sent on Banks's specimen of Terra Australis to the mineralogist, Martin Klaproth.[285]

To Banks the study of mineralogy formed a natural part of the proper exploitation of a gentleman's estate–an attitude of mind that was to be greatly strengthened by the fact that the Industrial Revolution was increasingly to draw attention to the value of mineral products. Hence Banks's extensive correspondence with William Milnes, the steward of his estate at Overton in Derbyshire, over the exploitation of lead and coal mines on that property and the possible uses of the new mining technology developed by Banks's friends, Boulton and Watt.[286] By 1811 we find Banks writing to the French naturalist, Barthélemy Faujas de St Fond, that 'Geology becomes more and more in Fashion. I hope we shall before long advance somewhat the Limits of this Science'. Significantly, Banks continued by attributing the growing interest in geology to its economic advantages which made possible a growing amount of employment for students of geology:

We have now some Practical men well versd in Stratifications who undertake to examine the subterraneous geography of Gentlemens Estates in order to discover the Fossils likely to be usefull for fuel as Grind Stones Mill Stones & c & c [as] employment begins to be given to these people the Consequence must be a Rapid improvement of the Labourers[?] in this great work.[287]

In 1808 Banks himself had employed such a practitioner, the geologist, John Farey, to draw up a map of the limestone district of Derbyshire where Banks's own mining interests were centred.[288] Banks's view that such surveys were valuable for their scientific as well as their economic significance is borne out by a letter to one of his stewards at Overton urging him to co-operate as much as possible with Farey in drawing up a coloured map of the stratigraphy of the area since 'it is an Object of some importance to me as a matter of science to have it next winter to Shew to my Friends in London'.[289] And, indeed, Farey's work on Banks's behalf led to the production of the earliest known geological section across England.[290]

Geology also intermeshed with gentlemanly culture in a more traditional manner, for the collecting or description of fossils and minerals could form part of a virtuoso's activities. The topographer, Benjamin Hutchinson, for example, requested Banks to join the company of other notable landowners, such as the Duke of Manchester and the Earl of Sandwich, in sponsoring a history of Huntingdon which would record the county's store of 'extraneous fossils' together with its antiquities.[291] John Pinkerton, a regular correspondent with Banks on antiquarian matters, was also a keen student of mineralogy describing it–in the manner of a virtuoso (or, as Pinkerton styled himself, as a 'connoisseur')–as 'a science not only amusing but instructive'.[292] However, Pinkerton was a virtuoso who also saw the necessity of bringing some system to bear on the collections of minerals he amassed, just as in his historical works he tried to sort his antiquarian findings into some sort of order. His efforts to classify his mineralogical collections were encouraged by his fellow mineralogist, Robert Townson, who had taken an MD at Göttingen in 1795 and had thus been exposed to German mineralogy. In 1800 Townson urged Pinkerton to emulate the systems of classification that had been employed with such success in the animal and vegetable kingdoms, and to 'copy the writing of that celebrated classifier of natural bodies, Linnaeus, and give us the characters of the classes, orders, and genera, as he has done in all his works. In my humble opinion, you cannot have a better model than the system of Mineralogy edited by Professor Gmelin'[293]–a Göttingen mineralogist who, as he wrote to Banks, often consulted Blumenbach's collection of minerals.[294] Pinkerton went at least some way towards realising these goals since, later that same year, Charles Hatchett acknowledged the receipt of his tract on mineralogy with the comment that 'the general arrangement appears to me to be judicious' even though Hatchett queried certain points of his classification, invoking the support of Werner and others for his views.[295]

In geology, as in other areas of natural history, Banks was much more concerned with building up a corpus of observations and exploring their possible practical applications than with attempting to develop a theoretical structure to explain such findings. On occasions, however, Banks gave some indications of his views about the way in which the earth had developed. In a letter to William Richardson, an Anglo-Irish clergyman-geologist, Banks, having thanked him for his memoir on the basalt pillars of Farhead, continued on to express his agreement with the view 'that all the material changes that have happened in the Superficial Surface [?] on which we inhabit have been effected by causes that are no longer in action'. Such an opinion might appear to undermine the possibility of placing geology on a scientific footing since it eliminated the possibility of drawing analogies between present and past geological causation, but Banks maintained that some sort of general understanding of the earth's development could be arrived at through a study of the effects of such bygone geological phenomena.

Predictably, however, Banks was cautious about subscribing to any particular geological theory. Overall he saw 'Geology [as] now making rapid strides' though he was sceptical of the claims of the Plutonians (who believed geological developments could be explained as the result of the action of heat). He was also only prepared to view the claims of Werner and the Neptunists (who emphasised the significance of the action of water) more sympathetically if they displayed a degree of eclecticism by also admitting 'the agency of fire in all places where the consequences of this action are demonstrable'. But Banks's chief counsel to Richardson was to be cautious in developing such theory and to accept that 'These Arcana of nature we can only hope to develop by slow degrees. [W]e must not wonder then if we remain utterly ignorant of matters which will be familiar to succeeding generations as we now are well acquainted with matters of which our ancestors were wholly ignorant'.[296]

Such a cautious attitude to scientific theory was characteristic of Banks and, more generally, of the class of gentlemen-scientists of which he was an archetypal embodiment. For those, like Banks, nurtured on the cultural ideal of the virtuoso, the fascination with collecting objects and scientific data for their own sake continued to weaken the impu'e to arrive at a general body of scientific theory. True, Banks and others of his order departed from the gentlemanly detachment of many of the earlier virtuosi in also emphasising the importance of applying such knowledge for practical ends; but this, too, could act as a brake on the development of hypotheses which were regarded as remote from the more immediate goals of scientific improvement. Part of the appeal of natural history was the view that it avoided the necessity for such theory-making since its practitioners could concentrate on the task of simply accumulating more data. In 1782 the conchologist, Da Costa, expressed the contempt of many of his fellow naturalists for scientific theory in his remark to the botanist, Thomas Martyn:

Systems & Systemmakers I most generally abhor. Facts I prize as you do but they must be truly & authentically respected . . . They are often perverted to prove what can never be deduced from them. Science is now in a bad company with pedantry & imagination & forsaking her former friends & associates Reason Judgement & Truth.[297]

Richard Brookes in his *A New and Accurate System of Natural History* (1763) was even more explicit in advancing the claims of natural history over other sciences as a field in which fact alone was supreme: 'Of all the studies which have employed the industrious or amused the idle, perhaps Natural History deserves the preference; other sciences generally terminate in doubt, or rest in bare speculation, but here every step is marked with certainty'.[298]

Banks himself was never quite so explicit in his advocacy of the empirical charms of natural history as against the speculative character of other sciences, nor as President of the Royal Society–a body with a history of dispute between practitioners of the mathematical and natural sciences–would it have been politic for him to be so. But, though Banks was cautious about dismissing the claims of areas of science other than natural history, his remarks often indicate a rather lukewarm attitude to scientific theorising and, *a fortiori*, anything that smacked of philosophical speculation. When responding to the work of the chemist and mineralogist, Richard Chenevix, in 1804 he commended his experimental work–which was intended to establish the composition of palladium by means of its reaction with mercury–since such investigations provided clear empirical data which 'must Establish the Fact beyond all Controversy'. However, he admonished him for having 'entered into a metaphysical controversy' for 'these meteors of the understanding Blaze during the life of the inventor burn less bright in the hands of his disciples & in general extinguish like a Candle Burnt out in due time'.[299] His suspicion of scientific theorising is evident, too, in a letter to Tom Paine in which he commended American practical ingenuity which he saw as being largely the result of the fact that the citizens of a young country were 'free from these shackles of Theory which are imposed upon the minds of our people before they are capable of exerting their mental faculties to advantage'.[300]

Another feature of the culture of the virtuoso which inhibited the development of a body of scientific theory was its eclecticism and omnivorous taste for almost any branch of learning. A virtuoso made no clear distinction between collecting antiquities or collecting natural history specimens, between promoting history or promoting science. Banks had, of course, done much to discipline and make more rigorous his own interests and collecting habits and those of some of his contemporaries and, as we have seen, he looked with some disdain on the happy muddle and lack of a proper system of classification of some of the virtuoso collectors of his age. Nonetheless, Banks's outlook was still coloured by the traditional gentlemanly preference for the generalist as against the expert, the man of leisure and cultivation as against the functionary–an attitude strengthened by the Enlightenment view that science should form part of the general culture of the age rather than be the province of the specialist. Such attitudes which naturally tended to retard the development of specialised disciplines were strengthened by the nature of the scientific organisations of the age[301]–the Royal Society was meant to be a club in which all the members could communicate with each other without the hindrance of too many disciplinary boundaries.

So, too, Banks used his influence to maintain the British Museum as an institution linked to the gentlemanly and clubbable world of the Royal Society and other London learned clubs. The very fact that Banks held office as a trustee of the Museum *ex officio*, from the year of his election as President of the Royal Society in 1778 until his death in 1820, is an indication of the way in which the activities of the Museum in maintaining and enlarging its collections of curiosities, both from the natural and human world, were regarded as a natural area of concern for the Royal Society. Indeed, just as the foundation and growth of the Society of Antiquaries or, subsequently, the Society of Arts allowed a harmonious division of labour to develop within the world of London learned society so, too, the Royal Society regarded the British Museum as naturally complementing its own activities. The Royal Society's early attempts at constructing its own museum were subsumed into the British Museum's holdings after its foundation,[302] a tradition which continued as the Museum grew in size. Thus in 1771 the Society's Council reiterated its view 'that it is expedient to present the Collections of Natural productions belonging to the Society to the British Museum for the use of the public'; similarly, in 1787, it was decided 'That the specimens of malleable iron from South America ... be presented to the British Museum'.[303]

For the Royal Society and elite society generally, then, the British Museum became more and more the natural repository for the new and curious. '[T]he British Nation', Banks remarked in 1814 apropos of the acquisition of collections of minerals, 'in matters of Curious Collections are Represented by the British Museum'.[304] As the British Museum's collections more and more outshone all others so there was less incentive for both institutions and individuals to amass their own collections. The new status of the Museum thus weakened the culture of the virtuoso or, at least, concentrated much of the virtuosi's collecting urge in a single national institution. As Banks wrote in 1794:

> Tho the study of natural history is certainly not upon the decline here but Continues to be prosecuted with Eagerness & Considerable success yet the business of making Private Collections of Animals is almost wholly laid aside, this Change has I believe been principaly brought about by the circumstances of a vast & national Collection existing here to which Every subject of the Country has a Legal right of admission.[305]

But though the British Museum might in theory be open to the public, Banks regarded its chief function as being to act as 'the Public Treasuries of Science preservd here for the honor of the Country & the use of students'.[306] The British Museum, in short, in Banks's view existed to facilitate the researches of the members of the Royal Society and other learned societies.

Under Banks's influence, the Museum continued to collect widely and omnivorously, thus maintaining the undifferentiated culture of the virtuoso–though it also brought greater system to bear on its holdings than was typical of a gentleman's cabinet of curiosities. To someone such as Banks, who viewed the Museum as the corporate collection of London elite learned society, the admission of the general public was a nuisance to be curtailed as much as possible. Hence his proposal that the Museum should charge admission in order to lessen the ill-effects of a situation where 'every person, whatever his station may be, has an equal right to demand & to receive Tickets' with the result that 'persons of low education, who visit the collections from mere motives of idle Curiosity, are therefore continually mixed in the same Company with those who have prepared themselves by reading to receive useful information'.[307] While under Banks's sway, then, the British Museum still retained something of the aura of a vast collection of a virtuoso to be restricted as far as possible to those who had the social and educational advantages properly to appreciate its worth. In the years after Banks's death it was, as Miller writes, to undergo a transition 'from being in effect a nobleman's cabinet of curiosities to being a truly national museum'.[308] By doing so the Museum became more fully a part of the national estate but its traditional ties with the Royal Society and the London learned clubs generally were loosened as the Museum moved away more and more from the cultural world of the virtuoso–a world to which Banks continued to owe many allegiances.

For Banks was too secure a member of his class to abandon altogether some of the attitudes of mind of a virtuoso. True, he did much to reshape the gentlemanly traditions of the virtuoso towards ends which were scientifically more productive, by promoting a degree of system and of classificatory rigour which had often been absent and by being ever vigilant in seeking to apply such knowledge, rather than viewing it as a form of ornament. But, despite his enormous contribution to promoting scientific exploration and the amassing of data about the natural world, he did little to encourage the development of scientific theories which would help to explain the significance of such materials. For Banks, as for the virtuosi, the amassing of collections frequently remained an end in itself even if the collections were to be organised along systematic lines and closely scrutinised for any practical applications. Moreover, for Banks, as for the virtuosi, such findings should, as far as possible, be readily accessible to a gentleman of wide culture rather than become the exclusive domain of a set of competing scientific specialities.

For all his importance as a statesman of science and as a promoter of natural history as a scientifically-based pursuit, Banks provides an instance of the versatility of the cultural ideal of the virtuoso: an ideal which had its roots in the world of the Renaissance courts but which survived transplantation to the divided society of seventeenth-century England and, over the course of the eighteenth century, succeeded in coalescing with the Enlightenment goal of a general culture which could incorporate science as well as the arts. But, as the nineteenth century progressed and the volume and complexity of scientific learning expanded, the virtuoso became more and more a relic of a bygone age-an age when the frontiers of science were still open to those with relatively simple equipment and the relatively simple training open to a gentleman expected to show some familiarity with the overall map of knowledge. Even the sheer volume of new specimens threatened to overwhelm the virtuoso collector and we find Banks remarking to his collector, George Caley, in 1808, that 'I cannot say that Botany continues to be quite as fashionable as it used to be. The immense number of new Plants that have every year accumulated seem to deter the people from making Collections as they have little hopes of making them perfect in any branch'.[309] By the time that Banks died in 1820, the future of the ideal of the virtuoso was beginning to look as uncertain as the unreformed constitution in Church and State which had sustained and supported such gentlemanly culture but which was overshadowed by the spectre of revolution and, less fearsomely, by the prospect of eventual change and reform.

CHAPTER FOUR

From Antiquarian to Anthropologist

ANTIQUARIANISM, NATURAL HISTORY
AND THE STUDY OF SOCIETY

Banks largely moved beyond the virtuoso's omnivorous and undiscriminating habits of collecting in the field of natural history. But his continued fascination with the study of antiquities is an indication of the extent to which his activities still bore some of the imprint of the culture of the virtuoso which was so widely diffused within his class. For the virtuoso often collected the rarities of human society as a natural complement to the amassing of the rarities of nature. The study and collection of antiquities, along with specimens of natural history, were both ways of coming to know the peculiarities of a particular region. This was true whether one was a traveller or a long-standing resident of England like Gilbert White, the title of whose *Natural History and Antiquities of Selborne* captures the way in which the study of these two realms of human and natural history were seen as being complementary. Earlier, John Aubrey had considered his *Templa Druidium* and his *Chorographia Antiquarie* as forming part of his *Natural Historie of Wiltshire*.[1] The study of antiquities was particularly suited to a leisured landed class since it was a natural outgrowth of their preoccupation with genealogy and frequently provided a means of demonstrating their families' long association with the neighbourhood on which their wealth and power was based.

The study of antiquities did not, however, lend itself readily to that systematic ordering which was to give the natural history pursuits of the virtuoso increasing scientific status in the latter half of the eighteenth century. Nonetheless, there were attempts to place the study of antiquities on a more scholarly footing and to bring order to the often random collections built up by the undiscriminating enthusiasm of some virtuosi. The industrious antiquary, Richard Gough, urged compilers of county histories to bring greater order and system to their works for in his view most examples of this genre consisted of 'crowds of epitaphs, lists of landowners, and such farrago thrown together without method'. 'Such works', he continued, 'bring the study of antiquities into disgrace with the generality'.[2] But in the study of antiquities, as in other areas of knowledge, the confidence in human progress which was such a salient feature of the Enlightenment asserted itself. In his 1782 apologetic for the study of antiquities Thomas Burgess, like Gough, took an unenthusiastic view of earlier students of the subject who 'confined themselves to a necessary, but elementary part of the Study, to which the collection and arrangement of their *curiosities* was only an introduction'. But, he continued, the study of antiquities had now reached greater heights: 'And what indeed may we not expect further from an Age in which every part of science is advancing to perfection'.[3]

One indication of the growing level of sophistication of antiquarian studies was the fact that the embryonic science of archaeology also had begun to demand a more systematic study of the way in which specimens were located relative to each other as a way of facilitating dating. Archaeology, however, did not develop into a separate discipline until the nineteenth century.[4] In the eighteenth century it was still regarded as an aspect of the study of antiquities: thus Banks's close friend, Lord Mulgrave, was described as being an 'antiquarian resurrection-man' because of his interest in excavating barrows[5] and the attempt to discover the Temple of Jupiter Ammon in Egypt in 1792 was termed 'an object of antiquarian research'.[6] Archaeology–the study of the material relics of the human past– was often linked by the virtuosi with the history of the earth more generally, helping to stimulate the growth of an interest in geology.[7]

The parallel between the study of human history and the history of the earth is evident in Robert Hooke's remark that shells and fossils were 'the Medals, Urnes, or Monuments of Nature'.[8] A knowledge of the earth and its forms could also act as an aid to better understanding archaeological remains, as Aubrey found when he was able to discern that the pebbles used in constructing Roman roads were often not of local origin but had been transported from a distant sea shore.[9]

But for all the natural symbiosis between the study of antiquities and that of natural history, as the eighteenth century advanced there was increasing recognition that these two areas of virtuoso culture could be distinguished both by their subject matter and the methods they employed. One symptom of the way in which the study of human society and its relics was beginning to be distinguished from the study of the natural world was the foundation of the Society of Antiquaries in 1707 with the subsequent granting of a royal charter in 1751. The Society's founders regarded such an institution as being particularly necessary 'in an age wherein every part of science is advancing to perfection'. They also saw its foundation as an indication of national maturity, since theirs was 'a nation not afraid of penetrating into the remotest periods of their origin, or of deducing from it any thing that may reflect dishonour on them, or affect either their civil or religious rights'.[10] Hitherto the Royal Society had encompassed the study of both the natural realm and human antiquities–though the Society's tolerance for antiquarian pursuits had waxed and waned. Under Newton's presidency (1703–1727), the Royal Society came close to sundering completely its association with antiquarians. Thus an advertisement setting out 'what subjects seem most suitable to the ends of its [the Royal Society's] institution' in 1718 placed the study of antiquities at the very end of its list of desirable activities after 'Husbandry, Gardening and Planting'.[11] 'Sir Isaac Newton', Spence reported in his book of anecdotes, 'though he scarce ever spoke ill of any man, could scarce avoid it towards your virtuoso collectors and antiquaries'.[12] But the divorce between the study of the natural world and antiquities never became absolute and under presidents such as Martin Folkes (President of the Royal Society, 1741–53 and of the Society of Antiquaries, 1750–4), James West (President of the Royal Society, 1768–72 and Vice-President of the Society of Antiquaries, 1750–72) and Sir John Pringle (President of the Royal Society, 1772–8 and a fellow of the Society of Antiquaries), the membership and the activities of the two societies frequently intermeshed. One indication of this close connection is that the Royal Society and the Society of Antiquaries arranged their meetings so that members could attend both.[13] Folkes, indeed, was praised for attempting to bring to bear on the study of antiquities something of the rigour which he had derived from his scientific (and especially mathematical) studies. As one of his eighteenth-century biographers wrote: 'He had turned his thoughts to the study of Antiquity and the Polite Arts with a philosophical spirit, which he had contracted by the cultivation of the mathematical sciences from his earliest youth'. This portrait of Folkes also drew attention to the need for the study of antiquities to be invested with the sort of system which gave natural philosophy its elevated standing as a form of knowledge: 'Too many of those who have engaged in the former branch of Literature have been too little exercised in Logic, and contented themselves with heaping up passages from a multitude of authors, without being able to connect them, or to draw the proper conclusions from them'.[14]

Banks continued this tradition of active involvement in both societies. From 1785 to 1787 and again from 1813 to 1820 he sat on the Council of the Society of Antiquaries[15] and within the Royal Society much of his support was drawn from fellows who, in the tradition of a gentlemanly virtuoso, combined membership of the Royal Society with that of the Society of Antiquaries. Thus, when he stood for the position of President of the Royal Society, he wrote to the antiquary, Thomas Astle (both an FRS and FSA), for support, assuring him that 'if my Friends of the Antiquarian Society will support me I have not the least doubt of succeeding in a very creditable manner'.[16] Though involved in both societies, Banks did draw a distinction between their proper spheres. A request to help sponsor a work on the genealogy of the English peerage resulted in Banks remarking that this would be better addressed to the President

The Antiquarian Society. Caricature by J. Gillray, 1812. Banks is second from left and Lord Aberdeen (President of the Society of Antiquaries 1812–16) is in the chair. Courtesy of the Trustees of the British Museum

of the Society of Antiquaries rather than 'The President of the Royal Society, whose business it is to encourage natural knowledge & who is in Truth a very superficial antiquarian'. Banks continued by commenting that 'for my own part the [collecting of] general antiquities has been always with me a favorite pursuit of Relaxation, [though] I have never delighted in the genealogical Parts'.[17] The request by the Abbé Grosley in 1785 for the Royal Society to sponsor the publication of an edition of a French twelfth-century manuscript prompted Banks to remark that 'The Royal Society do not meddle with matters of history or Belles Lettres' though the Society of Antiquaries might accept it.[18] Indeed, Banks in his capacity as a senior member of the latter society offered to submit it to that body–an indication of the extent to which any attempt at institutional separation of the world of science and that of scholarship was lessened by the fact that both areas of learning were frequently supported by the same people. Nor was the division between the activities of the two societies observed with quite the punctilio that Banks's comments suggest, particularly when antiquarian studies could be regarded as in some ways merging with the scientific. George Pearson's attempt to apply the techniques of chemical analysis to the study of some ancient metallic utensils unearthed in Lincolnshire in 1787-8 and passed on to Banks was published in the *Philosophical Transactions* for 1796. The same journal also published a copy of the report to the House of Commons issued by Humphry Davy, Banks and others in 1819 on their observations and experiments on the papyri found in the ruins of Herculaneum–a collection which they concluded 'must afford much curious & useful information respecting the State of Society, Literature, Science, & the Arts amongst the ancients'.[19]

In London the size and level of activity of the learned world allowed some institutional separation between the world of the antiquarian and that of the student of natural philosophy. In smaller centres, however, the two continued to be combined in one institution as they had been in the early days of the Royal Society. Maurice Johnson, who founded the Gentlemen's Society at Spalding in 1712, was associated with the early history of the Society of Antiquaries and saw his provincial foundation as promoting all forms of learning appropriate to the world of a leisured gentleman whether these were antiquarian or scientific. Hence the Spalding Society's description of itself as 'a Society of Gentlemen, for the supporting of mutual benevolence, and their improvement in the liberal sciences and in polite learning'.[20] Among its early members was Banks's grandfather and namesake who was also elected an FRS in 1730, thanks to the support of the antiquarian, Roger Gale.[21]

Both the study of antiquities and the study of nature were linked by a critical attitude to the available evidence. Antiquarians, for example, dispelled some of the myths that surrounded the origins of the English nation just as naturalists cleansed the world of fabulous animals.[22] Both fields of learning, then, were concerned with the accumulation of reliable factual data.[23] The influence of the Royal Society and its Baconian ideology helped to refashion antiquarian studies from their traditional bent to a field more concerned with material objects and their properties than with persons and events. The ends to which such data were put were generally of much less interest to the gentlemanly supporters of such learned societies who frequently made no clear distinction between reporting on oddities of the natural and human worlds of their neighbourhoods or of the areas they visited. But such unvarnished empiricism became less respectable as the natural sciences became more and more dominated by the need to organise data along the systematic lines which Linnaeus and others had laid down. The study of antiquities therefore came to seem less obviously a complementary activity for the natural historian and more as a field with its own methods and particular problems of organisation.

The young Banks joined the Society of Antiquaries, as he did the Royal Society, as a natural step for someone of his class attracted to the learned society of London. We need not take too seriously the declaration at his election in February 1766 (at the instigation of Dr Charles Lyttelton, President of the Society of Antiquaries) that he was one 'well versed in the Antiquities of this and other Nations'[24] though the youthful Banks did show signs of his lifelong interest in antiquities. In October the following year he excavated a barrow in Wales and his use of techniques such as the careful recording of the artefacts contained in the tomb with a view to dating the site indicates an attempt to approach the study of antiquities in a systematic spirit. Banks also used the evidence collected from this site to correct the work of previous antiquarians, challenging the view of Dr Plot that the ancient Britons never burnt their dead.[25] In the study of antiquities, as in the study of natural history, the importance of accumulating properly attested information for the benefit of others working in the field was becoming ever more evident prompting the establishment of the Society of Antiquaries' journal of record, Archaeologia, in 1770. We find, for example, in the 1774 volume an account of the Welsh archaeological site of Carn Braich by Governor Pownall which gives due credit to the previous findings of Banks and others of his circle, such as Pennant and Daines Barrington, who, like him, were active in the study of both antiquities and natural history. Their findings, Pownall notes, dispose of the view that it was a fortress and 'all confirm my opinion of what this place is not'.[26]

Banks took particular delight in archaeological digs as a means of providing relatively secure historical data. We find him noting, for example, in the journal of his West Country excursion of 1767 that it would be possible to settle the question of whether or not the ancient barrows were 'the common place of internment of the slain in a Battle' by 'Opening one or more of them, by which alone it can be determined for what use and when they were erected'.[27] Later he opened the tomb of another site around which the myths of the past had collected, the tomb of Little St Hugh, the alleged victim of Jewish ritual murder.[28]

Naturally, his archaeological and antiquarian activities were particularly focused on his native Lincolnshire. In October 1780 he employed two men to open three barrows near Revesby which had been described by Stukeley. Disappointed in not finding any druidical remains there he then turned to the excavation of the site of the abbey of Revesby.[29] Two years later, while on a visit to the Lincoln races, he took part in the excavation of the tomb of the medieval bishop, Robert Grosseteste. This he described to the antiquary, Richard Gough, as the beginning of his 'function of a collecting Antiquary ... since which time I have prepared regular places to put all antiquarian matters relating to Lincolnshire, in an order which will preserve them from being lost'.[30] Banks and many of his contemporaries, then, were attempting to bring order to antiquarian studies in a manner which resembled the way in which natural history had been placed on a systematic footing. But, of course, the study of antiquities lacked its Linnaeus and Banks's own attempts to systematise his work in the field did not extend much beyond organising his material around specific topics, particularly those which impinged on his native Lincolnshire. The limitations of such a system help to explain why Banks adopted a rather lukewarm tone in describing 'My Collections for the County of Lincoln' in a later letter to Gough as having 'not proceeded much, from the variety of more interesting occupations in which I have been engaged'.[31] And this rather dismissive view of the study of antiquities as being of secondary interest to scientific pursuits, such as botany, which lent themselves more obviously to systematic organisation can be detected in other remarks of Banks. In 1783 he remarked to Blagden, apropos of his annual vacation in Revesby away from the business of the Royal Society, that he would be glad 'to do somewhat in the way of Antiquity'[32]– clearly, then, he regarded it as more of a diversion than a serious study.

As Banks grew older and his involvement with the world of science and government became more peripheral, he turned back to the study of antiquities as a source of genteel amusement with no very obvious focus for his diverse interests. From around 1808 to his death he conducted an extensive correspondence with the antiquary, Francis Douce, on such recondite subjects as the etymology of ancient and obscure words. His antiquarian studies waxed as his political star waned–hence his remark to Douce that 'The Gov[ernmen]t has compelld me as usual to resume my Antiquarian Studies'.[33] He also pursued other unrelated activities, such as requesting the Royal Archives of Copenhagen for information on Scottish noblemen in the time of James I.[34] As a knight of the Order of the Bath, Banks (and his sister) paid particular attention to the history of chivalric orders, which helps to explain his authorship in 1813 of a manuscript 'On the origin of the Order of the Garter as related by the Duke of Northumberland'.[35] And, of course, subjects immediately connected with his home county continued to prompt his particular interest. The discovery of some antiquities in the bed of the River Witham, Lincolnshire, led to a communication from Banks to the Society of Antiquaries in 1815 on which he brought to bear antiquarian sources encompassing a variety of medieval English chronicles as well as a knowledge of Italian paintings of the fifteenth century in order to ascertain the probable date and function of the objects thus discovered.[36] On occasions, Banks combined his interest in antiquities and natural history by providing historical accounts of such botanical events as the introduction of the potato into Britain, something he attributed to the colonists sent to the New World by Sir Walter Raleigh.[37]

In Banks's mind the study of antiquities appears to have been a pursuit which could be distinguished from the writing of history–a common view throughout the early modern period.[38] The attempt by the orientalist, the Reverend Thomas Maurice, to interest him in a proposed history of India prompted Banks to respond that 'the course of my pursuits have not led me to pay any respect to the study of history other than as an amusement'.[39] Banks had a poor opinion of himself as a literary stylist and, in an age when history continued to be regarded, as it had been in classical times, as a branch of literature, he may well have distinguished his love of antiquities from the writing of history. Moreover, a work of history required the synthesis of data rather than the accumulation of often disparate pieces of information in the manner characteristic of much of Banks's antiquarian activities.

Despite such protestations, and despite Banks's rather dismissive view of antiquarian and historical pursuits as being a subject of 'amusement', Banks's approach to political and social problems was deeply coloured by a sense of the past. This may have owed much to the influence of the common law with its system of precedents. It would also have been reinforced by his experience as a landowner, since administration of estates and attempts to introduce such improvements as enclosure or fen drainage constantly required attention to precedents and custom. As Farnsworth comments in his excellent study of the administration of Banks's estates: 'successful management demanded extensive records and something of the tastes and abilities of the antiquary'.[40] This habit of mind, which attests to Banks's deep respect for tradition, can be seen in the way he approached a number of problems which fell to him as a Privy Counsellor. His work on the recoinage of copper coinage led to his compiling about 1797 a 'History of Copper Coinage' dating back to 1464;[41] subsequently, around 1816, he drew together from the manuscript collection in the Society of Antiquaries a list of 'Proclamations about Coin'.[42] His interest in matters relating to the Treasury also led to his compiling, around April 1800, collections on the ancient offices of the harbingers and the king's exchangers.[43] Earlier, when Banks went into action to defend the landed interest in the controversy over the Wool Bill of 1787, he again began by providing some historical foundations for his remarks, commencing his pamphlet by demonstrating, by recourse to such documents as Rymer's *Foedera*, 'That Wool was Formerly the most valuable produce of the British Islands'.[44] Like a lawyer mastering his brief, Banks regarded it as important to survey the historical precedents in a particular field and, of course, where possible, to invoke precedents in support of his proposals. The techniques of an antiquarian, then, were not simply for amusement but could also provide a means of legitimising a particular course of action in a society where an appeal to tradition retained considerable potency.

The techniques and interests of the British antiquarian were, naturally enough, generally devoted to his own immediate neighbourhood. But for all this natural insularity or even parochialism the methods and habits of mind of an antiquarian could provide a stimulus for the study of other cultures. The most natural extension of the scope of such antiquarian pursuits was to the study of the classical past, England's Roman heritage being a particular preoccupation of antiquarians. The interest in the classical world was further stimulated by the custom of the Grand Tour which did so much to promote the collecting habits of the virtuosi. It also focused the attention of many of England's elite on the extent and grandeur of the relics of the Roman world and, in the case of the few adventurous spirits who made their way to Greece or former centres of Hellenistic civilisation, those of Greece. Such interest was given institutional form with the foundation in 1734 of the Society of Dilettanti, formed by some of the gilded youth who had recently returned from the Grand Tour, among those most active in its foundation being Lord Sandwich, Banks's early patron. To begin with, the Society was largely devoted to the promotion of artistic taste–as one contemporary put it: 'Some Gentlemen who had travelled in Italy, desirous of encouraging, at home, a Taste for those objects which had contributed so much to their entertainment abroad, formed themselves into a Society, under the name of the DILETTANTI'.[45] And indeed the Society did much to help to promote the foundation of the Royal Academy on the patriotic grounds–which were very much in accord with Banks's thinking–that 'It is both a Disgrace and a Detriment to a Commonwealth to have any Want, having the proper Materials within itself to supply it'.[46] But the activities of the Society broadened to encompass the study of classical antiquity, particularly that of the Grecian world. By 1751 the Society had agreed to sponsor the publication of a three-volume set of plates of Athenian ruins and, in 1764, it raised two thousand pounds to mount an expedition to study the relics of the classical world in the Eastern Mediterranean, the results of this expedition eventually being published as volumes entitled *The Antiquities of Ionia* and *Voyages in Greece and in Ionia*.

Banks played an active part in the Society–no doubt largely because of his association with Sandwich–serving as 'Very High Steward' from 1774, Treasurer and Secretary until 1794 and Secretary alone until 1797.[47] In resigning the secretaryship in 1797 on the grounds of ill-health, he was at pains to convey his continuing good will towards the Society which he had served 'with much satisfaction to myself for 18 years'. He added that he would go on attending its meetings 'as often as it is in my Power so to do'.[48] In his capacity as Secretary Banks assisted in providing material for one of the Society's more outré productions, Richard Knight's *An Account of the Remains of the Worship of Priapus*.[49] This was a work that blended classical studies with fashionable infidelity by tracing Christian religious rituals back to ancient fertility cults. But, as so often, such elite flirtation with the more radical fringes of enlightened opinion was combined with caution about unsettling the faith of the masses. The work was only available to members of the Society and its author commented to Banks that 'I mean my discourse only for the Society of a few real Dilettanti–if it is to be in the smallest degree public many other parts must be suppressed'.[50]

A still further chronological and cultural extension for the virtuoso-antiquarian cultural interests of the late eighteenth-century elite was to turn to the study of Egypt, a natural development for those–such as the members of the Society of Dilettanti–with an interest in the Hellenistic world. Sandwich, for example, visited Egypt (along with Constantinople) in 1738-9 and published an account of his travels,[51] while Edward Wortley Montagu, a cousin of Sandwich, was one of the first to undertake archae-ological excavations in Egypt. Indeed, in 1741, Sandwich, along with William Stukeley, helped to establish a short-lived society to promote and preserve 'Egyptian and other ancient learning'. Although this society disbanded within two years its membership and its interests were absorbed into the Society of Antiquaries.[52] The link between antiquarianism and an interest in exotic civilisations is borne out by the number of virtuoso-collectors who added Egyptian mummies to their collections; these in turn were closely examined in order to provide some further insights into Egyptian civilisation at a time when hieroglyphics were still a closed book. The first published account of a dissection of a mummy was that by Dr John Hadley in the Royal Society's *Philosophical Transactions* of 1764.[53] This was later followed up by Banks's enthusiastic German correspondent, Johann Blumenbach, during his visit to London in 1791-2. For Blumenbach, a comparative anatomist and pioneering physical anthropologist, the close examination of Egyptian mummies was an adjunct to his fundamental goal of investigating and classifying the varieties of humankind. In undertaking such researches he was very much aided by Banks, who enabled him to gain access to mummies in both private collections and at the British Museum. Appropriately, Blumen-bach's account of his findings in the *Philosophical Transactions* took the form of a letter to Banks–a paper in which Blumenbach advanced the view 'that we must adopt at least *three* principal varieties in the national physiognomy of the ancient Egyptians'. However, Blumenbach added, with a remark that indicates his more general caution about the extent to which the different varieties of human beings could be clearly distin-guished in any classificatory scheme, that 'like all the varieties of the human species, [these] are no doubt often blended together, so as to pro-duce various shades'. Overall, he was inclined to place the Egyptians 'between the Caucasian and the Ethiopian'. In Blumenbach's view, such evidence of the physical anthropology of the ancient Egyptians was also relevant to the study of its cultural anthropology or, to put it in the less anachronistic terms Blumenbach himself employed, this information could be used 'for the determination of the different periods of the *style of the arts of the ancient Egyptians'.*[54] Blumenbach's work on this subject represented the application of German scientific and medical practice to the cultural artefacts made available by the English antiquarian tradition- we find, for example, Blumenbach praising to Banks the Egyptian artefacts in the collections of 'your great Antiquarians Mr Townley & Mr Knight'.[55] The range of Blumenbach's interests also suggests the way in which anthropology, in the sense of the study of new contemporary societies, was naturally linked with an interest in past societies–particularly those, such as the Egyptians, which, because of linguistic difficulties, had largely remained inaccessible to European scholarship. We find a similar con- junction of interest in the work of Blumenbach's compatriot and corres- pondent, Johann Forster, who was a keen student of Egyptology[56] as well as being one of the founding fathers of Pacific ethnology. James Prichard, Britain's first anthropologist of international significance, also produced in 1819 *An Analysis of Egyptian Mythology* which included studies of the hieroglyphic alphabet.

As befitted an active member of both the Society of Antiquaries and the Society of Dilettanti, Banks took an active personal interest in the study of Egyptian antiquity–one instance of which is his manuscript from around 1804 on an examination of a mummified ibis found in Egypt which 'exhibit[ed] some of the products of civilized life from a Nation whose Customs and Arts are little known'.[57] Through Blagden he kept in touch with the important findings made by Napoleon's armies in Egypt: in April 1802, for example, he was told of Cuvier's opinion that skulls of the mummies 'have the European or Western Asiatic proportions . . . none approaches to the Negro' while in the following month he learnt of the two different alphabets (hieroglyphic and hieratic) which had been found on two rolls of papyrus brought to France.[58] As a trustee of the British Museum, he also encouraged that institution to extend its col- lection of Egyptian artefacts, reporting with satisfaction to Blagden in 1818 that the statue of Memnon (the colossal head of Rameses II sent by the African explorer, Henry Salt) 'is arrived & lies in the Court yard of the British Museum . . . it is the very best workmanship of Egypt & has induced Combe [an FRS and antiquary] to think that the Egyptians taught Sculpture to the Greeks'.[59] Earlier, the Rosetta stone–the single most important object of Egyptian antiquity–had been acquired by the British Museum after briefly residing with the Society of Antiquaries. Thomas Young, whose important work on its decipherment was built on by the eventual discoverer of the hieroglyphic alphabet, François Champollion, was one of Banks's closest associates.[60] The case of Young again indicates the link between Egyptology and the study of antiquities for (as Banks reported to Blagden) he gave 'his Observations on the Hieroglyphics of the Rosetta Stone to the [Society of] antiquaries who have printed it'.[61]

Banks's interest in Egyptology is an indication of the way in which his antiquarian interests extended well beyond his natural habitat in Lincolnshire. Indeed, Banks and others of his circle extended their interest in antiquities beyond the European world to embrace the study of the peoples of the Pacific whom British naval power was making more and more accessible to the enquiring gaze of the gentleman collector. After all, the cultural phenomenon of the virtuoso-collector had largely originated as a consequence of genteel travel and Banks's *Endeavour* voyage was a variant of the Grand Tour. The association between travel and the collecting of both antiquities and ethnological data is evident in Lord Shaftesbury's inclusion among the characteristics of the virtuoso his interest in both the antiquities and the mores of the societies he encountered in his travels. Such a traveller returned having 'inform'd themselves of the *Manners* and *Customs* of the several Nations of Europe, searched into their *Antiquities*, and Records'.[62] The infant discipline of anthropology was to derive from a number of different intellectual forbears: physical anthropology was to grow out of anatomical studies (particularly in the highly professional medical schools of Germany and France), while cultural anthropology owed much to moral philosophy, which was particularly cultivated in the Scottish universities, a fertile ground for early comparative studies of society. In England, however, where the study of moral philosophy had only a limited impact and where medical education was less well developed than in many of the major European centres, one of the stimuli for an interest in other societies was the study of antiquities which formed part of the cultural ambience of the governing classes. As the physician and naturalist, Matthew Guthrie, pointed out to Banks, despite the narrowness of many antiquarian enquiries nonetheless such pursuits could promote 'the history of man and Civil Society'[63]–what a later age would call the social sciences. In 1782 Thomas Burgess made the same point arguing that although 'the name of ANTIQUARY has been long subject to the ridicule of vulgar prejudice' it was a pursuit which could contribute to the understanding of the development of society more generally: 'And while the Antiquary investigates the origins of the Arts, he is led back to the first dawnings of civil life, and the progressive rise of political institutions. It is obvious therefore how wide a compass of human learning is subject to the researches of the Antiquarian'.[64]

The collection of curiosities from one's own society helped to promote an interest in collecting curiosities from quite foreign societies. Significantly, Lightfoot's catalogue of the vast collection of the virtuoso Duchess of Portland bracketed 'Artificial curiosities from America, China, and the newly-discovered Islands in the South Seas' with 'antiquities' more generally.[65] Such exotic artefacts in turn helped to stimulate an interest in the way of life of the peoples who produced such objects. This the more so since British antiquarians themselves were becoming increasingly aware of the need not simply to unearth antiquities but also to indicate what role such objects had once played in the societies that made them. Such enquiries could even require a degree of field-work as the antiquarian, like the anthropologist, attempted to elicit from those native to the area its local customs and traditions. As the antiquarian, Richard Gough,

wrote in the preface to his *Topographical Antiquities* (1768): 'Our enlightened age laughs at the rudeness of our ancestors, and overlooks the
manners of that rank of men whose simplicity is the best guardian of
antiquity. Innumerable lights may be drawn from local customs and
usages, which are generally founded on some antient fact, and serve to
guide us back to truth'.[66] Banks confirmed the wisdom of Gough's remark
when he dug up a tumulus near the seat of his friend, Lord Mulgrave,
and found the local opinion that it 'had been a beacon & not a place
of burial' confirmed by the presence of charcoal and ashes.[67]

In his *Endeavour* journal, Banks devoted considerable attention to the
recording of what vocabulary he could collect from the different languages he encountered in the attempt to discern which languages, and
hence which peoples, were related. This pioneering exercise in cultural
anthropology was, in Banks's mind, linked to his antiquarian pursuits–
thus, at the conclusion of a set of such vocabularies where he draws
attention to the surprising similarities between some of the languages of
the East Indies and that of Madagascar, he wrote: 'and how any Communication can ever have been carried between Madagascar and Java . . .
is I confess far beyond my comprehension . . . But this point requiring
a depth of knowledge in Antiquities I must leave the Antiquarians to
discuss'.[68] And, indeed, antiquarians like Burgess did discuss such issues.
'An accurate knowledge of the primitive manners and customs of a
people', wrote Burgess in his *An Essay on the Study of Antiquities* (1782),
'tends much to illustrate the earlier periods of their language: While the
investigation and analysis of Language conduces to point out the genius
of a people'.[69] This connection between antiquarian interests and the
anthropological study of language is also brought out in the way in which
Banks's anthropological protégé, William Marsden, published his early
papers on human linguistic diversity in *Archaeologia*, the journal of the
Society of Antiquaries.[70] *Archaeologia* also included articles such as the
one by Governor Pownall on 'Vases found on the Mosquito Shore in South
America' which attempted, in the manner of a proto-social scientist, to
link these artefacts to the 'demands of his [Man's] advancing civilization'
concluding that they were 'the produce of the middle stage of civilization
which has just left nature and not arrived at taste in art'.[71] Another instance
of the Society's role as a forum for anthropological discussion was the
article by the Reverend George Gregory on some caves near Bombay
which 'have of late attracted the notice of the virtuosi'. Again the author
dwelt on the theme of the transition 'from barbarism to civilization' by
analysing the similarities and differences between ancient and modern
Indian religion and customs.[72]

In Marsden's most important work, *The History of Sumatra* (1783), there
are a number of suggestions of the way in which Marsden's knowledge
and interest in the antiquarian study of his own society suggested points
of comparison and ways of analysing that of Sumatra. When discussing
the role of oaths in Sumatran society, for example, he writes: 'these customs bear a strong resemblance to the rules of proof established among

our ancestors, the Anglo-Saxons, who were likewise obliged, in the case
of oaths taken for the purpose of exculpation to produce a certain number
of compurgators'. Interestingly, Marsden continued by suggesting that the
Sumatran practice showed greater sophistication since they selected such
witnesses with greater care and applied much sterner penalties for perjury
and thus 'there seems to be more refinement, and more knowledge of
human nature in the Sumatran practice'.[73] It is a passage which points
to a theme to which we shall later return: the lessening of European
cultural chauvinism in the early anthropology of the Enlightenment.
Another Sumatran legal practice, that of declaring a criminal an outlaw,
again prompted Marsden to point to an Anglo-Saxon comparison: 'In
the Saxon law we find a strong resemblance to this custom; the kindred
of a murderer being exempt from the feud, if they abandoned him to his
fate'.[74] Similarly, another of Banks's associates, Thomas Falconer, in his
Remarks on the Influence of Climate (1781)–a work which drew together
many of the recent accounts of the societies of the Pacific which British
naval and imperial power had exposed to a larger world–included in a
general discourse on the association between forms of punishment and
climate a section on the penalties prescribed by some of the Anglo-Saxon
kings.[75] Though Banks was less explicit in drawing parallels between the
Anglo-Saxon past and the Pacific present he also drew on his study of
English antiquities to provide the analytical categories, such as the
concept of feudalism, which he used to make sense of Tahitian society
in terms comprehensible to an eighteenth-century Englishman. When
describing the political system of Tahiti he wrote that

> the Subordination which takes place among them very much resembles the early state
> of the feudal laws by which our Ancestors were so long Governd, a System evidently
> formd to secure the Licentious Liberty of a few while the Greater part of the Society
> are unalterably immers'd in the most abject Slavery.

Banks continued this exercise in cross-cultural translation by giving
Tahitian equivalents for the terms 'king', 'baron', 'vassal' and 'villain'.
Needless to say, however, subsequent anthropological enquiry has revealed
how inadequate was a social model derived from medieval English society
for the accurate description of pre-contact Tahiti.[76]

Forster's relations with Banks (and, indeed, with most people) were
much pricklier than those of Marsden or Falconer but he, too, illustrates
the close link between the study of antiquities and early anthropology.
When Forster first arrived in England from his native Germany his first
contacts with the English learned world were largely through the medium
of the Society of Antiquaries to which he was elected on 22 January 1767
as 'a Gentleman well versed in Antiquities & in other Branches of Literature'.[77] The Society was prepared to accommodate the very broad view
of the scope of antiquities which Forster's wide education and interests
made possible. In 1767, soon after being elected as a Fellow, he published
in *Archaeologia* a paper on the burial customs of the Tibetans (or, as he
termed them, 'those who follow the religion of the Dalai-lama'). This

he later referred to in his *Observations made during a Voyage around the World* (1778) by drawing out points of comparison between Tibetan and Tahitian burial customs, an illustration of the way in which the activities fostered by English antiquarians helped to provide a frame of reference for Forster's pioneering anthropological studies. In the same section he also drew attention to the way in which the Tahitians, like the ancient Egyptians, 'agreed in thinking the soul to remain about the body as long as any flesh continued undecayed' even though the Tahitians did not follow the Egyptians in believing in the transmigration of the soul[78]– again an instance of the way in which Forster's wide education in the antiquities of the classical and Mediterranean societies helped to provide the foundation for his study of exotic contemporary societies.

Having approached the study of Pacific studies with the intellectual equipment provided by the study of antiquities, the process could sometimes be reversed with the students of English antiquities drawing parallels with the curiosities from Pacific societies that were becoming ever more prevalent in major British collections, both public and private. Banks compared the Roman urns and weapons found in Lincolnshire with those he had observed first hand in the Pacific.[79] In George Pearson's paper in the *Philosophical Transactions* about the chemical analysis of Banks's collection of Roman, Saxon and Danish antiquities uncovered by the scouring of the River Witham in Lincolnshire in 1787–8, he suggested points of comparison between the state of British society at the time of the coming of the Romans and 'that in which our late discoverers found the natives of the South Sea islands'. Thus both societies were very eager to acquire metal goods from the intruding power and the ancient Britons, like the 'inhabitants of Otaheite', abandoned some of the early metal goods they so obtained because they realised that they were of inferior quality.[80] In 1812 the Reverend Frederick Clarke, professor of mineralogy at Cambridge, wrote excitedly to Banks to report that labourers had unearthed an ancient weapon 'exactly resembling the Stone Hatchets of the South Seas'[81]–a comment which suggests the wide circulation of the Pacific anthropological curiosities brought back by Banks and later Pacific travellers. Among the institutions which held such collections was Trinity College, Cambridge, where Sandwich deposited the artefacts he received from Cook's voyages[82] and where Clarke may well have seen a specimen of a Pacific stone axe.

Part of the reason for the association between antiquities and anthropology in England was simply that the Society of Antiquaries was one of the few sources of encouragement and patronage for the study of history and human societies; by contrast, many of the Continental countries had State-supported academies and universities which provided an institutional setting for some of the early students of anthropology. But even in France, which provided considerably more State support than Britain for the embryonic discipline of anthropology, thanks to the Institut National and the medical schools, there was also some sense of intellectual affinity between the study of antiquities and anthropology. The Société des Observateurs de l'Homme (founded in Paris in 1799), the first anthropological society, drew much of its support from the medical profession but acknowledged the contribution of those who 'cultivate the science of antiquities' to the study of anthropology–a term which the Society was among the first to use in its modern sense.[83]

THE CONTRIBUTION OF NATURAL HISTORY AND MEDICINE TO THE DEVELOPMENT OF ANTHROPOLOGY

Along with the study of antiquities a closely-related stimulus for anthropological enquiry was that of natural history–closely-related since, as we have seen, the study of the antiquities and the natural history of an area often were regarded as complementary; both pursuits therefore formed part of the culture of the virtuoso. Gilbert White's great work–an archetypal example of the fusion of an interest in natural history and antiquities–also included a plea for what amounted to an anthropological study of Irish society couched in terms of English condescension. In letter XLII, White commented on the possible advantages of a well-born naturalist–or, as he termed it, some 'future faunist, a man of fortune'–extending his studies of Ireland to 'The manners of the wild natives, their superstitions, their prejudices, their sordid way of life, a study which would prompt many useful reflections'. Elsewhere he also offered some of his own observations on the language and customs of the Gypsies.[84] Pennant, to whom White addressed this letter, extended his own close interest in natural history and antiquities to include accounts of the native peoples encountered by British explorers. In his autobiography Pennant included what was in effect an anthropological treatise–'Of the Patagonians'. In it Pennant set out to support the widely-held belief that the Patagonians were giants by drawing on the testimony of a Jesuit missionary and those of a number of travellers, including a personal letter from Admiral Byron, one of England's first major Pacific navigators. At times Pennant discusses the habits of the Patagonians in much the same manner as his discussions of zoological subjects: 'Those who deny the existence of these great people', he writes, for example, 'never consider the migratory nature of the inhabitants of this prodigious tract'. However, he also includes information about their more distinctly human activities–their customs, government, and religion–as well as discoursing on the deleterious effects of the impact of the Europeans which has 'been a dreadful obstacle to their moral improvement'.[85]

The antiquarian studies of Pennant's fellow naturalist, Daines Barrington–the person who did most to prompt White to publish–did not venture beyond Britain but they did prompt some tentative moves towards a form of historical sociology of the sort much cultivated in Scotland (where there was much interest in the comparative material made available by the Pacific explorers). In Barrington's major work of antiquarian scholarship, *Observations on the Statutes, Chiefly the More Ancient, from Magna Charta to the Twenty-first of James the First* ... (1766), the cultural comparisons with England are generally limited to Scotland

and a few other European societies (though there is some discussion of Mexican society as described by the conquistadors[86]). However, this work did illustrate the way in which the study of antiquities was developing beyond an unsystematic collection of curiosities into an attempt to relate cultural practices, such as the forms of law, to the historical development of a society. At the outset he affirmed his belief 'that the old acts of parliament were (as far as they went) the very best materials for an English history; and that they were likewise strongly descriptive of the manners of the times' (p.iv)–a precept he built on with a close analysis of the way in which major pieces of legislation such as the Magna Carta reflected the customs of the period (for example in the treatment of women). In short, Barrington was attempting in his own limited way to arrive at a study of the spirit of the laws within England. He does acknowledge Montesquieu's great work which, despite his reservations about the Frenchman's history of torture, he praised for 'The very great ability and learning, which appear almost in every other part of it'.[87] And Barrington's work did help to promote the beginnings of a sociological study of the role of law, for Bentham later acknowledged his debt to the *Observations*.[88]

The example of Barrington, then, provides yet another example of the way in which the study of natural history and antiquities were frequently linked. It also suggests the way in which the study of antiquities could provide a stimulus for an attempt to arrive at something approaching a more generalised study of human society, an enterprise which could be extended beyond the borders of one's own culture to include the exotic societies encountered by Pacific travellers.

Barrington also helped to promote interest in the exotic societies which had recently come within the ken of the European world in a more concrete fashion by facilitating the distribution of curiosities collected by Pacific travellers. It was he, for example, who arranged for much of Cook's collection of ethnological artefacts to pass to Sir Ashton Lever, the owner of a vast but ill-arranged private museum of anthropological and natural history specimens.[89] Collectors of natural history specimens frequently also purchased anthropological curiosities, an indication of the extent to which the study of the natural history and the human society of new areas of the globe were seen as being linked. Thanks to Banks, Pennant acquired a number of Pacific artefacts[90] and earlier in the century Sir Hans Sloane had included in his vast collection (the nucleus of the British Museum) various ethnological specimens of which the largest group was described as 'made by the Indians-Esquemos in Hudsons Streights'.[91] However, such anthropological specimens were often undervalued since, unlike the new natural history specimens, they could not be linked to an overall system. As Kaeppler writes, 'because there was no *Systema Naturae* (Linnaeus, 1735) by which to arrange them and no precise terminology with which to discuss them, few took them seriously'.[92]

The association between antiquities and natural history as different aspects of the culture of the virtuoso suggests one reason for the fact that those interested in natural history often extended their interests to the collection of anthropological artefacts and even to some ventures in the direction of developing a 'science of Man'. Another, ultimately more significant, link between natural history and anthropology was the wide domain staked out for natural history by Linnaeus, Buffon and other major systematisers of the age.

For Linnaeus the true natural historian should take as his brief not only the animal, vegetable and mineral kingdoms but also the human world. Linnaeus himself set the example in his early voyage to Lapland in 1732, where he was as much interested in the study of human society as in the flora and fauna.[93] Other Linnaean disciples followed his example–Peter Kalm's account of his travels in North America[94] was, among other things, an account of the different societies he encountered there while Carl Thunberg's *Travels in Europe, Africa and Asia* included among other comments on human society a detailed and open-minded portrayal of Japanese culture.[95] Forster, who translated both these works into English, emphasised in his preface to the translation of Peter Kalm's *A Voyage to China and the East Indies*, the Linnaean character of such anthropological observations since Kalm was 'a pupil of the great Linnaeus . . . [who] followed punctually and literally the rules prescribed by his excellent tutor in his *Instructio Peregrinatoris*'–hence his close attention to such things as 'the antiquities, the religion, the manners, . . . [and] the character' of the societies he visited.[96]

For all his ambivalence about the Linnaean system of classification Thomas Pennant, too, saw his copious travel accounts (or his accounts of others' travels) as being formed by the Linnaean tradition with lengthy descriptions of different societies as well as the realm of nature. Thus his account of Western Hindoostan aspired to 'imitat[e], as far as my talents will admit, the great examples left by the disciples of the Linnaean school'.[97]

The theoretical basis for such an inclusive definition of natural history was the fact that Linnaeus's classification of the animal world took the controversial step of including human beings. Some sense of how momentous a step this was, and what an outcry it provoked, can be gained from Linnaeus's highly defensive preface to his *Fauna Sueica* where he wrote:

> No one has any right to be angry with me, if I think fit to enumerate man among the quadrupeds . . . indeed, to speak the truth, as a natural historian according to the principles of science, up to the present time I have not been able to discover any character by which man can be distinguished from the ape.[98]

In the classificatory system outlined in his *Systema Naturae* (1735) and developed in subsequent editions of this fundamental work, Linnaeus classified humankind with the primates and divided the genus '*homo*' into two species which were in turn broken up into several varieties based on physical and cultural distinctions. The first of these species, *homo sapiens*, embraced Wild Man, American, European, Asiatic and African; the second, *homo monstrosus*, 'Mountaineer, Patagonian, Hottentot,

American, Chinese, Canadian'. Such divisions were based partly on physical differences but also on cultural differences–in Linnaeus's account European man was governed by law in contrast to the American (regulated by custom), the Asiatic (governed by opinions) and the African (governed by caprice).[99]

The classificatory impulse of the eighteenth century had extended to the world of humankind and Linnaeus's attempt at system was to be further refined by other eighteenth-century pioneering anthropologists, most notably by the German physical anthropologist, Blumenbach. In contrast to Linnaeus, however, Blumenbach allocated human beings a genus to themselves quite distinct from that of their nearest animal neighbours, the apes. Nonetheless, Blumenbach warmly praised 'the immortal Linnaeus' for initiating the scientific study of humankind by including the human race in his *Systema Naturae*.[100] In Linnaeus's account the inclusion of human beings in his classificatory system was not an individual idiosyncrasy that could be removed at will but was integral to his whole conception of the working of nature.[101] All aspects of nature were linked by the Great Chain of Being which proceeded from the most lowly insensate object up to *homo sapiens*–hence the importance of including the human world in his systematic analysis of the natural world. Indeed, the study of humankind was in some ways the key to the rest of nature–as Linnaeus himself wrote in 1760: 'we must pursue the great chain of nature till we arrive at its origin; we should begin to contemplate her operations in the human frame, and from thence continue our researches through the various tribes of quadrupeds, birds, reptiles, fishes, insects and worms, till we arrive at the vegetable creation'.[102]

Though Banks was never formally a pupil of Linnaeus his conception of natural history (including the study of human society) was naturally shaped by the great Swedish naturalist with whom he corresponded enthusiastically and whose favourite pupil, Solander, was Banks's *alter ego* in his natural history endeavours. Banks's lengthy accounts of the exotic societies he encountered while on the *Endeavour* can be seen as a natural product of the activities of a compleat Linnaean naturalist. Nor was Banks's role as a recorder of ethnological information restricted to non-European societies. Banks's journal of his voyage to Scotland and Iceland in 1772 includes lengthy sections of what are, in effect, anthropological observations on these societies.[103]

As Banks moved from the role of traveller to that of patron of discoverers he continued to promote a conception of natural history which embraced the study of humankind. Thus Robert Brown, in his long letter back to Banks reporting on his work as a naturalist on board the *Investigator*, followed the listing of his botanical and zoological findings with a discussion of the character of the Australian Aboriginal society he had observed at Cape Arnhem of whose language 'we have collectd a small specimen'– a specimen that Brown compared with Aboriginal vocabularies collected elsewhere.[104] Brown also described the activities of Malay fishermen from the Celebes who fished for bêche de mer in the Gulf of Carpentaria.[105]

Likewise, Flinders, the captain of the *Investigator* and a client of Banks, recorded both the cultural and linguistic practices of the Aborigines, concluding that despite the varieties of language the uniformity of customs indicated that Australia was inhabited by a single race.[106]

Though Johann Forster's personal links with Linnaeus were even more tenuous than Banks's he was even more explicit than Banks in identifying with the Linnaean conception of the role of the naturalist–including the view that the true naturalist ought to encompass human society within his brief. His remark to Pennant of 1768 that 'Although I am not a pupil of Linnaeus, however I know his method, & reckon myself to be a kind of Linnaean being' was, appropriately, prompted by the request that he should undertake the translation of 'Journeys of the Linnean School'. Forster also proposed that he should also add some of his own ethnographical observations in the form of an account of his travels through Russia. Such material, he argued, would provide much valuable comparative data since in the Caucasus there were 'more than 50 little Nations living in ... separate valleys [and] each nation has a separate Language & manners, & all are the remainders of the several wandering Nations which spread over Asia & Europe'. Forster concluded his list of possible subjects for his account of Russia with 'The Natural history of the Volgae & that of the Orenburg Government'[107]–a usage that again underlines the association between the Linnaean vision of natural history and the beginnings of anthropology. Indeed, in his *Observations Made During a Voyage Around the World, on Physical Geography, Natural History and Ethic Philosophy* (1778), an account of his experiences on board the *Resolution*, Forster lamented that more naturalists had not devoted themselves to the study of the human as well as the animal and vegetable worlds. Those travellers, he wrote, who 'happened to be capable of collecting and communicating useful information, relative to the study of nature ... have usually confined themselves to the inanimate bodies of the creation; or have principally considered part of the brute organic; while Man ... is entirely neglected and forgotten, amongst less important pursuits'.[108] Furthermore, continued Forster, those writers who do concern themselves with human society tend 'to study mankind only in their cabinets; or, at best, to observe no other than highly civilized nations, who have over-run all parts of the world by the help of navigation and from commercial views; and are more or less degenerate and tainted with vice'.[109] And this generous conception of the role of the naturalist was to be passed on to Forster's son, Georg, who, in 1789, described 'my preoccupations hitherto' as having been 'Natural history in its broadest sense and particularly anthropology'.[110]

For all Johann Forster's enthusiasm for incorporating the study of humankind in the proper domain of the naturalist he nonetheless showed some uneasiness about the extent to which in Linnaeus's system human beings were placed almost literally on all fours with the animals. In his *Observations* he launched a spirited aside (which probably had as its immediate target the eccentric Scottish social theorist, Lord Monboddo) at those 'patrons and advocates of the long exploded opinion that monkies are of the same species with mankind' adding, with unaccustomed humour, that anyone who compared the human female with 'an ugly, loathsome ouran-outang' deserves that 'none but ouran-outangs vouch-safe and admit his embraces'. In support of this view that humankind was *sui generis*, Forster invoked the work of most of the major physical anthropologists of the late eighteenth century, among them Hunter, Camper and Blumenbach, pointing to their evidence 'that man is the only creature of the class which suckle their young ones, who is intended to walk erect'.[111]

Forster's patron, the naturalist, Thomas Pennant, was even more explicit in his rejection of Linnaeus's classification of the human race within the animal kingdom. At the outset of his *Synopsis of Quadrupeds* (1771), Pennant wrote of Linnaeus's work that 'I reject his first division, which he calls Primates, of foremost in Creation, because my vanity will not suffer me to rank mankind with apes, monkeys, maucaucos, and bats'.[112] Such a view had the august support of Pennant's correspondent, the great Buffon. Buffon acknowledged that in certain respects Linnaeus was correct to classify humankind with the animals:

> Man, it is true, resembles the other animals in the material part of his being; and in the enumeration of natural existences, we are obliged to rank him in the class of animals.

But, he continued,

> in nature, there are neither classes nor genera; all are mere independent individuals ... and, though we place man in one of these classes, we change not his nature; we derogate not from his dignity.

Despite the taxonomic convenience of linking human beings with the animal creation, then, Buffon was insistent that we should recognise that

> Between the faculties of man and those of the most minute animal the distance is infinite.[113]

But such reservations did not mean that Pennant, Buffon, or, still less, Forster, did not support the extension of the techniques and classificatory rigour of the Linnaean naturalist to the world of humankind. They might insist on the importance of emphasising the gulf between the animal and the human but nonetheless they included human society in the naturalist's domain. In his *British Zoology* Pennant, like Linnaeus, described zoology as gaining much of its intellectual coherence from the fact that it encompassed the gradations of the Great Chain of Being from humankind to the lowest form of animal life: 'Zoology is the noblest part of natural history, as it comprehends all sensitive beings, from reasoning man, through every species of animal life, till it descends to that point where sense is wholly extinct and vegetation commences'.[114] Appropriately, in his copious travel accounts Pennant devotes space to the description of the human societies he encountered along with an account of the features of the animal, vegetable and mineral realms. Buffon, too, devoted much space to an analysis of the human world and his great *Natural History* played a major part in fostering the infant science of anthropology.[115] It was largely thanks to his example that the neglect of the study of human society of which Forster complained was remedied, so that when Herder published his *Outlines of a Philosophy of the History of Man* in 1791 he could remark on the growing attention devoted to this area of natural history: 'And is human nature alone unworthy of that accurate attention, with which plants or animals are drawn? Yet in modern days the laudable spirit of observation has begun to be excited towards the human species'.[116]

Among those who extensively used Buffon's account of different human societies (based largely on accounts by travellers) were many of the major Scottish social theorists, among them Dunbar, Ferguson, Monboddo and Kames.[117] Such social theorists both increased interest in the possibility of what was termed 'a science of Man' and acted as a stimulus for further research. For it was commonly felt that theorising about human society had outstripped the properly attested body of data on which such a science should be based and that the firm empirical foundation for the study of human society had yet to match that established by naturalists concerned with the animal and vegetable worlds. Even Ferguson caustically remarked apropos of the study of human society in his *Essay on Civil Society* (1766) that 'In every other instance ... the natural historian thinks himself obliged to collect facts, not to offer conjectures'.[118] In the preface to his *History of Sumatra* William Marsden described it as his goal both 'to throw some glimmering light on the path of the naturalist' and

> more especially to furnish those philosophers, whose labours have been directed to the investigation of the history of Man, with facts to serve as *data* in their reasonings, which are too often rendered nugatory, and not seldom ridiculous, by assuming as truths, the misconceptions, or wilful impositions of travellers. The study of their own species is doubtless the most interesting and important that can claim the attention of mankind; and this science, like all others, it is impossible to improve by abstract speculation, merely. A regular series of authenticated facts is what alone can enable us to rise towards a perfect knowledge in it.[119]

Along with the study of antiquities and natural history, another stimulus for early anthropological enquiry was the study of medicine and particularly comparative anatomy. Given the rather somnolent state of the medical schools of Oxford and Cambridge this was of less significance in England than elsewhere in Europe. But in neighbouring Scotland the well-developed medical schools were of greater significance for science in general and, to some degree, for the development of anthropology than those in England. It is significant, for example, that James Prichard, the first British physical anthropologist of international standing, was a medical graduate of Edinburgh and his pioneering anthropological treatise, *Researches into the Physical History of Mankind* (1813), grew out of his Edinburgh MD thesis of 1808, *De Humani Generis Varietate* ('About the Variation of the Human Race'). However, after graduating, Prichard had to combine his anthropological investigations with running a medical practice, an indication of the lack of career opportunities within Britain for the early students of anthropology.[120] Such an interest in anthropological questions had been prefigured by a number of Edinburgh medical students, among them John Hunter (who died in 1809 while his better known medical namesake died in 1793). In 1775 Hunter took as the topic for his Edinburgh MD thesis *De Hominum Varietatibus et Earum Causis* ('About the Varieties of Mankind and their Causes')-a subject prompted in part by the controversy generated by Lord Kames's recent *Sketches of the History of Man*.[121] Hunter's work preceded by a few months Blumenbach's much more influential account of human variation, *De Generis Humani Varietate Nativa* ... ('About the Natural Variation of the Human Race'). The two works also adopted a broadly similar system of classification for the human race with the European, American and African being regarded as the primary forms.[122] But, after producing this promising early work, Hunter's energies were thereafter devoted to his medical practice at home and abroad in Jamaica (where he served as superintendent of a hospital from 1781-1783).

William Falconer, a kinsman of Pennant and brother of Thomas, the early correspondent of Banks, was also an Edinburgh medical graduate having taken an MD there in 1766. In between his duties as physician at the Chester Infirmary, Falconer found time to produce a work which blended medical and social theory, the weighty *Remarks on the Influence of Climate ... Nature of Food, and Way of Life on ... Mankind* (1781). The goal of this work was to supply an explanation for the differences in human society by recourse to the influence of climate, an enterprise which obviously owed much to Montesquieu's *Spirit of the Laws*. Falconer acknowledged his debt to the Frenchman whom he described as 'one of the greatest men of the age' (p.135) though not without including some criticism. Falconer was, for example, dismissive of Montesquieu's experiments on the effects of temperature on a dead sheep's tongue, pointedly contradicting them with his own deductions based 'on the known and acknowledged effects on the *living* human body' (p.3). Generally, Falconer was of the view that a hot climate 'naturally renders men tired and slothful' (p.iv) while 'The manners of the northern nations, in comparison with those of warm climates, appear rough and austere' (p.46)-thus placing the English and other occupiers of temperate zones in the most privileged position.[123] 'The intermediate climates', concluded Falconer, 'have always been esteemed, both in ancient and modern times, to be the most favourable to human nature'-a view shared by Adam Ferguson, who argued that civilisation was the product of neither very hot or very cold zones but rather of those with 'some intermediate degree of inconvenience'.[124] In Falconer's scheme those in temperate climates were prone to 'fickleness' and 'uncertainty of temper' (p.20) but even this could be an advantage: Falconer suggests, for example, that the 'fickle and uneasy disposition [of the English], also, is highly favourable to the advancement of science, as it leads them to be dissatisfied with the present, and of course, inquisitive after what is better in future. This disposition induces a spirit of examination and enquiry' (p.73). But Falconer was not a complete determinist in relation to climate recognising that the effects of climate could be outweighed by cultural factors. The Chinese, for example, 'inhabit a hot climate and are probably naturally disposed to be indolent and slothful; but the number of the people being very great, necessity compels them to labour, and thus overpowers the natural tendency of heat' (p.iv).

Falconer also argues that the effects of climate can be outweighed by other physical factors such as food–a vegetable diet he regards as producing people who 'are less bold and courageous than those who use animal food', something which helps to account for the easy conquest of the peoples of the East Indies (p.239).

Falconer's work brought into clear focus debates about the extent to which, as Montesquieu had suggested, the differences between cultures could largely be explained in terms of climate. This hypothesis was one of the first, and one of the most fertile, organising principles for a 'Science of Man'. However, as Falconer's work suggests, the growing interest in developing a body of theory to explain the diversity of human societies brought with it a more critical attitude towards Montesquieu's pioneering work and, in particular, to the question of the significance of climate. In listing the three causes which resulted 'in the production of those varieties which we have remarked among the different nations of the earth' the great Buffon continued to give primacy to climate, followed by food (a subject which also looms large in Falconer's work) which, Buffon pointed out, has 'a great dependence on climate' and, finally, manners 'on which climate has, perhaps a still greater influence'.[125] Buffon, then, very largely continued to accept climate as the critical shaping force in human societies with food and manners reflecting its influence. Even Buffon's reference to manners did not represent a real departure from Montesquieu, who saw the spirit of the laws as not only being shaped by climate but also by such cultural factors as religion, customs and manners.[126]

In Johann Forster's work, however, there is a greater scepticism about the primary role of climate. In his *Observations* he questions the view advanced by Buffon that 'The heat of the climate is the chief cause of blackness among the human species'[127] by arguing that such an explanation did not account for the fact that the Dutch settlers had been at the Cape for one hundred and twenty years without showing any sign of a change in skin colour.[128] After discoursing on the effects of climate on temperament and culture, Forster again questioned such explanations by pointing out that they did not explain why Tahitian society was more advanced than those of other peoples living in the same climate (p.295). Such observations led Forster to place a greater stress on cultural and moral influences in shaping the differences between human societies rather than on the mechanistic impact of climate.[129] Forster's influence within Germany helped to promote a rather more cautious attitude to the significance of climate that is reflected in Herder's remark:

> It has even been objected to the great Montesquieu, that he has erected his climatic spirit of laws on the fallacious experiment of a sheep's tongue. It is true, we are ductile clay in the hand of Climate; but her fingers mould so variously, and the laws, that counteract them, are so numerous, that perhaps the genius of mankind alone is capable of combining the relations of all these powers in one whole.[130]

And, as Falconer's work suggests, in England, too, social theorists were increasingly inclined to stress the importance of influences other than climate. Marsden in his *History of Sumatra* took the view that the effects of climate were more successful in explaining societies subject to the extremes of heat and cold but 'In the temperate zones, where this influence is equivocal, the manners will be fluctuating, and dependent rather on moral than physical causes'.[131] The Scottish social theorist, Henry Home, Lord Kames, was even more sceptical about the influence of climate. Citing Banks's and Solander's experience in Tahiti and Iceland he explicitly rejected Montesquieu's thesis by affirming that 'It is my firm opinion that neither temper nor talents have much dependence on climate'.[132]

Like that of Montesquieu and most eighteenth-century social theorists the analyses of Kames and Falconer relied heavily on the accounts brought back by travellers from hitherto little-known societies. As Gay writes:

> The prehistory of the social sciences had its beginning in the emergence of cultural relativism, the bittersweet fruit of travel. Whether realistic, embroidered, or imaginary, whether on ships or in libraries, travel was the school of comparison, and travelers' reports were the ancestors of treatises on cultural anthropology and political sociology.[133]

Perhaps William Falconer played a role in prompting his brother, Thomas, to encourage Banks to study the human societies he encountered as well as the flora and fauna. When Banks proposed to go to Sweden in 1768 'for the benefit of natural history' (as Thomas Falconer put it) he was urged by Falconer to emulate Linnaeus by extending his observations to 'the examination of the Laplanders themselves, viz their height Make & Oeconomy of features'. For Falconer such observations were relevant to the larger question of illustrating the physical similarities between the peoples of northern Asia and those of North America, with the Laplanders constituting a possible link between the peoples of northern Europe and those of northern Asia. Such an enquiry he considered particularly appropriate for Banks as 'one that has visited the Coast of Labrador and has such opportunities of comparing the one with the other'.[134] And, although Banks never made his way to Sweden, he does appear to have shared Falconer's interest in the physical features of the peoples of the sub-arctic region. When, in December 1772, a group of Eskimos arrived in England, Banks took the opportunity of observing closely a people with whom he had had no contact on his Newfoundland and Labrador voyage since, as he wrote in his journal of that voyage, regarding the Canadian Indians: 'They in return Look upon us in exactly the same light as we Do them killing our people whenever they get the advantage of them & Stealing or Destroying their nets wheresoever they find them'.[135] Banks and Solander made frequent vists to the visiting Eskimos and *Lloyd's Evening Post* reported that they were 'extremely well satisfied with the observations and behaviour of those people'[136]–what the Eskimos thought of the two naturalists is not recorded. Two years before his death Banks once again returned to the subject of the Eskimos and their origins. In a letter to Blagden in 1818 he reported that 'The most curious thing that has been met within the North Western Expedition is the Original Nation from whence all the Esquimaux who have travelled to the Southward seam [sic] to have migrated'.[137] Banks then launched into a description of the way of life of the Eskimos, an account which once again underlines the extent to which Banks saw the province of the naturalist extending beyond the animal and vegetable kingdoms to the human world.

Banks also appears to have encouraged William Anderson, yet another Edinburgh-trained surgeon, to extend his activities as surgeon and naturalist on board Cook's second and third great voyages to include ethnology. Anderson had undertaken to collect specimens on Banks's behalf on the third voyage but when he, like Cook, failed to return from the voyage his collection of 'natural curiosities' (which included specimens of the world of nature including humankind) was left to Banks.[138] Though Anderson studied at Edinburgh from 1766 to 1769, his highly detailed accounts of various Pacific societies appear to have been based simply on a natural association between medicine and an interest in natural history rather than on any more systematic training. Like Banks's ethnographical observations, too, they are largely innocent of any theorising, though Anderson does draw out some comparisons between European customs and those of the peoples of the Pacific as well as between the different Pacific societies he observed.

Anderson, Prichard, John Hunter and William Falconer were all products of a university where medical research, including comparative anatomy, was actively promoted and where there was considerable interest, especially among the professors of moral philosophy and law, in the possibility of arriving at some generalised explanations of the workings of human society. Such a situation found only the faintest echo in the two English universities which were very largely ecclesiastical seminaries. However, in the London medical world there was also some interest in physical anthropology, though the level of activity was limited by the lack of research posts of the sort supported by a number of the European (and Scottish) universities. The main focus of such activity in London was the figure of John Hunter (the surgeon as opposed to the previously-mentioned physician). Hunter and Banks had a long association–Banks aided Hunter in obtaining natural history specimens for his vast collection and helped to obtain for him a post with the East India Company in 1789.[139] Appropriately, in 1806 the Royal College of Surgeons presented to Banks a bust of Hunter to which Banks responded with an appreciative letter referring to his friendship with Hunter.[140] As early as 1774 Solander was involved with Hunter in investigations relating to animal comparative anatomy, Solander in turn passing on such information to Banks.[141] Hunter's vast private museum was a natural centre for students of natural history including Banks. In 1786, for example, Blagden commented of a specimen of a burnoke that its size 'considerably exceed[ed] that in Mr Hunters collection which is the largest Sir Jos Banks & myself have seen'.[142] However, when Hunter's museum was offered for sale in 1796, following his death, Banks did not attempt to persuade the government to purchase it for the British Museum, despite the plea of his old friend, William Eden, Lord Auckland, that Hunter's family desperately needed the money.[143] A pamphlet addressed to Banks also urged purchase on the grounds that Hunter's collection was not that of a virtuoso–that 'It was not hastily formed in a fit of caprice or vanity, as many heterogeneous collections have been'–but rather 'was the result of a well digested truly scientific scheme'.[144] Banks regarded the private museum as being primarily a medical collection rather than one of importance for the study of natural history or science more generally[145] and this he regarded as being inappropriate for a museum catering to the general educated public. But he did support its purchase for more specialised educational purposes and praised 'the Munificence of the Legislature [which] has most judiciously, purchasd the late Mr Hunters Anatomical & Physiological collections'–particularly since it enabled the British Museum to divest itself of specimens relating to these subjects.[146] After the Royal College of Physicians declined the government purchase in 1799, it was acquired by the newly-founded Royal College of Surgeons in 1800. Banks in his role as one of the Hunterian Museum's trustees helped to deal with the government of the day on its behalf[147] thus strengthening his links with the medical profession.

Among the branches of natural history which Hunter cultivated was an interest in physical anthropology which explains why his museum included a collection of human skulls. But Hunter's clinical commitments tended to push such interests to the periphery of his published works. There are, however, some faint traces of his anthropological researches: in his posthumously published work on fossils, for example, he hinted at the possibility of biological evolution and dwelt on the close connections between human beings and the animal kingdom.[148] Banks also reported that Hunter had argued that 'Black or dark Colors were in almost all cases the natural original ones of animals ... & [consequently] he maintaind warmly that adam & Eve must have been negroes'.[149] By contrast, Blumenbach and other influential physical anthropologists argued that the Caucasians had come first and that the so-called coloured peoples were later variants of the white original. Hunter also delivered a lecture entitled 'Remarks on the Gradations of Skulls' which, although it was never published, prompted Hunter's former student, Charles White, to devote himself to a study of human differences[150] which resulted in the publication of his *An Account of the Regular Gradation in Man, and In Different Animals and Vegetables ...* (1799).

Like Hunter and other would-be British physical anthropologists, White had to combine such interests in an uneasy combination with his more pressing clinical commitments; as he put it in his preface, underlining the association between natural history and anthropology, he did 'not profess to have a knowledge of natural history adequate to the extent of his undertaking' because of his 'fatiguing and anxious profession' (p.iv). Though White was personally opposed to the slave trade, his treatise presented one of the most unequivocal statements of white supremacy based on the assessment by the aptly-named White of the physical differences between the races. Indeed, his work was used within the United States as part of the ideological armoury of the pro-slavery camp.[151] The organising principle which ran through White's work–like that of so many eighteenth-century naturalists–was the Great Chain of Being, a principle extended by him to a hierarchical ordering of the varieties of humankind. 'Every one', he wrote, 'who has made Natural History an object of study, must have been led occasionally to contemplate the beautiful gradation that subsists amongst created being, from the highest to the lowest' (p.1). So much emphasis did White place on the gradual descent from humankind that he discoursed at some length on the similarity between some primates, especially orang-outangs, and human beings, even speculating on the possibility of orang-outangs and human beings mating. At the outset of Part Two–'On the Gradation in Man'–White again acknowledged his debt to Hunter, whose collection of skulls, both human and animal, organised in a steady gradation, had suggested to him 'that Nature would not employ gradation in one instance only, but would adopt it as a general principle' (p.41). Thus he set out to illustrate 'the extremes of the human race', the European and African, the latter White describing with unabashed racial supremacy as 'approach[ing] nearer to the brute creation than any other of the human species' (p.42). White then attempted to substantiate his thesis by adducing evidence related to the comparative bone structure of Europeans and Africans, arguing also that 'a similar gradation takes place in the cartilages, muscles ... size of the brain' (pp.56–7). The conclusion that White drew from such evidence comes as no surprise: that 'In whatever respect the African differs from the European, the particularity brings him nearer to the ape' (p.67).

White's emphasis on the gulf between European and African even led him to argue that the different races were separately created (p.125), a proposition that ran counter to the biblical account of the descent of humankind from one pair of original parents. This difficulty White dealt with, in a manner that was becoming increasingly widespread among eighteenth-century naturalists, by arguing that the biblical account of Creation was metaphorical and not intended as an accurate record of scientific events, or, as White put it: 'that Revelation was given to man for a different purpose than to instruct him in philosophy and natural history' (p.136). In advancing the polygenesist view, that the different varieties of humankind constituted different races, White was departing significantly from the views of his mentor, Hunter, who, in common with most of the major authors of the day, was a monogenesist upholding the essential unity of humankind. In advancing the polygenesist position, White was influenced by the physical evidence (which was later shown to be largely spurious) amassed by Edward Long in his *History of Jamaica* (1774), one of the major polygenesist tracts.[152] 'When we reflect on the nature of these men [negroes]', Long had written, 'and their dissimilarity to the rest of mankind, must we not conclude that they are a different species of the same genus'.[153]

White's departure from biblical orthodoxy prompted the American Presbyterian clergyman, Samuel Stanhope Smith, to add an appendix devoted to refuting White to his *An Essay on the Causes of the Variety of Complexion and Figure in the Human Species* (1788). The basic incompatibility in the positions of White and Smith is apparent in the declared goal of Smith's work: 'to establish the unity of the human species, by tracing its varieties to their natural course ... [thus] bringing in science to confirm the verity of the Mosaic history'.[154] The physical differences between Europeans and Africans Smith attributed to the fact that the Africans were in the process of changing to the higher form embodied by the Europeans. Smith's introduction provides yet another affirmation of the links between the infant science of anthropology and natural history, since in it he asserts that 'There is certainly no subject in the science of NATURAL HISTORY more curious and interesting than that which respects the variety of COMPLEXION and of FIGURE among mankind'. The 'natural history of man' he saw as now being based on more data than ever before–largely thanks to Cook's voyages which 'have especially contributed to eradicate former errors, and to establish permanent truths in the history of man'.[155]

Another of Smith's targets was the Scottish social theorist, Henry Home, Lord Kames, who had also suggested that the differences between the varieties of human beings were so considerable that they could be regarded as different species. Kames argued (as he put it in a letter to the Scottish physician, James Lind) that 'there are different species of men fitted for the different climates'. In the same letter Kames requested Lind to collect whatever evidence might be relevant to such a conjecture while accompanying Banks on Cook's second voyage–a voyage from which, of course, Banks withdrew, carrying Lind and the rest of the Banksian entourage to Iceland.[156] In arguing that the human race was comprised of a number of different species Kames was well aware that he was departing from the position advanced by the authoritative Buffon, that all human beings belonged to the one species, since they could procreate. For Buffon variations in human types could be explained in environmental terms and chiefly as a consequence of climate,[157] a position that Kames explicitly rejected in his *Sketches of the History of Man*.[158] Though Forster resembled Kames in rejecting such an explanation of human differences based on climate he was, nonetheless, a vigorous defender of the mono-genesist position. Despite the apparent differences between human beings, he maintained that 'if we examine the insensible gradations ... we shall find that they are by no means so widely remote from each others in the scale of being, as to form separate species' a remark he reinforced with the italicised affirmation *that all mankind are descended from one couple*.[159] Banks, too, remained a monogenesist accepting the position of Buffon that the test of a species was the ability to interbreed–hence he wrote in a letter about slavery in 1792 that 'the negroes ... [are] most certainly our fellow creature because we mutually breed together & the animal produced is not a mule'.[160]

In the course of his work White made ample use of the work of the Dutch physician and naturalist, Pieter Camper, who, with the goal of making the fine arts more realistic, had pioneered many of the techniques of craniometry–measurement of the human skull–which were to become basic to the study of physical anthropology.[161] As White conceded, Camper had been a monogenesist who (like Buffon) maintained, 'that all the varieties were occasioned by climate, nutrition, air, & c'. But White saw himself as undermining such opposition by extending Camper's own techniques of measurement asserting 'but what would he [Camper] have said, if he had known that the lower arm of the African was considerably longer than that of the European'.[162]

White's connection with Camper was not simply an intellectual one: though Camper came from Leyden he had studied under White's mentor and long-standing friend from student days, John Hunter.[163] The link with Hunter also helps to explain how Camper came to know Banks. In 1785 we find Blagden writing to Banks to express his high opinion of Pieter Camper who was then visiting London. Camper had indicated his abilities by showing to Hunter's satisfaction that a collection of bones in his museum were not those of some fabulous great bird but rather those of a tortoise.[164] On Camper's return to his native Netherlands, Banks continued to maintain contact with him. In January 1786 Camper wrote to thank Banks for his hospitality while in London; a later letter of June the same year links Banks with John Hunter by promising to send them both drawings of fossils.[165] Banks also received news of Camper from Broussonet, Banks's chief French correspondent, who, during a visit of Camper to France in May 1787, warmly praised Camper to Banks as 'a very learned man who knows about some very curious matters'.[166]

For Camper, Banks provided an entrée into a vast international natural history collecting network which could provide him with specimens otherwise difficult to obtain through Dutch sources. His letters to Banks mingle the courtesies of eighteenth-century scholarly correspondence with requests for a number of natural history specimens–the skull of the Asiatic rhinoceros, skulls of a walrus and other animals from duplicates in the British Museum. As well as requesting specimens Camper also looked to Banks to send him news of the London scientific world (and especially John Hunter). However, Camper declined the offer of Banks's good offices in obtaining for him foreign membership of the Linnean Society on the grounds that he had a poor opinion of Linnaeus being 'astonished how in these days his system can be adopted but for making a catalogue'.[167] Camper, however, endeavoured to repay such services in similar scholarly currency: thus he arranged for an exchange of specimens with the British Museum and sent accounts of his own scientific researches. Camper also sent Banks news of political developments in the Netherlands when, in 1787, the civil war forced Camper to move with his precious collections.[168] Banks's association with Camper, then, was that of a fellow naturalist interested in drawing the Dutchman into his European-wide network of scientific collecting and dissemination of information. Whatever may have been the subject of their discussions while in London, the correspondence between Banks and Camper does not reveal much explicit attention to specifically anthropological topics-though such a clear distinction between natural history and anthropology would have been quite foreign to Camper (or Banks), whose interests spanned the full gamut of what the eighteenth century understood by natural history, including the study of human society. In any case, the fact that Banks was in a position to send Blumenbach copies of Camper's plates of skulls[169] does suggest that there was some interchange between the two men on anthropological matters.

By contrast, Banks's relations with Blumenbach, Camper's admirer and fellow pioneer in the field of physical anthropology, were far more explicitly devoted to the advancement of anthropology *tout court*[170] and the extensive correspondence between the two men brings out some of the major points of contrast between the state of anthropology in England and on the Continent. In the first place, Banks–like most of his compatriots-acted in the role of an acquirer and disseminator of specimens and scientific knowledge and contacts rather than by promoting original investigations of his own. Secondly, like Camper (who took his MD from Leyden in 1746 and served as a professor of medicine successively at Franeker, 1751, Amsterdam, 1755 and Groningen, 1763), Blumenbach was a medical graduate who earned his living as a professor of medicine. He thus serves as a case study of the research possibilities offered by continental medical faculties in promoting, among other things, anthropology–in conspicuous contrast to those of England.

Blumenbach studied medicine at Jena and Göttingen taking his MD in 1775 from the latter with a dissertation entitled *De Generis Humani Varietate Nativa* ... ('About the Natural Variety of the Human Race'), a pioneering work of physical anthropology, which Blumenbach was to revise and supplement over the course of his career. The fact that Blumenbach chose such an original subject is testimony to the intellectual vitality of the newly founded University of Göttingen (f. 1734) and particularly its medical faculty which owed much to the stimulation of Albrecht von Haller, who had served there as professor of medicine from 1736 to 1753.

Blumenbach himself was appointed professor of medicine in 1778, a post he combined with that of curator of the natural history collection on which much of his research was based. The Electorate of Hanover gained great prestige from the accomplishments of its university but, as a relatively minor state, it offered little opportunity for the accumulation of natural history specimens which were so often the by-product of imperial expansion. However, the university benefited from the fact that since the Elector of Hanover and the King of Great Britain were one and the same, there was at least the possibility of benefiting from the natural history riches amassed by the British. Predictably, one of the main intermediaries in enabling Göttingen to so benefit was Banks, both because of his far-flung scientific connections and because of his personal ties with the king. One practical advantage that accrued to Banks as a *persona grata* at court was that Banks had access to the diplomatic mail between London and Hanover which provided him with a regular and relatively secure means of sending natural history specimens to Göttingen.

From Blumenbach's point of view there was everything to gain from an association with Banks and the network of scientific collecting and information of which he was the centre. The first extant letter in the lengthy correspondence between the two men dates from 30 July 1783, a reply to an earlier untraced letter from Banks which had requested information from Blumenbach about his experiments related to freezing.[171] Blumenbach's letter set the tone for much of the correspondence that was to follow by requesting Banks to obtain specimens for Blumenbach's museum, specifically ethnographic 'curiosities' from the first of Cook's voyages, to supplement its existing collection of items from the second and third voyages. By June 1787, Blumenbach was requesting that Banks obtain for him a skull from the South Seas to add to a collection of human skulls which he had been building up for some time and which formed the basis of much of his work in physical anthropology. Blumenbach attested to the scientific standing of the collection that it 'had already merited the admiration of several gentleman of your acquaintance, for example Mr De Luc and Mr Herschel'.[172] Banks was eager to help but wrote that 'since Mr Hunter here & P[iete]r Camper in Holland have written so much on that subject those who have possession of the Crania of the South Seas set a high value upon them'.[173] As Banks's remarks indicate, Camper's work had done much to stimulate interest in the field of physical anthropology which Blumenbach was to develop further–indeed, Blumenbach himself remarked in old age that he considered his correspondence with Camper as one of the most fortunate incidents in his life.[174]

Despite this initial setback, Banks's role in the ghoulish task of obtaining for Blumenbach crania for his collection was to be one of the main scientific links between the two men. At first Banks had to respond by simply sending Blumenbach casts from the collection of 'My Friend', John Hunter, and a promise to request a ship's captain bound for Tahiti to collect skulls in the South Seas and in New Holland.[175] Banks continued to put his scientific contacts at Blumenbach's disposal: in November of the same year he had, as he told Blumenbach, 'written to St Vincent's & Commissioned a Friend who is going to Otaheite to return[?] Crania'.[176] By July 1789 he could report proudly to Blumenbach that 'I have not been idle in my attempts to fulfill my Promise of supplying you with the Crania of different nations' and that he was sending the cranium of a chief from St Vincent–something which he owed to Alexander Anderson, keeper of the botanical garden there.[177] Though Anderson was primarily a botanist, like most eighteenth-century naturalists his interests and activities also extended to the study of humankind–thus he could report to Banks that, although he had been able to locate one specimen, skulls were difficult to obtain since 'the Yellow Caribs, the aboriginal race, had been almost extirpated by the Black Caribs'. Moreover, he added, 'any attempt to disturb the ashes of their Ancestors they regard as the greatest of crimes'–a sentiment which did not deter Anderson (or Banks) from obtaining such a specimen[178]. The arrival of a second Caribbean skull in 1790 prompted Blumenbach to thank Banks for 'the noble liberal way you promote any well minded attempt for the advancement of natural history'[179]–an indication of the way in which anthropology continued to be regarded as a branch of natural history.

Blumenbach continued his quest for further anthropological specimens through Banks's agency, particularly from that scientific *terra incognita*, New Holland–prompting the beginnings of a trade in Aboriginal skulls which has occasioned a movement for repatriation and ritual reburial in Australia today. Banks at first was a little pessimistic about obtaining such crania since, as he commented in a letter to Blumenbach of July 1792, 'the natives of that Countrey being in the habit as the Governor [Phillip] writes me word of Burning their dead to ashes'[180]–a remark that indicates both Banks's and Phillip's interest in the ethnological study of Australia.[181] In the same letter to which Banks referred, Phillip also discussed other Aboriginal customs he had observed in the six months since he arrived. He also remarked on how much more numerous the Aborigines seemed than he had expected[182]–perhaps a veiled comment on Banks's testimony to the House of Commons in 1779 that he 'had reason to believe the country was very thinly peopled'.[183]

Blumenbach maintained what pressure he could muster, writing to Banks on 6 April 1793 that 'I learn by the newspapers that Cpt'n Bligh is arrived in the W.Indies. How happy would I be if he by Your kind Intercession should have brought with him some acquisition for my collection from the South Seas'.[184] And by August 1793 Blumenbach achieved his goal, for Banks sent him the cranium 'of a male native of New Holland who died in our settlement of Sydney Cove' together with the promise to send by the 'next [royal] quarterly messenger' one from Tahiti, once Bligh had completed customs procedures.[185] A second such specimen from New Holland followed in June 1799.[186] Blumenbach acknowledged these services by noting in the third decade of his catalogue of crania that: 'My collection rejoices, owing to the liberality of the illustrious Banks, in the very rare skull of a New Hollander from the neighbourhood of Botany Bay'.[187] Blumenbach gave Banks advance notice of this tribute in a letter of November 1793 coupled with a request for further anthropological information. Thus he asked Banks if this cranium corresponded with what Banks had observed of 'the young New Hollanders brought over lately from Sydney Cove' a request prompted by the fact that the drawing by Webber of a Tasmanian Aborigine in the account of Cook's third voyage was 'very different from the scull you favoured me with'.[188] Banks's reply was of limited use since he had attempted vainly to seek the assistance of Governor Phillip (who had not returned from Bath) but he caustically remarked that Webber's depiction should not be relied on since 'that Gentleman indeed was by Profession a Landscape painter & what he has done in the portrait line I have given little credit to'.[189]

In Blumenbach's long letter to Banks of 1 November 1793, he also indicated the uses to which this trade in the dead was being put. Since his MD dissertation, Blumenbach's scientific energies had been largely focused on the attempt to develop a classification of human types which would extend to 'the Science of Man' the classificatory rigour which Linnaeus had brought to bear on the study of natural history more generally. In his 1775 thesis he had proposed four main divisions of humankind: Caucasian (European), Mongolian (Asian), Ethiopian (African) and American, viewing the latter three as examples of degeneration of the original Caucasian strain (as Blumenbach first christened it on the basis of a specimen from the Caucasus region).[190] Such 'degeneration' Blumenbach saw as being the result of 'the influence of climate and of food; and in the mode of life'.[191] However, Blumenbach, a staunch advocate of the unity and the physical and mental equality of mankind, used the term 'degeneration' more in a technical than in a pejorative sense.[192] Indeed, Blumenbach sought to refute the polygenesists by demonstrating that 'no bodily difference is found in the human race ... which is not observed in the same proportion among the swine race'.[193]

As European exploration gathered pace, Blumenbach found it increasingly difficult to maintain his original, relatively simple classification and the need to refine it further was one of the reasons Blumenbach relied on Banks's aid. By the time he came to publish the second (1781) edition of his *De Generis Humani Varietate Nativa . . .* he had added a fifth category to take account of the new ethnological information which had largely become available as a result of Forster's observations on Cook's second voyage.[194] After listing his existing four categories he added:

> Finally, the new southern world makes up the fifth . . . Those who inhabit the Pacific Archipelago are divided again by John Reinhold Forster into two tribes. One made up of the Otaheitans, the New Zealanders, and the inhabitants of the Friendly Isles, the Society, Easter Island, and the Marquesas, & c, men of elegant appearance and mild disposition; whereas the others who inhabit New Caledonia, Tanna, and the New Hebrides, & c. are blacker, more curly, and in dispositions more distrustful and ferocious.[195]

But, as this passage indicates, this proposed fifth division was rather sketchy and provisional largely because Blumenbach had insufficient data. He had nothing to say, for example, about New Holland where Forster had not been–hence the need for Banks's good offices. As he commented to Banks in the letter of 1 November 1793 apropos of the receipt of skulls from New Holland and Tahiti:

> As I am of the opinion that the most natural division of the human species in her varieties will be that which I have proposed in my 1st *Decas craniorum*, nothing in the world must be more interesting to me than to get likewise one or the other scull of those people which I refer to [as] the 5th variety ... by your generosity [I am] at once in the possession of 2 sculls of both the two principal Races which constitute this remarkable variety in the 5th part of the world; viz of the *black* race & of the *brown* one.[196]

In developing this fifth category, which he termed Malay, Blumenbach used not only the evidence derived from skulls provided by Banks but also drew on Banks's collection of ethnographical drawings. As Blumenbach himself wrote:

> During my happy stay in London You were kind enough to allow me the perusal of your inestimable portfolios of drawings of the South Sea curiosities & even the copying of many of them & so I brought with me by this your liberal allowance a Treasure of exact copies of those drawings of the Hottentots, Tierra de Fuego people particularly of many New Zealanders.[197]

Blumenbach also benefited from the ethnological data sent by Banks which helped to explain the particular specimens he sent. Thus Banks accompanied the dispatch of a Tahitian skull in 1794 with a letter indicating the close study he had made of Tahitian society and his more general interest in the study of humankind as a branch of natural history. The skull, he wrote, 'is the only one I have been able to procure with an under jaw the Custom of the natives being against Sculls being found Compleat in their mode of internment which is to wrap the body in multitudes of Folds of Cloth & expose it to Rot in the air'. As a consequence, added Banks, the sutures of the cranium soon separated 'as I myself have seen'. Banks could also bear personal testimony to the fact that 'in all cases of an Enemy being killd the Lower Jaw is the Trophy which the victor carries off . . . I have seen the front of a house ornamented by a half hoop on which a large number of such were displayd'.[198] Ironically, however, the fact that Banks made it possible for Blumenbach to study more closely the physical features of the peoples of the Pacific made him more cautious about the fixity of his classifications–thus he saw the Aborigines as occupying a 'middle place' between the Malay and the African and he even went so far as to suggest that they could be classed with the Africans 'if it was thought convenient'.[199] It is a comment that underlines Blumenbach's belief that the differences between the various types of humankind 'run so insensibly, by so many shades and transitions one into the other that it is impossible to separate them by any but very arbitrary limits'; for ultimately, as he insisted again and again 'There is but one species of the genus Man'.[200]

Given his debts to Banks it was appropriate,then, that Blumenbach should preface his third (1795) edition of the *De Generis Humani Varietate Nativa* with a dedicatory letter to Banks-a welcome opportunity, as he wrote to Banks, 'to acknowledge once publickly my gratitude for your favour & benevolence to me'. While amplifying these effusive thanks to Banks, Blumenbach made it apparent that he saw himself as contributing to a new discipline-which he actually terms 'anthropology', a word only just beginning to be used in its modern sense-and that Banks should be regarded as one of the new science's patrons: 'By perusing the Book a little you will, I fancy, find by Your name so often mentioned, that I am on more accounts indebted to You, even in these my anthropological researches, than you perhaps did imagine or remember Yourself'.[201]

Previously, when acknowledging Banks's co-operation in obtaining a second Tahitian skull in 1794, Blumenbach had expressed similar sentiments by again profusely thanking Banks 'for this new proof of the generous interest you take in so liberal a way for my anthropological study'.[202] Hitherto, the English word 'anthropology' had been used in the more generalised sense of the study of the human species, both its anatomy and psychology, but had lacked the comparative, cross-cultural element so basic to Blumenbach's work. Just how novel was Blumenbach's usage is brought out by the fact that at the beginning of the century James Drake could still term his general medical text, *Anthropologia Nova*, or 'A New System of Anatomy' (1706).[203] By the end of the century not only Blumenbach but also the French Society of the Observers of Man (founded 1800) was beginning to describe its activities as contributing to the study of 'anthropology'-though Blumenbach's earlier usage does call into question the view that it was within the Society that 'the term anthropology was first used in the modern sense'.[204] Brown, who encountered the Baudin expedition and, with it, Péron, a member of the Society of the Observers of Man, reported to Banks in May 1802 that the expedition included a 'zoologist, who is also anthropologist'[205]-an indication that the term had begun to gain currency within England or, at least within Banks's circle, perhaps partly as a consequence of Banks's links with Blumenbach and the Göttingen school more generally. In 1803 Banks reported to Governor King of New South Wales that the ghoulish consignment of a 'New Hollander's head' in spirits was 'very acceptable to our anthropological collectors, and makes a figure in the museum of the late Mr Hunter, now purchased by the public'.[206] Where previously such collectors would have simply been termed natural historians the growing use of the term 'anthropology' or 'anthropological' is an indication of the increasing awareness that the study of humankind, like botany and zoology and, most recently, geology, was beginning to emerge as a separate discipline within the general field of natural history. This was a transformation which in England owed much to the services of Banks as patron and organiser of an area of knowledge the importance of which had been emphasised through his contact with Blumenbach.

For all his awareness that the study of humankind was beginning to rise to the status of a separate discipline, Blumenbach still regarded himself as contributing to the more general field of natural history, a point underlined by the fact that the dedicatory letter to Banks of the third edition of the *De Generis Humani Varietate Nativa* included the outline of a system of natural history. A younger colleague recounted how Blumenbach's lectures 'drew the natural sciences out of the narrow circle of books and museums into the cheerful stream of life',[207] while the expatriate British physician, Alexander Crichton, prefaced a translation of one of Blumenbach's medical texts with a tribute to 'The great knowledge and extensive information, which my valuable and learned Friend the Author possesses, not only in physiology, and comparative anatomy, but in every branch of natural history'.[208] And this wide view of the domain of the natural historian was to be reflected in his correspondence with Banks. Along with the anthropological material, the scientific exchange between the two men included mention of the three kingdoms of natural history. Again Blumenbach could benefit from Banks's far-flung collecting network: as zoologist he received a specimen of that rare Australian oddity, the platypus, which Blumenbach, in a paper on the subject, christened '*ornithorhynchus paradoxus*';[209] as mineralogist Blumenbach also received specimens from Banks's Australian connections such as that of the 'rare earth'[210] which caused a controversy between Wedgwood and Hatchett;[211] and as botanist Blumenbach was the recipient of seeds from New Holland as well as of 'two cases of a substance brought from India . . . [which] Proves on analysis to consist entirely of Tanin'.[212] Some of this scientific largesse made its way into Blumenbach's publications, particularly his *Contributions to Natural History* (Part 1, 1791; Part 2, 1811); they were also available for study by 'our naturalists' (as Blumenbach put it) in his museum.[213]

What did Banks gain in return? Chiefly, Banks seems to have been content that the material he and his agents had collected was being put to good scientific use, particularly in a field such as anthropology where there was little expertise within Britain. Banks was well aware of the national importance of science as a source of improvement and of prestige but the little State of Hanover was not likely to rival Britain and, in any case, the two States of course shared the same ruler. Nonetheless, Blumenbach does appear to have been rather embarrassed by the generally rather one-sided character of the exchange. In a letter in which he asked Banks for a list of naturalist's desiderata which encapsulated the extent of Banks's global contacts–'for new volcanic products from Thibet', minerals from Nootka Sound and for a tail or any other part of a sea-otter's skin–Blumenbach was at pains to assure Banks that he stood ready to execute any commissions for him; he also sent Banks a copy of a new edition of his *Handbuch der Natürgeschichte*.[214] And, on occasions, Blumenbach did reciprocate with additions to Banks's collections. In August 1793 Banks wrote to convey his 'abundant thanks . . . for the many good things you have sent to me'. Blumenbach was evidently also prudent enough to aid Banks's beloved sister, since Banks added that 'my sister desires also her very best thanks for the Catalogue of ducats of Prof. Kohler'.[215] On specific points Banks would sometimes call on Blumenbach's wide-ranging scientific expertise. In January 1791, for example, he wrote to Blumenbach both to thank him for 'the Observations of the Last Eclipse of the moon' and to request some other observations on light 'differing from the reflected Light of the sun which gave occasion to believe more fully than before the existence of Volcanic Fires'. But Blumenbach had to concede that he was the principal beneficiary in the scientific commerce between the two men–hence his remark to Banks, 'But God beware that You would be ever so pitiless as to enter into account with me. Then I must become a ruined bankrupt'.[216]

Banks's close association with Blumenbach also gave him an entrée into the activities and range of expertise within Göttingen University, then among the most distinguished of universities in Europe. In particular Göttingen, as Blumenbach's interest in anthropology suggests, was a centre for the study of hitherto largely unknown cultures and peoples. It was at Göttingen that Carsten Niebuhr's expedition to Arabia of 1761–7 was planned and where Christoph Meiners (whom Banks praised for his energy and ability[217]) wrote his *Grundriss der Geschichte der Menschheit* ('Outline of the History of Mankind').[218] Blumenbach's use of comparative anatomy to develop a system of human classification owed much to the work of the anatomist, Samuel Sömmerring, who took his MD from Göttingen in 1778, before gaining a professorship at Kassel (1779) and, subsequently, at Mainz (1784). When Banks in his capacity as a founder of the African Association (or, more correctly, the Society for Promoting the Discovery of the Interior Regions of Africa) (f.1788) needed expertise and personnel to undertake such exploration, it was frequently to Blumenbach that he turned. From very early in its history Blumenbach took a close interest in the African Association, an obvious source of fresh anthropological data. Thus, in June 1790, we find him writing to Banks to enquire how to obtain the Association's publications[219] and, as Carter suggests, his visit to London in 1791–2 may have helped to prompt Banks to plan more actively for a major expedition to Africa.[220]

After returning to Göttingen, Blumenbach continued to look to Banks and the African Association as a possible source of rare anthropological data. In March 1794 he wrote rather apologetically to Banks that 'though I know very well that those Reports are only for the Members of the [African] Association, yet in case that those new ones should contain some particular news concerning the corporeal singularity of the Inhabitants (in regard to the complexion, hair, characteristical feature & c) I should be infinitely indebted to You for a kind information in a few lines'.[221]

After the disastrous outcomes of a number of expeditions led by English explorers (the Scottish Mungo Park being the only Britisher to achieve any notable success before he, too, eventually disappeared, suffering the almost inevitable fate of African explorers of this period) Blumenbach became a source of fresh recruits for these perilous undertakings.[222]

He was also in a position to arrange for them at Göttingen the kind of linguistic and scientific preparation which was not readily available in England. It was Blumenbach who, in 1796, recommended to Banks and the African Association the services of Friedrich Hornemann, ensuring that he first spent six months at Göttingen preparing himself for the trip. There, as Blumenbach assured Banks, he would be instructed in those elements 'of natural history which may make his expedition the more useful as for inst[ance] with the geognostical part of mineralogy ... But besides this he would spend his time principally with our orientalists for the Arabian Language & c with our Mathematicians & astronomers, & c'. Along with Blumenbach, Hornemann's crash course was supervised by Blumenbach's brother-in-law, Professor Benjamin Heyne, a fellow naturalist, who, as Blumenbach assured Banks, 'takes the greatest interest in that matter, [and] will with all his heart give him all information & hints in his power'; further assistance came from another family connection, Professor Heeren (the son-in-law of Heyne)[223]–a cameo example of the way in which German universities frequently housed academic dynasties. Hornemann also received assistance in the form of a manuscript entitled 'Index geographicus Aegypti criticus et etymologicus' from Johann Forster who, though at the University of Halle, continued to look to Göttingen and, specifically, to Blumenbach to sustain his natural history interests.[224] Blumenbach was to prove a loyal ally since it was he that helped to persuade Banks to cancel Forster's debt to him and thus to alleviate the parlous financial condition of Forster's widow.[225] While Hornemann was in statu pupillari at Göttingen his expenses were met by the African Association, with Banks acting as the Association's financial intermediary. Though Hornemann's expedition duly ended in his death in 1800 it proved to be one of the African Association's most successful expeditions and thus helped to pave the way for that led by another of Blumenbach's protégés, the Swiss Johann Burckhardt. In 1806 Burckhardt, who was educated at Leipzig and Göttingen, arrived in England with letters of introduction from Blumenbach[226] which led to an expedition which was still more successful in every respect except that it, too, resulted in the explorer's death (in 1817).[227]

In England, Blumenbach's main disciple was Sir William Lawrence, the translator of Blumenbach's Comparative Anatomy (1807), who is a further instance of the link between medicine and the beginnings of physical anthropology. As the title of this work indicates, Lawrence continued the tradition of John Hunter by developing anthropological studies based on his researches in comparative anatomy and in undertaking such an enquiry he had the support of Banks who used his influence within the Royal College of Surgeons to ensure that Lawrence gained access to Hunter's collections.[228] Lawrence also paid tribute to 'the unrivalled library of Sir Joseph Banks' and 'the more uncommon liberality with which it is opened to all who are engaged in scientific pursuits'.[229] Thanks to the work of Blumenbach, however, Lawrence was able to bring to this area new techniques and, more importantly, a well-developed body of theory. Lawrence's major work–*Lectures on Physiology, Zoology, and the Natural History of Man Delivered at the Royal College of Surgeons* (1819)– was dedicated to Blumenbach with the acknowledgement that it 'has received its most numerous and successful illustrations from your sagacity, industry and learning'. Lawrence, however, placed greater emphasis than Blumenbach on the gulf between races and, as a consequence, on white superiority–hence comments such as: 'The distinction of colour between the white and black races is not more striking than the pre-eminence of the former in moral feelings and in mental endowments'.[230] Lawrence also differed from Blumenbach in dismissing the influence of climate as an explanation for the differences in human skin colour.[231] Nonetheless, Lawrence emphatically agreed with Blumenbach in affirming the unity of mankind and regarded the work of White and other polygenesists as disseminating views which are 'as false philosophically, as the moral and political consequences, to which it would lead, are shocking and detestable'.[232] He also regarded Blumenbach's fivefold division of human-kind as the best available 'although it is not free from objection; and although the five varieties, under which he has arranged the several tribes of our species, ought rather to be regarded as principal divisions, each of them including several varieties'[233]–a verdict from which Blumenbach would not have dissented.

But Lawrence was working in a period when the reaction against the French Revolution had created an intellectual climate unfavourable to new ideas which might weaken the established order in Church and State, particularly in relation to so sensitive an area as the nature of humankind. Lawrence's *Natural History of Man* provoked an outcry on its appearance in 1819[234] since it dwelt on the similarity between human and animal anatomy and hence was regarded as attempting 'to prove by actual experiment, that the soul is mere matter'. Indeed, this same critic affirmed that 'we must attribute the French Revolution, with all its horrible attendants of anarchy, despotism and murder, to the persuasion that there was no future existence'.[235] Following this outcry, Lawrence abandoned the study of anthropology for more conventional medical research,[236] a decision which points to the less than encouraging environment for anthropological investigation in the wake of the French Revolution. It was not only in anthropology but also in other infant disciplines, such as geology, which also touched on sensitive issues of religious belief, that the English, after the watershed of 1789, tended to avoid theoretical discussions. Those with interests in such fields stayed on safer territory by largely confining their activities to the collection of data.[237] Such an attitude of mind further strengthened the strongly empirical bent of British anthropology–and natural history more generally–which those, like Banks, reared in the tradition of the virtuoso had already done so much to foster. Banks's relations with Blumenbach epitomise the character of much of the field of British ethnology generally in this period. British naval and imperial power made possible the collection of artefacts, of human specimens and of that sharply observed detail about other societies and customs of the sort that one finds in the journals of Banks and Anderson. But when it came to erecting theoretical structures on the basis of such empirical foundations Banks–and many of the British more generally–were largely content to leave such work to others, particularly the French and the Germans whose academic institutions provided more support for the development of a systematic anthropology which went beyond the ethnographical observation of Banks and other British naturalist-explorers.

For this tendency to eschew anthropological theory was strengthened by the character of learned societies in late eighteenth-century England–these being primarily gentlemen's clubs carrying on the virtuoso tradition of the gifted amateur, rather than bodies intended to support professional scientists or scholars.[238] As we have seen, anthropological discussion tended to be carried on in bodies such as the Society of Antiquaries or the Society of Dilettanti[239]–which, as their names suggest, were intended more as places where the leisured classes could meet and receive some degree of intellectual stimulation than as research institutions. By contrast, in France, institutions such as the Academy of Sciences or (as it was renamed in the period 1795 to 1815) the National Institute, together with the Grandes Ecoles and the reformed system of universities, provided full-time paid employment for naturalists or medical professors who regarded anthropological research as part of their professional duties. Similarly, the revitalised German universities–where Göttingen, Blumenbach's university, led the way–also provided opportunities for research in a number of new areas, including anthropology.

Such considerations as the continued dominance of scientific and intellectual life by the cult of the leisured virtuoso, together with the poor condition of medical education in England (though not in Scotland), help to explain why in England anthropology was slower to be acknowledged as a separate speciality than in France and Germany. It was in France, as we have seen, that the first specialist anthropological society, the Society of the Observers of Man, was established in 1800, later to be followed by the more long-lived Société Ethnologique of Paris in 1839 which, in turn, helped to prompt the formation of the Ethnological Society of London in 1843.[240] As in science more generally, British anthropology at the beginning of the nineteenth century reflected the amateur, unspecialised tradition which had been associated with the Royal Society since its foundation in 1660. Such a cultural ideal naturally predominated in a society where political power was largely in the hands of a group of landowners who were reluctant to extend the power (and taxes) of the central government; thus England offered few opportunities for government-funded full-time research and the specialisation associated with it. British educated opinion was influenced by the Enlightenment goal of applying to humanity the techniques derived from the physical sciences, but it was content for the time being to leave to others much of the cost and the intellectual labour of assessing the implications, for the study of human beings and society, of the contact with new cultures–contact which, ironically, British naval power had done so much to promote in the course of the eighteenth century.

THE EXPLORATION OF THE PACIFIC AND THEORIES OF
HUMAN LINGUISTIC AND RACIAL DEVELOPMENT

The same reliance within England on the tradition of the interested amateur can be seen in the way in which Banks helped to promote anthropological investigation of the new languages that Pacific and African exploration were making available for study. Again local antiquarian pursuits could mesh with distant anthropological studies: one of Banks's Anglo-Irish correspondents attempted to interest him in theories connecting old Irish and Arabic[241] and Banks's sister's interest in language took the form of compiling a large vocabulary of the Lincolnshire dialect,[242] a project that no doubt had Banks's support.

Along with the linguistic peculiarities of his own county, Banks also took a close interest in the languages of the native peoples he encountered on the *Endeavour* expedition. Indeed, he had been urged to do so by the Earl of Morton, the President of the Royal Society, who included among his *Hints . . .* for those on the expedition the suggestion 'Lastly, to form a Vocabulary of the names given by the Natives, to the several things and places which come under the Inspection of the Gentlemen'.[243] Banks's study of Tahitian–of which he developed sufficient mastery to converse with the locals–is evident both in the vocabularies included in his journal and in those which exist in the manuscript collection of his protégé, William Marsden, an early student of South-east Asian and Pacific languages. In typical English amateur fashion he at first combined his researches with service in the East India Company in Sumatra and subsequently with a secretaryship with the Admiralty. The vocabularies from the South Seas and New Zealand which Cook included in his *Endeavour* journal were also derived from those of Banks–as Cook acknowledged when writing of his Tahitian vocabulary, it came 'from Mr Banks who understands their Language as well or better than any one on board'.[244] The object of Cook's vocabularies was to show the close similarity between the Polynesian languages of the South Seas and of New Zealand–an instance of the way in which the Pacific explorers (and particularly Banks) attempted to use language as a guide to the diffusion of cultures and the human geography of the new realms they had penetrated.

Anderson, the surgeon-naturalist, who accompanied Cook on his second and third voyages and whose style of close ethnological observation, largely devoid of theorising, closely resembled that of Banks, also included in his journal extensive vocabularies with a view to comparing them. When discussing the language of New Zealand he noted that 'I have collected a great many words of this and several other Languages both now and in a former voyage which are in a Manuscript call'd Vocabularys of the Indian Languages among the Islands of the South Seas'.[245] Anderson compared such new languages, not only with each other, but also with European languages, commenting, for example, that the Maoris' tongue was 'in many respects deficient if compar'd with our European languages'; he also commented on the parallel between the 'several

Sydney Parkinson. *Portrait of a New Zeland Man* c.1770
(BL, Add. MS 23920, fol.55). By permission of the British
Library

degrees of comparison as us'd in the Latin Language' and in Tongan.
Similarly, Banks compared the 'soft and tuneable' pronunciation of
vowels in Tahitian with Spanish and Italian though he also added that
'In one respect however it is beyond measure inferior to all European
languages, which is its almost total want of inflexion both of Nouns
and verbs'.[246]

In developing his views on the extent to which the languages of the
Pacific were linked Banks used not only his own observations but, where
possible, also those of previous explorers. He noted, for example, that
'From the vocabularies given in Le Mair's voyage . . . it appears clearly
that the Languages given there as those of the Isles of Solomon and the
Isle of Cocos are radically the identical same languages as those we met
with, the greatest number of words differing in little but the greater
number of consonants'.[247] Later explorers were, in turn, to build on the
vocabularies which Banks and others on board the *Endeavour* had

provided. Johann Forster, for example, based his manuscript 'Vocabularies of the Languages spoken in the Isles of the South Seas ... with some Observations for the Better Understanding of Them' chiefly on the vocabulary compiled by William Monkhouse (surgeon on the *Endeavour*) at Banks's instigation. Banks also encouraged Parkinson to compile such vocabularies and these, too, were used by Forster who had them available in printed form in the controversial edition of Parkinson's journal published by Parkinson's brother.[248]

For Cook's second voyage Forster could draw not only on his own collections but also the vocabularies of Isaac Smith, mate of the *Resolution,* and those of Gibson, one of the marines. These recent English sources he combined with the vocabulary published in Bougainville's account of his voyage (which Forster had translated into English). Forster's motives for drawing together such a compilation were mixed–like those of Pacific explorers of the age more generally. In the first place the imperatives of empire played a role for, as Forster wrote, such a linguistic guide 'may one day or other become usefull, if the European especially should chuse to make settlements in these Islands or at least to erect here a new branch of commerce'.[249] But of greater importance to the scholarly Forster was the quest, so dear to the Enlightenment, for understanding the origin and nature of human language. In pursuing this goal the Germanic Forster showed a degree of scholarly rigour and breadth of reference that was to set him apart from interested amateurs like Banks and Anderson.

The belief that ultimately all languages could be traced back to a common source–with Hebrew, Chinese, Egyptian or Sanskrit being among the eighteenth-century contenders for the dignity of being this primal language–helps to explain that preoccupation with illustrating the linkages between different languages which can be found in the work of Forster, Banks and other Pacific explorers of the period. A further reason for such a preoccupation was the belief that linguistic evidence was one of the surest guides to patterns of migration and settlement. As James King wrote in his journal of Cook's third voyage:

> There doubtless cannot be a subject more liable to error than in deducting the origin of people from certain resemblances in their religious ceremonies, their arts & their manners ... The same language however hardly requires any other proof of those who speak it being the same People, & originating from the same Country; & that the Language which is spoke at these Isles, at New Zealand, at Easter Island & the Society & friendly Isles is the same is clear from the Specimens of each Annexd.[250]

Forster came to similar conclusions about the common origin of the languages, and hence the peoples of the South Seas (apart from those of New Holland), as Cook and Banks, arguing that what difference there was 'consists in the different pronunciation of the vowels & consonants'.[251] The extent of Forster's close study of the numerous Pacific languages is evident in the range and number of vocabularies he collected (often in conjunction with Anderson), many of which are preserved in the collection of William Lanyon who served on Cook's second and third voyages.[252] But again the German-trained Forster went further than his English counterparts in not only recording his thoughts on the common origin of the languages of the South Seas and the empirical evidence on which it was based, but also in attempting to integrate his findings into a larger interpretative framework. Thus he suggested that such linguistic evidence supported the hypothesis that 'these [South Seas] Nations came originally from the East India islands, & gradually spread to the East from Isle to Isle, & on one side to the South to New Zealand'. In support of this view he pointed to the fact that 'the more you go to the West & approach the East-Indies, the more Malay words are in the Language to be found'. But Forster was eager not to let such theorising get too far ahead of the available evidence and he hastened to add that 'I think not to use this correspondence of a few words, as an Argument to prove, that the Inhabitants of the Tropical Isles in the South Seas are descended from the Malayan: this would be proving rather too much'. He argued instead that though 'It would be very wrong to say these Languages & Nations were descended from the Malayans' nonetheless 'it is by no means improbable to believe, that all these languages have preserved several words of the ancient Languages which were formerly more universal & were gradually changed & altered into so many strange Languages'. The Malayan words, he continued, 'are the wrecks, of a much more antient, more universal Language' ultimately derived from Asia–a comment that underlines the eighteenth-century preoccupation with the possibility of tracing the diversity of modern tongues back to a few primal origins and possibly back to an original Ur-sprache. Forster demonstrated both his remarkable linguistic and cultural range and his theoretical caution by observing that the peoples of the South Seas were distinct from those of the Americas since 'if we look into the Vocabularies of the Mexican, Peruvian, Chilese, & some other Languages, we find their words so widely different from the Language of the South Sea-Isles, that there is not the least doubt remaining, that these Nations have no relation or Affinity to one another'.[253]

Appropriately, Forster's South Sea vocabularies and manuscripts on these languages were later used by Wilhelm von Humboldt when developing his seminal works on comparative philology.[254] His brother, Alexander von Humboldt, also drew on the linguistic findings of other members of Banks's circle in his philological investigations. In the section on the Guanches of Tenerife, in his *Personal Narrative of Travels to the Equinoctial Regions of the New Continent During 1799–1804* he cites 'the travels of Hornemann, and the ingenious researches of Marsden'[255] to indicate the parallel between the languages of the Guanches and that of the Berbers of North Africa. The examples of the philological researches of the Humboldts and that of the Anglo-German hybrid, Forster, again suggest the phenomenon brought out clearly in the relations between Banks and Blumenbach: the extent to which the anthropological fruits of English exploration were frequently gathered by continental (and specifically German) scholars belonging to an academic tradition which both provided the stimulus and the professional openings for concentrated research in new fields such as anthropology.

A partial exception to this generalisation is the case of Banks's close associate, William Marsden. However, the fact that his researches were limited by the demands of his post at the Admiralty from 1795 again points to the restricted opportunities for anthropological research or, indeed, scientific research more generally within England. Marsden's researches began as an avocation while he was in the service of the East India Company in Sumatra from 1771 to 1779. He returned to England, he tells us in his memoirs, partly because he had heard so much about the

> meetings, in London, of scientific and learned persons, of the attention paid to travellers who visited distant countries and communicated their observations, and especially of the enthusiastic spirit of curiosity excited, not in England only but throughout Europe, by the publication of the *Endeavour*'s voyage to the islands of the Pacific ocean and round the world.[256]

Marsden, then, was attracted by the learned London world where virtuoso culture remained strong. As with his patron, Banks, too, there are elements of the virtuoso about Marsden though, like Banks again, he also exhibited a degree of specialisation and application uncharacteristic of the virtuoso. On the one hand, Marsden indulged in such virtuoso activities as the amassing of a vast coin collection (which he left to the British Museum) and active involvement in the very miscellaneous activities of the Royal Academy of his native Ireland, which sought to combine the functions of the Royal Society and the Society of Antiquaries. On the other hand, however, he also produced such works of sustained scholarship as his *Dictionary and Grammar of the Malayan Language* (1812). His two published catalogues of his collections of books and manuscripts[257] also have a degree of system and scholarly order which was foreign to the collections of many virtuosi–even the title of the second of these catalogues reflects Marsden's clearly focused aims: *Bibliotheca Marsdeniana ... Collected with a View to The General Comparison of Languages, and to the Study of Oriental Literature.*

When he returned to London from Sumatra Marsden naturally gravitated to Banks as a focus of the learned society which he wished to enter and as someone who shared his interests in the languages and cultures of the peoples of South-east Asia and the Pacific. To cite Marsden's memoir once more: 'As it respected myself and my objects of pursuit, the most important introduction, and which tended materially to influence the character of my future life, was that to Mr ... Banks, the distinguished President of the Royal Society'.[258] Having met Banks, Marsden became a regular member of his scholarly breakfast meeting 'until the year 1795, when I ceased to have the command of my own time'– that is, until Marsden became second secretary of the Admiralty, a post he held (with a promotion to first secretary in 1804) until 1807 and which necessarily curtailed his scholarly investigations. Nonetheless, he continued to play an active role in the affairs of the Royal Society and acted as Banks's deputy when he was ill.

Marsden reports that at Banks's breakfast sessions one of the topics discussed 'was that of the languages of the Eastern and South-sea Islands, to which Mr Banks, during his voyage in the *Endeavour*, had paid much attention'.[259] Out of such discussions grew Marsden's first publication on the subject which became his lifetime interest, the linkages between the languages of the South-east Asian and Pacific regions. These Marsden subsumed under the general title of the Polynesian language, which he defined as 'that general tongue, which will be found to extend, through the inter-tropical region, from Madagascar, or, more obviously, from Sumatra, as its western, to Easter Island, in the Pacific Island, on the Pacific Ocean, as its eastern limit'.[260] Significantly, this first paper-'Remarks on the Sumatran Languages'-which took the form of a letter to Banks, was presented at the Society of Antiquaries, a choice of forum which, like Marsden's interest in such antiquarian pursuits as coin collecting, indicates the association between the new science of anthropology and the traditional gentlemanly study of antiquities. Marsden opened this paper by acknowledging Banks's encouragement; in his memoirs, too, he notes that he 'was materially assisted in making the collections necessary for the intended comparison' by Banks.[261] Predictably, Marsden's goal was that of Banks and Forster: to use the available linguistic evidence in order to demonstrate the links that existed between the different societies of South-east Asia and the Pacific. 'My chief design in these collections', as Marsden put it in his paper, was 'to trace, if possible, a common origin'.[262] But, as Marsden himself acknowledged, the linguistic data available to him enabled him to do little more than to state the problem and to point to the need for further research:

> The only general inference we can draw on this head, is, that from Madagascar eastward to the Marquesas, or nearly from the east coast of Africa to the west coast of America, there is a manifest connexion in many of the words by which the inhabitants of the islands express their simple ideas, and between some of the most distant, a striking affinity. The links of the latitudinal chain remain yet to be traced.[263]

Like Forster he was eventually to conclude (as he put it in his later 'On the Polynesian or East-Insular Languages') that the Malay language was not 'the parent stock from which the other dialects have sprung . . . their connexion is that of sisterhood'. Like Forster, too, he stressed the dissimilarity between the languages of the Pacific islands and those of the Americas.[264] But Marsden never carried these researches quite as far as he would have liked-no doubt largely because he lacked the time, since England offered no full-time professional opening for one with his interests.

Marsden's linguistic interests ranged beyond the Pacific to include other areas of the globe. In 1785 he published an article entitled 'Observations on the Language of the People Commonly called Gypsies' which, again, was published in the *Archaeologia* and again took the form of a letter to Banks. A further similarity with his earlier paper was the fact that Marsden was once more attempting to demonstrate the connections between languages and peoples, for its thesis was that the language of the Gypsies ultimately derived from Hindustani. Banks had provided much of the material on which this paper was based for, as Marsden acknowledged, 'Through the obliging assistance of Sir Joseph Banks, who has spared no pains to promote this investigation, I procured an opportunity of obtaining a list of words from our Gypsies'.[265] Banks's interest in the language of the Gypsies is also suggested by a letter from Sheffield of 1788 in which he writes of 'A Friend ... [who] was very desirous to know whether you had not begun to form a vocabulary of the Gypsy Language & whether you had not ascertained what it was'.[266]

As Marsden acknowledged in this paper, he was indebted to Banks not only for a vocabulary of the language of the Gypsies but also a list of Turkish words transmitted by Banks's regular correspondent, James Matra, secretary to the British Embassy at Constantinople, and, subsequently, British Consul in Tangier.[267] For information on Indian languages Marsden could draw on the work of William Jones and Christopher Wilkins, who were also among Banks's correspondents. In 1790, for example, he received a list of Sanskrit and Kashmiri words from Jones.[268] Marsden acknowledged his admiration for the work of these two pioneering English students of the Indian languages in the preface to his *Miscellaneous Works* (1834). It was a natural tribute from one who, like them, exemplified the tradition of English gentlemanly scholarship since they, too, had had to combine scholarship with service to the East India Company as Marsden had done early in his career. The connections between these students of languages was strengthened by Marsden's marriage in 1807 to the daughter of Wilkins who, having returned from India where he had assisted Jones in learning Sanskrit and in establishing the Asiatic Society of Bengal, was among the founders of the East India college, Haileybury. Marsden's interest in India is also apparent in his 1790 paper on 'the Chronology of the Hindoos' which, interestingly enough, was published in the *Philosophical Transactions*,[269] an indication that the Royal Society still maintained some interest in subjects which might be considered of antiquarian interest. Marsden's interest in both Hindu and Malay languages was brought together in his paper 'On the Traces of the Hindu Language and Literature Extant among the Malays' which was published in his *Asiatick Researches* for 1795[270]–a work in which Jones showed considerable interest.[271] Marsden's continued interest in linking his Indian and Malay researches can be seen in his statement in 'On the Polynesian and East-Insular Languages' that 'the Sanskrit or one of its least corrupted derivatives, was the language from which the Malayan dialect of the Polynesian received its first and most important additions'.[272] He also argued that much of the vocabulary of Malayan derived from Hindu as well as Arabic sources.[273]

Marsden's linking studies of Indian languages with that of Malay is one instance of the way in which his linguistic research expanded

outwards from his original relatively circumscribed study of the languages
of Sumatra and its immediate neighbours–thus prompting him to aspire
to an investigation of language on a global scale. A still further extension
of his linguistic interests was to Africa where again they intermeshed, if
rather more tangentially, with his Pacific researches. One of the linguistic
phenomena that most interested and puzzled Marsden was the similarity
between some of the South-east Asian languages and that of Madagascar–
as he wrote, it was an affinity 'the indisputable existence of which is one
of the most extraordinary facts in the history of language'.[274] Banks, too,
had commented on this remarkable similarity in his *Endeavour* journal
and it was no doubt a regular topic of discussion between the two men.
Banks also had produced lists of vocabulary illustrating this linguistic
conundrum–something which prompted him to exclaim:

> From this similitude of language Between the inhabitants of the Eastern Indies and
> the Islands in the South Seas I should have ventur'd to conjecture much did not
> Madagascar interfere; and how any Communication can ever have been carried
> between Madagascar and Java to make the Brown long haird people of the latter speak
> a language similar to that of the Black wooly headed natives of the other is I confess
> far beyond my comprehension.[275]

Marsden's curiosity about this issue led him to study further other African
languages to see whether Madagash was unique in this respect, concluding
that indeed it was: 'It is proper to observe, at the same time, that this
tongue [Madagash], where it differs the most from the Polynesian, does
not bear any resemblance whatever to that of Mozambique or others on
the opposite coast of Africa'.[276] Needless to say, in studying the languages
of Africa Marsden was chiefly reliant on Banks and the activities of the
African Association. As early as 1789, a year after the foundation of the
African Association, Banks's chief agent in North Africa, James Matra,
British Consul in Tangier, wrote to Banks both to send on a proposal
describing a route to the interior and to outline a plan for obtaining for
'our friend Mr Marsden' a list of words 'in the language of Twarg-y-
Timbuctoo'.[277] Though, like so many of the plans for African exploration,
this did not eventuate, Matra was able to send Marsden, via Banks, a
vocabulary of the Shilla Language.[278]

Another of Banks's correspondents who assisted Marsden in his African
studies was Blumenbach who sent Banks, for the benefit of Marsden,
pamphlets on the African geography of Herodotus together with 'a
philological book'.[279] When, in 1817, Banks was sent an African vocabulary, he naturally forwarded it on to Marsden for his comments as someone
'whose Experience in Languages he [Banks] believes to be superior to that
of any other Persons'.[280] It was Marsden, too, who, in 1802, contributed
'Observations on the Language of Siwah in a Letter to the Rt Hon. Sir
Joseph Banks' to the published version of Hornemann's travels, suggesting
that this language may have been 'the general language of all Northern
Africa before the period of the Mahometan conquests'.[281] Marsden also
provided the appendix on the vocabularies of the Malemba and Embomma

in the account of Tuckey's ill-fated attempt to explore the River Zaire, which was published in 1818. These were drawn up along the lines suggested by Marsden in the instructions issued to Tuckey[282]. Predictably, however, Marsden never fully integrated such African studies into his grand design of outlining the diffusion of language across the globe. Banks's own interest in African languages is apparent in the fact that his papers include material such as 'information collected at Mozambique . . . with vocabularies of the Makrana-Munjaui Noveli Somalia Galla & Hurra Languages' and a manuscript copy of the 'Observations on a Vocabulary of the Language spoken by a Woolly-headed tribe on the Eastern side of South Africa'.[283]

In the study of the languages of the Pacific, as of those of Africa, Marsden naturally looked to Banks with his well-established contacts in that area. Moreover, Banks could provide Marsden with access to his own collection of Pacific vocabularies compiled while on the *Endeavour*-manuscripts which Banks appears to have given Marsden. For among the Marsden papers is a manuscript entitled 'Vocabularies of the Languages of Tahiti, Prince's Island, Sulu, Samaran [Java], New Holland, New Zealand, Savu' together with another entitled 'Observationes de Otaheite . . . made by Sr Jos Banks . . .', both of which include vocabularies of the Tahitians and other Pacific peoples; the latter also includes observations on the size of Tahitian breadfruit, prefiguring Banks's eventual role in instigating the *Bounty* expedition. A further volume on Malay and Sumatran languages includes vocabulary collected by Banks while at Batavia.[284] Another indication that Banks and Marsden collaborated in the study of the languages of the Pacific is an enquiry by Banks to Marsden about a Tahitian vocabulary and grammar which he had sent him.[285] This was probably a reference to a guide to the Tahitian language produced by the London Missionary Society, the efforts of which to establish a mission in Tahiti had been greatly assisted by Banks. Marsden's collections also included another linguistic manuscript which, we may surmise, came to him through Banks's agency: the notebooks of William Dawes, lieutenant in the marines at Sydney, which were given the title, 'Grammatical Forms and Vocabularies of Languages Spoken in the Neighbourhood of Sydney'.[286] This work Marsden refers to in his article 'On the Polynesian or East-Insular Languages' when writing of the differences between the Polynesian languages and those of New Holland:

> So long ago, however, as the year 1792, I received from a Mr. Dawes, whose familiar habits of intercourse with the natives enabled him to acquire a competent knowledge of their tongue, a collection of memoranda that furnish a tolerable idea of their grammatical system (if such it may be termed), particularly as respects the inflections of the verbs, with their accompanying pronouns.[287]

As Marsden's slighting comments on the languages of New Holland suggest, he took a rather dismissive view of the Australian Aborigines. In Marsden, as in the Scottish social theorists whose aim, as Bagehot put it, was to illustrate the transition from savage to Scotsman, the organising principle is the idea of an evolution of more complex cultures from more primitive ones–a transformation he saw as being mirrored in linguistic change. At the beginning of the article on Polynesian languages he refers to the growth of philological research 'especially amongst our continental neighbours' who had studied the growing number of languages which European exploration had made available to scholars with a view 'to bring these languages within the scope of critical investigation, to examine their structure, compare their degrees of advancement from the rudest stage, to shew their analogies'.[288]

Something of the growing continental preoccupation with the classification of races which is evident in the work of Blumenbach can be seen in the way in which Marsden classifies the peoples of what today would be called Melanesia, as distinct from the Malay and Polynesian peoples, as negritos. He also included in this category the Australian Aborigines, writing of them 'With regard to the physical qualities of the natives, it is nearly superfluous to state, that they are negritos of the most decided class, and according to our ideas of comparative beauty and deformity, they must rank with the most ill-favoured species of the human race'. He contrasts the mainland Aborigines unfavourably with those of Van Diemen's Land whom he regarded as having 'much the advantage' 'in person and feature' but acknowledged that little was known of their language perhaps because of 'the state of hostility that from an early period has subsisted between our settlers and the native inhabitants'.[289]

Marsden's implied belief in a sort of human hierarchy can also be found in his most widely known work, his *History of Sumatra*, where he outlines a cultural pecking-order of the human race with 'the polished state of' the Europeans (and perhaps the Chinese) at the top and 'the Caribs, the New Hollanders, the Laplanders, and the Hottentots, who, exhibit a picture of mankind in its rudest and most humiliated aspect at the bottom'. Between the two ends of this spectrum he proposed five categories with the more civilised Sumatrans in the third (along with the Arabs), while the less civilised were in the fourth (together with 'the people of the new discovered islands in the South Seas').[290] As we have seen, such hierarchical conceptions were even more developed in the work of Marsden's contemporary, Charles White–with the difference that White's categorisation was based on physical rather than cultural differences. Interestingly, however, they do not figure in Banks's own work; Banks and Cook (who was greatly influenced by Banks's ethnological writings) took a much more favourable view of Aboriginal society than Marsden and generally do not appear to have been disposed to arrange the new societies they encountered in a system where European society was at the acme.

For Banks, Aboriginal society catered to the 'real wants of human nature' but avoided the 'anxieties attending upon riches, or even the possession of what we Europeans call common necessaries'. Aboriginal society revealed the basic simplicity of the natural order which had become obscured in European societies–the latter, continued Banks, attempted to defy the natural order by multiplying luxuries, but did so in vain since

Plate XXVII

Two of the Natives of New Holland, Advancing to Combat.

Two of the Natives of New Holland, Advancing to Combat. Engraving after Parkinson by T. Chambers in Parkinson, *Voyage to the South Seas* (1773), pl. xxvii. Courtesy of Cambridge University Library

'Luxuries degenerate into necessaries'. The result, then, was that, despite outward appearances, all societies were more or less on an equal footing: 'In this instance again providence seems to act the part of a leveler, doing much towards putting all ranks into an equal state of wants and consequently of real poverty'.[291]

The difference between Banks and Marsden may reflect the fact that Banks was the product of an earlier phase of the Enlightenment which, particularly in England, where the elite classes were generally fairly content with things as they were, had tended to place little emphasis on change and development; by contrast, the accelerating pace of change in the late eighteenth century–highlighted by the French and Industrial Revolutions–helped to promote systems of thought based on concepts of growth and evolution. The early Enlightenment, which was overshadowed by the great Newtonian achievement, emphasised the unchanging and constant laws of Nature–something which was reflected in the static and orderly character of its classificatory systems of which, by far, the most notable was that of Linnaeus. Those, like Banks, formed in such an intellectual milieu were more likely to measure the new societies they encountered against the yardstick of a set of perennially valid laws rather than attempting to evaluate them in terms of the extent to which they resembled European society. If it was discovered, for example, that nudity was quite acceptable within Aboriginal society–something on which Banks, Cook, Anderson and other late eighteenth-century explorers commented at length–then it was an indication that the traditional European taboo against nudity was not grounded on the laws of Nature but, rather, was socially conditioned. As Anderson remarked apropos of the nudity of the Tasmanian Aborigines: 'Indeed the custom of covering such parts is perhaps not an inclination or instinct implanted in mankind by nature, as some have suppos'd but only a custom acquir'd'.[292] Certain practices, however, Banks regarded as a contravention of the laws of Nature: thus he described the Tahitians' widespread practice of infanticide as being 'contrary to the first principles of human nature'; similarly, he regarded cannibalism, which he encountered in New Zealand, as being contrary to the laws of Nature since it denied the special importance of humankind in 'the admirable chain of nature in which Man, alone endowd with reason, justly claims the highest rank'.[293] As such instances of the far from universal nature of what had been thought of as fundamental natural laws began to accumulate so, too, the idea that all societies could be regarded as different reflections of the same basic laws began to weaken.[294]

Such a decline in a belief in a perennially valid set of natural laws helps to account for the increasing prevalence of attempts to explain the variations between different human societies in terms of a process of cultural evolution. Banks and Cook had viewed the Aboriginal way of life as a particular manifestation of the natural laws which could be discerned in all human societies; but a growing number of anthropologically-inclined students of natural history came to regard 'primitive' societies–and particularly the Aborigines–as forming an early stage in a gradual process of human amelioration. And since such systems of human development had an implied teleology, with the people of Europe at their apogee, the result was that tribal societies came to be viewed in a distinctly negative light as being a more primitive and less developed version of European society.

The prevalence of such developmental views of human society and their implied value-systems–evolutionary in the very general sense of arguing for increasing complexity and sophistication over time–has been traced in the thought of the French Enlightenment (and particularly in its later stages) by Duchet.[295] To give one instance from the influential pen of Buffon: in the section of his vast *Natural History* entitled 'Varieties of the Human Species' (written in 1778) he portrayed the Aborigines as 'perhaps the most miserable people of the world, and these who of all human beings are nearest to the animals'. This same view, that the Aborigines represented one of the lowest rungs of the ladder of human evolution, is apparent in one of the reasons which Buffon gives for his derogatory description of the Aborigines, that they 'live in groups of twenty or thirty', for, to Buffon, the size of a society's basic groupings was a virtual index of its level of development.[296] Ironically, Buffon's authority on the nature of Aboriginal society was probably Banks for Buffon drew heavily on Hawkesworth's account of the *Endeavour* voyage which, in ethnological matters, was based on Banks's journal[297]–an instance of the way in which the ethnological data could be placed in a very different conceptual framework than that envisaged by the original observer.

One finds an even more derogatory view of Aboriginal society in the work of James Burnett, Lord Monboddo, a Scottish social theorist who took to the point of a *reductio ad absurdum* the Scottish preoccupation with social evolution. Such a concern with explaining the dynamics of social change may have owed much to the Scottish experience of a growing divide between the traditional Highland society and the more Anglicised society of the Lowlands which had been accelerated by the effects of the Act of Union between England and Scotland in 1707. Such differences naturally made Scottish social theorists (who were drawn, of course, from the Lowlands) particularly inclined to dwell on the way in which societies developed from rude beginnings to the cultural heights which they saw themselves as representing. In Monboddo's work the human evolutionary scale extended as far down as the orang-outangs, and Aboriginal society he regarded as occupying a position towards the bottom end of such a scale. Thus he used the Aborigines as an example of the way in which a people 'living in the lowest stage of brutalisation' were devoid of intellectual achievements and remained in a state of 'brutish insensibility'.[298] But, though he described Aboriginal society in such demeaning terms, Monboddo regarded it, and other 'primitive' societies, as having a special importance to the student of society, since 'savages . . . are so much nearer the natural state of men than we, that it is from them only that we can form any idea of the *original* nature of man'.[299] As Casson writes, Monboddo was 'One of the few men in the eighteenth century to attempt to correlate the new ethnographical knowledge with the problem of the antiquity of man'.[300] We can see this same assumption that human society could best be explained in developmental or evolutionary terms with 'primitive' societies, therefore, being of particular importance as a means of measuring subsequent human advance in many of Monboddo's fellow Scottish social theorists. James Dunbar, for example, who, like Monboddo, drew eagerly on the recent ethnological observations from the Pacific, wrote in his *Essays on the History of Mankind in Rude and Cultivated Ages* (1780) that 'The history ... of some of the South Sea isles, which the late voyages of discovery have tended to disclose, enables us to glance at society in some of its earlier forms'.[301]

Banks first met Monboddo in Edinburgh in 1772 on his way to Iceland and thereafter the two men continued to correspond. Monboddo, like so many of the social theorists of the eighteenth century, was very dependent on travellers, and especially travellers to the new world of the Pacific, for information to support his speculations on the nature of human cultural and linguistic development. Banks's relations with Monboddo were similar to those between Banks and Blumenbach, with Banks providing the empirical data which the other party used as grist for his theoretical mill. But in the case of Monboddo Banks's data proved of only limited use. Monboddo placed a great deal of emphasis on the way in which Nature progressed steadily from the simple to the more complex–such a progression, he argued, could also be found in the development of humankind with the gap between animal and human societies being bridged by a form of human beings who possessed tails.[302] This view was strengthened by Monboddo's belief that 'the Ourang-outangs ... are of our species, and though they have made some progresses in the arts of life, they have not advanced so far as to invent a language'[303]–hence the anecdote recorded by Boswell: 'Went with Dr Solander and breakfasted with Monboddo, who listened with avidity to the Doctor's description of the New Hollanders, almost brutes–but added with eagerness "Have they tails, Dr Solander?" "No, my Lord, they have not tails"'.[304] It was probably Banks and Solander to whom he alludes in his remark that 'the huts of the New Hollanders are not near so well built as those of beavers, and serve only as a cover to the heads and shoulders, as I am informed by the travellers who have lately been in that country'.[305] Banks was also later able to console Monboddo by sending him an extract from a German traveller 'favorable to the system of mankind having in a former period of the Existence of their species been endowd with a tail or Tail like appendage'.[306]

When the first instalment of Monboddo's six-volumed *Of the Origin and Progress of Language* appeared in 1773 the historian, William Robertson, reported to Banks that 'You are frequently mentioned in it & in a proper manner' and that 'Amidst all these oddities, there are mingled ingenious & bold opinions'.[307] In this mammoth work Monboddo alluded both to his disappointment at the meagre ethnological dividends from Pacific exploration thus far and to his hopes for more in the way of confirmation of his theories in the future. He also indicated the extent to which he, like his contemporaries, continued to regard anthropology as a branch of natural history by writing:

This is all, so far as I have observed, that has hitherto been discovered in the South sea concerning the natural state of men there. But we have reason to expect from these countries, in a short time, much greater and more certain discoveries, such as I hope will improve and enlarge the knowledge of our species as much as the natural history of other animals, and of plants and minerals.[308]

Monboddo's quest for understanding the way in which language had developed also led him to enlist Banks's aid in observing instances of human beings who supposedly had grown up outside human society and who, in Monboddo's evolutionary scheme of things, were therefore a guide to the linguistic practice of early humankind. Of these the most celebrated was Peter the Wild Boy who allegedly had grown up alone in the forests of Germany before being discovered in a hollow tree in 1725 when George I was hunting. Peter was then brought to England and placed under the scholarly scrutiny of Dr Arbuthnot, who eventually decided that he was too backward to act as a fit subject for observing the transition from natural to cultivated man and placed him in the care of a Herefordshire farmer.[309] However, Monboddo, ever watchful for any insight into the origins of language–that scholarly Holy Grail of the eighteenth century–continued to regard Peter's history 'as a brief chronicle or abstract of the history of the progress of human nature, from the mere animals to the first stage of civilized life'.[310] But again Banks's observations (or, more accurately, those made on his behalf) provided little encouragement for Monboddo's theorising. Indeed, Banks expressed the view that 'For my own part what little I know of Peter has induc'd me to consider him an idiot who was by his parents plac'd in the woods' particularly since he had failed to learn to speak with any fluency despite 'his remaining among civilised men 50 years'.[311] Banks's scepticism about the case was later confirmed by Blumenbach who showed that Peter the Wild Boy had in fact been a retarded child abandoned by a hostile step-mother, concluding that 'Neither Peter nor any other Homo sapiens ferus of Linnaeus can serve as a specimen of the original Man of Nature'.[312] Ironically, Blumenbach's interest in the case may well have been prompted indirectly by Monboddo who had asked Banks to make enquiries in Hanover about Peter. But the belief that Peter the Wild Boy was an example of primal man was too important to Monboddo to be undermined by Banks's objections: to Banks's argument that Peter could not have survived for so long in the forest, for example, Monboddo countered by invoking Cook's account 'of the inhabitants of New Caledonia, part of whose food is the bark of a certain tree'.[313]

Monboddo's interest in the origin and progress of human language was one of the central concerns of eighteenth-century European intellectual life, particularly in Scotland where the issue was closely related to the various theories of human development: Adam Smith, for example, wrote a *Dissertation on the Origin of Language* and the issue was also addressed in the work of Hugh Blair, Thomas Reid, James Beattie and Lord Kames.[314] So much ultimately fruitless speculation was devoted to the problem that eventually in 1866 the Société de Linguistique de Paris took the drastic step of proscribing discussion of the subject. The interest in the development and the varieties of human languages evident in the work of Banks and his circle was, then, characteristic of the period more generally. The important work done by Banks's friend and correspondent, William Jones, on the nature and history of Indian languages, and particularly Sanskrit, again illustrates the extent of interest in linguistics in late eighteenth century British and, more generally, European society. Monboddo, a regular correspondent of Jones,[315] even attempted to link his work with the supposedly primal civilisation of Egypt by suggesting that Sanskrit was the original language which the Egyptians had introduced into India.[316] Monboddo's belief that 'Egypt was, of all the countries we have heard of, the most proper for the invention of language'[317] reflected a widespread belief in the significance of Egyptian culture which, by the late eighteenth century, was beginning to supplant the traditional biblically-based view that the central focus of ancient history was the civilisation of the Jews.[318]

Banks, too, appears to have shared at least some of Monboddo's enthusiasm for the central role of Egyptian civilisation as the core from which other languages and cultures derived. In the passage in his *Endeavour* journal where Banks pointed to the puzzling similarity between the languages of the South Seas and that of Madagascar, he very tentatively advanced as a possible explanation for this strange linguistic phenomenon the possibility that 'the Egyptian Learning running in two courses, one through Africa the other through Asia, [which] might introduce the same words, and what is still more probable Numerical terms, into the languages of people who never had any communication with each other'.[319] This view that ultimately all languages went back to a common source helps to explain Banks's and, *a fortiori*, Marsden's preoccupation with explaining how the languages of the Pacific and, ultimately, the globe were related. Hence Marsden's remark in his *History of Sumatra* that it was his goal 'To render this comparison of languages [of southeast Asia] more extensive, and, if possible, to bring all those spoken throughout the world, into one point of view' even though he acknowledged that 'my hopes of completing such a work are by no means sanguine'.[320]

Another indication of the central importance that Banks, like Monboddo, accorded to the language and civilisation of the ancient Egyptians comes in a letter of 1802 to Blumenbach, a close student of Egyptology and particularly the comparative anatomy of mummies. Announcing the dispatch of a mummified body from the Canaries, Banks pointed out the similarity which he saw in the structure of the jaw and the teeth of this specimen and that of 'those of the Egyptian mummies you describe as having Incisors of a Cylindrical Form'. Banks then attempted to connect the languages of the Guanches of Tenerife with that 'which is now spoken on Mount Atlas & as Hornemann [the African explorer] tells us all along the Continent of Africa'. Thus Banks made the link between the Guanches and the Egyptians suggesting to Blumenbach that 'Here then is a Scent of the 3d Set of People who have inhabited Egypt, their

origins you have not been able to trace'. As further collaborative evidence
Banks added that 'the Circumstance of both preserving their dead is a
strong indication of a similar origin'–that is the fact that the Guanches,
like the ancient Egyptians, practised mummification again pointed to
the wide diffusion of Egyptian culture.[321] Blumenbach responded enthusiastically writing that 'The singularity of the Teeth & the analogy of the
Scull with that kind of Egyptian face which You mention & which had
been till now enigmatical to me, struck me on the first sight of the
mummy'.[322] Banks returned to this issue in a later letter to Blumenbach
of 1806 hinting that Egyptian culture had penetrated even further afield.
This time Banks sent Blumenbach plaster casts of sepulchres of the
Peruvian Indians accompanying them with the observation 'but is it not
remarkable that the Preservation of the Bodies of the Dead should have
been anciently Practised in Egypt by the Guanches & in Peru by the
Aborigines all laying on a Strait Line East & West & no where Else in
the world'.[323] But Blumenbach appears to have become rather sceptical
about such speculations regarding the diffusion of Egyptian culture.
Indeed, Humboldt in his description of the Guanches cites Blumenbach's
support when arguing that the apparent physical similarities between
the mummies of Egypt and those of the ancient residents of the Canary
Islands were misleading.[324]

THE 'SCIENCE OF MAN' AND NON-EUROPEAN CIVILISATIONS

Such an interest and admiration for Egyptian civilisation was, in part,
an indication of the secularising trend of the Enlightenment. Traditionally,
the Christian West had looked back to the Jews, the Chosen People, as
the main focus of ancient history and the source of civilisation and
even language. A residue of this traditional belief was a paper in the
Archaeologia addressed to Marsden arguing that there was an 'Affinity
of certain Words in the Language of the Sandwich and Friendly Isles in
the Pacific Ocean with the Hebrew' thus confirming that 'there was a
time when all the inhabitants of the world spoke Hebrew'.[325] It was one
of the major purposes of Voltaire's *Philosophy of History* (1765) and the
Essai sur les Moeurs (1769) to challenge such a view by emphasising the
extent and influence of Egyptian culture and the relatively marginal
importance of the Jews. Voltaire's work also highlights the antiquity and
civilisation of China, again with the polemical intent of diminishing the
significance of the history of the Jews and of the biblical record more
generally. One feature of the Enlightenment, then, was a growing interest
and sympathy for non-Christian cultures. In part this was the product
of a growing willingness to entertain the view that non-Christian cultures
might not be completely riddled with error despite the lack of access to
the Judaeo-Christian revelation. Nor did such a position necessarily entail
the anti-Christian animus found in Voltaire. In his *Resolution* journal
the Lutheran minister, Johann Forster, appealed to both the ideals of

A Woman and a Boy, Natives of Otaheite, in the Dress of the Country. Engraving after Parkinson by T. Chambers in Parkinson, *Voyage to the South Seas* (1773), pl.v. Courtesy of Cambridge University Library

Protestantism and the Enlightenment–or what he called this 'refined age' with its greater 'light & principles'–in urging Europeans to avoid 'The blind Zeal for their religion' of the Spaniards with its assumption that non-Christian peoples were immersed in error.[326] Forster's sympathetic study of the beliefs and cultures of the peoples of the Pacific led him to suggest that some of the features of revealed truth could be arrived at through reflection on the natural order–a view with a long history in Christian tradition but which became particularly pervasive in the eighteenth century with its emphasis on natural religion. Nonetheless, he maintained that the Christian revelation purged man-made religions of the idolatrous practices to which they were prone and which, in Enlightenment fashion, he saw as chiefly the product of 'priest-craft'.[327]

Earlier, in 1721, another Lutheran, Christian Wolff, had seen no impiety in extolling the lofty ethical teachings of Confucius and suggesting that they derived from reason rather than revelation–a position that did lead to an outcry from the Pietists though Wolff was ultimately reinstated in the Lutheran university of Halle.[328]

This interest and sympathy for non-European and non-Christian civilisations also owed something to the more dispassionate and sometimes critical attitude to European practices promoted by increasing contact with other societies–an attitude of mind which helps to explain the emergence in the course of the eighteenth century of the beginnings of the social sciences. As Kiernan writes of the Enlightenment: 'One feature of it was a willingness to recognise civilizations outside Europe as fellow-members of a human family, equal or even superior to Europe in some of their attainments'.[329] As we have seen, such an openness to other non-European societies was, particularly in the late eighteenth century, increasingly off-set by the tendency to place different cultures and peoples in a hierarchical order with Europeans at its apex. Nonetheless, the view that Europe could learn much from other societies–and particularly the ancient civilisations of Asia–appears to have been more prevalent in the eighteenth than in the nineteenth century, when concepts of European supremacy were further strengthened by evolutionary anthropological theories and, more fundamentally, by the increasing scale of European imperialism. It is a change in attitude epitomised by the contrast between Voltaire's portrayal of China as a truly enlightened society and the remark of Francis Jeffrey, one of the founders of the *Edinburgh Review*, at the beginning of the nineteenth century that 'I had always a profound contempt for the Chineses'.[330]

Unlike Jones and his circle, who combined service in the East India Company with the study of Indian antiquity, Thomas Macaulay's time in India during the 1830s only served to strengthen his contempt for non-European cultures–thus he reproved a friend for devoting himself to the study of ethnology rather than undertaking a translation of Herodotus:

> Your talents are too great, and your leisure time too small, to be wasted in inquiries so frivolous (I must call them), as those in which you have of late been too much engaged; whether the Cherokees are of the same race with the Chickasaws; whether Van Diemen's Land was peopled from New Holland, or New Holland from Van Diemen's Land; what is the precise mode of appointing a headman in a village in Timbuctoo: I would not give the worst page in Clarendon or Fra Paolo for all that ever was, or ever will be, written about the migrations of the Leleges and the laws of the Oscans.[331]

By contrast, Banks displayed a remarkable interest in non-European societies combined with a willingness to learn from them. This attitude of mind no doubt owed much to the fact that, as we have seen, in Banks's work there is little indication of a tendency to adopt an evolutionary conception of human societies with its implicit or explicit notions of European supremacy. Though critical of some features of Tahitian society, Banks could cheerfully admit that in some respects the Tahitians had surpassed the Europeans. Of their ability to forecast the weather he wrote: 'we found them indeed not infallible but far more clever than Europaeans'. The Tahitian fishhooks he described as seeming 'far to exceed any thing of the kind which I have seen among Europaeans' while their surgical practices left a scar 'as smooth and as small as any I have seen from the cures of our best European surgeons'. Banks gave a detailed account of the Tahitians' procedure for dyeing clothes since he 'was not without hopes that my countrey men may receive some advantage either from the things themselves or at least by hints derivd from them'.[332] Conversely, Banks could compare aspects of European society unfavourably with those he had observed in the Pacific. In his account of the Scottish crofters, included in his journal of the voyage to Iceland, he wrote that 'Their huts are poor to admiration. I have seen few Indians live in so uncomfortable manners'.[333]

In his attitude to the ancient civilisations of China and India, Banks again displayed an openness to the possibility that in some respects they had advanced beyond Europe and that Europeans could learn from them. China especially Banks–like Voltaire and other *philosophes*–regarded with particular admiration. Of the proposed embassy to China led by Lord Macartney, Banks wrote in January 1792: 'I confess I feel much interest in the Success of an undertaking from whence the usefull as well as the ornamental branches of Science are likely to derive infinite advantage'. Though he regarded contemporary China as 'possess[ing] the Ruins of a state of Civilisation' they were heirs of a culture which 'had carried all kinds of knowledge to a much higher pitch of perfection than we Europeans have hitherto been able to attain'. Moreover, continued Banks,

> The great inventions which actualy serve as the basis of our present state of Civilization were all known to the Chinese long before they were either reinvented or stolen from them by us. Printing, Paper making, gunpowder & the arts of working & purifying the most Refractory metals were known to these people ages before, we pretend to have possessed them, their Porcellane remains a chef d'oeuvre in chemistry which the Labor of half a century aided by unbounded expenditure & the royal patronage of many Kingdoms has not been able to discover.

As Banks's comments on Chinese porcelain suggest, his admiration for the Chinese was combined with a determination to acquire for Britain– if necessary by surreptitious means–the mastery of such Chinese industries as porcelain-making or tea manufacture in which China still retained clear supremacy. Hence Banks's active role in recruiting for Macartney's embassy craftsmen who could observe and record Chinese methods. As he wrote to Macartney with a rush of enthusiasm: 'it is highly probable that a few practical men admitted among them would in a few weeks acquire a mass of information for which if placed in the industrious & active hands of English manufacturers the whole Revenue of the Chinese Empire would not be thought a sufficient equivalent'.[334] Thus Banks wrote to Wedgwood as one 'who have turnd the art of Pottery into a Science' to find a skilled potter for Macartney's entourage.[335] Such a person, Macartney remarked, 'might have opportunities by being in the train of the Ambassador of observing unsuspected a variety of processes and improvements which might redound greatly to the advantage of this Country at his return'.[336] Similarly, Banks approached Thomas Percival, an FRS and prominent Manchester physician, to find someone skilled in dyeing cloth (while maintaining as much secrecy as possible) since he hoped thereby 'many important improvements may be expected'.[337] In proposing such a 'technology transfer' Banks was concerned to promote agriculture and particularly horticulture. Thus in his 'Hints on the subject of Gardening suggested to the Gentlemen who attend the embassy to China'[338] he urged them to pay particular attention to various Chinese horticultural practices, such as 'the method of accelerating the blossoming of Plants' which the Europeans had not yet been able to master. Banks duly received a journal from a gardener by the name of Huxton who accompanied the embassy–though, to judge from Banks's extracts, the interests of both Huxton and Banks extended beyond the immediately practical to encompass subjects such as Chinese religion.[339] Banks's interest in the religion and mythology of China is evident, too, in his comments on his wife's collection of old China where he wrote that 'the Idolatry of the Chinese is far more extensive than that of the Japanese, they seem indeed to tolerate in the most comprehensive sense the more ancient Idolatry of the Country, which like that of the Romans & Greeks admits of a tutelar Divinity for every possible contingency of human life'.[340] The source for such remarks was probably John Reeves FRS, an East India Company official, who, as he wrote to Banks, had been commissioned by him 'to ascertain certain points connected with the religion or rather the Mythology of the Chinese as depicted upon the China ware of the Country'.[341]

In relation to India, too, Banks's interests ranged beyond the immediate economic advantages that could be derived from it. As well as being a friend of Jones and a supporter of his studies of ancient Indian language and culture, Banks also encouraged the work of Samuel Davies, a Fellow of the Royal Society and Accountant-General of Bengal, who attempted to investigate the scientific, and particularly the astronomical learning of the Brahmins.[342] Banks's papers also include notes on the customs of the Parsees of India, on Hindu funereal practices and beliefs concerning the transmigration of souls, together with excerpts of an essay on the rites of the Brahmins.[343] But needless to say Banks was anxious, wherever possible, to gain for Britain the benefit of any traditional learning which might be of use. Thus his 'A Project of a Botanic Garden in the Island of Ceylon' urges close study of the Ceylonese herbal doctors who 'are far more skillful than Europeans are willing to admit'.[344] In a letter to David Scott, a director of the East India Company, Banks described the civilisation of India much as he had written of China to Lord Macartney: 'I look upon the arts of India as the Ruins of a vast Fabric of Science raisd many ages ago to a height probably far superior to that on which we europeans now pride ourselves'. It followed, then, that Banks was anxious to promote the acquisition of Indian craft skills, difficult though this may be–as he wrote to Scott: 'Nothing in my opinion is more interesting to the progress of Arts in Europe than Communications from well informd men of the minute practise of Indian workmen but nothing I am confident is more difficult to Obtein'. By making available to Britain the ancient skills of India, he assured Scott, 'you are certein to contribute very Largely towards the Real advantage of your native Countrey'[345]–a remark which indicates once again both Banks's openness to the possibility that non-Europeans might be superior in their skills and learning and his determination to acquire such technological advantages for the benefit of Britain.

Banks's interest in ancient, non-European civilisations even ranged beyond Asia to the New World for he maintained a correspondence with Benjamin Smith Barton, who argued for the antiquity of pre-European North American civilisation. Like Banks himself, Barton was a naturalist who extended the range of his studies to include ethnology and even archaeology. Like Banks, too, Barton excavated some ancient barrows using the evidence thus obtained to support the view that the larger tumuli and fortifications in North America were the work of an ancient culture, either that of Mexico or 'a people nearly in the state of society and improvement of the Mexicans'.[346] Earlier, he wrote to Banks of the ancient fortifications found beyond the Alleghanies which indicated that the peoples there had 'relinquished the form of society which we denominate *savage*'.[347] Banks was evidently sympathetic to his arguments since, in one of his letters to Banks, Barton approvingly commented that 'Your opinion concerning the antiquity of the *American-world* has afforded me much pleasure'.[348] Banks's papers also include a copy of a lecture by another of his American correspondents, the physician and naturalist, Samuel Latham Mitchell, which had as its aim to show 'the original inhabitants of America . . . to be of the same family and lineage with those of Asia'–a subject in which, as we have seen, Banks had a long-standing interest dating back to his early Labrador and Newfoundland expeditions of 1766.

In support of this view, Mitchell referred to the work of Barton in illustrating the 'affinity of their languages'. In a nationalistic vein, he suggested 'that America was the cradle of the human race' and 'that on coming to America, he [the European] had left the *new* world behind him for the purpose of visiting the Old'.[349] While Banks may well have declined to follow Mitchell on such a speculative trail, his interest in the ethnology and archaeology of North America is another instance of Banks's relative lack of European chauvinism and his willingness to learn from and about non-European civilisations.

Banks's interests in non-European societies were partly those of the virtuoso desirous of new curiosities, partly those of the antiquarian concerned with the study of different human societies, both in their past and present manifestations, and partly those of the naturalist, who included the study of the human species in the study of the natural world more generally. His goals in pursuing such studies and, more importantly, in encouraging others to do so reflect both the ideals of the Enlightenment and the imperatives of Empire. Whenever possible Banks hoped to turn the study of different cultures and, in particular, their arts and manufactures to imperial profit by acquiring for Britain the mastery of such new and, he hoped, lucrative practices. The study of new peoples could also be a prelude to more direct forms of imperial control: thus, for example, Banks's testimony about the nature and extent of the Aboriginal population of Australia was a major consideration in prompting its settlement by the British, since it was thought that the native population was unlikely to offer much resistance. Both Marsden and Banks corresponded extensively with Raffles on the natural history and ethnology of the East Indies[350] and Raffles's own anthropological interests are apparent in his *History of Java*. Such studies provided Raffles with the familiarity with local conditions which enabled him to effect the purchase of Singapore Island for the East India Company in 1819, thus extending the effective reach of the British Empire.

But Banks's interest in the infant discipline of anthropology also reflected some of the aspirations of the Enlightenment. Though Banks largely contented himself with the collection of ethnological data and left others to draw such material into larger and more systematic theoretical frameworks, his encouragement of the work of such early anthropologists as Blumenbach and Marsden indicates his sympathy with the Enlightenment project of developing a 'science of Man'. Such a study should, as the Scottish theorist, Adam Ferguson, put it in his *Essay on Civil Society* (1766), have as its object the discovery of the 'laws of his animal and intellectual system' in order to promote human happiness.[351] For underlying the Enlightenment's advocacy of a 'science of Man' was the same assumption that had shaped its view of the natural sciences–that, in Bacon's words, such studies would yield fruit as well as light and that they would ultimately contribute to the 'relief of man's estate'. The study of different peoples, it was hoped, would direct attention to the well-springs of human progress and, conversely, make evident the social and cultural obstacles to improvement. Hence the claim of Georg Forster that an expedition such as Cook's second great voyage made possible observations of new societies which would 'enlighten the Understanding ... improve manners and morals ... eliminate prejudice; and in sum promote improvement'.[352] The founders of the French Society of the Observers of Man, the first anthropological society, held similar hopes that 'the science of man would certainly bring a new age in the intellectual history of mankind'.[353]

Such overweening optimism about the possibilities which could flow from the 'science of Man' was heightened by the realisation that the eighteenth century offered a particularly fertile field for its development, since so much of the world had been opened to European gaze. As Edmund Burke put it in a letter to the historian, William Robertson:

I have always thought with you, that we possess at this time very great advantages towards the knowledge of human nature. We need no longer go to history to trace it in all its stages and periods. History from its comparative youth, is but a poor instructour ... But now the great map of mankind is unrolld at once; and there is no state or gradation of barbarism, and no mode of refinement which we have not at the same instant under our view.[354]

In the introduction to his *A Narrative of the Voyages Round the World performed by Captain Cook* (1820)–a work prefaced with a tribute to Banks 'for the interest he has taken in the present publication'–Alexander Kippis waxed eloquent on the ways in which Cook's Pacific voyages had played a particularly important part in the extension of humanity's knowledge of itself. Not only had such voyages promoted sciences like astronomy and botany, but 'Another important object of study has been opened by them; and that is, the study of human nature, in situations various, interesting and uncommon'. Such observations 'could not but afford many subjects of speculation to an inquisitive and philosophical mind. Hence may be collected a variety of important facts with respect to the state of man'. Kippis particularly singled out the way in which Cook's voyage had drawn attention to the problem which had so intrigued Banks, the similarity of languages from South-east Asia to Madagascar. With a bow to the work of Marsden, Kippis expressed the conviction that 'The collections that have been made of the words which are used in the widely diffused islands and countries that have lately been visited, cannot fail ... to throw much light on the origin of nations and the peopling of the globe'.[355] As Kippis suggests, then, the voyages of discovery were intended to investigate the nature and diversity of humankind as well as the character of the terraqueous globe.

By sailing to new lands and new peoples eighteenth-century Europeans also saw themselves as approaching more closely to their own origins– thus the pioneering French anthropologist, Joseph-Marie Degérando, urged the Baudin expedition to Australia to grasp the opportunity to advance 'The Science of Man ... [as] a natural science, a science of observation'. By studying the people of the Pacific, he wrote,

we shall in a way be taken back to the first periods of our own history; we shall be able to set up secure experiments on the origin and generation of ideas, on the formation and development of language, and on the relations between these two processes. The philosophical traveller, sailing to the ends of the earth, is in fact travelling in time; he is exploring the past; every step he makes is the passage of an age.[356]

The voyages in which Banks participated and those which he promoted were, then, to become not only a means of charting the territories and seas hitherto unknown to the European world but also of better grasping the extent of what Burke had called the 'great map of mankind'. In venturing into these uncharted regions the European explorers were to become engaged in an exploration of human nature and in providing much of the ethnological cargo with which the Enlightenment attempted to construct a 'Science of Man'.

CHAPTER FIVE

The Principles and Practice of Improvement

THE NATURE AND EXTENT OF THE IMPROVING CREED

Along with the ideal of the virtuoso, within the world of eighteenth-century elite culture another stimulus for an interest in exploring both the world of Nature and of humankind was the increasing emphasis on the possibilities of improvement. The ideal of improvement came to embrace a wider and wider range of activities, but its origins were closely linked with an activity which was at the heart of landed society: the practice of agriculture. For the novel methods applied to agriculture over the course of the eighteenth century provided proof positive of the benefits of improvement as an outcome of human ingenuity and application. Indeed, the advance of agriculture provided an illustration of the possibility of that Enlightenment-charged concept, the idea of progress. As the land bore more, better, and increasingly diversified fruits as a consequence of patient experiment with new techniques and crops so, too, the need to apply comparable methods to other areas of the economy and society more generally came to seem more insistent. The confidence that the human condition could be improved rippled out from agriculture, the traditional centre of the nation's economic and social order, to most other areas of society.

From agriculture to manufacture was a natural extension, especially in fields such as tanning or textiles, which were directly dependent on agricultural products. But the improving impulse also extended to other areas and problems seemingly much more remote from agriculture. One such was the growing level of mass pauperisation in the late eighteenth century which was linked to the rapid increase in population. To members of a landed class that had experienced the success that experiment and rational management had brought in the world of agriculture, such social problems also seemed amenable to some sort of solution. Moreover, their determination to find one was strengthened by their awareness of the socially explosive consequences of allowing the problem to grow unchecked. Such an attitude of mind helps to explain why agricultural reformers were closely associated with a body known as the Society for Bettering the Condition of the Poor and why, in turn, a society such as this helped give rise to the Royal Institution, the early history of which was dominated by the quest to apply to agriculture the findings of science.[1] Appropriately, too, its chief founder, Count Rumford, while State Councillor to the Elector of Bavaria, had combined his scientific work with a wide-ranging project to reduce pauperisation in Munich by the establishment of workhouses and soup kitchens which dispensed a diet based on rigorous economy and scientific principles of nutrition.[2]

Improvement was in addition a creed that could be applied not only to many different fields of the economy but also to many different levels of activity on the part of individuals or government. Predictably, gentlemen improvers such as Banks or his close friend, Lord Sheffield, improved their estates with a view to improving their incomes; they also saw it as their social duty to improve the lot of their agricultural dependents. But such local pursuits were also paralleled by their activities within the governing structure of the British State. The possibilities of improvement, which they had experienced at first hand, helped to shape the policies they advanced to increase their nation's wealth and power. If new crops like the 'artificial grasses' which had conferred so many benefits on British landowners could be introduced within Britain why could new crops, and indeed whole new industries, not be introduced to territories of the British Empire? Crops such as cotton and tea, which were increasingly important staples of British trade, drained British wealth because they could not be produced within Britain itself. But if the plant life of Britain's colonial dependencies were re-organised (and, from a certain perspective, improved) to benefit the motherland, Britain could become self-sufficient in such products, with a consequent saving in both treasure and national prestige. Thus Banks combined his efforts to improve his Lincolnshire estates with his work as an unofficial adviser to government, promoting schemes to transplant tea from China to India or cotton from Persia to the British West Indies. The ideal of improvement, then, could be both local and imperial as the experience of economic growth welled up from the grassroot experiences of broad-acred gentlemen to shape their view about the uses to which Britain's expanding control over increasingly diverse portions of the globe should be put.

Though the ideal of improvement more and more coloured the outlook of the elite of late eighteenth-century England and, not least, of its head, 'Farmer George', its origins largely derived from England's poorer and less fertile northern neighbour and sister kingdom of Scotland.[3] Both kingdoms had, since the Act of Union of 1707, been integrated politically and this merger assisted the circulation of both goods and ideas between the two kingdoms. The Scots' awareness of their comparative backwardness strengthened their determination to promote schemes which would improve the productivity of Scotland's agriculture and put to better use both its land and its people. It was the Scottish improvers who did much to forge that alliance between science and agriculture which was to provide the basis for the improvers' optimism in Britain more generally. The Scottish virtuoso tended to be more mindful than his counterpart south of the Tweed of the need to shape his studies towards the production of useful knowledge.[4] National pride helped to prompt the search for applied knowledge in a country which since the Restoration had had to bear multiple indignities: exclusion from English overseas trade (for, under the terms of acts of 1660 and 1662, Scotland had, for commercial purposes, been relegated to the position of a foreign country[5]); the collapse of the Darien scheme, 1698–1700, and, with it, Scottish hopes for an independent presence in world trade; and the eventual rather reluctant acceptance of a legislative marriage with England as a means of redressing its relative economic backwardness. Severe famines in the late seventeenth century further strengthened the resolve of landowners to extract as much produce as possible from their estates to compensate for Scotland's agricultural deficiencies.[6]

Among the Scots agriculture came to be seen as the pre-eminent example of the merger of philosophy with practice or, as the pioneering social theorist, Lord Kames, put it: 'Agriculture justly claims to be the chief of the arts; it enjoys the signal pre-eminence of combining philosophy with useful practice'.[7] In 1763 we find him congratulating one of his correspondents on choosing 'the noblest plan for the conduct of life', that of an improver.[8] Kames later received a warm tribute from Sir John Sinclair, the doyen of Scottish agricultural improvers, as someone who 'deserves to be placed at the head of the list . . . of those distinguished patriots through whose brilliant exertions Scotland acquired that perfection in husbandry which is now [1825] so eminent'.[9] Lord Monboddo, Kames's rival in both the fields of law and social theory, also shared his interest in agricultural improvement and divided his time between the law, supervising agricultural experiments on his estates and writing copiously and controversially on the origins of human language and society.[10] Appropriately, in Aberdeen those wishing to cultivate enlightened values did so chiefly through two institutions, the Gordon's Mill Farming Club (founded 1758) and the Aberdeen Philosophical Society. The eponymous founder of the Farming Club, Thomas Gordon of Aberdeen University, emphasised the need to establish agriculture on a firm scientific footing. Thus he laid down for the club a Baconian programme based on the assumption that 'As agriculture ought to be considered as a noble & important branch of natural Philosophy, it should be pursued in the same method'.[11]

Such impulses were given political form by the establishment of a number of national instrumentalities for the improvement of Scottish agriculture. Private initiative led the way with the establishment in 1723 of the Society of Improvers in the Knowledge of Agriculture in Scotland, the first such body in Britain. It had a membership of about three hundred drawn from the more substantial representatives of the landowning classes.[12] Its activities helped prompt the government to establish in 1727 the Board of Trustees for Arts, Manufacture and Fisheries with a budget of about six thousand pounds per annum to promote schemes for improvement–though its largesse became more and more restricted to the promotion of the Scottish linen industry.[13] The rebellion of 1745 brought in its wake the establishment in 1752 of the Board of Commissioners for the Forfeited Estates, which had as its goal the administration and the improvement of confiscated Jacobite estates. Though, in practice, the Board was rather sluggish in promoting such ends, it remained confident that the gospel of improvement would bring with it not only economic benefits but also social and political enlightenment as the traditional Gaelic culture which had supported the Jacobite uprising was extinguished by the spread of scientifically-based agriculture. Thus Lord Milton, the lieutenant of the Duke of Argyll (Scotland's virtual viceroy from 1726 to 1742 and from 1746 to 1761) and an active member of the Board of Trustees, urged that the Highlanders should be dealt with by 'civilising them by introducing Agriculture, Fisherys, and Manufactures, and thereby by degrees extirpating their barbarity, with their chief marks of distinction, their language and dress, and preventing their idleness, the present source of their poverty, Theift and Rebellion'.[14] Others also endeavoured to promote the alliance between agricultural improvement and the spread of Enlightenment ideals. The Reverend Dr John Walker, professor of natural history at the University of Edinburgh from 1779 to 1803, regarded enclosure and the introduction of artificial grasses in the Highlands as the vanguard of a more wholesale assault on Highland backwardness and on its reluctance to acknowledge the benefits of Hanoverian civilisation. These two measures, he wrote, 'are the two leading steps of improvement, in the uncultivated parts of Scotland . . . They are introductory to every sort of polishd Culture'.[15]

THE FOUNDATION OF THE BOARD OF AGRICULTURE

The spread of such sentiments promoted a faith in the possibilities of improvement and, with it, a spirit of optimism and self-confidence in a nation which increasingly had to bear the indignity of living in the political shadow of its southern neighbour.

And, as the century progressed, there were more and more examples of the successful application of agricultural improvement to add momentum to the cause. In 1795 George Dempster, author of *Heads of a Plan for Improving the Waste Lands in the Highlands*, extrapolated from previous successes to envisage a time when 'it will hardly be believed that a Country so capable of Improvement was at that time occupied by a few indigent Cattle herds'.[16] The sixth (1815) edition of Lord Kames's *Gentleman Farmer* rejoiced that 'there never were greater agricultural improvements carried on in any country than there have been in Scotland during the last thirty years'.[17] By the end of the century the Scots were playing a major part in establishing new institutions for promoting agricultural improvement which captured the attention and the membership not only of Scots but of Englishmen as well–an illustration of the way in which the effects and benefits of the Act of Union were increasingly flowing in both directions.

The growing interest in the improvement of the Highlands led to the establishment of a Highlands Society which, in turn, promoted specialist societies narrower in focus but Britain-wide in their membership. George Dempster, the main promoter of the Highlands Society, founded the British Fisheries Society in 1786[18] and, thanks to the initiative of Sir John Sinclair, the Society for the Improvement of British Wool was established in 1791.[19] Another promoter of this latter body was Sinclair's ally, James Anderson, an indefatigable pamphleteer and promoter of agricultural improvement. He argued that previous bodies for the promotion of agriculture, such as the Society of Improvers in the Knowledge of Agriculture (which had faded away in the aftermath of the rebellion of 1745), had been too ambitious 'their efforts having been divided among such a multiplicity of objects, become feeble, and their effect imperceptible'. Hence the need for a society focused on one particular goal 'naturally susceptible of improvement by means of premiums'.[20]

Naturally, improvers such as Anderson and Sinclair made contact with Sir Joseph Banks, a fellow enthusiast for the improvement of British wool and indeed for the improvement of British agriculture, life and labour more generally. Banks, moreover, was an enthusiastic admirer of Scotland and its enlightened intellectual life. In 1819 he reminisced nostalgically of his visit to Edinburgh in 1773 when 'I spent my time so agreably that the Recollection of it has haunted me Ever Since . . . Edinboro was before that time & has been Ever Since a School of the Liberal Sciences which could not be Exceeded & Possibly was not Equald by any in England. [O]f Such a School I feel myself proud as a Briton'.[21] Banks and Sinclair began corresponding on the possibilities of improving British sheep in 1785 and, thanks to Sinclair, Anderson was also drawn into Banks's vast network of correspondents.[22] In the following year Banks assisted with letters of introduction for Sinclair's characteristically energetic tour of northern Europe where, as he acknowledged to Banks in a letter from St Petersburg in 1786, Banks's introductions greatly facilitated his investigations.[23]

Sinclair's European voyage formed part of his lifelong promotion of the gospel of improvement. As he himself wrote, it was his goal 'to ascertain the state of other countries, and to discover every means, which had been sanctioned by the experience of other nations, that could be successfully introduced for the improvement of Great Britain'. When Sinclair returned in 1788 he did so

> full of ardour, to establish, in my own country, all the beneficial institutions which were scattered over others; and to make this island, the centre of the various improvements, of which political society was capable, more especially those of an agricultural nature, to which a person of landed property is naturally partial.[24]

Sir John Sinclair (1754-1835). Painting by Sir Henry Raeburn. Courtesy of the
National Portrait Gallery

Sinclair's role in the establishment of the Society for the Improvement
of British Wool in 1790 proved to be but a prelude to his continuing
endeavours to give a more effective institutional form to the movement for
the promotion of agricultural improvement of which he was assuming the
position of chief promoter. Believing, as he did, that 'the peace and quiet of
the country, and the resources of the state depend, upon the progress of our
agricultural improvements'[25] Sinclair devoted his considerable energies

to persuading the British government that agriculture, like trade, should have a government board to promote its interests. In attempting to do so he was hampered by his uneasy political relationship with William Pitt but, nonetheless, the Board of Agriculture's charter was duly sealed on 23 August 1793, largely thanks to the support of Henry Dundas, Scotland's pre-eminent politician.[26]

Sinclair's commitment to the cause of improvement was reflected in the very title of this body, its full and formal name being the Board of Agriculture and Internal Improvement. A month after its foundation Sinclair outlined to the king–a fellow enthusiast for agricultural improvement–his hopes for the Board of which Sinclair himself was foundation president. It was an institution, he wrote, which 'will be the means of adding many millions to the annual produce of your Majesty's dominions, and of bringing the principles of agriculture and of national improvement to an unexampled height of perfection'.[27] Indeed, Sinclair saw the establishment of the Board, and the realisation of the ideals of improvement associated with it, as marking a milestone not only in the history of his own country but also more generally. Hence the claim in his 1797 address on 'the progress that has been made by the Board' that 'the establishment of a Board of Agriculture in Great Britain, (if the Institution shall be carried on with proper zeal and energy) will form an important era, not only in the History of this kingdom, but of mankind in general'.[28]

The Board of Agriculture had a peculiar constitution establishing it as a half private, half public, body not answerable to the Treasury for its accounts though it did receive three thousand pounds per annum from the government.[29] Despite its anomalous constitution it owed much to the example of the Board of Trade and its functioning. Thus Sinclair proposed at its foundation that it 'should consist of twenty-four members, in the same manner as the present Board of Trade' and in moving in Parliament for its establishment he commented on the anomaly that government could obtain information about commerce from the Board of Trade but lacked an equivalent source for agriculture when dealing with 'many points, in which the general interests of the country were deeply involved'.[30] Indeed, Sinclair saw the establishment of the Board of Agriculture as belated recognition of the importance of the landed interest which was becoming increasingly resentful at what it considered was the undue attention being accorded to commerce and manufacture. Thus his *A Plan for Establishing a Board of Agriculture* (1793) urged that 'It has long been justly complained of, whilst every attention has been paid to *Trade*, and every encouragement given to *Commercial Industry*, yet that AGRICULTURE has been totally neglected'. Furthermore, Sinclair continued, invoking the rhetoric which was ultimately to culminate in the debates over the Corn Laws, 'manufactures and commerce, are neither so permanent a source of national prosperity, as the proper cultivation of the soil'.[31] Such aspersions on the worth of trade may well help to explain the opposition of Lord Hawkesbury, President of the Board of Trade, to the foundation of Sinclair's brain-child.[32]

Sinclair's political tactlessness was to do much to reduce the significance of the Board as an instrument for influencing government. At the foundation of the Board in 1793 Sinclair was briefly and uncharacteristically in favour with Pitt but thereafter relations between the two men resumed their normally distant character. As a consequence, Pitt's government looked to the Board only for such humble tasks as the administration of bounties for drainage and potato growing.[33] In 1798 Pitt's influence, together with Sinclair's financial ineptness, resulted in Sinclair's deposition as President in favour of Lord John Sommerville, another Scottish laird with improving sympathies. Sommerville's term was brief–1798 to 1800– but it was he, together with his successor, Lord Carrington (1800-3), who largely oversaw the Board's most important incursion into parliamentary politics: the passage of the Enclosure Consolidation Act of 1801. This measure greatly simplified the process of enclosure which the Board and its officers, such as Sinclair and Arthur Young, saw as one of the major vehicles for promoting improvement. Sinclair had been defeated by one vote, with Banks being among those who voted against him, although he afterwards wrote to Sinclair expressing the hope that they would continue to 'meet together at the club, and talk over all matters that concern us, either as members of the Board, or fellows of the Royal Society'.[34] Sinclair eventually returned as President from 1806 to 1813–with, as Banks told Arthur Young, 'promises of good behaviour'[35]–but the Board's exclusion from the major concerns of government continued, prefiguring its eventual demise in 1822. But, though government was largely oblivious of the Board's activities, it left its mark in the series of county reports which, as Harrison puts it, 'remain a lasting memorial to the statistical aspirations of its founder'.[36] The aim of these surveys was both 'to ascertain the general state of the Agriculture, the Manufactures, and the Commerce of the Country' and, predictably, to ascertain 'the means of improvement of which they are respectively capable'.[37] In a letter to the king of 1796 Sinclair once again emphasised the contribution that such county surveys could make to the cause of improvement describing them as 'a foundation ... for carrying on the improvement of your Majesty's kingdom, which no other country was ever possessed of'.[38]

Naturally, Sinclair was keen to obtain the support of Banks for the Board, both as President of the Royal Society and unofficial scientific adviser to government and as a long-standing correspondent on matters relating to agricultural improvement. In April 1793 Sinclair sent Banks a draft of the plan for the proposed Board together with a covering letter urging the merits of its activities (and especially those of the projected statistical survey of England) as a means of 'turn[ing] the attention of the public from foreign possessions to our improvements at home, which are much more solid & permanent'. However, at first Banks's reaction was somewhat lukewarm. He commended the proposed Board chiefly because it was not a body 'armed with the powers of making regulations relative to the direction of agricultural industry' but rather 'calculated merely to examine the progress and encourage the improvement of agricultural efforts'. Indeed, Banks wished to see the Board stripped of any affiliations with government considering it 'far better suited for a private than for a public establishment'.[39] At first, too, Banks was wary of accepting an *ex officio* position on the Board as President of the Royal Society-something which Sinclair attributed to his fears that the Board might infringe on some of the Royal Society's scientific territory.[40] Banks may also have feared that the proposed Board's link with the State might make agriculture more of a politically divisive issue[41] for on 1 August 1793 he told the Reverend Richard Shepherd that 'I early gave my opinion that its institution as a measure was not likely to benefit the Landed interest'. Nonetheless, his comment that, as a consequence, 'there is no likelihood of my being consulted'[42] on the Board's affairs proved false, for Banks eventually became an active supporter of its activities-by 1811 the *Agricultural Magazine* could write that 'The institution of the Board of Agriculture has had its utility greatly increased by means of the counsels of the President of the Royal Society'.[43] When famine loomed in 1795, Banks used the Board's good offices both to draw attention to the scale of the problem and to suggest possible remedies-hence the comment of Banks's steward, Benjamin Stephenson, on 22 February 1795 that 'Your Board of Agriculture acts very wisely in flinging hints of alarm of an approaching scarcity ... I think there never was a time in my Memory, that there was so bad a prospect of scarcity as the present'.[44] At Sinclair's suggestion, Banks took charge of some of the trials of potatoes, a vegetable which, it was hoped, would provide a substitute for the badly depleted grain crops.[45] The fruits of experiments like these were embodied in such publications of the Board as its *Hints Respecting the Cultivation and the Use of Potatoes* (1795)-measures which, Sinclair claimed in a letter of September 1795 to the king, acted as 'the means of saving this country from the risk of famine this season'.[46]

The possibility that poor harvests and the disruption to trade caused by the French Wars might again bring Britain to the brink of famine continued to dominate Banks's relations with the Board of Agriculture, a body which he saw as the main institution for promoting changes to prevent such a calamity. When the spectre of dearth again surfaced in 1801, Banks's proposals to the Board on the need to extend the planting of potatoes became the subject of a formal submission to a committee of the House of Commons called to consider the 'High Price of Provisions'. This took the form of a request from Lord Carrington (President of the Board of Agriculture, 1800-3) for 'the particulars of the proposal ... made this morning at the Committee of the Board of Agriculture'.[47] For all its political impotence, then, the Board could act as a conduit to the inner workings of government for measures intended to promote improvement.

Banks linked the spread of potatoes with the increased use of common lands by individual farmers, an instance of the Board's enthusiasm for promoting agricultural change by altering traditional patterns of land ownership (especially through encouraging enclosure). Its report of 1795 of a 'Committee Appointed ... to Take into Consideration the State of the Waste Lands and Common Fields of this Kingdom' had described 'any intermixture of property in the same land, as being a great, and in many cases an unsurmountable bar to all improvement'.[48] Improvement, then, meant not only the application of the fruits of experiment and scientific agriculture but the remoulding of such basic social relations as patterns of land ownership to facilitate the application of such principles.

Though Banks was a warm advocate of the merits of the potato as a buffer against famine, he was well aware that the food stocks of the nation were chiefly reliant on the grain crops and particularly wheat. Consequently, most of his energies were devoted to extending the yield of wheat with the Board of Agriculture acting as his major vehicle for promoting and publicising such enquiries. Banks's papers from the period 1804-5 provide ample evidence for his preoccupation with different strains of wheat and the possibilities of improving their yield, a concern prompted by the renewed possibility of dearth. What particularly seems to have engaged Banks's attention was the widespread incidence of wheat blight in the crop of 1803-4. As he wrote in August 1804, 'Tho I have paid attention to this Calamitous disease in the wheat for some years I have never before seen it nearly so General or so severe'.[49] Banks's response to this national calamity took the form both of a series of experiments to counteract the blight and of a search for new strains of wheat. His investigations[50] of the cause of the blight led to the publication in January 1805 of his *A Short Account of the Cause of the Disease in Corn, called by the Farmers the Blight, Mildew, and the Rust, etc.* In this he argued that the incidence of rust was related to the spread of the barberry bush which, he suggested, acted as a host for a parasite. The Board assisted in the dissemination of these findings for, within two months of publication, Banks's pamphlet was included in its *Communications*.[51] With his credentials thus established, the Board in 1806 turned to Banks to comment on a series of papers on the course of the blight; he also proposed a cure for smut on wheat received from Sweden.[52]

Banks used the Board, too, to promote another of his schemes for the improvement of the wheat yield: the introduction of 'spring wheat'. The planting of this strain of wheat–as opposed to the traditional winter wheat–Banks saw as a ready means of ensuring a greater supply of food at a time when this was essential for Britain's social and political stability. Hence Banks's comment, in a document addressed to the Board of Agriculture, that 'in the present State of the Country there are few things of greater political importance than the introduction of Spring wheat ... [since] our population is rapidly increasing'.[53] Together with the advantage of an increase in yield Banks's patient investigations showed that spring wheat was more resistant to blight.[54] Armed with both an historical account of the progress of spring wheat and a chemical analysis of it conducted by Humphry Davy at the Royal Institution which showed 'that bread made of the flour of spring wheat is more nutritious than that of winter wheat, because spring wheat contains a larger proportion of the gluten or half animalised matter' Banks made known his findings in the

Communications to the Board of Agriculture of 1806. In this article he also praised the Board for having offered premiums over the previous years 'for the increase of its culture, which have had the effect of rendering it more generally known than otherwise would have been the case'.[55] It comes as no surprise, however, to find that the main agent in persuading the Board to offer such a premium was probably Banks himself for it appears to have been he who, in February 1805, added to the Board's list of prizes one for the person who could raise the greatest number of acres of spring wheat.[56] Banks also attempted to persuade the Board to send at its expense 'an intelligent Journeyman miller' to Sicily where spring wheat was widely used.[57] Such a measure he thought especially appropriate since 'The Political Relations between the Country & Sicily render such a measure at this time particularly Easy'[58]–a reference to the co-operation that existed between the kingdoms of the two Sicilies and Great Britain in the face of the threat from Napoleon.

Though there is no record of the Board parting with any of its meagre funds to send Banks's agricultural emissary to Sicily, Banks does appear to have been successful in winning over Sinclair to support his crusade for the introduction of spring wheat. In his *Observations on the Nature and Advantages of Spring or Summer Wheat* (1805?), Sinclair urged the need for 'some legislative encouragement, to augment the culture of Spring Wheat'. Sinclair's chief reason for doing so was a concern that Banks amply shared– that if domestic production did not increase then the landed interest's position would be weakened by an increase in the volume of imported grain. As Sinclair robustly put it in the same passage, 'How much better is it, to promote domestic cultivation and improvement, than to bestow bounties on the importation of mere trash, the refuse of foreign granaries'.[59] Two years later, in a letter to Banks, Sinclair once again emphasised the importance of spring wheat as a means of promoting national self-sufficiency affirming that he, like Banks, was 'convinced, that we never can be independent of foreign supply, without cultivating spring wheat'.[60]

Along with spring wheat Banks attempted to interest the Board in other schemes for augmenting the nation's food supply. In January 1809, two months after Sinclair's letter on spring wheat, Banks sent the Board an essay on the way in which 'inferior grains' (those which were shrivelled or underweight) could be used for human consumption, urging that 'There are few subjects on which the members of this useful Board can be more advantageously employed in the service of the Public' than in promoting experiments to investigate such a problem. For, he continued, 'no consideration so intimately involves in itself the Future Destiny of the Country as the necessity of securing by every measure the sagacity [?] of men can devise a sufficient supply of ... food for the whole population of the Country at a reasonable & adequate Price'.[61] For Banks, then, as for Sinclair, agricultural improvement offered the possibility of transforming the face of the nation; its methods might be mundane, with recourse to better crops or more turnips and manure, but its results could save the nation from the historical fate of having a population increase followed by dearth and misery–a fate which their contemporary, Thomas Malthus, was prescribing for Britain.

Despite Sinclair's financial extravagances, and political ineptness, Banks retained a lasting respect for him as someone who shared his own belief in the possibilities that agricultural improvement offered for 'the relief of man's estate'. As he wrote in 1798 to William Tatham, a military engineer and enthusiast for promoting agricultural drainage (one of the major means of improvement in Banks's native Lincolnshire), Sinclair's 'whole pursuit is the advantage of his Country'. He also commended Tatham for submitting his scheme 'to the Board of Agriculture as the excellent president of that board [Sinclair] ... will be both able & willing to give a satisfactory report concerning the public utility & national importance'.[62] In 1800 Banks's unwillingness to take part in Sinclair's ill-fated plan for a Joint Stock Farming Company strained the friendship[63] but, by 1805, Sinclair was again looking to Banks to supply him with news of the Board of Agriculture and, in particular, the circumstances surrounding Sheffield's retirement from the presidency. Banks also chose to dedicate his 1809 pamphlet on merino sheep–a subject particularly dear to his heart–to Sinclair, expressing the hope that it would be valuable to 'the very useful Institution over which you preside, with so much advantage to the agricultural interests of this country'.[64] In 1814 another of Sinclair's ill-considered financial schemes, in which he had invoked Banks's name, led to a more serious breach in relations, with Sinclair writing to 'express his regret at so unfortunate a termination of an intercourse, arising from similar pursuits, and calculated for the public benefit'.[65] But harmony was again restored for, in 1819, a year before his death, Banks sent Sinclair both his warm personal regards and, appropriately, a tribute to the traditions of Scottish agricultural improvement which had animated Sinclair's whole career. Writing of Sinclair's *Account of the Systems of Husbandry adopted in the More Improved Districts of Scotland* (which had first appeared in 1812), Banks commented:

> I rejoice to hear that your Scottish Agriculture has met with so extensive a sale. The adoption of it in England will probably be the consequence, and a more beneficial one scarce can be conceived. That a Scots farmer can get more crop from the earth than an English one seems a fact not to be disputed. To have been the cause of imparting to Englishmen the skill of Scots farmers is indeed a proud recollection.[66]

IMPROVEMENT AT HOME AND ABROAD

Though the Scottish had done much to promote the ideal of agricultural improvement throughout Britain, it was a movement that also derived from extensive native English roots. Scotland may have led the way in promoting improvement but the number of local and specialised bodies within England[67] and among the English abroad was an indication of the extent to which the Board of Agriculture could draw on English as well as Scottish support. Part of the function of the Board was, for example, to co-ordinate the activities of the county and local agricultural societies which grew in number and extent from around the 1770s: the Bath and West of England Society, for example, was founded in 1777 and the Kentish Society for Promotion of Useful Knowledge (of which Banks, in his capacity as a minor Kentish landowner, was made a member at the initiative of William Shipley, the founder of the Society of Arts[68]) in 1788.[69]

These, in turn, stimulated the formation of colonial replicas, though these usually had a short life-span. Most long-lived was the Jamaican Society for the Cultivation of Agriculture and other Arts and Sciences, which lasted two decades.[70] The improvement of agriculture was also the chief goal of some of the more general and learned societies, such as the Society of Arts of Barbados, which wrote to Banks in 1781 asking his assistance in promoting the aims of their society, which had been formed for the purpose 'of discerning the usefull Qualities of the native Productions, Animal, vegetable & Fossil, of Barbados'.[71] The Literary and Philosophical Society of Cork which, as a gathering point for the Anglo-Irish ascendancy, was, in effect, a colonial body, also wrote to Banks on its formation in 1803 asking for his patronage for it as a body dedicated 'to apply[ing] what is already known to the improvement of this part of the British Empire'.[72]

The activities of the Board were also supplemented by a number of specialised societies to promote agricultural improvement, underlining the truth of Ashton's remark that 'In the eighteenth century the characteristic instrument of social purpose was not the individual or the State, but the club'.[73] Predictably, Banks played an active role in promoting such bodies. In 1804, for example, he was a founding member of the Society for the Improvement of Horticulture, which he served as chairman of the committee to frame its constitution and as its vice-president.[74] Most of the Society's other inaugural members were also drawn from Banks's circle.[75] When the veteran gardener, William Forsyth, superintendent of the Royal Gardens at St James and Kensington, approached Banks in 1801 about setting up such a body, he responded enthusiastically, writing that 'I know of no Trade that conceals so many valuable branches of knowledge as that of a gardener & Few subjects where the Public will be more benefited by the disclosures which such a society will immediately occasion'.[76] Banks's enthusiasm for the Society's goals of promoting agricultural improvement through the dissemination of better horticultural methods is evident in the fact that of his fifty-one publications twelve were sent to the *Transactions of the Horticultural Society of London* a figure surpassed only by the seventeen he sent to the *Annals of Agriculture*.[77] Banks was the patron, too, of the Society for the Promotion of Animal Chemistry, founded in 1808 with Banks's close Royal Society confrère, Charles Hatchett, as president.[78] One of this society's first resolutions was to affirm 'That the branch of the Science of Chemistry which comprehends the Analysis and examination of animal substances, and which may properly be called Animal Chemistry, has not hitherto been sufficiently extended; and that the advances already made in it clearly demonstrate its great importance'.[79] An even more specialised body for advancing the cause of agricultural improvement was the Merino Society, which Banks served as its President from its foundation in 1811 until his death in 1820.

Such English-based endeavours to extend agricultural improvement made it appropriate that, along with the Scottish Sinclair, the other major figure active in promoting and sustaining the Board of Agriculture was an Englishman, the indefatigable improver, Arthur Young, who served as Secretary of the Board from its foundation in 1793 until his death in 1820. Fittingly, the Board also virtually expired in the same year. Young had come to know Banks when they both served as stalwart champions of the landed interest during the controversy over the export of wool in the 1780s. *The Annals of Agriculture*, which Young founded in 1784, helped to give voice to the demands of this landed interest and, moreover, gave this still-protean group some sense of identity. Naturally, Banks shared with Young an enthusiasm for promoting the political and economic interests of landowners which both viewed as the mainstay of the nation. When Banks, for example, wrote to Young on the subject of vegetables blocking drains, this mundane subject served as a point of departure for suggestions on how 'the increasing prosperity of the landed interest of this kingdom' might be served by developing 'the theory of draining whole districts, by tapping the mother springs that overflow their surface'.[80]

Both men also shared the Baconian view that science should take the form of useful knowledge and that theoretical speculations should be restrained by practical observation. As Arthur Young put it in 1793: 'Science is never better or more liberally employed, than when exerted in pursuits that assist the more necessary occupations of mankind'.[81] When discussing with Young the gradual dissemination of some of the agricultural improvements dearest to his heart, Banks relegated himself to the position of a theorist–not a complimentary term in his lexicon–to underline the point that his suggestions on such topics as the salvaging of shrivelled corn or the introduction of merinos or spring wheat had to stand the test of agricultural experience: 'I am well aware that information given to practical men by theorists like myself, ought always to be received with hesitation and acted upon with the utmost Caution ... it is by a Long Series of Experiments alone that the adoption of a new custom in agriculture can be established'.[82]

For the gentlemanly promoters of agricultural improvement it was a point of pride that their endeavours were based on the scientific principles which an enlightened age had cultivated and disseminated. As the Reverend Mr Peirson put it in his essay 'On the Connection between Botany and Agriculture': 'Indeed, to do justice to the present age, our improvements in agriculture seem to be built more firmly upon the foundation of philosophy and natural knowledge'.[83] But the improver was also insistent that such scientific respectability should be combined with utility: that science should not only spread enlightenment but also produce bigger and better crops. As Lord Kames wrote, one of the main reasons why 'Agriculture justly claims to be the chief of arts' was that it enjoyed 'the

signal pre-eminence of combining deep philosophy with useful practice'.[84]
More pointedly, the botanist, William Curtis, urged the claims of his
subject on the grounds of its utility–especially in the field of agriculture–
arguing that the ultimate test of the worth of any science was its ability
to confer practical benefits: 'It must be allowed, that all human knowledge
ought to be subservient to the good of society, and in proportion as this
is advanced by any science, so ought that science to be held in esteem'.[85]

The ideals of improvement, then, reflected the values of a leisured class
which was highly conscious of its social position and responsibilities–
responsibilities which included the application of knowledge for the
benefit both of themselves and society more generally. The very different
ideal of scientific knowledge for its own sake ran counter to the view of
such a class, which held that all knowledge had a social function. It also
ran contrary to the Enlightenment's conception of science as 'useful
knowledge' which would serve to liberate humankind both from its self-
imposed 'mind-forged manacles' and the natural scourges of famine and
disease. As the *Tatler*–that journal of enlightened and elite culture–put it
as early as 1710: 'It is the duty of all who make philosophy the entertainment
of their lives, to turn their thoughts to practical schemes for the good of
society, and not pass away their time in fruitless searches which tend rather
to the ostentation of knowledge than the service of life'.[86]

Though President of the Royal Society, Banks clearly subscribed to this
view that scientific knowledge should be applied knowledge or, as one
of his admirers put it, his scientific studies were not 'a mere barren and
speculative amusement' since he was 'ever ready to render them subservient
to purposes of general utility'.[87] Another of Banks's early biographers
made the same point, writing that 'Every thought of Banks was practical:
it tended every where and always to the application of the physical
commodities of nature, to the improvement of the condition and the
multiplication of the physical resources of mankind'.[88] To Matthew
Boulton's enquiry about a mathematically-based paper on naval architecture, he replied that it was insufficiently rigorous for publication in
the *Philosophical Transactions* but nonetheless he endorsed its importance
because of its potential practical benefits. Indeed, Banks made it plain
that he considered such a contribution to the improvement of the trades
of greater significance than a properly-constructed scientific paper,
writing that 'although we lose the benefit of the publication in the
Philosophical Transactions the Public may gain the use of the Boats
which is a matter of infinitely greater Consequence'.[89]

Nor was Banks's view of the Royal Society as a body which provided
a forum for practical improvements as well as scientific findings at variance
with the Royal Society's Baconian origins and much of its early practice.
True to the precepts of its mentor, Francis Bacon, the early Royal Society
had attempted to compile a history of the trades and, as early as 1664, had
set up a Georgical Committee with the goal of 'composing a good History
of Agriculture and Gardening, in order to improuve the practise thereoff'[90]–
it achieved little, however, because of a lack of public interest.[91] Though

the business of promoting improvement was largely delegated by the Royal Society to other bodies, such as the Society of Arts, the Board of Agriculture and the Society for the Improvement of Horticulture, the Royal Society still retained a residual role in the task of promoting practical knowledge. Charles Hatchett, for example, published his paper on the eminently practical subject of 'A Description of a Process, by which Corn Tainted with Must may be Completely Purified' in the *Philosophical Transactions* of 1817 with Banks's endorsement.[92]

For, in an age of improvers, few were more passionately wedded to the cause than Banks who, as one of his obituarists put it, was 'connected with nearly all the improvements of the age in which we live'.[93] The pursuit of improvement gave unity and direction to his myriad activities and offered his contemporaries an example of the way in which knowledge and social utility could be combined in fruitful harmony. Thus the *Agricultural Magazine* of 1811 praised 'his attentions to the improvement of the breeds of our sheep and other domestic animals' as an instance 'of that scientific patriotism, which has long been the best benefactor of our country'.[94] As for most landowners, improvement for Banks began at home on his estates, for Banks *qua* Lincolnshire squire was, like his father before him, an active promoter of schemes, such as drainage and navigation projects, which improved both the yield from the land and the ease with which agriculture and other produce could be moved around the county.[95] As a consequence of such activities the value of Banks's Lincolnshire estates almost doubled in his lifetime.[96] We find him, for example, writing to Blagden from Revesby Abbey in 1814 that 'I am here overwhelmed with the winding up of various improvements'. But, for all the labour involved, such local improvements had shown their worth, for the 'drainage of the fens' by the prominent civil engineer, John Rennie, had proved 'a most beautifull work the Extent is 40,000 acres which were 20 years ago an useless swamp'. Moreover, such improvement was fuelled both by self-interest and patriotism, for the French blockade had resulted in an increase in the value of domestically-produced agricultural produce, thus providing more resources and more incentive to proceed with 'our improvement of the Fens'. Thus 'The cheif support of this Great improvement is owing to the mistaken Policy of Bonaparte'.[97] Within his own county, then, Banks acted as a catalyst for the promotion of improvement and, as a contemporary local historian put it, 'laudably set an example to the gentlemen of the neighbourhood, by the numerous agricultural and other improvements he made, or suggested in the surrounding districts'.[98]

Improvement of one's estate could cover not only crops produced on the surface but also underground, as Banks's extensive involvement in developing the mineral resources (lead, coal and some copper) on his Overton estate in Derbyshire indicates.[99] Characteristically, Banks's interest in this form of improvement extended from his own estate up to the affairs of the nation. He advised other improving landlords, such as Lord Palmerston, a former Lord of the Treasury and a keen clubman, on how best to conduct 'the tryal intended to be made for Coal in your Lordships neighbourhood'. In return, he requested scientific information: 'an exact account of the Strata passed through with the depth of Each'.[100] Such involvements led him, in turn, to study the coal trade as a national interest and, presumably in his capacity as a Privy Counsellor, he produced in 1797 an 'Essay regarding the coal trade, the number of persons it employs, revenue gained from it & the importance of the coal trade to the naval strength of Great Britain'.[101] From the national level Banks's interest in coal extended to the imperial. When Governor Hunter was informed that coal had been discovered near the Hunter River in New South Wales in 1798 he sent samples to Banks. Banks, in turn, prompted the Navy Board to send in 1799 'two borers and six bitts in the *Porpoise* to New South Wales, for the purpose of trying for coals at a more convenient place than where the present mine has been discovered'.[102]

As the example of Banks's promotion of coal mining suggests, the philosophy of improvement drew its sustenance from local roots but it was a creed capable of operating at different levels and in different contexts. Through his work for the Board of Agriculture and other bodies, such as the Society for the Improvement of Horticulture or the more short-lived Merino Society, Banks, the improving Lincolnshire landowner, endeavoured to promote and disseminate measures calculated to advance agrarian development throughout the nation. Predictably, Banks's frequent complaint was that his countrymen were slow to embrace the improvements which seemed to him so obvious and so necessary. As he complained to Benjamin Thompson, Secretary of the Merino Society, 'in the case of improvement the progress is always retarded in the full Ratio of its value'.[103] It was a sentiment he had earlier voiced in 1798 in relation to the fact that potatoes had taken two centuries to become a staple part of the English diet. It recurred in 1806 when, in his discussion of the need to introduce spring wheat, he had discussed the ready acceptance of tobacco in contrast to potatoes with the remark that 'the progress of agricultural improvements has in some instances advanced in the inverse ratio of the utility of the novelty recommended to the public'.[104]

Such frustrations in promoting improvement at the national level by voluntary means help to explain why Banks was naturally attracted to schemes which involved governmental action and the possibility of more expeditious and programmatic implementation. This applied particularly to schemes for improvement at the imperial level where government was somewhat less constrained by local traditions. Banks was one of the most enthusiastic advocates of the view that the territories under the British crown could and should have their flora and fauna improved partly for their own benefit but, more compellingly, for that of Britain. As early as 1775, Banks received the praise of the agriculturalist, Richard West, as someone whom 'Future ages will revere ... when they see the valuable productions of distant colonies naturalised here & in our colonies, which must prove of great advantage to the commerce of these kingdoms'.[105]

Among the institutions which Banks used to promote his plans for imperial improvement was the Board of Agriculture. In March 1799, for example, Banks invoked the good offices of the Board to send seeds from Sumatra to the West Indies; as well he retained some samples for the Royal Gardens at Kew, the great centre of Banks's imperial botanical designs.[106] Indeed, the presidents of the Board of Agriculture appear to have looked to Banks when matters of an imperial nature came their way. In 1799 Banks provided Lord Sommerville with his opinion on the samples of 'Dry or Mountain Rice' received by the Board 'from the Neighbourhood of Serinagur' together with a disquisition on his belief that 'the introduction of new esculent vegetables [was] a matter of material importance to the agricultural interest of this country'.[107] In 1801 Lord Carrington referred to Banks seeds from India presented by the East India Company and, after examination, Banks responded with suggestions about which areas of the Empire would best favour their transplantation.[108] Two years later Banks was requested by Carrington to comment on which of the botanical specimens recently sent from Sumatra 'would prove Desiderata in the West Indies'.[109] Banks was even prepared to promote improvement outside the boundaries of the British Empire, especially if Britain gained a reciprocal advantage thereby. Hence in 1810 he urged the Board to send seeds of a South American grain-bearing plant in return for samples of Sicilian corn (and, particularly, no doubt, its spring wheat), since he believed that the grass would 'succeed in the warmer parts of the Island of Sicily & make an important addition to the Agricultural resources of that Country'.[110]

Sinclair, too, favoured the spread of improvement to encompass the wider Empire contributing, for example, in 1814 a paper entitled 'Hints on the Agricultural Advantages to be Derived from our East India Possessions'[111] which described the attempts of the Board of Agriculture to improve farming in India notably through the introduction of the potato. But Sinclair appears to have been more of a little Englander (or, at least, as a good Scotsman, a little Britainer) than Banks in matters to do with improvements. For Sinclair improvement at home should be the overriding priority of the Board and indeed that of the nation–as he wrote in the report of the Board's committee on enclosures in 1795: 'it surely is desirable that internal improvements should at least be considered as an object fully as much intitled to attention as distant speculations, and when they come into competition, evidently to be preferred'.[112] Sinclair also seems to have been slow to respond to suggestions by the East India Company botanist, Charles Campbell, who was based in Fort Marlbro on Sumatra, about the possibility of 'Transfer[ring] the useful vegetable productions of this Coast to such of our transatlantic Colonies, or other Countries, as the Board of Agriculture might think most eligible'. After a long delay, Campbell wrote again to Lord Somerville, Sinclair's successor as President of the Board of Agriculture, with further samples asking if the 'Institution, over which he [Sinclair] then presided, did not limit its patriotic views alone to the Economies of Britain'.[113] Sinclair's inaction seemed to indicate that it did.

For Banks, however, the activities of the Board of Agriculture, and the mission of improvement generally, spanned the Empire. Just as improvement was to be promoted in the Lincolnshire fens so, too, it was to be promoted through any of the agencies of British rule which impinged on the wider world. An enquiry from the East India Company about their station at St Helena elicited a long policy document outlining plans for new crops, gardeners, and the enclosing of the commons–a project particularly dear to all improvers. In discussing enclosure Banks linked local with imperial improvement by advocating for St Helena 'the system adopted in the Inclosure Acts for the Fens of Lincolnshire'. He also commended the planting of timber that had already taken place 'both at the Public expense and at the Cost of Individuals' since it showed plainly 'that the business of improvement' there was likely 'to be of a Permanent & by no means of a Temporary nature'.[114]

Two years earlier, in another report to the East India Company, he had complimented the governor of the island for 'the improvement . . . owing to this spirit of industry which he has put into motion'.[115] To George Yonge, Minister for War, 1782–3, 1783–94 (and therefore the person responsible for the island of St Vincent which was a military garrison), Banks wrote in 1787 urging a scheme for the transplantation of crops from the Botanical Gardens at Calcutta to those at St Vincent. It was a measure which he described as likely to prompt the inhabitants of both areas to 'look up with veneration to the Monarch who protected, & the Minister who carried into execution a Plan, the benefits of which are above appreciation to the present Generation'.[116]

In August of that same year Governor Phillip, commander of the First Fleet (which was to initiate European settlement in Australia), was busy in Rio de Janeiro collecting the plants which Banks had specified as being likely to be of benefit to the new colony.[117] This was to be but the first of a series of attempts by Banks to make Britain's newest and most distant possession self-supporting and, if possible, of economic benefit to Britain through the techniques of agrarian improvement.[118] Reciprocally, Banks attempted to transplant from New Holland plants which might survive in Britain. Though these ultimately provided little economic benefit they did promote a horticultural art which he regarded as being 'likely to prove advantageous' 'that of inuring plants, natives of warmer climates' to the British climate. 'The settlement lately made at New Holland', he continued, 'gives a large scope to these experiments; many plants have been brought from thence which endure our climate with very little protection'.[119]

Around 1807 Banks also pondered on what introduced crops would best suit the colony of Newfoundland and how best these could be adapted to local conditions.[120] Such global transplantations were, of course, intended primarily to benefit British trade but Banks, in the Baconian and Enlightenment tradition of utilising science for the 'relief of man's estate', rejoiced that what was good for Britain was often good for humanity more generally. As he wrote in a letter to a member of the House of Assembly in Kingston, Jamaica, in 1791, apropos of Bligh's second (and successful) voyage to transplant breadfruit from Tahiti to the West Indies:

> It is difficult, in my opinion, to point out an undertaking really replete with more benevolence, more likely to add comforts to existing people, and even to augment the number of those for whom the bounties of creation were intended, than that of transporting useful vegetables from one part of the earth to another where they do not exist.[121]

Banks was not alone in viewing the ideal of improvement in such a wide, imperial perspective. Among his contemporaries who urged the necessity of bringing the Empire within the pale of the improver's activities was Sir John Dalrymple. In a characteristically Scottish manner he combined practice of the law with the promotion of agrarian improvement (including among his successes the promotion of a technique for making soap out of herrings). Dalrymple sent his fellow Scot, Lord Bute, then the king's first minister, 'a plan by the Transplantation of plants for raising in one or other part of the British dominions every article of commerce that depends upon vegetable production'.[122] There is no evidence that the letter had a practical effect on the deliberations of HM Government but it may have played some role in creating the climate of opinion which was later to make Banks's imperial botanising possible. Lord Sheffield, Banks's close ally in protecting the interests of the landed interest and a President of the Board of Agriculture, was, like Banks, active in promoting improvement both within his county of Sussex and, through his influence in government, at the level of imperial policy. His proposed policy for implementing the terms of peace at the conclusion of the War of American Independence, for example, included measures for promoting 'The rapid progress in the improvement of Surinam & Demerary with their dependencies', which he saw as being 'capable of producing any quantity of Sugar'.[123] Another ally in the cause of imperial improvement was Sir Thomas Raffles, the founder of Singapore, who corresponded with Banks on both botanical and anthropological matters. To Raffles the spread of empire and the spread of improvement should accompany each other—hence in his *History of Java* he insisted that under the Dutch 'the arts of agriculture, and the improvement of society' had made little progress[124] as a way of justifying British expansion into the Dutch East Indies.

Furthermore, the work of the Board of Agriculture in promoting agricultural improvement at home and, to a lesser extent, abroad had been prefigured by another body, The Society for the Encouragement of Arts, Manufactures and Commerce (founded in 1754), which differed from the Board in having no direct ties with government. As its name suggests, this Society was devoted to promoting improvement in all aspects of society. Thus its founding charter began by affirming 'Whereas the Riches,

Honour, Strength and Prosperity of a Nation depend in a great Measure on the Knowledge and Improvement of useful Arts, Manufactures Etc'.[125] True, its title did not specifically include agriculture which its founder, William Shipley, regarded as being outside its province, but in practice the Society came to regard the promotion of agrarian improvement as one of its primary tasks.[126] The arch-improver, Arthur Young, for example, was one of the Society's keenest supporters, having been elected as a member in 1769 after winning a gold medal for a paper on raising hogs; in 1779 he was awarded another gold medal by the society for his work on the 'clustered potato'.[127] In the face of the near famine of 1795, the Society joined with the Board of Agriculture in persuading the population of England to accept the potato as a substitute for grain. The Society's motives for promoting improvement were the outcome of that mixture of patriotic and mercantilist sentiment which played so large a part in shaping Banks's views about the need, wherever possible, to replace foreign imports with products grown or manufactured within Britain or its Empire. Appropriately, one of its short-lived predecessors bore the robustly John Bull title of the Anti-Gallican Society, having been founded in 1745 'to promote British Manufactures, to extend the commerce of England, to discourage the introduction of French modes and oppose the importation of French commodities'.[128] In the first volume of its *Transactions* (1783) the Society made plain its mercantilist motivations. Commenting on its system of premiums for colonial products, it declared that

> The Society, influenced by the tenor and spirit of sundry acts of parliament subsisting for more than a century past [is] of opinion that to encourage in the British Colonies the culture and produce of such commodities as we must otherwise import from Foreign nations, would be more advantageous to the navigation and commerce of this kingdom, than if the like things could be raised on the island of Great Britain.[129]

Such motives help to explain why the Society played an active role in promoting the introduction of new plants to Britain's colonies and why, too–despite the regular incantation of the phrase 'offered for the advantage of the British colonies'[130]–it did nothing to foster manufactures in the colonies which became simply suppliers of raw materials. The Society was, then, one of the major agencies in spreading the ideals of agrarian improvement to the larger Empire and in many of its projects it prefigured the later work of Banks. Using a system of prizes known as 'premiums' to promote innovations the Society's colonial schemes included measures later associated with Banks, such as the transplantation of breadfruit from Tahiti to the West Indies, cochineal insects from the Spanish dominions to Jamaica[131] or the growing of hemp (an essential item for the Navy and hence for British power) within the Empire. The botanical gardens on the island of St Vincent, which formed an integral part of Banks's world-wide network of bases for the transplantation of plants, owed their origin to the fact that in 1762 the Society offered rewards 'to any one who would cultivate a spot in the WEST INDIES, in which plants, useful in medicine, and profitable as articles of commerce might be propagated'.[132] Like Banks, too, the Society sought to make Britain more self-reliant in industries closely allied with agriculture, industries such as tanning and dyeing.[133]

In undertaking such schemes for the promotion of imperial botany, the Society was encouraged by Ellis, Collinson and Fothergill, that trio which had done so much to revive British botany from its soporific condition in the mid-eighteenth century. Their work did much to link botany with the cause of agrarian improvement and, in particular, improvement in its imperial dimension–a tradition on which Banks was to build.

Ellis was a member of the Society from its beginnings until 1761 (when he probably left because of bankruptcy) and served on various of its committees. At his instigation the Society in 1758 offered premiums for useful plants which could be grown in the then-British colonies of Georgia and the Carolinas, a prize which established a precedent for a whole series of such imperial awards. It was he, too, who helped to initiate the establishment of colonial botanical gardens by persuading the Society to establish such a garden in the Carolinas.[134] Ellis also attempted to enlist political support for such aims, addressing to Lord Shelburne 'A Catalogue of such Useful Foreign Plants as will Thrive in the Different Climates of our American Dominions' which, again, clearly stated the mercantilist ideals which animated the Society: 'That the encouraging our Colonies in North America and the West Indies to raise those commodities, which we take from Foreigners, would be a means to extend and promote the exportation of our own Manufactures, and to lessen the Ballance of Trade against us in our commerce with other Nations'.[135] Collinson, too, looked to the Society to promote aspects of imperial botany which might enhance British economic well-being. In 1763, for example, he wrote to the Society suggesting that it encourage the planting of tea in West Florida, since 'no vegetable Production deserves more our Care and Culture, than the Tea Tree, for which we pay annually such immense Sums'. He also urged the Society to concern itself with 'the producing of Silk in our Colonies' as a measure which was 'of such great Importance to the Interest and Trade of Great Britain, such vast sums being paid in ready Money for the same'.[136] Fothergill, similarly, advocated the planting of a greater range of useful plants in the British colonies in North America, including the cultivation of sago in Georgia using techniques brought back from China.[137] In contending that botany had a crucial role to play in the economies of empire, then, Banks could draw on an already well-established set of arguments and practices which his botanical predecessors had helped to disseminate through the institutional mechanisms of the Society of Arts.

Though there was such a close parallel between both the aims and the specific measures advanced by the Society and by Banks, the latter's involvement in the affairs of the Society of Arts appears to have been less than whole-hearted. As part of his entry into London learned society the young Banks joined the Society in 1761 and he may have made at least one decisive intervention in its affairs. For it may have been he who, after receiving a letter from the Governor of St Vincent island on the subject of breadfruit,[138] persuaded the Society to offer a prize for its introduction to the West Indies in 1777.[139] If so, he probably enlisted the support of John Ellis who, in 1775, dedicated a pamphlet to the Earl of Sandwich proclaiming the merits of the breadfruit as 'a most necessary and pleasant article of subsistence to many' which 'must be easily cultivated in our West Indian islands'.[140] In support of these claims Ellis invoked the opinion of 'a gentleman of distinction who accompanied Captain Cook'-plainly a reference to Banks.[141] Appropriately, the Society's breadfruit premium was ultimately awarded to Bligh in 1793 after a voyage prompted and organised by Banks. Overall, however, Banks's energies were concentrated on the Royal Society rather than the Society of Arts. For the growth of the Society of Arts also appears to have led to some form of a demarcation with the Royal Society from at least around 1775: the former focusing more on 'the applied arts' (what a later age would call 'technology') and the latter on the promotion of science and 'useful knowledge'.[142]

After Banks became President of the Royal Society in 1778 his relations with the Society of Arts continued to be cordial though rather formal. A year after taking office as President the Society of Arts asked him, in his official capacity, to assist in the judging of standards of weights and measures.[143] In 1783 Banks coupled an attempt to persuade the Society to offer a reward for the growth of senna in British Antigua with a tribute to it as a body 'to whom this Country is indebted for so many valuable additions to Her Commerce which but for their laudable exertions would now have remained unknown or at least unoccupied by our Countrymen'.[144] Banks supported the Society's activities in the field of agrarian improvement at home by sending it, in 1788, a recipe for the cure of scab in sheep along with a tribute 'to the patriotic views which have ever guided their [the Society's] conduct'.[145] He helped, too, in the liaison between the Society and some of the outposts of empire: it was he, for example, who, in 1789, conveyed the thanks of the Society of Arts of Barbados-'instituted', as Banks put it, 'for similar purposes' to its metropolitan counterpart-for the gift of volumes of the *Transactions of the Society of Arts*.[146] Banks also conveyed the thanks of Dr Thomas Dancer, Superintendent of the Jamaica Botanic Gardens, for an award in 1791 which, he added, would encourage Dancer's 'exertions' which 'in due time [would] effect some desirable improvements in the culture of the valuable spices and drugs committed to his care'.[147] Overall, then, though Banks shared many of the goals of the Society and valued its work, he appears to have been largely content to leave it to its own devices while he pursued similar aims through different channels-these being principally the mechanisms of government, which his position as President of the Royal Society and confidant of the king enabled him to utilise.

IMPROVEMENT AND INDUSTRY

The fact that the Society of Arts sought to foster the spirit of improvement both in agriculture and in the trades underlines the extent to which the ideal of improvement came to engulf almost all sections of the economy.

For the landed gentlemen, who were the chief promoters of the reforming ideal, agrarian improvement was the first, and most obvious, area where the techniques of improvement should be applied but they favoured an extension of such methods to manufactures as well, particularly since most manufactures were directly reliant on agriculture for their raw materials. Besides, as a number of publicists for the improving cause protested, agriculture was a form of manufacture, turning raw materials into more valuable products. As the Scottish agriculturalist, James Anderson, wrote: 'And is it not sufficiently obvious, that agriculture, although it has been distinguished by another name, is, to every intent and purpose, a manufacture in as strict a sense of the word as the forming a yard of broad cloth'.[148] The example of agriculture, then, helped to promote the spread of improving zeal to the field of manufactures and economic life more generally. The Breconshire Agriculture Society, for example, rechristened itself in 1756 'A Society for Encouraging Improvements in Agriculture and Manufactures, and for Promoting the General Good of the County'. As one of its promoters wrote in 1755 to the Society of Arts–on which it plainly drew for much of its inspiration–if such bodies were founded in every county the result would be 'one of the most flourishing kingdoms in the World; as it would draw the attention of the nobility and gentry . . . to objects truly worthy of it–the encouraging and establishing manufactures, and the promoting improvements . . . cultivating a true public spirit, a spirit of universal benevolence'.[149]

In the spirit of such ideals a gentleman agricultural improver such as Banks naturally also devoted himself to promoting improvements in manufactures. When his friend and fellow agriculturalist, Lord Sheffield, wrote to him on the subject of wool, Sheffield also included 'a Parcel of Sheffield Manufactures' (knives, forks, razors and scissors) illustrative of the 'comparative State of Manufactures'. For he knew that 'It is your way to understand everything that is usefull & provided it be usefull, nothing comes amiss to you'.[150]

And, indeed, Banks's interest in promoting utility and improvement did extend to the world of manufactures and particularly to areas such as the woollen industry where there was a natural association with his endeavours to promote agrarian improvement through the introduction of new breeds of sheep. Even as a young man, Banks had taken a keen interest in the beginnings of the mechanisation of textile production, a subject of obvious relevance to a sheep-farming squire. His journal of his excursion to Wales records his getting up early on 26 December 1767 'to See the famous Shuttle [presumably that devised by John Kay] with which Broad Cloth is wove by one man sitting still which was used to be done by two or more throwing the shuttle from one to another'. He added that 'its contrivance is simple and ingenious' and included a lengthy description.[151] Appropriately, two decades later, Banks was associated with the early moves to mechanise the spinning of wool. At the instigation of his friend, Josiah Wedgwood, Banks met with Arkwright, with a view to obtaining for him a parliamentary reward for setting up machinery capable of spinning wool. In the event, however, there was no direct outcome from this meeting and Wedgwood in a letter of 21 February 1786 vainly attempted to prompt Arkwright into action, since Banks wanted to 'have something certain to lay before his parliamentary friends'.[152]

Banks's interest in promoting the woollen industry–both through the improvement of breeds of sheep and through the use to which the resulting wool was put–extended to other aspects of the manufacturing process, such as the finishing of the cloth. Thus, in 1787, a woollen merchant by the name of John Wallace wrote to Banks with a sample of a new form of woollen cloth, since he was 'sensible of the very active and laudable part you take in promoting the improvement of the Manufactures of this Country'. In the mercantilist spirit which was so commonly linked to the improvers' endeavours, Wallace apologised for the fact that the cloth was of French manufacture adding that he had purchased it 'with no other view than to improve our own'.[153]

But though Banks, as a Lincolnshire woolgrower, naturally showed particular interest in improving the manufacture of wool he was also eager to promote the growth of the cotton industry. Here the link with Banks's own agricultural interests was less direct for the raw cotton was grown abroad. However, Banks did do all that he could to facilitate the growth of cotton in territories under the British flag[154]–a further instance of the way in which Banks gave the movement for agrarian improvement an imperial dimension. Happily, too, the improvement of the woollen and cotton industries could frequently be combined, particularly in relation to the processes of dyeing and bleaching, where Banks was active in directing new scientific developments along channels which might assist the improvement of manufactures. In 1787, for example, Banks was able to report with satisfaction to Blagden that their close Royal Society associate, the chemist, Richard Kirwan, had informed him of a new method of preparing the dye, Prussian Blue, which 'he considers ... to be of great importance ... as it realy improves of that useful material & renders it cheaper at the same time'.[155]

Four years later one of the pioneering cotton manufacturers set out to enlist the interest of Banks 'in the rising Cotton Trade of this Kingdom'. He added that 'a mind like his; (active in general interests & indefatigable in important enquiries)' would rejoice in 'its wonderful & daily improvements', particularly 'the efforts in Mechanism to produce its thread & the late extraordinary success in Chymistry in establishing its Colors & the process of Bleaching'.[156] Banks continued to promote these latter improvements by publicising recent French chemical work which bore on the art of bleaching, being much assisted in this endeavour by his friends, Blagden and Lord Auckland, who had a wide acquaintance in French scientific circles.[157] Thus, in 1788, Banks was thanked at a Manchester public meeting to which he sent a letter 'giving an account of the improvement of the known process of M.Bertollet' for his 'readiness to promote the Interests of Commerce'.[158] He also ensured that his botanical collectors paid particular attention to the dyeing industry or to already established local techniques for dyeing. As late as 1815, for example, Banks received from Ceylon an account of the process used there to dye cloth red, together with samples of the materials used, following investigations by the Royal Society chemists into the chemical basis of Ceylonese dyeing techniques.[159]

Banks's interest in the mechanisation of spinning and the techniques of dyeing and bleaching was one example of the way in which his enthusiasm for agrarian improvement extended to the processes by which agricultural products were processed. Another such example is his interest in early attempts to mechanise the milling of grain. In 1782, at the instigation of Matthew Boulton, a charter was sought to establish a mill, known as the Albion Mill, on the Thames near Blackfriars Bridge and, despite opposition from the millers, it was granted. Predictably, the mill's engines were manufactured by Boulton and Watt; the mill also engaged the talents of another luminary of the early Industrial Revolution, the Scot, John Rennie, for whom the project marked the beginning of an illustrious career as a civil engineer in London. The mill made a considerable impact, both because of its central location and because it provided an early and graphic illustration of the possibilities of the new-fangled steam engine. However, after beginning production in 1786 it was burnt down in 1791 and, though it had for a time reduced the price of flour, its owners were left with a large debt.[160] Hence Boulton and Watt's enthusiasm to offer the site and its remains for sale when, in 1798, Banks made enquiries on behalf of the government about erecting mechanical mills on the banks of the Thames.[161]

From its beginnings Banks had taken a close interest in the project and the possibilities it offered for cheaper flour. On 23 October 1785 he reported to Blagden that Boulton was in town on business connected with the Albion Mill and that 'The Steam Engines at Albion Mills are to be worked with Watt's new invented furnaces to burn all the smoke'.[162] By 1798, the need to reduce the cost of foodstuffs had become ever more pressing, which no doubt accounts for government moves to investigate the possibility of erecting the new power-driven mills. It was probably on Banks's initiative that the Privy Council Committee on Trade (with Banks as one of its members) considered in November 1797 'the advantages which had accrued to the Public from the Operations of the Albion Mills',[163] for a similar printed document to that on which the committee based its deliberations is included among Banks's papers.[164] But, despite Banks's interest in this early application of steam power to the improvement of the processing of grain, the project does not appear to have received the blessing of government, perhaps because it became a casualty of the French Wars which were, by 1798, more and more occupying the energies of the State.

Banks's interest in the Albion Mills was but one instance of his early awareness of the possibilities offered by the steam engine. As early as 1778–within a few years of the development of the first Boulton and Watt steam engine around 1775–Banks began negotiations with Boulton regarding the installation of one of his machines at the Gregory mine on Banks's

(Above, left) Banks by Thomas Phillips, 1814. The Corporation of Boston commissioned this portrait as a tribute to one whose 'judicious and active exertions improved and enriched this borough and neighbourhood'. Appropriately, Banks is depicted perusing sketches and plans which no doubt relate to the improvement of Lincolnshire. Courtesy of the Guildhall Museum, Boston, Lincolnshire

(Above) Matthew Boulton (1728-1809). Painting by an unknown artist. Courtesy of the National Portrait Gallery

(Left) James Watt (1736-1819). Painting by C. F. von Breda. Courtesy of the National Portrait Gallery

Overton estate.[165] It was finally in operation by 1784, replacing an old Newcomen engine built in 1748; true to Watt's claims for the separate condenser, it consumed less than a third of the fuel of its predecessors.[166] In December 1783–two years before the steam engine was applied to cotton manufacture–Banks was corresponding with Boulton about the possibilities of further improving this motor of the Industrial Revolution, sending Boulton a report of a London mechanic who claimed to be able to construct steam engines suitable for 'smaller mechanical purposes'. Boulton proved sceptical of the claims of this would-be 'improver of Steam Engines', having 'seen the schemes of a hundred projectors or improvers prove abortive' but, nonetheless, replied to Banks that 'if any Improver, discoverer or Inventor of Steam Engines can promote my Interest or I promote his I am ready to conform to what candor & justice dictate'.[167]

OLD SOHO FOUNDRY.

Matthew Boulton's Soho Works (established near Birmingham in 1762). Courtesy of the Ironbridge Gorge Museum Trust

Banks's interest in steam engines, then, derived in the first place from the wish to exploit the resources on his own estates in the form of the mineral deposits at Overton though this fascination with the possibilities of steam power soon became more general in character. This is an instance of the way in which the improving impulse could extend from agriculture to the land and its products more generally and thence to other sectors of national economic life. One aspect of Banks's activities as an improving landowner, then, was an interest in mining technology. His journal of an excursion to Wales in 1767–8, for example, included a detailed account of 'a Copper mine belonging to the duke of Devonshire probably the richest in the Island this year' for, he added enthusiastically, 'Every Circumstance of this mine & the hill it is in are so wonderfull that they merit a very particular description'.[168] Banks's expertise in applying recent technology to the problems of mining led to his being consulted by neighbouring landowners. Thus in 1794 Matthew Montagu expressed his pleasure at meeting Banks who 'promised me a lesson on mining in a neighbouring mine belonging to himself'. Montagu added that he was 'happy in an opportunity of laying the foundations of an intimacy which may be very useful to me'.[169]

Closely associated with his preoccupation with mining was an interest in metallurgy. On this same youthful expedition to Wales, for example, Banks closely inspected the famous Darby iron works at Coalbrookdale which, he wrote, 'Probably cast greater Quantities & better metal than any other in the Kingdom. [H]ere all Large Casting work is done in the Greatest Perfection'.[170] Later, while visiting Scotland in 1772, Banks made sure to inspect the Carron iron works and the home of its founder, Dr Roebuck. Appropriately, he combined this with a trip to the Barrowness coal mine, which produced the coal on which the Carron works and Roebuck's patent for using pit coal in iron manufacture were based. His visit further encapsulated the character of the early Industrial Revolution by taking in the nearby canal locks and drawbridge.[171] In his less peripatetic days after he became President of the Royal Society in 1778, Banks continued to maintain an interest in the spread of improvements in the field of metallurgy. Blagden, for example, informed him in 1791 that 'In Glamorganshire I found they had made an improvement in the manufacture of coak iron, which seems likely to be of consequence. It consists in melting the raw pigs in a finery, till they carry a good Cinder, & then running the metal off into moulds, which in that state is called refined or prepared metal'.[172] In this area, as in others, Banks's inclination to favour those aspects of science likely to result in practical improvements is evident. When, around 1801, he advised the British Museum on the need to build up a collection of minerals, he did so on the grounds that it would benefit 'those persons who pursue the study of mineralogy a science of the utmost importance to the mining interest & consequently to the prosperity of the metallic manufactures of their kingdoms'.[173] It was to Banks, too, that government would, on occasions, turn when its policies impinged on the metallurgical industries. Thus in 1798 Banks provided George Rose, the Secretary to the Treasury, with an account of the quantity of pig-iron made in Great Britain in 1796, together with an estimate of the likely revenue from a proposed tax on pig-iron.[174]

Banks's enthusiasm for the better use of the earth and its products also extended to an interest in the making of pottery. His interest was quickened by the fact that recent improvements in British manufacture had opened the possibility of greater national self-sufficiency and a lessening of the drain of bullion to China to pay for fine porcelain–always a painful loss to one, such as Banks, inclined towards a mercantilist view of national economic life. Thus Banks favoured retaining a heavy tariff of seventy-five per cent on Chinese imports 'to protect our Potteries at home', which still found it difficult to compete with Chinese imports even though they had been greatly improved both in their production methods and labour practices–or, as Banks put it: such potteries 'are now conducted on the extensive scale of Manufactories & enjoy all the advantages that are derivd from large Capital & the subdivision of labor'. As a result of such improvements, Banks noted with satisfaction, 'Our Potteries have however already awakened the jealousy of our Neighbors by materially excelling the rest of Europe in their Manufacture & underselling them at Market; the Art is now become a National object & no inconsiderable source of British prosperity'.[175]

In the improving of pottery it was, of course, Banks's friend, Josiah Wedgwood, who led the way, as Banks had come to appreciate after a visit to his potteries on his way to Wales in 1767. He recorded, for example, that 'Mr Wedgwood has lately introduc'd into this manufactory the use of Engine Lathes which work upon the Clay with the greatest Ease'.[176] As the years went by his admiration for Wedgwood's ability to transform a traditional craft by the application of more scientific methods of production and organisation (or, as the eighteenth century would have put it, by thoroughgoing 'improvement') increased. In 1787 Banks described Wedgwood as someone 'whose genius & ingenuity has put the business of Pottery in England so much above its original mechanical rank ... excelling both as an art & a Science'.[177] In the same vein Banks had written to Wedgwood in 1784 about the way in which some French visitors were so 'struck with the high state of improvement in which they found your manufacture that they determined without delay to visit the Father of so valuable a National Treasure'.[178] In the previous year Banks had been the recipient of a letter from Wedgwood (later published in the *Philosophical Transactions*) illustrating the extent to which Wedgwood had sought to combine science and utility. For Wedgwood outlined some of his 'long course of experiment, for the improvement of the manufacture' which resulted in the development of a thermometer to measure very high degrees of heat.[179]

As in the field of agrarian improvement so, too, in his efforts to improve manufactures Banks attempted, where possible, to use the resources made available to Britain by its imperial expansion. Thus, in 1787, Banks sent on to Wedgwood some samples he had received from India within 'the Territories of the East India Company' of what was supposed to be 'the real Caoline [i.e. kaolin or "China clay"] ... of the Chinese'–thus opening the exciting possibility of Britain freeing herself from dependence on China. Hence Banks's request to Wedgwood that he would undertake experiments on the material 'as this appears an object of some national concern'. But, in the event, Wedgwood's experiments showed that the material was of no use. Experiments with clay from St Helena sent by Banks to Wedgwood also appear to have had little success.[180] Wedgwood was more sanguine, however, about the possibilities offered by clay

ETRURIA WORKS.

Josiah Wedgwood's Etruria Works (established near Stoke-on-Trent in 1769).
Courtesy of the Ironbridge Gorge Museum Trust

samples which he received, thanks to Banks, from the newly-founded
colony of New South Wales. After analysis Wedgwood concluded that the
material 'might certainly become the basis of a valuable manufacture for
our infant colony there'.[181] Banks also enlisted Wedgwood's aid as
someone 'who have turnd the art of pottery into a Science'[182] in attempting
to reduce Britain's dependence on China by an act of industrial espionage:
the inclusion of a skilled potter in the delegation accompanying Lord
Macartney on his embassy to China from 1792 to 1794 in order to learn
about the techniques the Chinese employed for making fine china.

    Banks's interest in the possibilities of improvement, then, extended well
beyond the central core of his activities as a landowner interested in
improved agriculture and in areas of manufacture, such as woollen or
wheat mills, immediately dependent on agriculture. His enthusiasm for
the application of improvements extended to areas such as mining,
metallurgy and potteries which had a much more tenuous connection

with the activities of an improving landlord concerned to put to good use the mineral resources of his estate as well as its land. Banks could also display an interest in trades quite removed from the ownership of land. In 1814, for example, he wrote to Blagden about the way in which the printing press 'has been very materialy improved by a variety of Persons & is now become a very usefull implement'.[183] Banks's work as an improver is an instance of the way in which the governing elite of England, though its political roots and much of its economic sustenance came from the land, were also well aware of the extent to which national prosperity was dependent on the efforts of manufacturers and others outside the gilded circle of the landed classes. As Banks's efforts to promote improvement in all sectors of the economy indicate, the landed classes were well aware of the importance of the middling orders in creating a nation which was, as far as possible, self-sufficient thanks to the judicious use of the resources within its own shores and those over which it had control as a result of its imperial expansion.

This same awareness of the importance of improvement both of agriculture and manufacture on the part of some of the prominent members of the landed classes can also be seen in another project with which Banks was closely involved, the Royal Institution. The full extent to which the Royal Institution was envisaged by its founder, Count Rumford, as being a vehicle for the promotion of the improving spirit is borne out by his original proposal for the body as 'a Public Institution for Diffusing the Knowledge and Facilitating the General Introduction of Useful Mechanical Inventions and Improvements'. He also saw it as providing 'for Teaching, by Courses of Philosophical Lectures and Experiments, the Application of Science to the Common Purposes of Life'-a phrase which underlines the extent to which Rumford shared with Banks the view that the proper function of science was chiefly to provide some 'relief of man's estate'. Indeed, Rumford, in the tradition of Bacon, saw it as the Institution's mission to overcome the gulf between 'philosophers and those who are engaged in arts and manufacture'. He also hoped that it would overcome 'The slowness with which improvements of all kinds make their way into common use, and especially such improvements as are the most calculated to be of general utility'.[184]

Though Rumford was the main founder of the Royal Institution he was out of Britain some forty per cent of the time between 1799 and 1802 (when he finally parted company with the Institution), so that much of the work involved in its founding fell on the shoulders of prominent agricultural improvers such as Banks.[185] This association between the early Royal Institution and the cause of agricultural improvement is brought out by Berman's calculations that of the first fifty-seven proprietors of the Institution-those who provided its financial base-eleven were official members of the Board of Agriculture, while fifteen were honorary members of that body; furthermore, of the inner core of managers and visitors, fourteen belonged to the Board and eight 'were among the most outstanding agricultural improvers or industrial entrepreneurs of the age'.[186] The original meeting held to establish the Royal Institution was held at Banks's home in Soho Square on 7 March 1799 and, following a motion moved by Rumford, Banks was 'requested to take the chair, and ... to preside at all future meetings of the managers, until, a charter shall have been obtained from his Majesty for the Institution'.[187] Banks also served as one of the original managers. As Martin points out, his support was essential both to avoid any possible conflict with the Royal Society, which was very jealous of any competitors–and particularly so under Banks's presidency–and also to obtain the support of the king of whom Banks was a confidant.[188] In 1801, at Banks's recommendation, the Royal Institution appointed Thomas Young as professor of natural philosophy, a post he held only until 1803, having proved to be 'not adapted for a popular lecturer'.[189]

More successful was the appointment in the same year of Humphry Davy as lecturer in chemistry, in which capacity he delivered, on behalf of the Board of Agriculture (and at Banks's instigation), a series of lectures on the application of chemistry to agriculture.[190] This common commitment to the cause of agricultural improvement on the part of both the Board of Agriculture and the Royal Institution was also brought out in Davy's lectures. In them he described 'Agriculture, to which we owe our means of subsistence' as 'an art intimately connected with chemical science'.[191] Such a statement was in accord with his more general thesis that 'Science has done much for man, but it is capable of doing still more; its sources of improvement are not yet exhausted'[192]–a view which summarised the aspirations of the Royal Institution. Davy also commended his patrons from the landed class–'The guardians of civilization and of refinement, the most powerful and respected part of society'–for taking on the responsibility for promoting the process of improvement and 'for giving up many of their unnecessary enjoyments, in consequence of the desire to be useful'. By so doing, he wrote in a phrase that indicates how closely intertwined were the goals of improvement and of enlightenment, 'the human species is capable of becoming more enlightened and more happy'. But Davy also made it clear that his conception of enlightenment had nothing in common with the utopian 'Republic of Virtue' which had so recently and so bloodily been established across the Channel. Rather he looked to the patient processes of improvement, the building on what had gone before to provide better hope for the future:

> In this view we do not look to distant ages, or amuse ourselves with brilliant, though delusive dreams concerning the infinite improveability of man, the annihilation of labour, disease, and even death. But we reason by analogy from simple facts. We consider only a state of human progression arising out of its present condition.[193]

In one of his lectures later delivered to the Board of Agriculture Davy again underlined his conviction that it was part of the *noblesse oblige* of the landed class to promote improvement for it 'was the higher classes of the community ... the proprietors of land ... who are fitted by their education to form enlightened plans ... it is from these that the principles of improvement must flow to the labouring classes of the community'.[194]

In a number of ways the practical realisation of this goal of linking science with the cause of agricultural improvement strengthened Davy's association with Banks. Banks well realised the benefits which chemistry offered for agriculture, commenting in a letter to Arthur Young (Secretary of the Board of Agriculture) of May 1803 that 'the Com[mitt]ee [of the Royal Institution] are aware that at present the Science of agriculturall chemistry is in its infancy'. Appropriately, in the same letter he also proposed both that Davy should undertake analysis of soils and that he should be appointed as a professor of agricultural chemistry with a salary of one hundred pounds per annum.[195] In the following year Davy analysed wheat specimens for Banks[196] a practice he repeated for the Board of Agriculture the following year.[197] Thanks to Davy's 'ingenious analysis' Banks was able to conclude triumphantly 'that bread made of the Flour of Spring Wheat is more nutritious than that made of winter wheat'.[198] With due deference Davy, in turn, responded to Banks's comments on his experiments by remarking that 'I had no idea when I performed them that You would have made so curious an application of them'.[199]

Along with their partnership in promoting agricultural chemistry, Banks and Davy were also drawn together by their common interest in improving tanning. This was an area of manufacture of obvious concern to the landed interest, a fact which helps to account for the particular emphasis it received in the affairs of the early Royal Institution. Banks's involvement in attempts to improve the tanning trade and to reduce its reliance on the increasingly expensive commodity of oak bark (which by the end of the eighteenth century accounted for three-fifths of the tanner's manufacturing costs)[200] predated the formation of the Royal Institution. This may partly have derived from the fact that Banks's native Lincolnshire contained many tanneries[201] but probably more important was his association with Lord Hawkesbury, the energetic President of the Board of Trade. For the increasing problems of the tanning trade in finding the necessary raw materials had become a matter of concern to government: in 1790, for example, Hawkesbury sent his thanks to Banks for supplying him with a list of queries to be put to the tanners.[202] In 1798 the two men again discussed the subject of tanning since, following consideration of the matter before the Board of Trade,[203] a bill was before the Parliament to repeal the clause in an act of James I restricting the tanning of leather to oak bark.[204] Banks appears to have had an ambivalent attitude towards such a proposal. Among his papers was a copy in his own hand of a submission urging that the proposed bill be rejected, both on the grounds that it would result in a decline in the quality of leather and because 'This indulgence might be the means of discouraging the growth of Oak Timber in this Country'[205]–the latter consideration being one that would have weighed heavily with Banks because it might weaken Britain's naval strength. For, among the many improving societies with which Banks was involved was the Society for the Improving of Naval Architecture founded in 1791 with Banks as vice-president–a society which, as its proposal for establishment acknowledged, derived its inspiration and methods from 'that Patriotic Society, the Society of Arts which had shew[n] the advantages which the husbandmen of this kingdom have derived from the invention of new and the improvement of old instruments of husbandry of various kinds'.[206]

Such an approach to the issue of the repeal of this ancient statute reflects the view held by Banks and most of his contemporaries that the workings of the economy ultimately ought to be controlled in the interests of the state as a whole–for nothing was more essential for British power than the maintenance of naval strength. His lukewarm attitude to the tanners' demands suggests why the lobbying of Samuel Purkis, a leading tanner who became one of the first life subscribers to the Royal Institution, had, at first, little success. For Purkis in 1798 had applied to Banks as someone who took an interest 'in every thing that concerns the Trade & Manufacture of the Country' to support the repeal of legislation 'if the subject should come before you at the Board [of Trade] officially'.[207] Perhaps because of Banks's ambivalent attitude, Purkis followed this up with a second letter urging, in language that was likely to appeal to Banks, that it would be 'impolitic to shut the door against *all possible improvements* or discoveries in any branch of Manufacture'.[208]

The attempt to repeal the act in 1798 failed, though eventually, following a Board of Trade enquiry launched in 1803, the traditional restrictions on the leather trade were abolished in 1808–a minor instance of the increasing dismantling of traditional and paternalistic controls on economic life which characterised the early nineteenth century. In these proceedings Banks played a major role and by this time he actively promoted the abolition of such traditional restrictions. If Banks had indeed moved from early ambivalence to positive support for the new proposal, such a change in attitude may well have been due to the realisation that the insistence on using oak bark was leading to a great increase in the importation of oak bark rather than the planting of more English trees. It was Banks who, in February 1803, provided Lord Glenbervie, Vice-President of the Board of Trade and Surveyor-General of Woods and Forests, with a digest of the 'Life Character & Behaviour of the Statute' together with a recommendation that it be repealed.[209] He was later, in 1806, to be commended by John Reeves, the King's Printer, for the encouragement he gave to the new process of tanning leather in the hope that he would also expedite changes in the printing industry.[210] Purkis also lavished praise on him in 1810 as the modern patron of tanners.[211]

But the tanners' commitment to the liberalisation of State controls over their industry was a limited one. For they looked to Banks not only for help in repealing traditional restrictions but also to invoke the aid of government in reducing foreign competition. In the submission which the tanners sent to the Board of Trade via Banks in 1801, they alluded to the fact that the recently concluded Peace of Amiens with France would again expose them to foreign and, in particular, French competition. Their wording reflects the increasing self-confidence and sense of self-importance of manufacturers and merchants: in their view of the British economy it was not agriculture but 'our Manufacture [which] may be considered as the chief Sources of National wealth'; consequently, its 'Encouragement becomes a primary object of National Concern'. After this preamble the memorial then proposed an increase in tariffs on foreign leather 'to afford that Degree of Encouragement to our Home Manufacture which it is the National Interest to support'. It also drew attention to Britain's relative backwardness in promoting technical innovations in the leather trade or, as the tanners' memorial put it: 'In the progressive State of Improvement which the Arts of late have attained, Tanning has abroad been particularly attended to. France has furnish'd a succession of Chymists, the most experimental in Europe, who have made discoveries applicable to their art of the greatest Importance'.[212] Banks duly sent this memorial on to the Board of Trade, receiving the thanks of Lord Hawkesbury for so doing. With a tribute to the importance that he accorded to Banks's advice on issues related to manufacture, Lord Liverpool (as Hawkesbury became after 1796) added that 'I do not however think it right to take any Step in this Business, without your previous Consent'.[213]

Predictably, Banks devoted particular efforts to remedying the relative scientific backwardness of the British tanning trade to which the memorial had alluded. Thus, on 29 June 1801–no doubt largely at Banks's instigation–the managers of the Royal Institution resolved that a course of lectures on the 'Chemical Principles of the Art of Tanning be given at the Royal Institution by Mr Davy'.[214] Davy also set in train a series of experiments which culminated in the publication in the *Philosophical Transactions* of 1803 of a paper entitled 'An Account of some Experiments and Observations on the Constituent Parts of some Astringent Vegetables; and on their Operation in Tanning'–a paper that won for him the Royal Society's Copley Medal. In the course of this paper Davy paid tribute to Banks for the discovery of a new tanning agent. 'The discovery of the tanning properties of catechu', wrote Davy, 'is owing to the President of the Royal Society who, concluding from its sensible properties that it contained tannin, furnished me in December 1801 with a quantity for chemical examination'.[215]

The route by which this substance, catechu or *terra japonica*, reached Davy at the Royal Institution was a roundabout one reflecting Banks's imperial network of scientific collectors. As Davy himself described it 'This substance is the extract of the wood of a species of the mimosa, which grows abundantly in India'[216] and its arrival in Britain was a consequence of Banks's connections with the East India Company. Banks was interested in its possibilities because he was aware of the way in which it was used in India–an example of his willingness to learn from other cultures. Thus his papers include 'A description of a new plant from which the Terra Japonica is extracted', which outlines the way in which the extract was obtained and its use in India in dyeing, in tanning and as a medicine.[217] The success of Davy's experiments prompted the managers of the Royal Institution to attempt to persuade the East India Company to import the substance in commercial quantities, an enterprise in which Banks took the lead. On 2 February 1802 Banks's request that the East India Company consider importing catechu was officially recorded[218] and the wheels of the East India Company slowly turned, with requests to various officials in India to conduct experiments. By January 1804 the East India Company finally responded to Banks, sending him further samples of the substance together with a piece of leather tanned by one of the company's employees, Dr Berry, with the request that 'you [Banks] will have the goodness to procure the Opinions of Chemists and other Scientific Persons thereon as speedily as may be convenient'.[219] Banks did indeed proceed with all due haste and in the following month reported on 'the probability of Cutch [catechu] becoming an article of consumption in this Country'.[220] True to its traditions, however, the East India Company remained cautious of change. Its Bengal Despatches of the following August included an item on *terra japonica* (which was derived from catechu) together with a copy of 'some important observations of the Right Honble Sir Joseph Banks on that article'. While noting that 'The increasing scarcity of Oak-bark renders the Importation of other Tanning Materials an object worthy of Consideration' the report added that 'we do not wish for any larger consignment of the article from you than may be sufficient for full & complete experiments of its qualities'. Part of the reason for such hesitancy is suggested by a remark preceding this passage which was deleted, namely that 'the Subject is of importance to the landed Interest of these Kingdoms'.[221] For the East India Company was wary of promoting imports, such as an alternative to the bark of oak or elm trees, which would bring it into conflict with the landed gentlemen who were, in many cases, its own shareholders. Furthermore, as Berman points out, the company had a ready market for catechu in India where, among other things, it was used in adulterating tea.[222] Such considerations help to explain why–despite Banks's advocacy–the company did not promote the import of catechu.

Another attempt by Banks to use his imperial connections to advance Davy's work on tanning also appears to have borne little fruit. In 1804 Davy conducted some experiments on leather tanned in New South Wales with mimosa bark which, no doubt, he obtained through Banks, but this led to no commercial consequences.[223] Subsequently, in 1816, Banks supplied William Brande, Davy's successor as professor of chemistry at the Royal Institution, with yet another possible tanning agent from his network of collectors: 'Oong Poey' or Chinese galls. However, it, too, proved a disappointment, Brande's experiments showing that 'leather produced by their infusion [was] extremely brittle when dried'.[224]

Banks was, however, more successful in promoting, both through the Royal Institution and the Royal Society, further research on tanning to assimilate and, if possible, to surpass improvements of the French chemists to which the tanners had referred in their memorial of 1801. One French chemist they had mentioned by name was Armand Séguin and it is no surprise, then, to find in 1803 Banks requesting Blagden (then in Paris) to obtain a copy of his report on tanning.[225] As Banks's close Royal Society colleague, Charles Hatchett, showed in his series of papers on tanning published in the *Philosophical Transactions*, Séguin's work was important in showing that the 'chief characteristic property' of tannin was 'that of precipitating gelatine or glue from water in a State of insolubility'. But, using substances supplied by Banks, Hatchett was also able to indicate areas where Séguin's work had been surpassed by English chemists like Davy, Chenevix and (by inference) himself. Hatchett also suggested the possibility of manufacturing a tanning agent from animal as well as vegetable substances. Most beguiling of all was his supposed demonstration 'that a tanning substance may be artificially formed by exposing carbon to the action of nitric acid'. Such experiments Hatchett regarded as showing the worth of chemistry and its ability to 'render great and essential services to the arts and manufactures'.[226] It was a comment that underlined the natural connection between the investigation of the scientific basis of tanning and the work of a body such as the Royal Institution, which was dedicated to the promotion of improvement both in agriculture and manufacture. And tanning, which impinged so directly on the interests of both the landowner and the manufacturer, was a natural focus for the Royal Institution's endeavours to encourage such improvements.

Despite Banks's active role in promoting activities such as research into agricultural chemistry and tanning–activities which embodied so well the aspirations of Rumford for the Royal Institution–both he and Rumford grew increasingly disenchanted with the Institution. From 1804 the Royal Institution appears to have concentrated more on its role as an educational rather than as a research institution. One major symptom of this was that in February 1804 the Institution's printing office was closed and the publication of its journal suspended.[227] Moreover, an increasing emphasis was being placed on philanthropic rather than scientific pursuits. That, at least, is the inference to be gathered from remarks made by Wilberforce in praise of Sir Thomas Bernard, the two men having worked together in establishing the Society for Bettering the Condition of the Poor in 1796, a body active in the establishment of the Royal Institution. For in July 1806 the diarist, Farington, records Wilberforce as speaking 'highly of Mr Bernard as the principal cause of many useful establishments. He said the Royal Institution was almost ruined under the management of Sir Joseph Banks & Count Rumford, but Bernard had recovered it & it was now more flourishing than before'.[228] It was such a disagreement over the direction of the Royal Institution to which Banks must have been referring when, in June 1804, he wrote to Rumford that the Royal Institution had 'fallen into the hands of the Enemy & is now perverted to a hundred uses for which you and I never intended it'. Banks alluded to the fact that Rumford had in effect severed ties with the Institution when he left for the Continent in May 1802, after what appears to have been a disagreement with Thomas Bernard and Sir John Cox Hippsley,[229] by adding:

> I could have successfully resisted these innovations, had you been here; but alone, unsupported, & this year confind to my house for three months by disease, my spirit was too much broken to admit of my engaging singly with the host of H[ippsley]s & B[ernard]s who had possession of the fortress.

Poignantly, he concluded,

> Adieu, then, Institution! I have long ago declard my intention of attending no more.[230]

That Banks saw the Royal Institution as having surrendered its scientific credentials is brought out, too, by a letter of the following year replying to Sir Francis Baring, who had vainly attempted to interest him in playing a part in the establishment of the London Institution, a body similar in character to the Royal Institution.[231] '[T]he Royal Institution', wrote Banks, 'was at first wholly under the Direction of Persons entirely addicted to Science & has not improved since the management of it has passed into other hands'.[232]

Such divisions within the Royal Institution reflect the different goals of its founders. On the one hand there were the hopes of those like Bernard and other members of the Society for Bettering the Condition of the Poor that the institution might alleviate the increasing pauperisation that rapid population growth and rapid economic change was bringing in its wake; on the other, the belief of Banks, Rumford and others that the Institution existed to promote a fruitful marriage between science and the trades. Both goals could be and, for a time, were accommodated beneath the umbrella of the improving ideology which animated the Royal Institution. Improvement could embrace not only better agricultural or manufacturing techniques but also improvement of society through the application of a rational and orderly approach to its problems. Thomas Bernard, in his introduction to the first volume of reports of the Society for Bettering the Condition of the Poor urged: 'Let us therefore make the enquiry into all that concerns the POOR, and the promotion of their happiness, a SCIENCE–let us investigate practically, and upon system ... let us unite in the extension and improvement of those things which experience hath ascertained to be beneficial to the poor'.[233] Understandably, then, the supporters of the Society for Bettering the Condition of the Poor were drawn to Rumford and the early Royal Institution by projects such as Rumford's earlier success in alleviating the condition of the poor of Munich through a highly organised system of public works and soup kitchens, using Rumford's own design of fuel-efficient stoves to prepare a broth based on a rigorous application of both scientific and economic principles.[234] Thus in 1797 Rumford was made a member of the Society's general committee for life 'in consideration of [his] extraordinary services for the benefit of the poor'.[235] Both Rumford and Banks grew disenchanted with the direction of the Royal Institution, not because they no longer subscribed to such philanthropic aims, but rather because they regarded the Institution as having lost contact with the scientific foundations on which its activities should be based.

Nonetheless, Banks remained in sympathy with the aspirations of those who wished to deal with pressing social problems, such as mass pauperisation, through the orderly methods associated with the ideals of the true improver. When famine threatened in his own area of Lincolnshire in 1800 he dealt with it in a manner not dissimilar to Rumford's approach to poverty in Munich, by attempting to provide basic supplies which could be stretched as far as possible by the application of scientifically-based principles. Thus he provided over a ton and a half of the relatively novel food, rice–presumably because it was easy to store and transport. Because it was unfamiliar he also had to supply printed sheets detailing ways of cooking rice, together with suggestions of how rice and wheat might be combined to make a kind of bread. Predictably, given his enthusiasm for potatoes as an alternative to grain, he also supplied sheets of recipes for using grated potatoes instead of flour.[236] These vegetables were also supplemented by barrels of herrings. The business of overseeing the distribution of the food was entrusted to his under-steward, James Roberts, who was given instructions as to which groups should benefit from his largesse. On 13 April 1801, for example, he wrote with instructions that the supply of rice should be reduced to half for those families of labourers now able to work, but full rations should be continued for 'those who are feeble and unable to do without the whole, women especialy'.[237] The experience of dealing with such famine relief prompted him to correspond in 1803 with the French chemist, Antoine Cadet de Vaux, who supplied him with a recipe for a nutritious and highly economical bouillon made from pulverised bones.[238] Banks replied by describing such an application of experimental techniques to so basic a social problem as being a 'discovery [which] is very interesting to humanity & [which] will in time become highly advantageous to all nations'. Banks had to acknowledge, however, that when, two years before, soup kitchens had been established because 'a bad harvest threatened us with Famine', the poor had declined such soup the following year. Nonetheless, he had some hopes that Cadet de Vaux's brew would prove more successful since he promised to 'do my endeavour to make your usefull discovery public'.[239]

IMPROVEMENT AND SOCIETY

The example of Banks, together with the concerns of the founders of the Royal Institution, are instances of the extent to which the problem of poor relief was linked with the cause of agricultural improvement. The system of parochial relief provided for by the Poor Law was most firmly rooted in the countryside and it was among the agricultural labourers of the 1790s that the consequences of population increase, low wages and harvest failures became most obvious. In its publication *On the Present Scarcity of Provisions*, which appeared in the black year of 1795, the Board of Agriculture added its voice in support of a form of poor relief which was similar to that instituted by the Justices of the Peace of Buckinghamshire at Speenhamland in the same year with such important long-term consequences. Thus the Board recommended that 'the labouring poor should be supplied with the necessaries of life at a reasonable rate' by subsidising their wages 'by private subscriptions or the parochial funds'.[240] The Board was also the forum in which Sir John Call, FRS, chose to present some of his speculations about the demographical pressures underlying the increasing incidence of poverty. In a paper of 1800, which he later sent to Banks, he suggested, in the manner of modern demographers, that the rise in population could be linked to changes in marriage patterns which, in turn, resulted in an increase in births. Thus he saw the rise in population as being associated 'in country parishes at least [with] the more frequent Marriages of Labourers & Mechanics'; he also linked it with changes in death rates caused by the spread of inoculation.[241]

Banks, together with other improving landlords such as Lord Sheffield, took a close interest in the Poor Law both because it was one of the most important instruments for maintaining social order and because it was a major item of expenditure for any landowner. It was, moreover, a burden that was greatly increasing–in Lincolnshire the poor rates in the period 1783-5 averaged £43,024 per annum but by 1813-5 they had reached £230,191 per annum.[242] In 1787, for example, we find Thomas Gilbert–the author of Gilbert's Law of 1782, which allowed parishes to combine to form unions to establish workhouses–asking Banks to consult with the gentlemen of Lincolnshire about 'the state of the poor and ... the measures propos'd on that head'.[243] Banks and his Lincolnshire neighbours continued to keep a close eye on developments which might concern the Poor Law and therefore their taxes. His old friend, Thomas Coltman, wrote to him in 1797 about Pitt's proposed reforms of the Poor Law, warning that 'Mr Pitt has engaged in a serious undertaking to meliorate the Condition of the Poor-The Fabrick of the 43d of Elizabeth [the original Poor Law] will stand better by itself, than with any addition, under the perturbed state of Mind the Country is in at present'.[244] With the end of the Napoleonic Wars the pressure for a wholesale change-or improvement-of the Poor Laws increased, with Banks's close friend and fellow agricultural improver, Lord Sheffield, being among the loudest voices for reform. In Sheffield's view the system needed root and branch change-as he wrote in a pamphlet of 1818: 'An attempt to patch up and amend a system, which is defective in its very principle, and still more in practice, will deceive and mislead the country'. This was not to say that Sheffield had abandoned the improving principle that the new should be built on the old with no sudden attempt to erect a totally new social order as the French revolutionaries had sought to do. For, he argued, 'The system must be ... gradually ... abandoned' and that it was 'highly necessary to obviate the mischief and desolation that would arise upon suffering the hasty abolition of those laws'.[245] In place of the traditional system with its heavy reliance on outdoor relief Sheffield-in common with the Poor Law Amendment Bill (which was finally passed in 1834)-wished to see an extension of indoor relief based around the workhouse. For the institution of the workhouse lent itself to that orderliness and system which was a part of the improver's outlook-as it also was to be of the outlook of Utilitarians, like Chadwick, who eventually framed the provisions of the New Poor Law of 1834.

Sheffield acknowledged that workhouses were poorly run at that time but, nonetheless, urged that 'we know from repeated experience, that well-regulated houses of industry are productive of great benefit'. Needless to say, Sheffield also emphasised the importance of agricultural improvement as a means of providing work and therefore of reducing the burden of the Poor Law. As he wrote in a subsequent pamphlet: 'The extension of agriculture is by far the best mode of furnishing employment to those who are in want of work'. But Sheffield qualified his hopes for such a remedy by pointing to obstacles in the way of an extension of agricultural improvement such as the cost of implementing the necessary changes. Furthermore, Sheffield pointed to the impoverished state of the country and the great expense of obtaining parliamentary acts permitting enclosure and of 'rendering the land when inclosed productive'.[246]

As Sheffield's comments suggest, enclosure was one of the most tangible ways in which the goals of the improvers impinged on the larger society. For improvers like Young or Sheffield, enclosure offered the best way forward from the confusion of traditional farming practices to the orderly and productive methods of improved agriculture. Hence the impatience evident in Sheffield's comments about the difficulty and cost of effecting enclosures. Sheffield had also earlier bemoaned the fact that so much of the country was left as common land without being enclosed, for he regarded the extent of enclosure as being a guide to the level of improvement more generally. Thus in his *Remarks on the deficiency of grain*, written in 1801 when England still faced the spectre of famine, he wrote: 'We seem to indulge the idea, that England is a highly-improved country; not one fourth of it is, however, cultivated as it should be; and no civilized country has so large a proportion of waste lands'.[247]

Predictably, too, Banks was an enthusiast for enclosure as a means of promoting more orderly agriculture. Where it could be shown to be both profitable and socially advantageous, he also supported enclosure's close cousin, the draining of fens, which was of considerable significance in Banks's native Lincolnshire. His concern with enclosure is evident in his remark on visiting the island of Staffa: 'The first principle of improvement is however on this island totally neglected I mean that of dividing the lands'.[248] Nonetheless, Banks recognised that if enclosure was to promote social as well as agrarian improvement it needed the support of the neighbourhood-hence the remark of his steward, Stephenson, that Banks 'disliked an enclosure unless it was with the consent and approbation of the generality of the commoners'.[249] Generally, the assumption of Banks

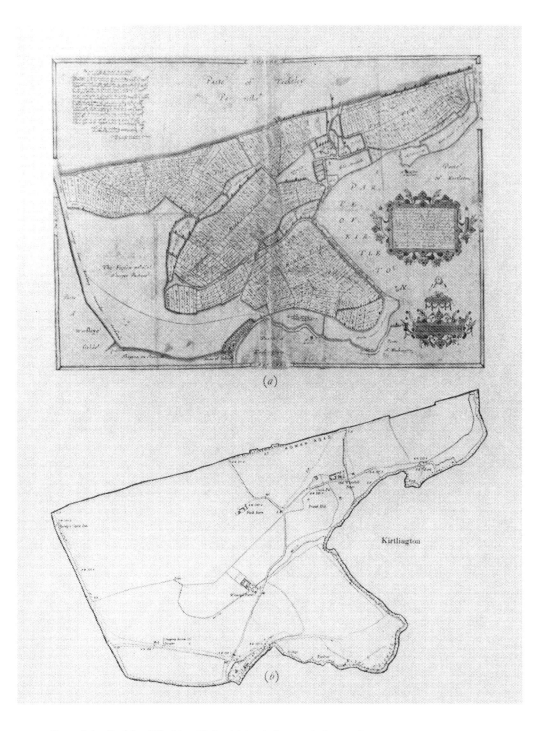

Part of the Parish of Tackley, Oxfordshire, before and after enclosure.
Map (a) Courtesy of the President and Fellows of Corpus Christi College, Oxford
Map (b) Courtesy of Ordnance Survey (Crown copyright)

and his fellow improvers was that improvement of agriculture or of industry brought with it improvement of society more generally. But Banks was capable of recognising, however, that the benefits of improvement had sometimes to be balanced against the hold of tradition or the need to maintain social harmony.

Improvement, then, was a creed elastic enough to stretch beyond its origins in agriculture to encompass industry and even social policy. It was also elastic enough to draw together the landholders, who were the original advocates of improvement, and members of the middling orders associated with the commercial and industrial advances of the eighteenth century. Thus improvement was one source of that remarkable degree of co-operation and cohesion which–generally speaking–characterised the relations between the traditional landed governing class and the mercantile and industrial classes who, more and more, were producing the wealth on which Britain's increasing imperial power rested. The goals of improvement at home assisted by expansion abroad (particularly into areas capable of supplying such vital raw materials as cotton or requisites such as tea) were goals that helped to unify the landed and commercial classes, softening the tensions that rapid social and economic change inevitably brought in its wake. As Bayly writes, there was 'a remarkable consensus in national aims between a revived and prosperous landed class with an emboldened professional and business class. All these elites had the common aim of domestic, and especially agricultural, "improvement", and national aggrandisement overseas'.[250] Of course, such a union of classes around the altar of improvement was not without its strains. The nineteenth-century debates about the Corn Laws–that symbol of the political power of the landed classes–had their dress rehearsal in the late eighteenth century.[251] Another area of conflict between the landed and the manufacturing classes in the late eighteenth century was the debate in the 1780s over whether or not wool should be exported–a controversy in which Banks figured prominently.[252] But such tensions did not fundamentally undermine the partnership between these two classes; the increasingly numerous and wealthy members of the commercial and manufacturing classes were generally content to leave the business of politics to the traditional governing classes since both groups shared common goals in domestic as well as foreign policy: the enlargement of the nation's wealth at home through the application of the principles of improvement and the expansion of its trade abroad. Industry and commerce were generally not seen as challenging the traditional social order but rather as increasing the wealth and, therefore the power, of the nation and its traditional leaders, the landowners. Thus the new profession of civil engineers enlisted for their society such landed patrons as the Earl of Morton (a former President of the Royal Society) and Banks–together with other 'men of science & gentlemen of rank and fortune, who had applied their minds to subjects of Civil Engineering'–in the confidence that theirs was a profession which was entitled to 'the encouragement of a great and powerful nation'.[253]

As an active promoter of improvement in both the agricultural and industrial spheres, Banks provided a conspicuous example of the way in which a landed gentleman could share many of the aspirations of the increasingly articulate middling orders. Like them, he valued efficiency and regarded the production of new and improved industrial products as a major source of national pride and power. Banks enjoyed a lifelong friendship with Boulton, probably the most important figure in directing the innovative techniques of such inventors as Watt along productive and profitable channels. The two men came to know each other in January 1768 when, on the way from his excursion through Wales, Banks visited Soho 'where Mr Boulton to whom I had a Letter Lived & Carried on his Manufacture which he does in a very noble way'.[254] The warm relations between the two men were further strengthened in 1781 by Banks's admiration for the methods and machinery employed by Boulton and Watt in the improvement of the Gregory Mine in which Banks had an interest–hence Banks's praise of Boulton and Watt for 'The candor & liberality with which you have conducted yourselves in the whole of this business'.[255] Out of these early beginnings developed a lifelong partnership. Banks, in his capacity as an adviser to the government on scientific issues, looked to Boulton to provide the technical advice and innovative industrial techniques which might serve the interests of the British State. Reciprocally, Boulton gained from his association with Banks access to the inner workings of government which was to prove particularly important in promoting the use of Boulton's techniques and machinery to replace many of the antiquated procedures at the Mint.

It was a partnership which reflected in miniature some of the characteristics of the relationship between the landed and manufacturing classes more generally–Banks, as a representative of the former, provided access to the skills of government and administration while Boulton, the industrialist, provided advice on the wealth-producing techniques which were to enhance the power of the British State for the benefit of both social groups. In 1786, for example, Banks wrote to Boulton about the commercial possibilities of platina since 'I know no one so able as yourself to inform me whether such a thing would be usefull in manufacture & no one so ready to Oblige his Friends'.[256]

By 1786 Boulton had begun his long involvement with the business of coining, an enterprise which was to involve him more and more closely with government and with Banks who served as his main advocate in the relevant circles. Boulton's limited involvement in the issuing of new gold coinage in 1785 served (as Watt put it) 'to revive his ideas on the subject of coinage which he had considered as capable of great improvement'. Such improving zeal in the management of coinage, an area so vital to the economic health of the country, was evident, too, in the way in which Boulton undertook the minting of a hundred tons of copper coins for the East India Company in the following year for (to cite Watt once more): 'Much ingenuity, time & great expence were required to perfect the application of the steam engine to coining'.[257] This, in turn, led to a number of other orders, including one on behalf of the early revolutionary government of France. Naturally, Boulton hoped that such successes would lead to large-scale orders from the British government but this was to prove a long and tortuous process. By June 1789 he was attempting to enlist Banks's support in his dealings with government by providing him with a memorandum on copper coinage, pointing out that the shortage of legal tender had led to such consequences as counterfeiting and an increasing reliance on private tokens. Naturally, too, he emphasised that he had the necessary equipment and expertise to remedy this situation, being capable of producing coins of a quality not 'having been attained in any Mint in Europe, nor being attainable by any coining Machine but his'.[258] A month later Boulton followed this up with a letter to Banks outlining the way in which the tardiness of government threatened to frustrate this 'the most capital improvement that was ever made in the art of coining'. For, as yet, government had made no real attempt to avail itself of Boulton's techniques though he had 'first entered on the subject with zeal in consequence of Mr Pitt's expressing to me a desire that some means might be found to put an end to so great an evil [as the shortage of copper coinage]'. Furthermore, complained Boulton, 'I have expended many thousand pounds in the completion of my invention, and necessary preparations for a new copper coinage'. Boulton concluded with an appeal to Banks's good offices, arguing that he would benefit the public, as well as Matthew Boulton, if Banks took advantage of 'any opportunity [which] offers wherein you can forward this necessary business'.[259]

Banks shared Boulton's view that his method of coining was indeed a 'capital improvement' and thus used his influence to promote Boulton's proposals within the recently-established Privy Council Committee on Coin (founded 1787) and to enlist the support of its energetic chairman, Lord Hawkesbury. He commended the arguments that Boulton had advanced in his memorandum and letter; indeed, he asked him to forward on 'any new ones that may occur to you at any future period'.[260] But the delays continued, to Boulton's great vexation; by the middle of the following year he was again expressing to Banks his hope that eventually 'my improvements [might be] rendered usefull to the publick by an application of them in his Majesties Mint'.[261]

In the event Boulton's schemes for remedying Britain's shortage of copper coinage were not endorsed by the government until 1797.[262] It was perhaps not coincidental that in March of the same year Banks was formally made a member of the Privy Council Committee on Coin; it was he that was to provide much of the liaison between Boulton and the Committee. A visit to Birmingham in August the same year provided Banks both with an opportunity to provide the Coin Committee with a report on the workings of Boulton's machinery[263] and to renew an acquaintance 'with everything that bears relationship to so old a Friend as you are who if I am not mistaken received me into your house & shewed me the town of Birmingham more than 39 years ago'.[264] The visit–and Banks's friendship with Boulton–bore tangible fruit in Banks's enthusiastic description of Boulton's industrial processes in a letter to Hawkesbury.[265] Banks remarked on the 'incredible Quantity' of twenty to twenty-five tons of coins a week that Boulton could produce and (though he was doubtful whether silver coins could be produced with quite the same rapidity) he urged the Committee to order more copper coins. Banks continued to smooth Boulton's path in his dealings with the labyrinthine workings of the late eighteenth-century British State. Two years later, he arranged for the Master of the Mint 'to see your excellent workings'.[266] When, shortly afterwards, Boulton suspected that the officers of the Mint were involved in a form of industrial espionage with a view to using his techniques themselves it was to Banks he turned, writing that 'I shall be very thankfull for your advice which I will certainly follow'.[267] A few days later Banks wrote to let Boulton know that he stood ready to help him overcome some of the delaying tactics of the Treasury, assuring him that 'I shall now be better & better able every day to be usefull to you & I shall always be very willing I promise you'.[268] Thanks to Banks's good offices Boulton's manufactures were even granted a royal viewing, for in 1804 the king was given one of Boulton's new specimen gold coins and (as Banks put it) expressed 'His Royal Approbation of it'. This led Banks to express the hope to Boulton that he would be permitted to mint gold as well as copper coins–'that you will on this Occasion, be permitted to shew your Skill as a Coiner & your Patriotism as a Man'.[269] His hopes were, however, a little dashed when he attempted to expedite the adoption of Boulton's coinage by the Bank of England and found the directors 'as torpid as toads'. Banks, however, 'persuaded them that the king had approved of your coin & the country in my opinion expected it'.[270] Banks also continued to lobby government on another front by urging the merits of Boulton's 'improvement in Gold Coin' in the Privy Council Committee on Coin.[271] This close working relationship with Boulton also extended to his partner, Watt: later that same year, for example, Banks requested Boulton 'to thank Mr. Watt for the very intelligent manner in which [you] were so good as to explain to me the Principles & Powers of your admirable manufactory'.[272]

All these examples are instances, then, of the way in which Banks, as a representative of the landed governing class, could help to facilitate the work of Boulton and Watt, representatives *par excellence* of the new manufacturing class–a class which, over the course of the next century, was to undermine the traditional social order and, with it, the position of the landed class. But in the late eighteenth century, when the Industrial Revolution was in its infancy, the class antagonisms between the middling and upper orders which were to emerge in the nineteenth century were constrained by patterns of traditional deference and by the reciprocal benefits both groups still gained from the existing social order.

Boulton, a conservative in politics, does not appear to have questioned the division of labour whereby the landed classes dealt with issues of government while he devoted himself to the development of manufactures. His friendship with Banks enabled him to gain access–albeit at one remove–to the government bodies which determined state policy on the issue of coinage, an area in which Boulton had invested much capital and expertise. And, despite numerous frustrations, Boulton's relations with government proved advantageous to both sides. This partnership between Banks and Boulton was founded, in turn, on a common adherence to the ideal of improvement, a word which Banks commonly employed in his correspondence with Boulton on coinage matters. As we have seen, like most of his class, Banks's enthusiasm for improvement had arisen out of his experience of agricultural improvement but had later been extended to embrace other sectors of national life such as manufacturing. Banks admired Boulton (and Watt) as major figures in promoting improvement in industry–hence his high praise for Boulton as 'one of the best and most useful men that has appeared in my life time in any country in Europe'.[273] The comment also underlines the warm personal bond between the two men and the absence of any class-originated condescension or distrust. When Banks's mother died in 1804, he turned to Boulton as 'an Old Friend' for solace;[274] two years later, in a letter to Boulton's son on mint business, he added 'my very kindest Remembrances to your good Father my very old & much respected Friend. I long to see him once more at least before we part'.[275] The relations between Boulton and Banks, then, typified the fruitful partnership which could exist both on the professional and personal planes between men of the late eighteenth-century landed and middling orders when they were united in a common purpose by goals such as the promotion of improvement. This partnership of landowner and industrialist could also take a very local form, as the landowner benefited from the increase in the value of his land as a result of industrial development, whether this took the form of mining or the erection of factories.[276]

The Anglican Boulton and Banks were fellow conservatives politically[277] but, as we have seen, Banks also enjoyed good relations with the more radical dissenting Wedgwood, another major representative of the embryonic manufacturing classes. Again, the link between the two men owed much to their common enthusiasm for the goals of improvement–an ideal which Wedgwood attempted to implement in the many different facets of his famous Etruria works, from the finishing of his pottery to the way in which he deployed his work force as productively as possible.[278] His belief in the possibilities of improvement was clearly expressed in an early letter to his cousin and future partner, Thomas Bentley:

> Many of my experiments turn out to my wishes, and convince me more and more, of the extensive capability of our Manufacture for future improvement. It is at present (comparatively) in a rude uncultivated state, and may easily be polished, and brought to much greater perfection.[279]

Commercial success as a result of such improvement also enabled Wedgwood to gain an entrée into the oligarchic world of the landed classes–thus in 1765 he could write to Bentley that 'I scarcely know without a good deal of recollection whether I am a Landed Gentleman, an Engineer or a Potter, for indeed I am all three and many other characters by turns'.[280]

Wedgwood's easy bearing in the clubbable world of the elite is apparent in a chatty letter from Banks in 1784 about the affairs of the Royal Society Club. Banks evidently valued Wedgwood's participation in the Club for he told him 'You are believe me good Sir much wanted here'. He also took Wedgwood into his confidence about the internal politics of the Royal Society and the way in which the number of 'disaffected' had diminished from forty-seven to two so that 'I think we have a fair prospect of Peace returning'.[281]

Though Wedgwood was one of the principal organisers of the commercial classes' first major lobbying organisation–the General Chamber of Manufacturers[282]–Banks nonetheless looked to him as an ally in some of the late eighteenth-century conflicts between the commercial and the landed interests. When immersed in the battle between the wool manufacturers and the wool producers, Banks sought to enlist his aid by complaining of the way in which 'Mr Anstie & the woolen manufacturers seem determined to give battle to us poor miserable growers' in an effort 'to draw the chains of monopoly tighter'.[283] Banks's fellow defender of the landed interest, Lord Sheffield, also looked to Wedgwood as a bridge between the commercial and the landed orders–hence his remark to Banks, apropos of the recent 'extravagance on the subject of wool', that he had 'desired Wedgwood to signify at the Chamber of Manufacturers, while it was busying itself on that head that I beleived, there was no ground for their apprehensions, that it was injudicious to require more sacrifice from the landed interest'.[284]

The fact that Sheffield chose Wedgwood as his intermediary with the Chamber of Manufacturers is testimony to Wedgwood's importance in the founding and promotion of that body. Among its other functions the Chamber served as a partial remedy for the fact that Birmingham–the commercial base for Wedgwood and Boulton (another supporter of the Chamber)–lacked a parliamentary representative. Its foundation in 1785 derived from the agitation about trade matters stirred up by the Irish Trade Treaty of the same year, with the Chamber acting as an effective brake on Pitt's attempt to permit freer commercial intercourse between the two kingdoms–something which the manufacturers saw as an encroachment on their English markets.[285] The Chamber was also vocal in the debates surrounding the French Commercial Treaty of 1786, brokered by William Eden, a close associate of both Banks and Sheffield. The French Treaty was indeed an occasion when the interests of at least some manufacturers generally coincided with those of government, for by facilitating a freer exchange of goods between the two countries the treaty increased the potential market for the Birmingham manufacturers. Hence the Chamber's praise for the treaty as one based upon 'liberal and equitable principles, [which] promises to be advantageous to their manufacturing and commercial interests by opening a new source of fair trade to both nations'.[286]

Outside the inner ring of innovative Birmingham manufacturers, however, other more traditional industries regarded the treaty in a more hostile spirit seeing it as facilitating an increase in French competition. The result of such a conflict of interests was that the Chamber became divided and, consequently, its political significance subsided.[287] Plainly, then, the middling order was no monolithic class interest locked in combat with the traditional landed elite. As a promoter of freer trade, Wedgwood was involved in conflict with such traditional commercial interests as the wool manufacturers who feared any measure that would increase foreign competition. So, too, representatives of the landed interest such as Banks and Sheffield also opposed the wool manufacturers for endeavouring to impede the free trade in unprocessed wool. On occasion, then, common economic interests could lead to alliances which crossed the divide between the commercial and landed orders.

On the one hand, Wedgwood's role in the founding and promotion of the Chamber of Manufacturers indicates the growing self-assurance of the industrialists and their belief that their interests could not be left entirely in the hands of the traditional landed class. On the other hand, however, Wedgwood's relations with Banks and Sheffield over so contentious an issue as the Wool Bill underline the fact that the Chamber's foundation did not lead to a polarisation between the classes. For Wedgwood could continue to employ the chameleon-like skill of moving with ease in both the world of the landed gentlemen and that of his fellow manufacturers while retaining the respect of both.

Naturally, there were some areas of conflict between the commercial and landed interests. Indeed, Banks was at the centre of the landed interest's agitation for legislative change regarding two contentious issues: the controls on the export of unprocessed wool and the increasingly vexed matter of restrictions on the importation of corn. But though in hindsight it may be possible to discern in these conflicts the embryonic beginnings of the bitter class divisions of the nineteenth century, they would have seemed to most contemporaries relatively small squalls which did little to impede the smooth passage of the ship of state. The traditional organic metaphors for society–much loved by Banks and other defenders of the landed interest–still dominated much of the thinking of the age and thus reinforced the view that, as in the human body, the interest of one member must necessarily complement the interest of another. During the controversy over the export of wool in the 1780s, for example, the MP for Boston described 'the dispute between the growers of wool and the manufacturers' as being 'like the dispute between the members of the same body: their real interests can be but one'.[288] And even if this organic metaphor for society was replaced by the more up to date analogy with a machine, the same moral applied. Such an emphasis on social harmony was supplemented and strengthened by the ideal of improvement with its assumption that improvement in any sector of the economy would ultimately be of benefit to all. Moreover, the language of improvement served to create a bond between the agriculturalist and the industrialist as both saw themselves as aspiring towards similar goals. The fact that improvement was a cultural ideal which had been first nurtured by the

landed interest and then promoted in other areas of the economy, such
as manufacture, further helped to strengthen such a sense of common
purpose. Britain's reputation as a land where improvement had proceeded
furthest also generated a glow of patriotic pride in which both agriculturalist and manufacturer could bask. Thus Banks, when presenting
the Copley Medal for 1791, spoke of England as being 'proud . . . of being
esteemed by surrounding nations the Queen of scientific improvement'.[289]
Even when a clash of interests was apparent, then, the natural instinct
was to paper over the cracks by invoking the language of social harmony.
Pitt attempted to conclude the parliamentary debate on the Wool Bill of
1788–a manifest defeat for the landed class at the hands of the manufacturing interest–by reapplying such a comfortable veneer. Thus Pitt
remarked that despite 'any difference[s] between the commercial and the
landed interest on the present occasion . . . their interests . . . ought
undoubtedly to be considered, as one and the same'.[290]

One of the great benefits of improvement as a social ideal was that it
allowed such a complacency to be combined with an ethic which
promoted change–change which, inevitably, would benefit some groups
more than others. Improvement, the rhetoric ran, was ultimately good
for all since the fuller use of the earth and its products which improvement
brought with it offered the chance of more wealth for all. The ideal of
improvement, too, offered the opportunity to blend knowledge with
practice, and the pursuit of learning with the maintenance of both one's
social position and responsibilities. This association of social utility with
the secular, this-worldly qualities of improvement also meant that the
values naturally intermeshed with those of the Enlightenment. We find,
for example, Sir George Staunton, secretary to the Macartney embassy
to China (with which Banks was closely associated), recoiling from the
popish Spanish culture of Tenerife (where he stopped en route to China)
with a mixture of enlightened anti-clericalism, residual Protestantism and
faith in improvement. 'Religion here', he wrote, 'engrosses much of their
leisure which might be devoted to instruction and improvements'.[291]
Fortified by the confidence in human reason that the scientific achievements which culminated in Newton's great work had brought and the
practical successes that were more and more evident throughout the land,
Britain's elite embraced the ideal of improvement as a means of
reconciling the possibility of economic progress with the maintenance
of a well-regulated society. The ideal of improvement, because it was
gradual and controlled, did not threaten the governing classes in the way
that later incarnations of the belief in progress–particularly those
emanating from the French Revolution–were to do with their attempts
to construct rapidly and, if necessary, violently, a totally new social and
intellectual order. The very word 'improvement' with its connotations of
building on what was already there was reassuring, while the practice
of improvement with its attention to the reassuringly mundane–turnips,
manure and better breeds of stock–drained it of any socially-unsettling
associations. Because improvement implied change without disturbing

innovations it elicited the co-operation of constituted authority and, in particular, of Parliament; this was needed to facilitate the process through myriad pieces of legislation which enabled improvements such as enclosure, drainage and navigation to be accomplished while maintaining the respect for the rights of private property which was so basic to eighteenth-century society. And as the legal mechanisms for improvement became better established the process gathered momentum, so that as the century advanced improvement became more and more the prevailing fashion.[292] 'Agrarian improvement', writes Bayly, '... was the dominant faith of the elite much as evangelicalism was to be after 1780'.[293] Improvement was a way of illustrating the truth of Pope's maxim that 'self-love and social mean the same', since the improvers benefited both through a better return from their estates as well as enriching society more generally. The improvers, then, were true patriots–hence the Marquis of Sligo's praise of the prominent agriculturalist, the Duke of Bedford, in a letter to Banks, as one who cultivated 'laudable & Patriotick pursuits ... to the infinite advantage of the Empire'.[294] And in promoting agrarian improvement the British elite could look to the example of their sovereign, 'Farmer George', who further strengthened the association between improvement and patriotism as well as that between improvement and social stability. Thus in a pamphlet on merino sheep Banks praised those landowners who had purchased the improved breed of sheep from the royal flock as having put 'a due value on the benefit his Royal patriotism offered to them'.[295]

Improvement, indeed, could be seen as the practical application both of biblical injunctions to use nature for the benefit of humanity and the Baconian mission to utilise science for the relief of man's estate. That improvement also brought with it potentially vast social, demographic and even environmental problems was not a subject on which the eighteenth century showed much inclination to reflect or even to recognise. Such wrinkles on the fair face of improvement were left for subsequent centuries to attempt to smooth out; for Banks and his circle the benefits which had accrued and would continue to accrue from the enlightened use of improvement seemed almost pure gain.

CHAPTER SIX

The Waning of the English Enlightenment

THE FRENCH REVOLUTION AND ITS IDEOLOGICAL IMPACT

The confidence of Banks–and the English Establishment more generally–in the values of the Enlightenment rested on the belief that they provided a secure defence for the constituted order in Church and State. Such a view could most readily be sustained in the middle decades of the century–Banks's formative period–for in that period the Hanoverian dynasty could be regarded as a bulwark against the forces of tradition and popery embodied in the Jacobites. Such Jacobites had been defeated (so the supporters of the Protestant succession argued) not only by force of arms but by the resources of a superior civilisation based on ordered liberty, rational belief and habits of industry: virtues that readily meshed with those of the Enlightenment. But the assertion that enlightened values offered a ready defence of the constituted order became more hesitant as the century progressed and the old regime in England faced the enmity of other forces who proclaimed that their cause was based on enlightened values. The American revolutionaries, the Irish Volunteers and many of the rational dissenters who challenged the position of the Established Church in the 1780s were all confident that their cause could be justified by an appeal to reason in contrast to the traditional obfuscations, entrenched irrationalities and injustices of the Establishment. But it was, of course, the French Revolution which most clearly, and most insistently, challenged the view that England's traditional order could be defended by recourse to enlightened values. The debate between Burke and Paine epitomised such a clash of values as Burke turned to tradition rather than reason as the bedrock of social and political stability and Paine used the values of the Enlightenment as a stick with which to beat the constituted order in Church and State.

But for others, like Banks, whose minds had been formed in the Augustan calm of the mid-century, the choice between Enlightenment and the defence of the existing order was less stark. The menacing shadow of the French Revolution made Banks more reverent of tradition but he also continued to hope for some measure of change and even progress through the patient techniques of improvement. The French Revolution further strengthened his already strong veneration for the monarchy but it did not lead to his investing the king with the attributes of divine right in the manner promoted by his old Royal Society adversary, Bishop Horsley. Though Banks became more solicitous about the defence of the Established Church as a bastion of good order, he was largely untouched by the religious revivals which the shock of the French Revolution helped to stimulate and strengthen. The threat from France prompted Banks to play an active part in such patriotic endeavours as helping to organise the Lincolnshire militia but it did not weaken his determination to maintain scientific links with the French Academy of Sciences and its successor, the National Institute, nor his belief that, where possible, voyages prompted by scientific goals should be kept free from the trammels of national conflict.

With his extensive network of international correspondents and, in particular, his close association with the Royal Society's French equivalent, the Academy of Sciences, Banks was particularly well placed to receive reports of the early stages of the French Revolution as that great historical whirlwind unleashed itself on an unsuspecting Europe. With his omnivorous curiosity Banks naturally watched the events across the Channel closely and as early as October 1788 was thanked by the French botanist, Charles L'Héritier de Brutelle, for his interest in 'our political news'.[1] Even in the early stages of the Revolution, when many of England's elite looked favourably on the Revolution as a constitutional upheaval destined to bring France more closely in line with the glories of English political life, Banks's correspondents sounded a more sombre note. In July 1789 L'Héritier lamented the execution by the mob of Berthier, the Intendant of Paris—a man whom Banks knew—with the dire words: 'We are living in a state of anarchy. We have neither King, nor law . . . nor government'.[2] L'Héritier's disapproval of the ever-increasing pace of change and upheaval continued. In August 1789 he lamented the destruction of aristocratic chateaux and likened the French to 'young runaway horses who singularly abuse their liberty'.[3]

Banks's close friend and political ally, Lord Sheffield—who was kept well-informed of events in France by their mutual friend, William Eden, Lord Auckland, the architect of the Anglo-French commercial treaty—strengthened Banks's forebodings. '[W]e have generally agreed in Opinion', wrote Sheffield to Banks in January 1790, '& I think we shou'd not disagree on the subject of France . . . The French nation had a great opportunity, but they have abused & may lose their advantages. If they had been content with a liberal Translation of our System . . . they might have raised a solid Fabric on the only true foundation, the natural Aristocracy of a great

Country'. But, continued Sheffield, such an opportunity to benefit from sound English practice had been lost as the Revolution began to pursue chimeras like 'the Establishment of a pure & perfect Democracy of 25 millions, the virtues of the Golden Age & the primitive rights & equality of Mankind'. Sheffield presciently added that 'the comfortless State of so large a neighbourhood, must ultimately be prejudicial to us'.[4] Sheffield's distaste for the Revolution was strengthened still further by a visit to Paris in mid-1791. 'The Nation seems eminently contemptible', he wrote to Banks from Lausanne in September 1791, 'If it cou'd possibly be at once restored to a state of quiet, there does not seem to be materials, of which sufficient administration cou'd be formed'.[5]

Though Banks shared Sheffield's dismay at the course of events across the Channel he was rather more complacent about its consequences for England. Indeed, he took the sanguine view that France's troubled state would serve as an object lesson to English radicals of the dreadful consequences of tinkering with the established order. 'England was never more Quiet more happy or more satisfied with her happiness', he wrote to the Florentine naturalist, Giovanni Fabroni, in November 1790, 'than [since] she has seen the miserable consequence of the French revolution where the people [like] Esops Dog in his Fable have Dr[opped a] piece of meat from their mouths by stretching at the shadow of another'.[6] Such smugness even survived the outbreak of war between France and Austria in April 1792 and the beginnings of the Terror that year, prompted by Parisian fears of foreign invasion. On 17 August, a week after the uprising in Paris which marked the effective downfall of the monarchy, Banks rejoiced that, despite the events in France, 'our nation is in a state of temperate health'. He was particularly glad that the country was resisting 'the pride of Democracy' and optimistically attributed this to the fact that 'we are all getting so rich that few if any would now vote for a scramble each fearing to lose of his own more than he hopes to gain of his neighbor's prosperity'.

Even though at this stage Banks felt that England had resisted the contagion of revolution, his dismay and outrage at events in France was becoming ever more strident. 'Our neighbors', he wrote, 'have I think now showd themselves in their Real Colors [as] a people who Prefer the Pleasures of Anarchy & Confusion to all other Delights of this Life'. The source of such anti-social behaviour Banks partly attributed to the *philosophes* of the Enlightenment, arguing that the French 'have of late spent so much time in imbibing the atheistical & Democratical Opinions of their Philosophes that they have spard none to trace back the page of their history or they never would have gone the Lengths they have'.

Such a comment suggests that Banks, like Burke, took the view that tradition rather than the forms of reason associated with the *philosophes* provided a more secure basis for what he called 'necessary order & Prudent subordination'. But Banks's hostility towards the French Revolution was also based on the belief that it was fundamentally irrational–a point he underlined by using medical metaphors for the Revolution as a sickness upsetting the natural balance of the body. After deploring the influence of the French *philosophes*, he argued that the Revolution was likely to result in a civil war for 'Bleeding is the only remedy that can subdue the republican fever which now Rages in their veins & a large Quantity of Blood must be taken away or a sufficient lowering of the Constitution cannot be obtained'.[7] Banks again invoked the language of pathology in February 1793, as the Terror gathered pace, to emphasise what he perceived as the fundamental irrationality of the Revolution. 'The French nation', he wrote, 'are certainly in a state of canine madness, very desirous of biting all mankind and by that means infecting them with the disease they themselves are vexed with'.[8]

Like his friend, Charles Burney, who, after the September Massacres of 1792, lamented 'Is this the end of the 18th Century, so enlightened & so philosophical',[9] Banks regarded the French Revolution as the betrayal of enlightened principles rather than their fruit. In a letter to the Swedish botanist, Adam Afzelius, in January 1793 Banks once again harped on the theme that the French Revolution represented a flight from order and rationality to 'a state of anarchy that is unparalleled as far as I know in the history of all that has passed hitherto in this world'–a state which included among its casualties that of 'human reason'.[10] Banks's old school friend, Lord Auckland, took a similar view lamenting in 1795 the fact that

It was reserved for the eighteenth century to see a great and enlightened nation, in which All, who were not shedding tears, were rejoicing in the sufferings of others.

But, continued Auckland, a long-time resident and admirer of France,

it would be unjust to attribute to the national character of France a distinctive alacrity in crimes ... I willingly believe that France is not in her natural state, but in a temporary delirium.[11]

For Auckland, then, as for Banks, the Revolution represented a national psychosis and a victory for the forces of irrationality.

On the one hand Banks (and Auckland) could thus dismiss the French Revolution as being fundamentally irrational and therefore a departure from enlightened principles. But, on the other, both men were aware that the Revolution justified its actions by recourse to principles such as an appeal to human equality or the need to judge traditional institutions before the bar of reason–principles which drew on the enlightened values to which they themselves subscribed. This ambivalence is apparent in Auckland's pamphlet of 1795. After cataloguing the changes that the Revolution had wrought throughout French society Auckland dismissed such reforms as a warning to follow the path of tradition since they 'were all admonitions to other countries to look with revived attachment to their own governments'. In particular, the example of France should prompt the English 'to cherish the whole system of their own civil and ecclesiastical establishment'. But–in contrast to most of his contemporaries (including Banks)–Auckland also warned that the spirit of counter-revolution could

The Contrast. Engraving by Thomas Rowlandson. Courtesy of the Trustees of the British Museum

go too far, extinguishing the enlightened credentials of the English constitution: that the 'salutary check to the dangerous spirit of innovation, may not hereafter prove favourable to abuses of power, by creating a timidity in the just cause of liberty'.[12]

Banks, however, was far more preoccupied with the disintegration which might result from applying such enlightened solutions to the fabric of the British constitution in such a troubled period, deploring the actions of 'those who wish for a scramble ... [and who] raise the lower orders into a wish for Equality'.[13] Banks indeed continued to hope that the example of France would serve as a graphic warning to would-be English reformers. As he wrote to Blagden in February 1793:

> Our minds are much heated here & the dreadfull State into which reform has plunged France will I think act [as] a very salutary lesson to prevent People from listening to those politicians who under the Semblance of Parliamentary reform & c would not scruple to plunge this Country into the First stage of anarchy & Rebellion.[14]

The following month he rejoiced in a letter to Lloyd that 'all things go on here as we could wish Democrats are almost annihilated Constitutionalists abound'.[15]

Though Banks continued to take the optimistic view that France might serve as a useful deterrent to would-be reformers about the dangers of unleashing popular discontent, he was also becoming increasingly aware of the threat posed to England, particularly after the declaration of war by France against Britain in February 1793. Banks may have regarded the fervour of the French revolutionaries as being irrational but, more and more, he was coming to appreciate its force and, consequently, the menace it posed to England and other old-regime states. 'The present situation of France', he wrote in his memorandum of March 1794 on the subscription by the Lincolnshire landowners to raise a force as a defence against invasion, 'has raised as much enthusiam among individuals as a good Cause could have done'. The revolutionary armies produced by 'The Volcano of Equality' were 'convinced by their Execrable Leaders who sit in safety at Paris that Europe is in League to overturn their Favorite system of Equality. [T]hey Fight like Tygers not only to Preserve that but to destroy all who oppose it'.[16] The extent and intensity of this revolutionary conflagration was underlined by the impotence of the forces of old-regime Europe in attempting to check it. 'I fear', he wrote to William Hamilton (a prominent virtuoso but better known as the husband of Nelson's mistress, Emma Hamilton) in July 1794, 'unless this Jacobine Fire which consumes all it reaches extinguishes itself by its own efforts all Europe at Present seems incapable of putting on an extinguisher'.[17] Elsewhere Banks acknowledged that even if France were defeated it was unlikely that the old order could be restored and that while ever it remained a republic 'it will be Formidable to us in the extreme'.[18]

Following the downfall of Robespierre and the end of the Terror in July 1794 the intensity of Banks's denunciations of the Revolution abated. France still remained the national enemy but the Revolution no longer appeared such an affront to human rationality and the basic fabric of society. As he wrote to Fabroni in November 1795, 'the French seem to Feel an abatement of that ill founded enthusiasm which alone has rendered them terrible to their well meaning neighbors'.[19] Two days later he also commented to the British consul in Lisbon that 'The French must be tired of Blood sucking[;] if so the Reign of Terror is at an end'.[20] Further and, from the point of view of the English propertied classes, more comforting reassurance of an increasing retreat from revolutionary fervour came in September 1797 with a coup d'état on the part of the oligarchic French Directory annulling popular elections. In the same month Banks's protégé, the African explorer, Hornemann, sent back word that when he passed through France on his way to Egypt he discerned that, though 'A large party still exists, who wish to see the Jacobine system of terror reestablished in France . . . the number of well disposd persons, who anxiously look for the restoration of peace, is still greater'.[21] Among the dissidents within England, too, enthusiasm for the goals of the Revolution was being drained away by the threat of foreign invasion. As Banks commented to Hamilton in March 1798: 'as danger approaches foreign danger I mean domestic harmony increases & I realy have a better Idea of the permanency of this Country now than I have had at any period for 5 years preceding the Commencement of the Present Year'.[22]

While the threat of invasion persisted, the greater predictability of the French government under the Directory and Napoleon–as compared with the affronts of the Terror–prompted Banks to attempt to re-establish scientific links with France.[23] When, in 1796, the French Directory applied to the British government for the return of a vast collection of natural history specimens collected by the French botanist, Labillardière, on the D'Entrecasteaux expedition to rescue La Pérouse–a collection subsequently captured by the British–Banks intervened energetically and, ultimately, successfully on behalf of the French scientific community. In his submissions to government Banks distinguished sharply between the behaviour of French political leaders and that of its scientists. The Revolution may have put France beyond the pale of civilised nations but the quality of its scientists and the fact that, under the Directory, they were once more receiving aid from the State provided some basis for civilised intercourse between France and Britain. As Banks wrote to the Foreign Secretary, Lord Grenville, apropos of the Labillardière affair, France was 'a country where however humanity may have been outragd by popular Leaders, Science is held in immeasurable esteem'.[24] Banks's success in obtaining in 1797 a passport for the African explorer, Hornemann, from the French government further strengthened his opinion that France was once again in rational, albeit still hostile, hands. As he wrote to the French Commissioner for the exchange of Prisoners of War, who had arranged the passport as well as an exchange of scientific materials: 'I have a perfect confidence in the executive directors of France derivd from the uniform protection they have given to Science'.[25] He echoed a similar sentiment in 1806, after Napoleon had become Emperor, when reassuring one of his collectors of French co-operation for his botanical endeavours in China. 'I do not doubt from the knowledge I have of the French nation', wrote Banks, 'where respect for Science & Scientific men was never for a moment abated during the most Horrible parts of their Revolution, in Case of capture, that you will Easily gain your Personal Liberty'.[26]

The signing of the Treaty of Amiens in 1801 provided a brief respite from the conflict between the two nations and an opportunity for Banks to consolidate his ties with the French scientific world after the merely intermittent relations permitted while war had raged. He was well aware that the treaty was likely to prove only a temporary respite in the conflict between France and Britain: as he wrote to Robert Brown in April 1803 'our peace with France proves no more than a turbulent and quarrelsome truce'.[27] But the fragility of the peace only increased the importance of opening up the channels of scientific communication between France and Britain before war once again impeded such a civilised interchange. Such a view helps to explain why Banks responded with such enthusiasm–indeed, in the minds of a number of his contemporaries, with such fawning indelicacy–when he was elected to the National Institute of France in January 1802.

When the National Institute published Banks's letter acknowledging this honour it offended the sensibilities of his compatriots for a number of reasons. In the first place his (surely well justified) reference to the National Institute as 'the first Literary Society in the World' was interpreted as a slight to Banks's own Royal Society. Hence comments to Banks such as one from a caustic clerical critic that his letter represented a 'hyperbolical, disgusting, fulsome Flattery on the French National Institute'.[28] Even more objectionable to some was Banks's refusal to damn the Revolution root and branch. For Banks distinguished between the excesses of the Revolution–what he had considered as the irrationalities of the Terror–and the more stable and orderly style of government that had emerged during the Directory and the Napoleonic periods. Predictably, Banks's letter condemned 'the horrible convulsions of the late tremendous Revolution' but assured his French correspondents that France was 'a nation which ... I have never ceased to esteem, well aware even in the worst periods, that good men in abundance were still there & that they would in time resume their superior stations & replace virtue Justice & honor in the hearts of their country men'.[29] The inference of Banks's letter was, then, that such a desirable transformation had taken place–that the worst excesses of the Revolution were over and that the 'good men' in whom he had such confidence were once again assuming positions of power and influence. In short, Banks was indicating that he, and the Royal Society of which he was head, could accept the present regime in France and conduct business with it even though it had been produced by a revolution that had overthrown a monarch, an established church and so many other traditional features which Britain shared with old-regime France. Plainly, then, Banks's revulsion against the Revolution took a much less strident and sweeping form than that of many of his contemporaries, which helps to explain why the experience of revolution did not fundamentally alter the overall tenor of Banks's thinking on such fundamental issues as the nature of society, religion or government.

Others, however, regarded Banks's letter and his implied acceptance of the present regime in France as an affront–especially since it came from the pen of a President of the *Royal* Society. The most swingeing and public attack was from a writer with the *nom de plume* of Misogallus who Banks believed was John Woodford, the British agent in charge of fomenting the French Counter-Revolution by financing émigrés. He was, as Banks wrote, 'violently angry with me' over Banks's role in returning the Labillardière collection to France.[30] Misogallus, in his diatribe published in the first (1802) volume of Cobbett's *Annual Register*, firstly criticised Banks for uttering such complimentary remarks to an institution which formed part of the apparatus of government of a republican nation when he had been 'distinguished as you are by repeated (out of respect to His Majesty I will not say unmerited) marks of royal favour'. For Banks's remarks could be regarded as implying acceptance of the ideological stance of France and, therefore, as Misogallus put it in characteristically hyperbolic language, as 'incense . . . before the altar of Atheism and Democracy'.

Banks was particularly taken to task for his neglect of established religion which had been such a spectacular casualty of the Revolution: 'As to religion, you seem yourself to despair of its restoration, since you do not even mention it; or perhaps you deemed it a matter of too little importance to merit the consideration of philosophers'. Banks was singled out, too, for his implied lack of respect for that other pillar of old-regime society which, in Britain, was being refurbished to withstand the onslaught of Revolution: the institution of the monarchy. For the writer was quick to point out that the 21st of January, the date of Banks's letter, was the anniversary of 'the day on which the ill-fated Louis XVI was executed by his traiterous subjects; and it is the anniversary of that day which you select to assure his assassins that *"they never ceased to possess your esteem"*!!!'.[31] The attack on Banks's lack of respect for traditional religious and political institutions was renewed later that same year in the next volume of the same journal by Cobbett himself. Banks's offence this time was his hospitality to the Abbé Grégoire on his visit to London. For, objected Cobbett, Grégoire was 'a Member of the Regicide Convention' and, though a Roman Catholic clergyman, 'he was the first man to vote for the pillage and destruction of that church'. Moreover, 'he has openly vilified and blasphemed, not only the Roman Catholic, but the Christian religion and its founder'. Cobbett concluded by remarking with heavy sarcasm that 'We should be glad to know whether it be the *politics* or the *religion* of Grégoire, that Sir Joseph Banks most admires'.[32]

The fact that Banks's letter stirred up such a hornets' nest is an indication of the gulf between Banks's response to the Revolution and that of many of his contemporaries. To Banks the Revolution was regrettable and the excesses of the Terror were intolerable, but he did not regard the forms of government which had emerged from the overthrow of the French old regime as ideologically abhorrent. Banks, it is true, regarded the person of Napoleon as the inveterate foe of Britain with extreme hostility, but this hostility did not extend to a denunciation of the religious or political bases of the Napoleonic regime or to any expression of nostalgia for the French old regime. Banks regarded the

French nation-even in its Napoleonic guise-with some sympathy, reserving his venom for Napoleon himself. 'The French nation wishes to be at rest', he wrote to Governor King of New South Wales in April 1803, but 'the Chief Consul wishes to be at war; and in order to bring about this event he assails us with uninterrupted affronts of the most serious nature'.[33] After Waterloo, Banks went so far as to suggest privately that Napoleon be tried as 'a wretch who has entaild such a mass of misery upon a Larger Extent of this Globe & a greater Number of his Fellow men, than any Former Tyrant'. He thought, however, that the French nation would also concur in such a verdict for he proposed that the trial be conducted by a joint French and English court.[34]

Nor had Banks always regarded Napoleon as quite such a sanguinary figure. For all his animosity towards Napoleon as his country's mortal foe, Banks had a certain admiration for him as a ruler who-in contrast to his British counterpart-was a generous patron of science. As he had commented to Dolomieu in July 1801:

> We English, tho' much attached to Science, have not, as your Chief Consul did, sent learned men with our Army, our successes therefore ... will be productive of political advantages only, while Science, unthought of by Rulers, must look to France alone for having blended Learning with her Arms.[35]

And such admiration was reciprocated by Napoleon who, on a number of occasions, told Blagden-Banks's virtual scientific representative in Paris-of his regard for Banks and his desire to see him in France.[36] Banks did not, however, take up Blagden's singular suggestion that the Royal Society should elect Napoleon a Fellow of the Royal Society 'in the most honourable manner that could be done ... as being a patron & protector of the sciences'.[37] But Banks had earlier that year conveyed the Royal Society's thanks to Napoleon for sending a scientific work. In the draft of the letter he also added (though he appears to have subsequently deleted it) a tribute from the Society to Napoleon 'for his uniform Patronage of Men of Science'. The Society, continued Banks, 'look forward with the more pleasure to the return of peace that they may express without restraint or reserve the sentiments of Esteem & admiration which his vast Talents inspire'.[38]

Such courtesies were largely prompted by hopes of scientific co-operation after the signing of the Treaty of Amiens in March 1802. But even after war was resumed in May 1803, Banks was still capable of acknowledging Napoleon's merits as a patron of learning, despite his overall hostility to Napoleon-hostility which he had the discretion to vent only to his friends lest it mar his scientific-diplomacy with France. When writing to Delambre in support of the English botanist, Thomas Manning, for example, Banks opened by acknowledging that he was 'Well aware of the unceasing interest your Emperor continualy feels for the advancement of Literature'.[39] Overall, then, Banks was enough of a pragmatist to accept the Napoleonic regime as one from which the world of learning and even, to a more limited extent, the British scientific community, could derive some benefit despite the bellicose behaviour of Napoleon. Though there was much that Banks found abhorrent about Napoleon himself, he had no ideological objection to dealing with him and his government when Napoleon's inclinations as a patron of learning offered Banks the opportunity to advance the cause of science.

Nor did the experience of Revolution prompt Banks to reshape his attitude to the institutions of his own nation. He continued, of course, to be (as he always had been) a loyal supporter of the monarchy and to pay public respect to the Established Church as a guardian of good order while generally keeping his reservations about its doctrine and the position and privileges of its ministers to himself. The Revolution did not, however, prompt Banks to imbue either institution with the aura of divine sanction in the manner of some of his contemporaries.[40] Banks's old Royal Society opponent, Bishop Horsley, for example, had attempted to revive the Anglican cult of passive obedience to the Lord's Anointed which had pervaded the Restoration Church in the aftermath of the execution of the Royal Martyr. '[T]he peaceable submission of the subject to the very worst of kings', proclaimed Horsley, 'is one of the most peremptory precepts of Christianity'.[41] The French *philosophes*, whom Horsley regarded as the source of the revolutionary canker, he went so far as to describe as 'those children of hell'.[42] Moreover, in Horsley's view, it was the duty of the English intelligentsia to combat the infection of such ideas. In particular, it was the duty of the scientific community since France's scientists were especially active in promoting infidel principles-so much so, wrote Horsley to John Robison (a contributor to the *Encyclopaedia Britannica* and author of the graphically entitled *Proofs of Conspiracy against all the Religions and Governments of Europe*), that '"Philosophe" and "Athée" are synonymous in the vocabulary of modern France'. Since Banks, as President of the Royal Society, was the nation's senior scientific spokesman, Horsley may well have had him in mind in criticising the lack of an English scientific counterattack. 'I wish', wrote Horsley to Robison, 'they [French scientific and philosophical ideas] met with more resistance from the learned of this Country than they do'.[43]

In more temperate language the first Earl of Liverpool, with whom Banks had worked so closely in directing the affairs of the Board of Trade and the other organs of government, also sought to invest the conflict between Britain and France with something of the aura of a religious crusade. Hence his assertion in his pamphlet, *The State of the Country in the Autumn of 1798*, 'That OUR CAUSE will finally triumph: that Religion will subdue Atheism; Virtue, Vice; and Order, Anarchy; we may consider as certain'.[44] Hence, too, his reference in a speech to the House of Lords in 1805 to France as 'a Republic of Atheists'.[45]

Where the experience of the Revolution left its deepest mark on Banks was in strengthening his opposition to doctrines of equality-doctrines which threatened to undermine the traditional hierarchical ordering of society and, consequently, the position of himself and other members of the landowning, governing classes. Banks still continued to acknowledge-as he had in calmer times–that there might be some theoretical basis for the concept of human equality but the Revolution made him dwell more and more on the practical mischiefs that the application of such a doctrine might cause. When criticising Adam Smith's laissez-faire principles, for example, he described them as being 'like Liberty & Equality in Politicks ... specious in theory but destructive in Practice'.[46] The practical realisation of political equality in the form of democracy incurred Banks's particular condemnation–hence his outburst in 1797 that though 'I am not an aristocrat yet I hate democracy'.[47] Banks's distaste for democracy extended to a determination to play his part in stamping out any of its manifestations, particularly in his native Lincolnshire where his influence counted for much. The activities of a local political activist, whose lectures Banks and the local magistrates agreed had a 'tendency [which] is dangerous in the extreme', resulted in Banks sending in 1794 a copy of one such offending lecture to some unnamed authority.[48] The influence that such political radicals could exert–even in the rural depths of Lincolnshire–had been brought home to Banks two years earlier when he had been warned by a local surgeon from the town of Horncastle (near Banks's seat at Revesby) that 'The Royal Party when compared with Paine's adherents, make them in point of number insignificant, but their audacity wants curbing'. These dissidents, it was said, had been responsible for circulating 'many inflammatory papers, many of which are said, to be furnishd by a late certain Major'.[49] Banks's suspicions of the intentions of the veteran political reformer, Major Cartwright (to whom his correspondent was no doubt referring), help to account for Banks's role in prompting the local magistrates to view with caution a meeting which Cartwright had helped to call for the seemingly innocuous purpose of agitating for a standard measure of corn in late 1792. The magistrates, wrote Banks on their behalf (in a draft that he seems to have later cancelled), were 'Convinced of the illegality of Associations in General without any exceptions being mindful of how liable such meetings are to be led astray if there be among them men who hold opinions inimical to the Constitutions of this happy Countrey'.[50] As a fellow gentleman and near neighbour, Banks had to deal more circumspectly with Major Cartwright than with a popular political activist, but Banks later exercised what sanction he could by formally breaking off relations with him. Cartwright, in turn, responded with gentlemanly formality writing in the third person 'to assure Sir Joseph Banks he is much obliged to him for putting an end to a familiar intercourse which it seems was no longer likely to have been cordial'. But he also registered his disapproval of Banks's hostility to the cause of political reform, writing that he was 'truly sorry to see in Sir Joseph Banks, an apparent bias towards political notions, which J[ohn] C[artwright] cannot reconcile with any ideas he has yet been able to form of free government in general, or of the English constitution in particular'.[51] In London, too, Banks took his place among the propertied defenders of order, acting in December 1792 as the chairman of an inaugural meeting of a branch of the Association for the Preservation of Peace, Liberty and Property (John Reeves' 'Anti-Levelling Association') in the parish of St Anne, Westminster.[52]

Behind Banks's vigilance in using his influence where possible to stamp out manifestations of agitation for political reform was the fear, so prevalent in his class, that freedom would slide into revolution. As his friend, Gibbon, put it: 'If you begin to improve the constitution, you may be driven step by step from the disfranchisement of Old Sarum to the King in Newgate, the Lords voted useless, the Bishops abolished'.[53] In a letter of 1794 Banks conceded that reform might be 'proper ... to be brought forward & supported in times of peace & quietness' but, he insisted, it 'ought not in my opinion to be inculcated in times like the present' when the country was threatened by 'the turbulence of a neighbouring Country in which all order Religious & Civil is destroyed'. To tinker with the established order at such a time was to court disaster since it 'gives encouragement to the disaffected ... to use their efforts towards the destruction of our present Government under which the Mass of the People live & grow rich'.[54] For, at the root of the demands for reform, lurked notions of equality which, as the French example showed, could explode into a cataclysm that consumed the very pillars of society. The attempt by moderate, aristocratic reformers like Lord Grey to contend that it was 'not fair to condemn principles, such as those which have of late been established in France, because they may have been abused' was strongly condemned by the second Lord Hawkesbury (son of Banks's old colleague at the Board of Trade and, as the second Earl of Liverpool, the future prime minister) in a speech to the House of Commons in April 1800. Hawkesbury argued that in so far as the principles of the Revolution were based on the notion of equality they were 'fundamentally false'. 'Government', he contended, 'is not founded on the equality, but it is a regulation of the natural inequalities of man ... The object of Government and of Society is not to counteract that order of things which Providence has established':[55] a sentiment with which Banks would, no doubt, have heartily concurred.

THE ROYAL SOCIETY, ITS RIVALS AND THE ECLIPSE OF THE IDEAL OF USEFUL KNOWLEDGE

The association of reform with revolutionary notions of equality which the French Revolution so dramatically and so pervasively strengthened was to permeate all aspects of English society. 'Everything rung and was connected with the Revolution in France', wrote Lord Cockburn of his youth, 'Everything, not this thing or that thing, but literally everything, was soaked in this one event'.[56] The conduct of intellectual and scientific enquiry and the institutions which sustained such enquiry naturally fell under the shadow of the Revolution. Speculations concerning the nature of humankind, of society and even of Nature now came under ever closer

Official portrait of Banks as President of the Royal Society at age 65. Painting by
Thomas Phillips, 1808. Courtesy of the Royal Society of London

scrutiny for their implications in the battle to maintain the ideological supports of the established order in Church and State. Institutions, such as the Royal Society, which were so closely intertwined with the operations of the British State and with its ruling elite naturally reflected the prevailing attitudes of that elite and, in particular, its hostility to reform. Given Banks's antagonism to the cause of political reform in the period of the French Revolution it is no surprise that he was also determined to resist change within the Royal Society: the old-regime institution with which he was most closely associated.

One obvious strategy for a President of the Royal Society anxious to avoid the taint of radical politics was to strengthen the links between the Royal Society and the governing elite and, in particular, the aristocracy, Burke's 'great oaks' supporting the traditional constitution. There is some evidence that Banks pursued such a policy–though, given that the Royal Society had always been anxious to cultivate the nobility in order to dispel any hint that science was subversive, this did not represent a very dramatic change from established practice. Carter's figures show that the percentage of aristocratic Fellows of the Royal Society in 1780 was 19.4; by contrast, the percentage of new aristocratic Fellows elected from 1766, when Banks became a member, until his death in 1820 was a little higher with a figure of 22.5. The number of spiritual peers, whose presence in the Royal Society assuaged fears that science and religion were not, as the French *philosophes* had claimed, mutually antagonistic, showed a more appreciable increase from 0.7 to 1.4 per cent, though the percentage of other clerics made fellows in the two periods showed only a slight change from 9.7 to 9.3 per cent.[57] Miller's evidence also suggests that during the 1790s Banks was actively recruiting to the Council new members who would further consolidate the Society's links with government and the constituted order in Church and State more generally.[58] Overall, then, it can be said that under Banks the Society's links with the upper echelons of society were certainly maintained and to some degree strengthened.

Recruitment from the ranks of the temporal and spiritual peers was the more significant since it occurred in a period when the centre of gravity of English science was beginning to move away from the gentlemanly world of the London scientific clubs and the two ancient universities to the fast-growing provincial towns and their scientific and literary societies. Banks's relations with such new scientific societies were marked by propriety mixed with condescension. Since they were not a challenge to the traditional pre-eminence of the Royal Society he was prepared to maintain cordial relations between them and the Royal Society. William Roscoe, for example, was rewarded for his energy in establishing a scientific society in Liverpool, with the comment that such a body was one of 'the most important supports of the Reputation your Town has obteind as being as Ready to promote Science as to carry on Trade'.[59] And promoters of such provincial societies generally appear to have had the prudence to seek the good will of the Royal Society by acknowledging its role as the nation's pre-eminent scientific society and Banks's position as its undisputed leader. The Manchester Literary and Philosophical Society accompanied its request that Banks should become an honorary member of the Society with an effusive acknowledgement that by doing so they were 'seeking a connection with a Gentleman so highly distinguished, for his own literary acquirements, for his zealous & munificent patronage of Sciences & for the station he holds as President of the first learned Institution of Europe'.[60] Banks graciously accepted the honour, though adding the cautious qualification that he would be happy 'to obey such of their commands as I shall judge compatible to the interest of the Royal Society'.[61]

While Banks might extend his sense of *noblesse oblige* to these lesser satellites of the Royal Society, he was cautious about allowing representatives of provincial scientific culture to intrude into the Royal Society if they brought with them some of the unsettling ideas about the need for reform. For such ideas naturally tended to be more prevalent in provincial centres which were frequently populated by Dissenters and had often grown into an early maturity outside the sustaining framework of many of the traditional institutions and practices of old-regime society. Banks's caution in promoting provincial scientists with radical leanings is illustrated in his ambivalent dealings with that would-be reformer of both science and society, Dr Thomas Beddoes, who, though he was based in the ancient chartered city of Bristol, drew much of the support for his Pneumatic Institute from the burgeoning Midlands. In 1791 Banks accepted papers from Beddoes on behalf of the Royal Society but thereafter was more cautious in his dealings with the 'Doctor of Revolution'.[62] Beddoes's attempt to extract financial support from Banks for his Pneumatic Institute failed, with Banks expressing both his scepticism about Beddoes's scientific methods and wariness of his politics. The Duchess of Devonshire wrote to assure Banks that Beddoes had 'abjur'd his political opinions [which] had occasioned his leaving Oxford'[63] and this prompted Banks to declare that his doubts had now lessened 'concerning the propriety of his giving public countenance, of any kind, to a man who has openly avowed opinions, utterly inimical to the present arrangements of the order of Society in this country'[64]–but the very vigour of Banks's language suggests lingering caution. Certainly, contemporaries were in no doubt that Banks's lack of support for the Pneumatic Institute was based on more than scientific objections. James Watt's son wrote that Banks had 'seen Beddoes's cloven *Jacobin* hoof and it is the order of the day to suppress all *Jacobin innovations* such as his is already called'.[65]

When Priestley attempted to propose Thomas Cooper as a Fellow of the Royal Society in 1790 he was rejected, much to Priestley's outrage.[66] Banks waxed indignant at the suggestion that Cooper's political or religious sympathies played a part in his being thus blackballed[67] but it is difficult to resist the suspicion that Cooper's strong sympathies with the French Revolution (later evidenced in a visit to Paris in 1792 and an exchange of pamplets with Burke) did not play some part in his exclusion. For even if Banks himself was indeed not influenced by such considerations many of the fellows were to become even more vigorous than he in excluding the politically suspect from the Society. Banks supported the election in February 1793 of the Milanese Count Andreoni, despite the fact that he was said 'to have held very imprudent Conversation relative to the government of England & to have descanted publicly in Praise of Republicanism'-rumours that Banks attributed simply to 'his Milanese enmity to his Present Sovereign'.[68] The bulk of the Society was not, however, disposed to take such a charitable view and duly blackballed him, prompting Banks to exclaim that 'I am verily of opinion that if Sir Isaac Newton had held Republican language that all the influence I have could procure him three votes as a Fellow'.[69]

As the Revolution pursued its bloody course and as France became Britain's enemy, Banks-and the Royal Society-became ever more anxious to distance themselves from radical political activity. By 1804 Banks could proudly inform Rumford that 'we shall not now I trust goe astray as I think we have not one attending member who is at all addicted to Politicks'.[70] 'Politics' in this context meant, of course, radical politics, for in Banks's mind politics was equated with change so that the maintenance of the established order was an apolitical position. And under Banks's leadership the Royal Society continued to avoid the radical taint. The year before he died Banks could rejoice with his old friend, Lord Sheffield, that 'my Freinds of the Royal Society have not been infected with the Mania of Reform'. Such distancing of the Society from the perils of reform owed much to Banks's unchallenged dominance of the Royal Society during this turbulent period. Appropriately, then, Banks's letter to Sheffield continued on by indicating his ascendancy in the affairs of the Society. 'I have no doubt', wrote Banks, 'of Carrying my Election of Treasurer without troubling any one of my Friends'.[71]

However, Banks's opposition to change within the Royal Society and the scientific establishment generally reflected more than simply the opposition to reform which was so pervasive a characteristic of the age. It was also linked to his conception of the proper domain of science and the role that it ought to play in society. Banks, as we have seen, was an exemplar of the Enlightenment in his view that science should be the chief instrument in achieving the great Baconian goal of 'the relief of man's estate'. Science, in Banks's view of things, should prove its worth through the practical benefits that it promoted, for improvement and science were naturally partners. In the manner of the Enlightenment, too, Banks took the view that science should form part of the public culture of polite society. As far as possible, then, science should not be cordoned off from the purview of the educated by abstruse terminology and over-specialisation for these were a bar both to the integration of science into the larger culture and an obstacle to its practical application. As Miller has emphasised,[72] too, such a view of science and its social role was strengthened within the Royal Society by the dominance of Banks's fellow landowners who naturally favoured scientific activities which had an obvious application or which were attuned to the clubbable world of learned London society with its vestiges of the omnivorous and collecting mentality of the virtuoso.

By the beginning of the nineteenth century, however, such an amalgam of science with polite culture was under challenge from the increasing tendency for such traditional all-embracing pursuits as natural philosophy or natural history to fragment into disciplinary specialities. As we saw in Chapters Three and Four, Banks's own wide scientific interests–and, *a fortiori*, those of his protégés–could less and less be contained within the generalised world of the cultivator of natural history and began to move towards a more self-conscious identification with specialised disciplines such as botany, zoology, geology and even anthropology. In the mathematical sciences the extent of specialisation and the gulf between the expertise of the researcher and the knowledge of an educated layman was, of course, greatest. Not surprisingly, then, much of the opposition to Banks's conduct of the affairs of the Royal Society came from the mathematically-inclined, as the disputes of 1783-4, led by Horsley, Newton's posthumous editor, indicate. Such resentment by the practitioners of the mathematical sciences continued and, as Miller shows,[73] after Banks's death much of the impetus for reform of the Royal Society came from mathematicians operating from such various institutional bases as Cambridge University, the military academies at Woolwich and Great Marlow (later moved to Sandhurst) and government instrumentalities such as the Ordnance Survey.

But the image of Banks as the dictator of the philosophers casting into scientific darkness all but the practitioners of his favoured pursuits will not stand the scrutiny of the Royal Society's publications during his period in office as President. Indeed, as Carter's analysis of the articles in the *Philosophical Transactions* from 1781 to 1820 shows, the non-biological sciences predominated, accounting for 72 per cent of papers. Of these 17.25 per cent were in astronomy, 6.3 per cent in mathematics and 15 per cent in physics.[74] Such figures indicate that the Royal Society reformers of the 1820s and the 1830s tended, like most reformers, to exaggerate the faults of the old regime they wished to reshape in their own image. However, the mathematicians' sense of exclusion was not entirely without foundation. The general tenor of the Royal Society reflected the values of Banks and his fellow gentry, anxious to turn science to practical account rather than to cultivate it for its own sake. Where mathematical pursuits were encouraged they tended to be in areas with obvious application. The author of an apologetic account of Banks's work as President of the Royal Society suggested as much when he wrote defensively after the disputes of 1783-4 that 'Those parts of mathematical science, upon which depends the perfecting of astronomy and navigation, the forming of canals and bridges, and the construction of mill machinery, have been cultivated [within the Royal Society] with diligence and success'.[75]

Though Banks was too intelligent not to see the importance of mathematical research he tended to value it as an adjunct to more accessible forms of science, preferably those that could help promote the great business of improvement. The pursuit of mathematics for its own sake he appears to have regarded as a little self-indulgent. As he privately noted during the dispute with Horsley and his fellow dissidents:

> Those gentlemen might easily be informed that howsoever respectable mathematics as a science might be it by no means can pretend to monopolize the praise due to learning. [I]t is indeed little more than a tool with which other sciences are hewd into form. Sir Isaac Newton demonstrated it is true the discoveries which made him immortal by the help of mathematicians but he owes his immortality to his discoveries in Natural Philosophy not mathematics.[76]

Not surprisingly, then, the Royal Society under Banks's presidency did not prove particularly fertile ground for the increasing mathematisation of natural philosophy and its reconceptualisation as the discipline of physics which was the great scientific achievement of the French Academy of Sciences (and its revolutionary successor, the National Institute) in the same period. Belatedly, the discipline of physics took root in England in the 1830s[77] after Banks and his conception of science as a natural part of the polite and improving cultural values of a landed elite had been eclipsed by other, more professionalised and disciplinary-linked views of science. One index of this change was that, as Lyons has calculated, the percentage of 'non-scientific Fellows' fell from 71.4 in 1800 to 67.7 in 1830 and eventually to 47.4 in 1860.[78] The accompanying decline in the traditional dominance of the landed classes within the Society is underlined (as Miller points out) by the fact that while in the last twenty years of Banks's rule 40 per cent of the Council was drawn from the aristocracy and gentry, by the decade 1831–40 this figure had fallen to 10 per cent.[79]

So undisputed was Banks's dominance of the Royal Society after the dissidents of 1783–4 had been roundly defeated that the tensions generated by such changing conceptions of science were largely played out beyond the portals of the Society itself. Though the Society was deeply divided– so much so that Davies Gilbert described it in 1819 as 'a volcano augmenting its power'[80]–there was no one willing to stage a mutiny against the Society's existing course while the aging Banks remained at the helm. In Banks's declining years the chief bone of contention was not the affairs of the Royal Society itself but the attempt to found new scientific societies–societies which reflected the status of individual sciences as separate disciplines with needs that could not be fully met by a more generalised scientific body such as the Royal Society. Banks had acquiesced with good grace in the foundation of a number of new scientific societies in London–notably the Linnean Society (1788), the Royal Institution (1799), the Society for the Improvement of Horticulture (1804) and the Merino Society (1811)–but these were not based on one particular scientific discipline and they duly acknowledged the supremacy of the Royal Society. In any case, they were all in some way linked with the study of Nature and the improved use of its products and so were naturally viewed with sympathy by Banks and other members of the landowning class who dominated the Royal Society.[81] We find, for example, Banks in 1804 indulgently praising both the work of the Royal Society and 'All our subordinate societies [which] also seem to prosper, and labour diligently in their respective departments; we have newly formed one for the improvement of horticulture, which promises to become very numerous'.[82]

The foundation of the Geological and Astronomical Societies was, however, interpreted by Banks as a challenge to the traditional role of the Royal Society as the clearing house for the scientific capital of the nation. For the establishment of disciplinary bodies such as these made it apparent that the clubbable ideal of the Royal Society providing a forum where all branches of science could be represented and made available to those with the interest, education and leisure to profit from them was passing. Science was now beginning to demand specialised audiences with specialised expertise–and, as it did so, the view of both the virtuoso and the Enlightenment *philosophe* that science should form part of polite culture along with literature and the arts also began to wane.

In any case, though the Linnean Society was founded with Banks's support, the fact that it became an effective, if unintentional, rival to the Royal Society had made Banks increasingly cautious of new institutional scientific rivals.[83] Such wariness was, no doubt, also heightened by his increasing age and, with it, a greater tendency to autocratic behaviour–particularly since he had no real rival as the dominant figure in representing the institutional and public face of science. When it was proposed in 1809 to found a small and highly specialised Society for the Promotion of Animal Chemistry (what today would be called bio-chemistry) its founders went to great pains to assuage any fears that Banks might have entertained about any possible challenge to the dominance of the Royal Society. Thus one of the first resolutions of the embryonic body was 'That the President of the Royal Society be requested to take such steps as he shall think proper to induce the Royal Society to take this Society under its Protection as an assistant Society constituted for the sole purpose of advancing the study of animal Chemistry'. It also resolved that 'it be our first fundamental Law, that all Discoveries and Improvements in Animal Chemistry, made by any of the Members, after they have received the approbation of this Society, be presented to the Royal Society'.[84]

Having dutifully paid such homage, the Society for the Promotion of Animal Chemistry was duly accepted as an assistant society under the overlordship of the Royal Society. Banks appears to have expected that other such societies would also meekly accept the role of satellites around the sun of the Royal Society. His early support for the formation of the Geological Society appears to have been based on this assumption. After the Geological Society metamorphosed itself from an informal dining club into a constituted society in November 1807, Banks accepted an honorary membership.[85] It was, however, a position that he resigned with some dudgeon in March 1809 after he became convinced that the Geological Society aspired to greater institutional autonomy from the Royal Society. This was despite the fact that the Secretary of the Society had attempted to mollify him by assuring him that the members 'were not conscious of having deviated from the principles which they entertained at their first establishment'.[86] Banks's stand helped to bring to a head the long-simmering issue of the Society's relationship to the Royal Society. The chief advocate for the Banksian view that the Geological Society should remain a subordinate society of the Royal Society was the wealthy collector, the Honourable Charles Greville, a long-standing member of the Royal Society and correspondent of Banks on matters mineralogical. Greville proposed two classes of membership with the first class being made up of Fellows of the Royal Society with the power to elect members, make bye-laws and to conduct 'the intercourse with the Council of the Royal Society, and all the affairs of the Society'. The Society itself Greville termed 'the assistant Society to the Royal Society for the advancement of Geology'. He also envisaged that the Royal Society should have the right of first refusal in publishing any papers presented to the Geological Society. In short, Greville was attempting to place the Geological Society in the same mould as the Society for the Promotion of Animal Chemistry.

The members of the Geological Society, however, roundly rejected these proposals, thus both clarifying the Society's constitutional position and strengthening the hostility of Banks. For, on 10 March 1809, the members resolved that 'any proposition tending to render this Society dependent upon or subservient to any other Society, does not correspond with the conception this Meeting entertains of the original principles upon which the Geological Society was founded'. They resolved, furthermore, that Greville's proposals 'having a direct tendency to render this Society dependent upon and subservient to the Royal Society, are inadmissible.' There was, however, also an attempt to hold out an olive-branch to the Royal Society and its formidable President, for the members declared that 'it has never entered into the contemplation of this Society to impose upon its Members the performance of any duties inconsistent with the obligations of those among them who may be Fellows of the Royal Society'. They also affirmed 'the high respect and deference they entertain toward that learned and scientific body'.[87]

Banks, however, was not so easily mollified and continued to regard the Geological Society, rather than the Royal Society, as the aggressor. For, in Banks's eyes, the Geological Society was breaking with earlier understandings that it would act as a society subordinate to the Royal Society. As he wrote to Greville in April 1809: 'No one of the R.S. members have any wish to Quarrell, but I am well informed the Geological Society wish to make war against us in the hopes of bringing themselves into public notice by the Contest'.[88] Nor was Banks entirely wrong in suspecting that some members of the Geological Society regarded him with less than complete cordiality and in some ways welcomed the contretemps as a way of more clearly establishing the Society's position and moving it from out of the shadow of the Royal Society. On a visit to Edinburgh one prominent member of the Geological Society reported back to the President that he was

> happy to find, that among all our honorary members I have had an opportunity of conversing with, the attempt made by a few meddling officious members of the Royal Society, to introduce petty intriguing into a society of men brought together for the advancement of science, has met with the same contempt it did at the last general meeting, and which is so justly merited. I find Sir J. Banks's character of courtier is in full force here. I am quite satisfied that, if we chuse, this business will go a great way to establish our Society on a firmer footing.[89]

In the following year Banks himself politely but firmly closed the door on the one remaining possible institutional linkage between the two societies: the publication in the *Philosophical Transactions* of papers presented to the Geological Society. In response to an enquiry by the President of the Geological Society, Banks replied that

> Being personally a well wisher to [the] Geological Society, I certainly can have no objection to look over and give my opinion on such of the Papers as have been read at their meetings ... but I must confess that I do not at present see any regular method, by which the papers of a Society entirely unconnected with the Royal Society can be presented to or received by, the persons who have the management of the Royal Society.[90]

The Geological Society, then, was left as a body quite separate from the Royal Society able to pursue its own disciplinary path without direction or interference from Banks and other members of the Royal Society's Council who still hoped to accommodate all useful scientific knowledge within their Society.

The divorce between the Royal Society and the Geological Society brought into clear focus a number of the developments of the age. Firstly, the very formation of the Geological Society underlined the way in which individual sciences had grown to the point where their disciplinary demands could no longer be so easily met within a general body such as the Royal Society. It meant, too, that the Royal Society and its journal, the *Philosophical Transactions*, no longer could be regarded as the nation's unchallenged repository of scientific knowledge. Thus Greville, Banks's chief ally in the early Geological Society, objected that a separate publication would undermine 'the duty and inclination of all its [the Royal Society's] Fellows ... to enrich the Philosophical Transactions, justly considered as the record of National progress in Science'.[91] Secondly, the form that the Geological Society took marked something of a defeat for the gentlemanly collecting tradition which the Royal Society, with its long associations with the virtuoso tradition, had accommodated. Symptomatically, Greville had built up one of the best collections of minerals in England. Given that the polite and improving functions of science had been closely linked together in the minds of the gentlemanly members of the Royal Society, it is not surprising that the Geological Society, with its quite different outlook, did not prove to be a very fertile environment for promoting the practical applications of geology to concerns such as mining. It was Greville's forlorn hope, for example, that the Society would assist in the formation of a 'National Collection and Office of Assay' which would act as a stimulus for 'the mining concerns of these kingdoms'. Among those who grew disenchanted with the Geological Society were the mineral surveyors, John Farey and William Smith, the latter of whom Banks praised for being able to apply his 'extensive and enlightened theory' to realise 'economic purposes'.[92] The formation of the Geological Society, then, marked not only something of a rejection of the Royal Society's aspirations to act as a forum for all sciences but also of the interests and outlook of the landed class who were its backbone under Banks's presidency.[93] The foundation of this new society was thus a symptom of the waning of the genteel scientific culture of the eighteenth century which had so naturally accommodated itself to the ideals of the Enlightenment with its emphasis on the need for science to be put to work for the advancement of society and its belief that science should form part of the cultural ambience of a leisured class.

The foundation of the Astronomical Society in 1820–the year of Banks's death–again raised the issue of the function of the Royal Society and once again provoked the ire of Banks, ever protective of his beloved Royal Society. 'I see plainly', the aging Banks caustically remarked to Sir John Barrow, 'that all these new-fangled associations will finally dismantle the Royal Society, and not leave the old lady a rag to cover her'.[94] Banks had no real expertise in astronomy–as so many of his critics had delighted in pointing out–and so, in contrast to geology, had no particular view about the goals towards which this discipline ought to be directed. Nonetheless, the formation of the new society was an obvious challenge to the Royal Society's status and purposes. Geology, after all, was a new discipline which had never been at the centre of the Royal Society's concerns but astronomy had long been a central focus of the Royal Society's activities and was closely associated with the Society's deity, the great Sir Isaac. Thus the formation of the Astronomical Society underlined even more unequivocally the limitations of the Royal Society in accommodating the increasing move towards disciplinary specialisation of its members. To add insult to injury the founders of the Astronomical Society included many of the major proponents of the need to reform England's old regime, with Banks being one of their chief targets of criticism. One such supporter of the formation of the Astronomical Society was Olinthus Gregory, a protégé of Hutton, whose eviction from the position of Foreign Secretary of the Royal Society had been a central issue in the disputes of 1783–4. As professor of mathematics at the new Royal Military Academy at Woolwich (a post in which he succeeded Hutton), Gregory looked with a jaundiced eye on the Royal Society and, in particular, its President whose role in deposing Hutton he had neither forgiven nor forgotten. After

Banks was safely dead Gregory published anonymously a blistering attack on his character and work concluding that 'If genuine science and philosophy have gained ground in England, during the last 40 years . . . it must have been from the operation of circumstances over which Sir Joseph, his habits and propensities, had no controul'.[95]

Gregory directed much of his venom at Banks's attempts to prevent the formation of both the Geological and Astronomical Societies, writing that Banks 'regarded the Royal Society as the "Aaron's rod" of scientific institutions which was to swallow up the rest'. Banks's actions in relation to the Astronomical Society, declared Gregory, were characterised by 'the most puerile and pitiable jealousy'.[96] And, indeed, Banks did do all in his power to prevent its formation, including dissuading both the Duke of Somerset and Davies Gilbert from acting as the Society's inaugural president.[97] Somerset actually acknowledged in his letter of resignation that he had taken the step since Banks to whom 'I have been long and sincerely attached, not only by the ties of public regard, but those of private friendship' 'apprehends the ruin of the Royal Society'.[98] Such moves on Banks's part prompted the eminent astronomer, Francis Baily, one of the main proponents of the Society, to comment to Charles Babbage that Banks was repeating the mistakes he had made earlier in regard to both the Royal Institution and the Geological Society which strengthened the Society's determination to stand alone: 'after the fruitless and *more violent* attempt, which Sir Joseph made aginst the Geological Society, & the Royal Institution (and which only tended to unite more firmly the original members), I wonder that he should again endeavour to oppose the progress of science in this particular instance'.[99] In the event, the opposition of the septuagenarian Banks availed little and the Astronomical Society was duly formed in the year of his death.

When the presidency of the Royal Society passed to Davy later that same year, he was at pains in his inaugural address to indicate that a new regime now prevailed and that the Royal Society no longer viewed such specialist societies as competitors. 'I trust', said Davy, 'that with these new societies, we shall always preserve the most amicable relations, and that we shall mutually assist each other'. To drive home further the contrast with his predecessor he added rather pointedly that 'there is no desire in this body to exert anything like patriarchal authority in relation to these institutions'.[100] Unlike his predecessor, then, Davy was prepared to recognise and accept that the Royal Society could no longer be scientifically all things to all men, that the age of the specialist had arrived requiring disciplinary institutions with a different ethos and aspirations from those of the Royal Society. The Royal Society continued to act as a source of prestige and a major clearing house for scientific information but it was no longer quite so unequivocally bound up with the cosy clubbable world of London learned society. The Royal Society continued, as it always had, to draw fellows from the leisured classes but less and less were they to have a role in determining the direction of the Royal Society and its scientific priorities. Banks's passing was also to mark the passing of the ideal of the

Society as the scientific arm of genteel society looking to the study of Nature to provide rational amusement and the sources of improvement. Science was to become more and more divorced from the generalised polite culture which owed so much to the Enlightenment's veneration for science as a source both of rationality and progress and to become more and more the province of the disciplinary expert answerable to his or her peers rather than to the educated public at large.

BANKS AND THE ENGLISH ENLIGHTENMENT: THE DECLINING YEARS

By the time that Banks died in 1820, too, other familiar landmarks of this cultural world and its Enlightenment-linked values were beginning to be eroded. Science was more and more viewed as a source of progress but the improving ethic which had been so closely associated with the values of a landowning elite was giving way to ideas of progress propagated by an increasingly self-confident bourgeoisie. The view that agriculture and a landowning class could set the pace for the improvement of society in general was being outstripped by the increasing dominance of a class that relied on more fluid and fluctuating sources of wealth from industry or commerce, a class which looked to technological processes largely removed from the land to act as the engine of progress.

The belief, too, that improvement could be combined with the maintenance of the existing traditional social and political order was more and more questioned as the middle-class beneficaries of trade and industry began to demand more of a say in the running of the nation's affairs. Industrialisation, too, brought in its wake a host of social problems–from rapid urbanisation to the reordering of poor relief–that no longer could be solved by the informal methods based on common ties within a governing oligarchy, methods of which Banks had been such a master both at the national level and in his capacity as a Lincolnshire squire. The challenge to such networks of privilege and patronage left their mark, too, on the London learned world with its long connection with the values of the leisured gentleman and virtuoso. Not only was London learned society fragmented by the increasing number of discipline-based societies but it also had less in the way of a common core of members drawn from the leisured class. One indication of this is the way in which the long-standing virtuoso tradition of linking the study of antiquities and the study of Nature finally unravelled as the number of joint members of both the Royal Society and the Society of Antiquaries dropped markedly after 1820.[101]

In many ways Banks's longevity, together with his stature as the nation's chief spokesman of the scientific estate, helped to keep alive the gentlemanly and virtuoso tradition of the Royal Society into the nineteenth century when so many forces, both scientific and social, were at work to undermine them. But Banks's resistance to change was strengthened by the general hostility to reform prompted by the English Establishment's reaction to the French Revolution, just as, conversely, the eventual reform of the Royal Society and English scientific institutions generally owed much to the movements for political reform which culminated in the Great Reform Bill of 1832.[102] Banks, then, was of the same mind as most of his elite contemporaries in interpreting the experience of the French Revolution as a warning against tinkering with the constitution of the old regime. Nonetheless, as we have seen, the French Revolution did not fundamentally alter the tenor of Banks's thought on such basic issues as the nature of religion or political authority. Formed in the mid-eighteenth century when the English elite's confidence in enlightened values was at its height, Banks retained a basic belief in the potentialities of human reason and the possibilities of social improvement. Though he worked closely with the London Missionary Society in furthering his own imperial designs, the evangelical revival of the late eighteenth and early nineteenth centuries passed him by. Nor did he appear to have been influenced by other forms of religious renewal–such as the High Church revival–which were stimulated by the French Revolution and the reaction against it. Banks's willingness to deal with France in either its republican or Napoleonic imperial guises was an indication, too, that he did not share the view of many others that by deposing an ancient and anointed monarchy and an Established Church the French nation had placed itself outside the pale of civilised international intercourse.

The renewed belief in humankind's basic corruption which was strengthened by both the French Revolution and the Evangelical revival also appears to have left no mark on Banks's thought. For no idea was so basic to the Enlightenment as a rejection of the doctrine of original sin or, at least, a refusal to invest it with great significance. Hence the importance of Locke's epistemology with its assumption that the mind was not marred by inherited faults but rather was a *tabula rasa* to be shaped by experience–a view that opened up the optimistic possibility that human beings exposed to good influences would become good. It was, for example, a view of human nature which underlay the hopes of some of the proponents of a penal settlement at Botany Bay.[103] In the preface to his life of Cook (which included effusive acknowledgements of Banks's help), Kippis praised the settlement since it opened up the possibility of moral improvement by exposing former criminals to a new environment and new experiences:

> One evident advantage arising from it is, that it will effectually prevent a number of unhappy wretches from returning to their former scenes of temptation and guilt, and may open to them the means of industrious subsistence and moral reformation. If it be wisely and prudently begun and conducted, who can tell what beneficial consequences may spring from it in future ages? Immortal Rome is said to have arisen from the refuse of mankind.[104]

The fundamental divide between Banks's Enlightenment-tinctured view and that of the evangelical missionaries he aided in establishing in Tahiti is apparent in their differing responses to the way of life of the Polynesians. For Banks, with his underlying belief in the basic goodness of humankind, Tahitian society–despite such blemishes as infanticide–was an instance of the way in which human beings could naturally conform to many of the moral principles embodied in natural law and dispense with many of the artificial constraints of European society. By contrast, for the London Missionary Society, Tahiti, with its sexual licence and practice of infanticide, was an example of the way human beings naturally behaved without the influence of Christianity to tame their essentially corrupt nature. Thus the instructions given to the missionaries to Tahiti exhorted them to 'Cultivate the tenderest Compassion for the wretched conditions of the Heathen, while you see them led captive of Satan at his Will. Do not resent their abominations as affronts to yourselves, but mourn over them as offensive to God'.[105]

Destruction of the Idols of Otaheite; pulling down a Pagan Altar, and building a Christian Church. Engraving in *Missionary Sketches*, no. 6 (July 1819).
Courtesy of the Mitchell Library, State Library of New South Wales

Banks's willingness to learn from other non-European societies, whether in Tahiti or elsewhere, helps to account for the close observation apparent in his ethnological writings. This openness to non-European cultures owed much to the Enlightenment: one of the favourite devices of *philosophes* like Montesquieu or Voltaire being to contrast the practices and beliefs of Europe with the allegedly more rational characteristics of ancient, non-Christian civilisations such as those of Persia or China. However, such an approach to the study of other societies waned during the course of the nineteenth century as the experience of European imperialism made Europeans less inclined to value other cultures. Anthropology also changed accordingly. Approaches like Banks's, with his reluctance to regard any one society as being superior to another, gave way, more and more, to anthropological theories and practices intended to demonstrate why some races were superior to others. The increasing success of European (and especially British) methods of manufacturing also weakened the incentive, which had been so strong in Banks, to study closely other societies in the hope of learning useful techniques.

The time of Banks's death in 1820 was a time when many of the familiar landmarks of the cultural and social landscape which had shaped and animated his work were beginning to fade or to be transformed. The challenge to the constitutional dominance of the landed classes was beginning its long and eventually successful course–though Banks's fellow landowners were to fight a very successful rearguard action before losing their traditional political pre-eminence. The prevailing influence of the landed classes in the world of learning had already been eroded and was to recede quickly as the pace of scientific change demanded more training and application than most members of a leisured class were prepared to invest. But, like the constituted order in Church and State, the scientific old regime with which Banks's career had been intertwined showed a capacity for change and growth. Despite the plethora of new scientific societies–of which the Geological and Astronomical Societies were merely harbingers–the Royal Society retained its pre-eminence as the nation's chief scientific forum and fount of honour. It also remained well into the twentieth century the chief source of scientific advice to government, a role for it that Banks had done much to promote.

And, ultimately, many of the distinctive features of the Enlightenment survived in changed form to shape the civilisation of nineteenth-century Britain. For, just as the cause of political reform proved more durable than the political reaction that followed the French Revolution, so, too, many of the values of the Enlightenment survived the ideological onslaught generated by the Revolution. Belief in human rationality may no longer have been linked to the values of a genteel culture which had subsumed the study of Nature into its canons of the socially desirable; but that belief, nonetheless, provided the well-spring for the vast scientific enterprise of the nineteenth century.

Improvement gave way to the more socially-unsettling belief in progress, as confidence that it was possible to achieve some 'relief of man's estate' was strengthened by technological success. And, just as the eighteenth-century gentlemanly improvers sought to promote social stability by improving the society around them as well as their lands, so, too, the nineteenth-century apostles of progress could argue that, for all its imperfections, nineteenth-century society had progressed sufficiently to avoid the spectre of revolution. Progress, then, in nineteenth-century

Britain proved as consistent with social order as 'improvement' had in the eighteenth. The practices and possibilities of Enlightenment which Banks had done so much to implant in the soil of eighteenth-century elite landed culture continued to bear fruit well into the following century.

Notes

INTRODUCTION

1. PRO, Prob. 10/box 4514 (Copy in BM(NH), GL MSS BAN). For further discussion of Banks's posthumous reputation see Gascoigne 'The scientist as patron and patriotic symbol: the changing reputation of Sir Joseph Banks'
2. Smith E., *The life of Sir Joseph Banks*
3. Lysaght, *Banks's Newfoundland diary*, p.42
4. Carter, *Sir Joseph Banks*
5. On the dispersal of his papers and early attempts to write his life see P. Mander Jones, 'History of the papers of Sir Joseph Banks', Dawson, *The Banks letters*, pp.xiii–xviii and Carter, *Bibliography*, pp.15–28
6. Cuvier, *Recueil*, III, p.49

CHAPTER ONE   JOSEPH BANKS: A BIOGRAPHICAL SKETCH

1. Farington, *Diary*, IV, p.193
2. Weld, *A History*, II, p.116; O'Brian, *Banks*, p.201
3. Barrett and Dobson, *Diary and letters of Madame d'Arblay*, I, p.318
4. O'Brian, *Banks*, pp.159–60
5. Rauschenberg, 'The journals', p.196
6. *ibid.*, p.196
7. Lyons, *The Royal Society*, p.194
8. DTC, 1:198–9, Solander, 11 Aug., 17 Aug. [1778]
9. O'Brian, *Banks*, p.196, Cullum to the Rev. Michael Tyson, 7 Dec. 1778. Earlier, Tyson, a fellow naturalist, had informed Cullum that 'Mr Banks is talk'd of to succeed him [Pringle], if no Nobleman takes it' ESRO, E2/20/2, Tyson to Cullum, 11 Sept. 1778
10. Lyons, *The Royal Society*, p.198
11. *ibid.*, p.194
12. *ibid.*, p.198
13. Kippis, *Observations*, p.96
14. For two recent analyses of the Royal Society disputes of 1783–4 see McCormmach, 'Henry Cavendish' and Heilbron, 'A mathematicians' mutiny'. (I am grateful to Prof. Heilbron for providing me with a preprint of the latter.)
15. DTC, 3:31, *Planta, 8 April 1783
16. DTC, 3:76, Blagden, 11 Sept. 1783
17. Weld, *A history*, II, pp.155–6
18. Anon, *An history*, p.3
19. Fitz., Blagden, [27 Dec. 1783]
20. RS, B.98, *Blagden, 27 Dec. [1783]
21. Fitz., Blagden, 30 Dec. [1783]
22. Weld, *A history*, II, pp.162–3
23. Kippis, *Observations*, p.145
24. Weld, *A history*, II, pp.161–6
25. BL, Add.8095:307, Mann, 4 June 1784

26. APS, *Franklin, 19 Nov. 1784
27. APS, *Franklin, 6 Dec. 1786
28. BrRO, MS 8030 (4) b, Goodenough to Ford, 13 Oct. 1805
29. O'Brian, *Banks*, p.299
30. Lyons, *The Royal Society*, p.199
31. RS, CMO, IX: 219, 18 May 1820
32. Dawson, *The Banks letters*, p.xxviii
33. BL, Add.427144: 10v-11, 'Memoirs of the early life, of John Elliott . . . Lieut. of the Royal Navy . . .'. (I am grateful to Dr Nigel Ramsay for a transcript of part of this document.)
34. Foster, 'William Sheffield', p.13
35. DRO, *Perrin, 20 Nov. 1767
36. DRO, *Perrin, 28 Feb. 1768
37. Carter, *Banks*, p.67
38. Coke, *Journals*, III, p.437 (14 August 1771)
39. ATL, Barrington to Pennant, 24 August 1771
40. Lee, *An introduction*, p.xviii, According to Johann Forster, Miss Blosset received the sum of £5000. PLS, Forster to Barrington, 13 August 1771.
41. Beaglehole, *Endeavour journal*, pp.55-6
42. Carter, *Sheep and wool*, p.xix
43. Anon, *A history*, p.20
44. Dawson, *The Banks letters*, pp.xx-xxi
45. Wisc., 'The Goldsmith's Garland'
46. DTC, 19:113-4, * T. Dundas, 23 Dec. 1814
47. KAO, U951/C141/2
48. Kew, Hooker Corr., 1:39, *Hooker, 19 June 1813
49. NMM, FL 1/26, MS 60/017, *A. Flinders, 4 June 1804
50. Carter, *Banks*, p.425
51. KAO, U951.C160/1, *E. Knatchbull, 25 May 1784
52. See the graph of periods of inactivity due to gout in Carter, *Banks*, p.525
53. Suttor, *Memoirs*, p.11
54. *HRNSW*, V:460, *King, 29 August 1804
55. Mackaness, *Bligh*, p.353, *Bligh, 15 March 1805
56. DTC 19:252-4, *Knight, 1 March 1816
57. DTC 20:15-6, *Knight, 15 Feb. 1817
58. DTC, 1:30, Johnson, 27 Feb. 1772
59. O'Brian, *Banks*, p.154
60. DTC, 13:99, Fox, 7 May [1802]
61. DTC, 18:106-7, *Home, 15 Sept. 1811
62. DTC, 1:33-4, Clerke, 31 May 1772
63. DTC, 1:266-7, Clerke, 18 Aug. 1779
64. Fitz., Lind to Maskelyne, 30 Jan. 1775
65. Kippis, *Observations*; O'Brian, *Banks*, pp.203-4
66. BL, Add.33272:59, Blagden, 28 March 1789
67. RS, B40, *Blagden, 31 July 1789
68. DTC, 20: 149-50, Temple, Lord Palmerston, 9 Dec. 1818
69. RS, MS 114, 'Cook Medal Papers', *E. Cook, 12 Aug. [17]84
70. Kew, 2:118, *Meiners, 1 Dec. 1794
71. BL, Add.8098:486-7, Sprengel (née Forster), 4 June 1799
72. Barrett and Dobson, *Diary and letters of Madame d'Arblay*, III, p.481
73. Farington, *Diary*, I, p.136
74. Bickley, *Diaries*, II, p.206
75. Carter, 'Sir Joseph Banks the man and myth' p.27; Home, *The Hunterian oration*, pp.10-1
76. Smith J.T., *A book for a rainy day*, pp.229-31
77. Y, S. Banks, [c. Aug. 1777]

78. BRO, D/RA/A/1B/4/35, *Charlotte Seymour, Lady Somerset, 20 Oct. 1818
79. BAO, 36, *Boulton, 19 Dec. 1791
80. LAO, 2 Haw 2/B/64, Copy of will of Miss Banks dated 21 Sept. 1818
81. NLW, 12422, Solander to Lloyd, 5 June 1779
82. KAO, U 951/235/1 (28)
83. Wisc.
84. DTC, 14:111–3, *Lance, 30 August 1803
85. Carter, *Banks*, pp.150, 234–5
86. Only in 1798, 1813, 1816 and 1818 did ill-health prevent this annual migration. Carter, *Sheep and wool*, p.xxi
87. Weld, *A history*, II, pp.111–2
88. SL, Ru 1:11, *Burges, 19 Jan. 1796
89. LAO, Hill 22/2/15, *Hobart, 18 Oct. 1793

CHAPTER TWO   THE LIMITS OF ENLIGHTENMENT

1. Lough, 'Reflections on "Enlightenment"', p.36
2. May, *Enlightenment in America*, p.xiv
3. Spadafora, *Idea of progress*, p.235
4. SL, C1.21. 'Observations and opinions relative to the recoinage of the silver money' [1796]
5. NLS, MS 9818: 16, *Leslie, 19 April 1805
6. DTC, 10(2): 197, 'An essay on the means of framing Lord Grenville's excellent idea of transcribing the triumph of the English nation, on the copper tokens furnished to her colonies into a regular system of historical record'
7. Banks, 'A report of . . . Spanish sheep', p.84
8. KAO, U951.Z38: 21, 'A commentary and annotation on *Five hundred points of good husbandry* by Thomas Tusser'. The edition of 1610 was collated with that of 1585, and edited by Sir Joseph Banks
9. SL, Ru 1: 53, Draft in clerk's hand with corrections by Banks, of a response to either the President of the Imperial Academy of Sciences in St Petersburg and/or the College of Ministers of Justice concerning English law and monarchy
10. Cullum, *The history . . . of Hawsted*, p.iv
11. Payne, *Philosophes*, p.19
12. SL, BG 1: 48, *Macquarie, July 1818
13. Bovill, *Missions to the Niger*, p.4
14. DTC, 2: 97, *Hasted, [1782]
15. Beaglehole, *Journals of Cook*, II, i, p.xlv
16. Saine, *Georg Forster*, p.53
17. Thiselton-Dyer, 'Historical account of Kew', p.305
18. Dancer, *Some observations*, pp.3–4
19. BL, Add.33982:286, A. Watt [1786]
20. YB:OF, *Sheffield, 20 Jan., 1818
21. Venturi, *Utopia and reform*, pp.126–32; Palmer, 'Turgot', p.608
22. Porter, 'Enlightenment in England'
23. Plumb, 'Reason and unreason', p.24
24. Ellis, 'Original letters', p.417, Mann, 31 Dec. 1779
25. *ibid.*, p.434, Mann, 16 Feb. 1790
26. *ibid.*, p.417
27. O'Connor, *Weights and measures*, p.253
28. Jacob, *The cultural meaning*, p.143
29. Evans, 'The diffusion of science'; Jacob, *The cultural meaning*, pp.157–9
30. Owen, *The minute-books*, p.1
31. ANL, MS 5674, *Lit. and Phil. Soc., 23 Sept. 1799; Watson, *The history of the . . . Society of Newcastle-upon-Tyne*, pp.45, 296–7

32. Jacob, *The cultural meaning*, p.152
33. Y, Atkinson, 7 May 1776; *?, 15 Jan. 1782
34. Beaglehole, *Endeavour journal of Banks*, I, p.352
35. YB:OF, *[John Rickman, 1805]
36. SL, BR1:25, *?, 29 March 1800
37. Hampson, *The Enlightenment*, p.154
38. Currey, *George Caley's reflections*, p.19, *Caley, 4 Sept. 1798
39. *HRNSW*, V:460, *King, 29 August 1804
40. Newcombe and Forsyth, *Menzies' journal*, p.x, *Menzies, 10 August 1791
41. Beaglehole, *Endeavour journal of Banks*, II, p.315, *Rolim de Moura, 17 November 1768
42. Y, *Macartney, 29 January 1792
43. Carter, *Sir Joseph Banks*, p.308
44. Fitz., Blagden, 28 December 1783
45. Miller, 'Royal Society', p.60
46. Pindar, *Poetical works*, II, p.82
47. Gay, *The Enlightenment*, II, p.412
48. *ibid.*, p.417
49. *ibid.*, pp.418-9
50. RHO, Br. Emp. MS r.2, *[T.Coltman, March 1792]
51. SL, CL2:64, Sheffield, 3 April 1790
52. Holroyd, *Observations*, pp. [1], 2, 56
53. ESusRO, Gage 5440/160, Sheffield to North, 12 April 1790
54. CL, Sheffield MSS, R. Millington to Sheffield, 4 March 1807
55. *ibid.*
56. BL, Add.41855:251, *T. Grenville, 7 June 1799
57. Bodl., MS Wilberforce c.44, *Wilberforce, 20 Nov. 1815
58. Gascoigne, *Cambridge*, pp.221-4
59. DTC, 18.257-8, *A. Park, 29 June 1813
60. Strauss, 'Paradoxical co-operation'; Gunson, 'Co-operation without paradox'
61. DTC, 16:265-7, *G. Staunton, 7 May 1806
62. RS, Misc.MS, 8.89
63. Wilberforce, *A practical view*, pp.114-5
64. Strauss, 'Paradoxical co-operation', p.251, *Haweis, 11 Sept. 1798
65. BL, Add.35128:145-6, *Young, 1 Sept. 1799
66. NRO, D(CA) 363 *F. Dryden, 20 Oct. 1807
67. LAO, Hill 22/1/14/16
68. LAO, Dixon 16/3: 168, Rev John Parkinson diary
69. Well., Banks file, *G. Kenyon, 27 April 1805
70. Sinclair, *Correspondence of Sir John Sinclair*, I, pp.226-7
71. Gazley, *Life of Arthur Young*, p.268
72. Beaglehole, *Endeavour journal of Banks*, I, p.379
73. Langford, *Polite and commercial people*, p.242
74. Barrow, *Travels in China*, p.459
75. BL, Add.56299:104
76. Beaglehole, *Endeavour journal of Banks*, I, p.381
77. BL, Add.33977:279, P. Russell, 26 December 1784
78. NLS, MS 9819:16, *Leslie, 19 April 1805
79. LAO, Dixon 16/3:168, Rev John Parkinson diary
80. Anon, 'Memoir of Banks', *Asiatic Observer*, p.152
81. RS, Misc. MSS, 6.71, *W. Marsden, 20 Oct. 1810
82. BAO, 127, *M. Boulton, 31 August 1804
83. BRO, D/RA/A/IB/4/3, *Charlotte, Lady Somerset (née Douglas Hamilton), 20 December, 1813
84. Well., MS 1049:33
85. Rauschenberg, 'Journals of Banks's voyage . . . to Iceland', p.215

86. Lysaght, *Joseph Banks in Newfoundland*, p.265
87. DTC, 10(2):232, R. Shepherd, 6 March 1798
88. SL, As 1.1
89. Gascoigne, *Cambridge*, pp.280-1
90. Jones W., *Religious use of botanical philosophy*, pp.2-3
91. Lysaght, *Joseph Banks in Newfoundland*, p.265
92. DTC, 2:218, Memorial to His Majesty King George III on behalf of Mr Francis Masson [?1782]
93. Arber, 'Sir Joseph Banks and botany', p.103
94. Banks, *Short account of . . . blight*, p.107
95. YB:OS, *Blagden, 11 May 1818
96. Knight, *Physiological and horticultural papers*, p.29, *Knight, 10 April 1800
97. Bodl., MS. Eng. Misc.b.38.pp.133-4, *T. Percy, 11 Nov. 1783
98. *ibid.*, pp.137-8, *Percy, 30 December 1783
99. *ibid.*, pp.139-40, *Percy, 7 Feb. 1784
100. Fitz., *Merck, 29 June 1784
101. Gött., 3:49, *Blumenbach, 8 July 1806
102. Rolfe, 'William and John Hunter', p.318
103. ML, Doc. 2502, *Jenkinson, 15 Sept. 1795
104. Beaglehole, *Endeavour journal of Sir Joseph Banks*, II, p.20
105. Anon, 'Account of Lord Sandwich', p.327
106. Carter, *Sir Joseph Banks*, p.152
107. *ibid.*
108. ML, MSS. C.181, *J. Wilkes, 18 July 1788
109. Roderick, 'Sir Joseph Banks, Queen Oberea and the satirists'
110. Anon, 'Histories of the tête-à-tête annexed', pp.457-8
111. Anon, *Mimosa*, p.12
112. Carter, *Sir Joseph Banks*, p.150
113. Extract from 'Banksiana', a collection of anecdotes about Banks allegedly 'written at the request of my friend Dawson Turner' by one 'CH' (probably Charles Hatchett, FRS), in Sotheby's, *English literature*, item 206
114. ATL, Barrington to Pennant, 24 August 1771
115. Fortescue, *Correspondence of King George III*, II, 372-3, J. Cook to ?, 1 August 1772
116. Y, Mackenzie, 24 Sept. 1777
117. Ryden, *The Banks collection*, p.28
118. NLW, 12422, Solander to J. Lloyd, 5 June 1779
119. Black, *The British and the Grand Tour*, pp.109-16
120. DRO, D239M/F15883, *Perrin, 21 March 1767
121. Porter, 'The exotic as erotic', pp.132-6. Though, according to an anecdote recorded by one of his contemporaries, Banks admitted that his experiences there did not always redound to his glory for 'he was severely Mortified when having passed the Night with the Queen Oberea, she dismissed him with evident Contempt, informing him that he was not to be compared with her own Men and requesting that for the future he would devote his attentions to the Girls of her suite, who being comparatively ignorant might perhaps be better satisfied with him than she was'. Sotheby's, *English literature*, item 206 (I owe this reference to Dr Nigel Ramsey).
122. Beaglehole, *Endeavour journal*, I, p.382
123. *ibid.*, II, p.331
124. Y, *M. A. Radcliffe, 18 April 1799
125. BRO, D/RA/A/1B/4/8, *Charlotte Seymour, 10 September 1814
126. DTC, 10(2):239-9, R. Shepherd, 9 May [1798]
127. APS, *Vaughan, 21 Feb. 1790
128. Kew:BC 2:9, *Priestley, 26 April 1790
129. PRO, WO 30/54, *Roy, 19 February 1790
130. BM(NH), BC 19, *Lancaster, 28 March 1806
131. SL, NF 1:3, Notes on Newfoundland

132. Harris, *Political ideas 1760-1792*, p.159
133. HRO, *Knight, 16 Feb. 1816
134. Payne, *Philosophes and the people*
135. BM(NH), 17v,19 *Lancaster, 20, 28 March 1806
136. BL, Add. 8100:178-9, *Jomard, 16 August 1816
137. KAO, U951/Z32/57, Delimonade, 18 November 1816
138. BL, Add. 8100:219, H. Christophe, 29 July 1819 (author's translation)
139. BRO, D/RA/A/1B/4/18, *Lady Somerset, 15 October 1815

CHAPTER THREE   FROM VIRTUOSO TO BOTANIST

1. Houghton, 'The English virtuoso', p.52
2. Shaftesbury, Boyle quoted in *OED*, 'virtuoso'
3. *ibid.*, pp.54, 55
4. Maddox, 'Gilbert White', p.47
5. Norton, *Letters of Edward Gibbon*, III, p.146, Gibbon to Elmsley, 28 March 1789
6. Miller, '"Into the valley" . . .', p.160
7. Plumb, 'The Grand Tour', p.57
8. Smith, E. *Banks*, p.16
9. Anon, 'Biographical memoir of the late Sir Joseph Banks', pp.40-1
10. *OED*, 'macaroni'
11. Langford, *A polite and commercial people*, p.577
12. *OED*, 'macaroni'
13. Stephens and George, *Catalogue of . . . satires*, IV, pp.11-83 and V, pp.70-108, 132-136
14. *ibid.*, IV, p.782
15. *ibid.*, IV, pp.82-3, 712, 742, 781-2 and V, p.86
16. Fitz., Blagden [27 Dec. 1783]
17. Anon, 'The Right Hon. Sir Joseph Banks', p.104
18. O'Brian, *Joseph Banks*, p.209
19. Academicus, *An authentic narrative*, pp.72-3
20. Snip, *The philosophical puppet show*, p.32
21. Brett-James, *Peter Collinson*, p.189
22. Lee, *An introduction to botany*, p.[v]
23. Curtis, *Proposals for . . . the London Botanic Garden*, p.7
24. Forster, *Observations*, p.203
25. Houghton, 'The English virtuoso', p.54
26. Altick, *The shows of London*, p.22
27. Anon, *A history of instances . . .*, p.25
28. Hill J., *The usefulness*, p.1
29. Griffiths and Williams, *Department of prints and drawings*, p.82
30. BM, 234.c.14, case J No. 5: 38-67
31. Kew, 1:147, Strange, 31 July 1783
32. MHSO, 14.30, W. G. Smith, 7 April 1819
33. Pindar, *The poetical works*, I, p.231
34. Kew, 2: 128, Hove, 20 Sept. 1795
35. Sprigge, *Correspondence of Bentham*, p.246, J. to S. Bentham, 6 March 1779
36. Anon, 'Sir Joseph Banks', pp.400-1
37. DRO, *Perrin, 16 August 1768
38. CUL., Add. 6294, 20 Jan. 1768
39. ML, A1594: iii, James Roberts, *A Journal of a Voyage to the Hebrides or Western Isles of Scotland, Iceland and the Orkneys undertaken by Joseph Banks, Esq., in the year 1772*
40. BL, Add. 38310:144, Jenkinson, Sept. 1795
41. ML, Doc.2502, *Jenkinson, 15 Sept. 1795
42. Anon, 'Letters from Sir Charles Blagden . . .', p.413, Blagden, 28 Oct. 1777

43. Miller, '"My favourite studdys": Lord Bute as naturalist', p.236
44. Farington, *The Farington diary*, III, p.273
45. Weld, *A history of the Royal Society*, II, p.153
46. Anon, 'Obituary. Sir Joseph Banks', pp.88-9
47. Stone, *The crisis of the aristocracy*, p.326
48. Marsden *A brief memoir*, p.46
49. Arber, 'Sir Joseph Banks and botany', pp.104-5
50. Berman, '"Hegemony" and the amateur tradition'
51. Farington, *Diary*, I, p.79
52. Cobban and Smith, *Correspondence of Burke*, p.220; Bodl.,MS Malone 36:1-6
53. Cannon, *The letters of Sir William Jones*, I, p.280, Jones to Althorp, 30 Nov. 1778
54. Houghton, 'The English virtuoso', pp.205-7
55. Farington, *Diary*, I, p.27
56. HSP, Galt's West, *[B.West] n.d.
57. HIBD, *William Smith, 14 May 1805
58. Wor., *Worsley, 29 June 1804
59. Kew, 2:114, *Band, 1 August 1794
60. Gillespie, 'Natural history'
61. Raven, *John Ray*, p.477
62. Nichols, *Literary anecdotes*, III, p.322
63. Miller, 'The Royal Society of London', p.108
64. Piggott, *Ruins*, p.117
65. BL, Egerton 1970: 80, Martyn to Strange, 8 April 1782
66. Stephen, *History*, I, p.322
67. ANL, MS 9(129), Perrin, 15 April 1768
68. Allen, *The naturalist in Britain*, p.7
69. Stieber and Karg, 'Guide to the botanical records', p.55
70. Smith J. E., *Correspondence of Linnaeus*, I, p.583, Ellis to Gordon, 2 Jan. 1771
71. Weld, *A history*, I, p.471
72. Carter, *Sir Joseph Banks*, p.25
73. Wall *et al.*, *A history*, I, p.170
74. Hollman, 'The Chelsea Physic Garden', p.91
75. Anon, *Memoirs . . . of the Botanical Garden at Chelsea*, pp.62, 86
76. Smith D., *Sir James Edward Smith*, I, p.499, Banks to Smith, 25 Dec. 1817
77. Fothergill, *The works*, p.628
78. Corner and Booth, *Chain*, p.54
79. Labaree *et al.*, *The papers of Benjamin Franklin*, III, p.116
80. Fothergill, *The works*, p.625
81. Brett-James, *Peter Collinson*, p.56
82. *ibid.*, p.105
83. ML, MSS 743/1, Fothergill, 4 August 1777
84. Lettsom, *John Fothergill*, p.x
85. Brett-James, *Peter Collinson*, p.235
86. Lettsom, *John Fothergill*, p.xi
87. HIBD, Fothergill to Bartram, 7 Jan. 1774
88. Tuke, *John Fothergill*, p.33
89. Hingston-Fox, *Dr John Fothergill*, p.384
90. Rauschenberg, 'John Ellis FRS', pp.153-4
91. *ibid.*, p.149
92. Smith J. E., *Correspondence of Linnaeus*, I, pp.279-80, Linnaeus to Ellis, 20 Jan. 1772
93. Cornelius, 'Ellis and Solander's *zoophytes*', p.38
94. Ellis and Solander, *Natural history*, p.[i]
95. Darlington, *John Bartram and Humphrey Marshall*, p.184
96. Hingston-Fox, *Dr John Fothergill*, p.163
97. Le Rougetel, 'Philip Miller/John Bartram', p.32

98. Nichols, *Illustrations*, IV, pp.635-6
99. LS, Collinson to Smithhurst, 9 Sept. 1742
100. Hingston-Fox, *Dr John Fothergill*, p.163
101. Darlington, *John Bartram and Humphrey Marshall*, pp.157, 365
102. Merrill, *Victorian natural history*, p.258
103. Bowden, *John Lightfoot*
104. Riddelsdell, 'Journal of a botanical excursion', p.293, Lightfoot, 24 August 1773
105. Lightfoot, *Flora Scotica*, pp.vi,xv
106. ML, Doc. 1120, Bentinck, 12 June 1782
107. Stuart, *Botanical tables*, p.4
108. *ibid.*, pp.16-7
109. *ibid.*, p.12
110. Thiselton-Dyer, 'Historical account of Kew', p.291
111. Smith J. E., *Correspondence of Linnaeus*, I, p.33
112. Henrey, *British botanical . . . literature*, II, p.242
113. LS, Collinson to Bute, 29 Oct. 1761
114. Miller, 'Lord Bute as naturalist', p.222
115. Curtis, *William Curtis*, p.82, Goodenough to Curtis, 2 March 1788
116. DTC, 1.140, Stuart, 7 Jan. 1777
117. Stuart, *Botanical tables*, p.14
118. Bretschneider, *History*, I, p.287
119. Smith J. E., *Correspondence of Linnaeus*, I, p.583
120. Home, *The Hunterian oration*, pp.10-11
121. Allen, *The naturalist in Britain*, p.19
122. Bill, *Education at Christ Church*
123. Martyn, *Lectures in botany*, p.vi; ESRO, MS 2785
124. Barrow, *Sketches of the Royal Society*, p.16
125. BL, Add. 5875: 95
126. O'Brian, *Joseph Banks*, p.26
127. Allen, *The naturalist in Britain*, p.45
128. MacGregor and Turner, 'The Ashmolean Museum', p.657
129. Lightfoot, *Flora Scotica*, p.xiv
130. Webster, 'The medical faculty and the physic garden', p.706
131. Y, Parsons, [March 1768]
132. DRO, D239M/F15886, *Perrin, 21 March 1767
133. Lysaght, 'Letters', p.92
134. Carter, 'Sir Joseph Banks: the cryptic Georgian', p.54
135. CUL, Add. 6294
136. PSLO, MS Sherard 218, *Sibthorp, 15 June 1793
137. ML, MSS 743/1:189, 10 June 1793
138. PML, R-V Autob. misc., *?, 21 July 1819
139. Anon, 'Obituary: Sir Joseph Banks', p.86
140. Anon, 'Biographical memoir of the late right Honourable Sir Joseph Banks', p.40
141. Allen, *The naturalist in Britain*, p.45
142. Anon, 'The Right Honourable Sir Joseph Banks', p.98
143. Willson, *James Lee*, p.24
144. Thornton, 'The late James Lee', p.xxvii
145. Lysaght, 'Banks's artists', p.15
146. Kew, 1.3, Hope, 14 Feb. 1767
147. Y, Banks Hodgkinson, 2 July 1767
148. DRO, *Perrin, 21 March 1767
149. Evans, 'Thomas Pennant', p.397
150. Pennant, *British zoology*, I, p.70
151. HIBD, Buffon to Pennant, 3 Oct. 1765; 30 Jan. 1766
152. Pennant, *The late Thomas Pennant*, pp.4-5
153. ESRO, E/2/22/2, Pennant to Ashby, 29 April 1779; 21 October 1770

154. Urness, *Peter Simon Pallas*, p.4
155. Pennant, *British zoology*, p.[i]
156. Pennant, *Synopsis of quadrupeds*, p.iii
157. Gordan, *Reinhold and Georg Forster*, pp.140-1
158. Pennant, *The late Thomas Pennant*, p.10; Ferguson, 'John Gideon Loten', pp.254-5
159. Pennant, *Arctic zoology*, I, p.[5]
160. Pennant, *The late Thomas Pennant*, pp.29-30
161. Pennant, 'An account of the turkey'
162. Pennant, *The late Thomas Pennant*, p.8
163. BM(NH), L/MSS/Pen
164. PML, Pennant, 19, 27 June 1767
165. ATL, *[Pennant], June 1767
166. PML, Pennant, 3 July 1768
167. PML, Pennant, 9 May 1773
168. Kew, 1.21, Pennant, 10 April 1768
169. Kew, 1.9, Pennant, 12 July 1767
170. Kew, 1.11-12, Pennant, 26 July 1767; 4 August 1767
171. Kew, 1.18-9, Falconer, 15 Feb. 1768
172. Kew, 1.22, Falconer, 16 April 1768
173. HC, Falconer, 2 April 1773
174. Kew, 1.42, Falconer, 8 Dec. 1773
175. ML, Safe 1/11:349-52, Falconer, 4 February 1772
176. Forster, *Observations*, p.ii
177. Marshall and Williams, *The great map of mankind*, p.92
178. Williams, *The British search*, pp.162-7
179. RS, CMO, VI:158-9, 19 Jan. 1773
180. Fry, *Alexander Dalrymple*, p.189
181. Foster, 'The honourable Daines Barrington', p.77
182. DTC, 1:23-4, White, 21 April 1768
183. Holt-White, *Gilbert White*, I, p.210, White to Barker, 21 Dec. 1772
184. PLS, Forster to Pennant, 12 Dec. 1768
185. PLS, Forster to Pennant, 30 Nov. 1768
186. ML, Doc. 489, Forster to Pennant, 23 June 1772
187. Gordan, *Reinhold and Georg Forster*, p.70
188. ANL, MS 760/17, Forster, [Dec. 1778]
189. eg PLS, J. R. Forster to Pennant, 3 July 1782
190. ML, Doc.359, G. Forster to Pennant, 5 March 1787
191. ATL, S. Banks to Pennant, n.d.; 6 Oct. 1770
192. NUL, Pw E 17, Lightfoot to Pennant, 12 Aug. 1772
193. Pennant, *The late Thomas Pennant*, p.36
194. Low, *Tour through Orkney and Shetland*, p.xxvii
195. HSP, Dreer MS, Low, 14 Feb. 1773
196. Lysaght, 'Letters', p.225
197. Low, *Fauna Orcadensis*, p.viii
198. BL. Add. 33981:212, 'Incola Orcadensis', 30 June 1805
199. Pennant, *Tour on the Continent*, p.[iii]
200. Pennant, *The late Thomas Pennant*, p.38
201. BL. Add. 8094:33, Linnaeus, 8 August 1771
202. LS, Linn. Corr., XI, Pennant to Linnaeus, 14 Oct. 1772
203. *ibid.*, VI, 1 August 1773
204. Kew, 1.79, Pennant, 14 Dec. 1778
205. Kew, 1.139, Pennant, 11 May 1783
206. Kew, 1.140, Pennant, 15 May 1783
207. PML, Pennant, 18 May 1783
208. Lysaght, 'Letters', p.229
209. ML, A 300, *Lacépède, 29 March 1803

210. Pennant *The late Thomas Pennant*, p.9
211. PSLO, MS Sherard 219:39
212. Allen, *The naturalist in Britain*, p.40
213. Henrey, *British botanical . . . literature*, II, pp.651ff
214. Pulteney, *A general view*, p.51
215. Stafleu, *Linnaeus and the Linnaeans*, p.11; Russell, *Science and social change*, p.82
216. Stoever, *Sir Charles Linnaeus*, p.89
217. Smith J. E., *Correspondence of Linnaeus*, II, p.152, Dillenius to Richardson, 25 August 1736
218. LS, Collinson to Linnaeus, 20 April 1754
219. Watson, 'An account', p.558; Stearn, 'Introduction to Linnaeus' *Species plantarum*', p.75. On Watson's importance in keeping alive interest in botany when it 'was feebly supported in these kingdoms' see Pulteney, *Historical and biographical sketches*, II, p.295
220. Stillingfleet, *Literary life*, I, p.252
221. *ibid.*, p.109
222. *ibid.*, p.186
223. Da Costa, 'Notices', p.513, Russell, *Science and social change*, p.82
224. Stearn, 'Introduction to Linnaeus' *Species plantarum*', p.78
225. Henrey, *British botanical . . . literature*, II, p.110
226. Lee, *An introduction to botany*, p.viii
227. Stafleu, *Linnaeus and the Linnaeans*, p.109
228. Smith J. E., *Correspondence of Linnaeus*, I, pp.124, 134, Linnaeus to Ellis, 30 May 1759; 11 August 1760
229. Marshall, 'Daniel Solander'; Rauschenberg, 'Daniel Solander'
230. Pulteney, *Progress of botany*, II, pp.350–1
231. Rauschenberg, 'A letter', p.65
232. NLW, MS 12415: 24, *Lloyd, 16 June 1782
233. PLS, Forster to Pennant, 17 Oct. 1768
234. Hoare, *Johann Reinhold Forster*, I, p.32
235. Gorham, *John and Thomas Martyn*, pp.37, 117
236. Whewell, *History*, III, pp.329–30
237. Stillingfleet, *Literary life*, p.123
238. LS, Linn. Corr., I: 291, Balfour to Linnaeus, 5 July 1762
239. Smith J. E., *Correspondence of Linnaeus*, II, p.46, John Hill to Ellis, n.d. [c.1761]
240. Stearn, 'Introduction to Linnaeus' *Species plantarum*', p.80
241. Brookes, *A new system*, I, p.xi
242. Berkenhout, *Outlines*, p.vii
243. Kew, 1.7, Pennant, 10 June 1767
244. Pennant, *British zoology*, I, p.xiii
245. Pennant, *Synopsis of quadrupeds*, p.vii
246. Anon, 'Review of *A new system*', p.315
247. Martyn, *Elements of natural history*, p.i
248. Beaglehole, *The wandering scholars*, pp.5–6
249. Smith J. E., *Correspondence of Linnaeus*, I, p.231, Ellis to Linnaeus, 19 August 1768
250. DRO, *Perrin, 16 Aug. 1768
251. Carter, *Sir Joseph Banks*, p.72
252. Hope, 'The autobiography of John C. Fabricius', viii–ix; Brock, 'Dr Hunter's South Sea curiosities', p.9
253. Smith J. E., *Correspondence of Linnaeus*, II, p.574, *Linnaeus, 5 Dec. [17]78
254. DTC 2: 52–4, Darwin, 24 October 1781
255. Fitz., Darwin to Codell, 2 Dec. [17]81
256. DTC, 8: 13, *Saint-Amans, 27 Feb. 1792
257. Brown, *Prodromus*, pp.xxxiii–iv
258. Carter, *Sir Joseph Banks*, p.454

259. Smith P., *Sir James Edward Smith*, I, p.498, *Smith, 25 Dec. 1817
260. Smith and Sowerby, *English botany*, I, p.[iii]
261. BL, Add. 56299:29, *Campo d'Alange, 10 April 1796
262. SUL, D/177, *Thunberg, 29 April 1796
263. This table has been reproduced with permission from Emerson, 'The Edinburgh Society'. The table was compiled from a sampling of the bibliography edited by Henrey, *British botanical . . . literature*, vol.3. All entries dated under the letters A-D, M and S were included except those referring to magazines and serials. Conjectured dates have been treated as certain.
264. Smith J. E., *Modern state of botany*, p.5
265. ANL, MS 9 (15)
266. Carter, *Sir Joseph Banks*, p.540
267. SUL, D/177, *Swartz, 28 Feb. 1788
268. LS, Smith 13.51, Smith to Cullum, 4 April 1814
269. Hankins, *Science and the Enlightenment*, p.169
270. Randall, *The making of the modern mind*, p.264
271. Hahn, *The Paris Academy of Sciences*, p.88
272. Barrington, *Miscellanies*, p.262
273. Martyn, *Heads*, p.v
274. *HRNSW*, V: 88-9, *Brown, 8 April 1803
275. *HRNSW*, IV: 240, Caley, 12 Oct. 1800
276. Kew, 1. 295(2), *Ferryman, 5 Feb. 1788
277. Palmer, *The works of John Hunter*, I, p.29
278. Shaw, *Zoological lectures*, I, p.i
279. Hill, *Fossils*, p.73. In eighteenth-century usage the word 'fossils' was frequently synonymous with 'minerals'; the term 'figured fossils' was sometimes used to distinguish fossils in the modern sense.
280. Miller, 'Lord Bute as naturalist', p.224
281. Anon, 'Obituary. Sir Joseph Banks', I, p.638
282. Wedgwood, 'On the analysis of a mineral substance'; Nicholson, 'Doubts concerning the existence of a new earth'
283. Hatchett, 1799, p.80
284. Porter, *Making of geology*, p.129
285. Nicholson, 'Doubts concerning the existence of a new earth', p.404
286. ICL; Carter, *Sir Joseph Banks*, pp.342-7
287. GPL, MS suppl. 367: 33v, *Faujas de St Fond, 7 Feb. 1811
288. SL, Geol. 1.2 Map, 9 Sept. 1808
289. Well., 67766(c), *Nuttall, 9 Sept. 1808
290. Sherborn, 'The earliest known geological section'
291. Kew, 1.260, Hutchinson, 6 March 1787
292. Pinkerton, *Literary correspondence*, II, pp.156, 158, Pinkerton to M. Laing, 4 May, 24 May 1800
293. *ibid.*, II, p.157, Townson to Pinkerton, 20 May 1800
294. BL, Add. 8098:49, Gmelin, 27 Nov. 1791
295. Pinkerton, *Literary correspondence*, II, pp.197-8, Hatchett to Pinkerton, 29 Dec. 1800
296. Kew, 2.289, *Richardson, 20 March 1804
297. BL, Add. 28539: 248v, Martyn to Da Costa, 1 July 1782
298. Brookes, *A new and accurate system*, I, p.[ix]
299. YB:OF, *Chenevix, 19 Sept. 1804
300. Foner, *Thomas Paine*, II, pp.1291-2, *Paine, [-June 1789]
301. Berman '"Hegemony" and the amateur tradition'
302. Hunter, *Establishing the new science*, p.155
303. RS, CMO, VII:170, 289, 29 March 1771, 20 Dec. 1787
304. BM(NH), GL, MSS RAM, *Rampasse, 8 Sept. 1814
305. APS, *Peale, 1 Oct. 1794

306. Wisc., MS 3:102, *[Aall], [c.1812]
307. DTC, 12:217, 'A Draught of some arguments against all Persons, who apply gratis for permission to see the British Museum, with a plan for receiving admission money for Tickets at the Porter's Lodge', 13 May 1801
308. Miller, 'Between hostile camps', p.44
309. Smith B., *European vision*, p.217, *Caley, 25 August 1808

CHAPTER FOUR   FROM ANTIQUARIAN TO ANTHROPOLOGIST

 1. Hunter, *John Aubrey*, p.193
 2. Evans, *Society of Antiquaries*, p.136
 3. Burgess, *An essay*, pp.34–5
 4. Levine, *The amateur and the professional*, pp.31–6
 5. Colman, *Random recollections*, I, p.189
 6. Kew, 3.25, Grant to Browne, 15 August 1792
 7. Schneer, 'The rise of historical geology', p.263
 8. Shapiro, 'History and natural history', p.14
 9. Hunter, *John Aubrey*, p.193
10. Anon, '. . . Account of . . . the Society of Antiquaries', p.i
11. Evans, *Society of Antiquaries*, p.49
12. Levine, *Dr Woodward's shield*, p.111
13. Gordan, 'Reinhold and Georg Forster', p.20
14. Nichols, *Literary anecdotes*, II, p.591
15. Smith E., *Life of Sir Joseph Banks*, p.159
16. ML, C181:5–6, *Astle, 22 Nov. 1778
17. Kew, 2.292, *T. Banks, 10 Aug. 1804
18. BL, Add. 33978: 24–5, *Grosley, 23 Aug. 1785
19. DTC, 20: 163, Davy, 12 Feb. 1819
20. Moore, *The Gentlemen's Society*, p.6
21. Carter, *Sir Joseph Banks*, p.13
22. Shapiro, 'History and natural history . . .', p.29
23. Hunter, 'The Royal Society'
24. Carter, *Sir Joseph Banks*, p.30
25. CUL, Add. 6294, 19 Oct. 1767
26. Pownall, 'Description of the Carn Braich y Dinas', pp.307–8
27. Perceval, 'Journal of an excursion to Eastbury . . .', pp.13–4
28. Hill, *Georgian Lincoln*, p.47
29. Well., MS 5215/2, 'Account of excavations near Revesby', October 1780
30. Nichols, *Illustrations*, IV, pp.694–5, *Gough, 18 Feb. 1784
31. *ibid.*, IV, p.695, *Gough, [?1784]
32. RS, B.13, *Blagden, 21 Sept. 1783
33. Bodl., MS Douce d 29: 41, *Douce, 13 Jan [1820]
34. EUL, *Thorkelin, 26 July 1810
35. SL, KB 1:26, 'On the origin of the Order of the Garter etc'
36. RS, Misc MSS, 6.36
37. Banks, 'An attempt to ascertain the time . . .'
38. Levine, *Humanism and history*, p.101
39. Kew, 2.83v, *Maurice, [9 Nov. 1792]
40. Farnsworth, 'A history of Revesby Abbey', p.11
41. SL, Co 1: 50, 'History of copper coinage'
42. SL, Co 1: 7, 'Proclamations about Coin'
43. Y
44. Carter, *The sheep and wool correspondence*, p.524
45. Daniel, *A hundred and fifty years of archaeology*, p.24
46. SD, D MSS I: 125

47. Cust, *History of the Society of Dilettanti*, p.114
48. SD, D MSS I: 409-10, *Soc. of Dilettanti, 6 Feb. 1797
49. Carter, *Banks bibliography*, p.143
50. ANL, MS 9(102), R. Knight, 18 June 1785
51. Montagu, Earl of Sandwich, *A voyage*
52. Wortham, *British Egyptology*, pp.26-38; Dawson, 'The first Egyptian society'
53. Thomson, *History of the Royal Society*, p.543
54. Blumenbach, 'Observations', pp.191-3
55. BL, Add. 8098: 213-4, Blumenbach, 8 Jan. 1794
56. Gordan, 'Reinhold and Georg Forster', pp.102-3
57. SL, Or 1: 2-3, 'Notes on a mummified ibis found in Egypt c. 1804'
58. BL, Add.33272: 175; 180, Blagden, 12-3 April; 4 May 1802
59. Y, *Blagden, 25 April 1818
60. Wortham, *British Egyptology*, pp.49-55
61. RS, B.48, *Blagden, 2 Jan. 1814
62. Houghton, 'The English virtuoso', p.219
63. BL, Add. 8099: 65v, Guthrie, [-June 1801]
64. Burgess, *An essay*, pp.117-8
65. Lightfoot, *A catalogue*, pp.58-60
66. Evans, *Society of Antiquaries*, pp.136-7
67. MHSO, Gunther MS 14.5a
68. Beaglehole, *Banks's Endeavour journal*, II, p.241
69. Burgess, *An essay*, p.32
70. Marsden, 'Remarks on the Sumatran languages'; 'Language of the people commonly called gypsies'
71. Pownall, 'Observations ... of the vases on the Mosquito Shore', pp.318, 322
72. Gregory, 'An account of the caves of Cannara', p.281
73. Marsden, *The history of Sumatra*, p.242
74. *ibid.*, p.245
75. Falconer, *Remarks ... on climate*, p.95
76. Beaglehole, *The Endeavour journal*, I, p.384
77. Hoare, *Resolution journal*, I, p.23
78. Forster, *Observations*, p.565
79. Hunt, 'The role of Sir Joseph Banks', p.46
80. Pearson, 'Observations on some metallic arms', pp.402-3
81. Y, Clarke, 26 Jan. 1812
82. Shawcross, 'Cambridge University collection of Maori artefacts'
83. Jones, 'Images of natural man', p.37
84. White, *Natural history ... of Selborne*, pp.114, 196
85. Pennant, *The literary life*, pp.58, 60
86. Barrington, *Observations*, pp.275, 278
87. *ibid.*, p.293
88. *DNB*, 'Barrington'
89. Kaeppler, 'Hawaiian Cook voyage artefacts'
90. Kaeppler, '*Artificial curiosities*', p.40
91. Braunholtz, *Sir Hans Sloane and ethnology*, p.19
92. Kaeppler, '*Artificial curiosities*', p.37
93. Linnaeus, *Lachesis Lapponica*
94. Kalm, *Travels into North America*. Kalm was in North America from 1748 to 1751.
95. Thunberg, *Travels in Europe*, III. Thunberg visited Japan in 1775 and 1776.
96. Osbeck, *A voyage to China*, I, p.vii
97. Pennant, *Outlines*, I, p.ii
98. Bendyshe, 'History of anthropology', pp.444-5
99. Linnaeus, *General system*, I, p.9
100. Blumenbach, *De generis humani*, p.viii
101. Broberg, 'Homo sapiens', p.173

102. Slotkin, *Readings in early anthropology*, p.180
103. Rauschenberg, 'Journals of Banks's voyage . . . to Iceland . . .'
104. BM (NH), Brown MS, J 8551: items 1,2,5
105. *HRNSW*, V:83, Brown, March 1803
106. Mulvaney, 'The Australian aborigines 1606–1929', p.140
107. PLS, Forster to Pennant, 17 Oct. 1768. The term 'government' in Russia meant a province or region.
108. Forster, *Observations*, p.212
109. *ibid.*, p.213
110. Hoare, *The tactless philosopher*, p.134
111. Forster, *Observations*, p.254
112. Pennant, *Synopsis of quadrupeds*, p.v
113. Buffon, *Natural history*, II, pp.360–1, 366
114. Pennant, *British zoology*, I, p.xii
115. Duchet, *Anthropologie et histoire*
116. Smith B., *European vision*, p.139
117. Wood, 'Natural history of man', p.100
118. Smith B., *European vision*, p.101
119. Marsden, *History of Sumatra*, p.vii
120. Cunningham, 'Anthropology in the eighteenth century', pp.27–8
121. Hunter, *Disputatio inauguralis*, p.2
122. Curtin, *The image of Africa*, p.38
123. *ibid.*, pp.65–6
124. Marshall and Williams, *The great map of mankind*, p.275
125. Buffon, *Natural history*, VIII, p.132
126. Shackleton, *Montesquieu*, p.310
127. Buffon, *Natural history*, VIII, p.203
128. Forster, *Observations*, p.271
129. Hoare, *The tactless philosopher*, p.143
130. Herder, *Philosophy of the history of man*, p.173
131. Marsden, *The history of Sumatra*, p.207
132. Home, *Sketches*, I, p.48
133. Gay, *The enlightenment*, II, p.319
134. Kew, 1: 18–9, Falconer, 15 Feb. 1768
135. Lysaght, *Banks in Newfoundland*, p.132
136. McCormick, *Omai*, p.77
137. Y, *Blagden, 24 Nov. 1818
138. Lysaght, 'Eighteenth-century bird paintings', p.261
139. Adams, *Memoirs . . . of Hunter*, 1817: pp.88, 103
140. RCS, Lib.275.h.12. *RCS, 27 April 1806
141. Fitz., Solander, 17 Nov. 1774
142. Y:OS, Blagden to Clarke, 9 May 1786
143. DTC, 10(1):11–12, Eden, Lord Auckland, 25 Jan. 1796
144. Anon, *An appeal*, p.7
145. DTC, 10(1):11–12, Eden, Lord Auckland, 25 Jan. 1796
146. Fitz., 6, Memorial regarding the British Museum
147. SL, Me1:2, Addington, 1 April 1802
148. Slotkin, *Readings*, p.204
149. HRO, *Knight, 23 Aug. 1807
150. White, *An account*, p.[iii]
151. Greene, 'American debate', p.390
152. Curtin, *Image of Africa*, pp.43–5
153. Long, *History of Jamaica*, II, p.356
154. Slotkin, *Readings*, p.214
155. Smith S. S., *An essay . . . on the human species*, pp.[v]–vi
156. Ross, *Lord Kames*, p.334

157. Buffon, *Natural history*, VIII, p.203
158. Home, *Sketches*, I, pp.9, 19
159. Forster, *Observations*, p.257
160. RHO, * [Coltman, c.10–12 March 1792]
161. Burke, 'The wild man's pedigree', p.271
162. White, *An account*, p.55
163. Cunningham, 'Anthropology in the eighteenth century'
164. DTC, 4: 182–4, Blagden, 16 Oct. 1785
165. BL, Add. 8096: 257–8, 261–2, Camper, 23 Jan., 8 June 1786
166. Carter, *Sheep and wool correspondence*, p.110, Broussonet, 14 May 1787 (author's translation)
167. BL, Add. 8097: 18–9, Camper, 12 Sept. 1788
168. BL, Add. 8096: 413–4, Camper, – Oct. 1787
169. Gött., 3:29, *Blumenbach, 22 Nov. 1787
170. Lysaght, 'Banksian reflections'
171. BL, Blumenbach, 30 Jan. 1783
172. Dougherty, *Commercium epistolicum J.F. Blumenbachii*, p.114, 20 June 1787 (author's translation)
173. *ibid.*, p.116
174. Cunningham, 'Anthropology in the eighteenth century', p.16
175. Dougherty, *Commercium epistolicum J.F. Blumenbachii*, p.116
176. Gött., 3:29, *Blumenbach, 22 Nov. 1787
177. Gött., 3:30, *Blumenbach, 15 July 1789
178. DTC, 6: 159–60, Anderson, 3 May 1789
179. BL, Add.8097: 264–5, Blumenbach, 22 Sept. 1790
180. Gött., 3:36, *Blumenbach, ?July 1792
181. Frost, *Arthur Phillip*, pp.184, 261
182. ML, C213: 16–20, Phillip, 27 July 1788
183. Harlow and Madden, *British colonial developments*, p.427
184. BL, Add. 8098:114, Blumenbach, 6 April 1793
185. Gött., 3:38, *Blumenbach, 16 August 1793
186. BL, Add. 8099:13–4, Blumenbach, 12 June 1799
187. Bendyshe, *Anthropological treatises of Blumenbach*, p.239
188. BL, Add. 8098:116–7, Blumenbach, 1 Nov. 1793
189. Gött., 3:40, *Blumenbach, 31 Dec. 1793
190. Bendyshe, *Anthropological treatises of Blumenbach*, p.9
191. Blumenbach, *A manual*, p.16
192. Burke, 'Wild man's pedigree', p.269
193. Blumenbach, 'Human race compared', p.288
194. Plischke, 'Die malayische varietät'
195. Frost, 'The Pacific Ocean', pp.35–6
196. BL, 8098:116–7, Blumenbach, 1 November 1793
197. BL, Add. 8098: 216–7, Blumenbach, 10 March 1794
198. Gött., 3:42, *Blumenbach, 7 Feb. 1794
199. Frost, 'The Pacific Ocean', pp.36–7
200. Blumenbach, *A manual*, p.36
201. BL, 8098:223, Blumenbach, 1 May 1795
202. BL, Add. 8098:216–7, Blumenbach, 10 March 1794
203. *OED*, 'anthropology'
204. Jones R., 'Images of natural man', p.37
205. *HRNSW*, IV: 779, Brown, 30 May 1802
206. *HRNSW*, V: 835, *King, 8 April 1803
207. Hallett, *Penetration of Africa*, p.189
208. Blumenbach, *An essay*, p.vii
209. Blumenbach, 'Some anatomical remarks'
210. BL, Add. 8097:362–3, Blumenbach, 9 Jan 1791

211. see Ch.3
212. Gött., 3:32, *Blumenbach, 28 Dec. 1790; 24 Feb. 1802
213. SL, A4:38, Blumenbach, 22 May 1803
214. BL, Add. 8097:366–7, Blumenbach, 14 April 1791
215. Gött., 3:38, *Blumenbach, 16 August 1793
216. BL, Add. 8098: 215, Blumenbach, 18 Feb. 1794
217. Kew, 2:118, *Meiners, 1 Dec. 1794
218. Ackerknecht, 'George Forster', pp.83–4
219. BL, Add. 8097: 261–2, 9 June 1790
220. Carter, *Sir Joseph Banks*, p.372
221. BL, Add. 8098: 216–7, Blumenbach, 10 March 1794
222. Plischke, *Blumenbachs einfluss*
223. Fitz., Blumenbach, 12 May 1796
224. Hoare, *The tactless philosopher*, p.144
225. BL, 8098: 436–7, Blumenbach, 19 Jan 1799; 8099:13–4, 12 June 1799
226. Rutherford, 'Banks', p.246
227. Sim, *Desert traveller*
228. RCS, Stone Coll. 54, *Clift, n.d.
229. Lawrence, *Lectures on physiology*, p.30
230. Curtin, *The image of Africa*, p.232
231. Lawrence, *Lectures on physiology*, pp.390, 521
232. *ibid.*, p.126. Though in later life Lawrence appears to have leaned towards the polygenesist position. The craniologist, Joseph Davis, reports Lawrence as saying that 'he has never made any additions or alterations in the editions of his N.H. of Man recently published from the first in fact. That his views concerning the unity doctrine are quite changed. And were he to write now, he would write very differently. In truth is now quite decided as to diversity of origin, and a great admirer of its advocates.' RASA, MS 140/4, Sept. 1857. (I owe this reference to Dr Paul Turnbull.)
233. *ibid.*, p.550
234. Goodfield Toulmin, 'Some aspects'; Mudford, 'William Lawrence', p.435
235. Anon, *The radical triumvirate*, pp.19, 20
236. Haddon, *History of anthropology*, p.55
237. Porter, *The making of geology*, pp.205–6
238. Berman, '"Hegemony" and the amateur tradition'
239. Casson, *The discovery*, p.202
240. Darnell, *Readings*, p.170
241. DTC, 13: 168, Vallancey, 17 June 1802
242. Matthews, 'The Lincolnshire dialect'
243. Beaglehole, *Journals of Cook*, I, p.519
244. *ibid.*, p.286
245. *ibid.*, III, pt ii, p.817
246. Beaglehole, *Endeavour journal of Banks*, I, p.370
247. *ibid.*
248. Parkinson, *Endeavour journal*
249. SPK, 62: 4
250. Beaglehole, *Journals of Cook*, III, ii, p.1392
251. SPK, 62: 8
252. Lanyon-Orgill, *Vocabularies*, pp.55–130
253. SPK, 62: 9–13
254. Hoare, *The tactless philosopher*, I, p.114
255. Darnell, *Readings*, p.117
256. Marsden, *History of Sumatra*, pp.25–6
257. Marsden, *A catalogue of dictionaries*
258. Marsden, *A brief memoir*, pp.44–5
259. Marsden, *ibid.*, p.47

260. Marsden, *Miscellaneous works*, p.3
261. Marsden, *A brief memoir*, p.151
262. Marsden, 'Remarks', p.154
263. *ibid.*, p.155
264. Marsden, *Miscellaneous works*, pp.8, 61
265. Marsden, 'Observations', p.383
266. Carter, *Sheep and wool correspondence*, p.161, Holroyd, 17 August 1788
267. Marsden, 'Observations', p.383
268. Marsden, *A brief memoir*, p.151n
269. Vol.LXXX, pp.560-84
270. Vol.IV, pp.221-7
271. Cannon, *The letters of Sir William Jones*, II, p.888, Jones to S. Davis, 11 Oct. 1791
272. Marsden, *Miscellaneous works*, p.6
273. Marsden, *A dictionary of the Malayan language*, p.xviii
274. Marsden, *Miscellaneous works*, p.32
275. Beaglehole, *Endeavour journal of Banks*, II, p.241
276. Marsden, *Miscellaneous works*, pp.32-3
277. BL, 33978: 274, Matra, 5 Dec. 1789
278. Fitz., Matra, 24 Sept. 1791
279. BL, Add. 8098: 434-5, Blumenbach, 20 Dec. 1798
280. Y, Henison, 19 Dec. 1817
281. Marsden, 'Observations on the language of Siwah', p.92
282. Tuckey, *Narrative of an expedition*, pp.xxxvii, 388
283. SL, A5: 16, 'Information collected at Mozambique ... with vocabularies of the Makrana-Munjaui Noveli Somalia Galla & Hurra languages'; *ibid.* p.28, Copy of Henry Salt, 'Observations on a vocabulary of the language spoken by a woolly-headed tribe on the eastern side of South Africa'
284. SOAS, MSS 12153, 12892, 12139
285. DTC, 18: 112, *Marsden, -1811·
286. SOAS, MS 41645 a-d
287. Marsden, *Miscellaneous works*, p.71
288. *ibid.*, p.1
289. *ibid.*, p.74
290. Marsden, *The history of Sumatra*, p.204
291. Beaglehole, *Endeavour journal of Banks*, II, p.130
292. Beaglehole, *Cook's journals*, III, ii, p.787
293. Beaglehole, *Endeavour journal of Banks*, I, p.351; II, p.20
294. Smith B., *European vision*, p.86. In this section I am drawing on material from Gascoigne, 'British anthropology'
295. Duchet, *Anthropologie et histoire*
296. *ibid.*, pp.254, 240
297. *ibid.*, pp.62-3
298. Williams, 'Reactions on Cook's voyages', p.47
299. Slotkin, *Readings*, p.448
300. Casson, *The discovery of man*, p.164
301. Slotkin, *Readings*, p.456
302. Cloyd, *James Burnett*, p.65
303. Slotkin, *Readings*, p.208
304. McCormick, *Omai*, p.73
305. Smith B., *European vision*, p.170
306. NLS, 5378/22/7, Burnett, Lord Monboddo, 7 May 1784
307. DTC, 1:47-8, Robertson, 18 Feb. 1773
308. Burnett, *Of the origin*, I, p.234
309. Fitz., Mello, 16 Feb. 1776
310. Bewell, *Wordsworth and the Enlightenment*, p.62
311. NLS, 5378/22/6, *Burnett, 29 July 1782

312. Bendyshe, *Anthropological treatises*, p.339
313. Fitz., Burnett, 30 Jan. 1783
314. Cloyd, *James Burnett*, p.65
315. Cannon, *Letters of Jones*, I, p.359
316. *ibid.*, II, p.818
317. Slotkin, *Readings*, p.452
318. Gascoigne, 'The wisdom of the Egyptians'
319. Beaglehole, *Endeavour journal of Banks*, II, p.241
320. Marsden, *History of Sumatra*, p.200
321. Gött., 3:47, *Blumenbach, 24 Feb. 1802
322. BL, Add. 8099: 142, Blumenbach, 21 March 1802
323. Gött., 3:49, *Blumenbach, 8 July 1806
324. Darnell, *Readings*, p.117
325. Glass, 'Letter to Marsden', p.81
326. Hoare, *Forster's Resolution journal*, IV, p.613
327. Forster, *Observations*, p.550
328. Hazard, *European thought in the eighteenth century*, pp.51–2
329. Kiernan, *The lords of humankind*, p.21
330. Burrow, *Evolution and society*, p.50
331. *ibid.*, p.51
332. Beaglehole, *Endeavour journal of Banks*, I, pp.368, 362–3, 376, 351
333. Rauschenberg, 'Journals of Banks's voyage . . . to Iceland', p.212
334. Y, * [Macartney], 22 Jan. 1792
335. SL, C2: 45, *Wedgwood, 6 Feb. 1792
336. SL, C2: 43, Macartney, 17 Feb. 1792
337. Y:B, OF, *Percival, 7 Feb. 1792
338. LS, Misc MSS
339. SL, C1: 11 Nov–Dec 1793
340. KAO, U951/Z34: 3, 'Collections on the subject of old china'
341. Well., 5217/2, Reeves, 27 Dec. 1812
342. Kew, 2:38, Davies, 10 March 1791
343. SL, EI 1:67, 77–8
344. SL, Bo 1:39, 1811?
345. DL, MS Q 158:23, *Scott, 17 March 1791
346. BL, Add. 8098: 415, Barton, 23 Jan., 1796
347. BL, Add. 8098: 208–9, Barton, 26 May 1783
348. HSP, Barton papers: 12, Barton, 26 May 1793
349. SL, Am 1:19, pp.1, 4, 11
350. Dawson, *The Banks letters*, p.692; Marsden, *History of Sumatra*, p.331
351. Voget, 'Progress, science, history', p.135
352. West, 'The limits of enlightenment anthropology', p.149
353. Jones, 'Images of natural man', p.37
354. Marshall and Williams, *The great map of mankind*, p.93
355. Kippis, *A narrative*, pp.360–2
356. Degérando, *Observation*, pp.61, 63

CHAPTER FIVE   THE PRINCIPLES AND PRACTICE OF IMPROVEMENT

1. Berman, *Social change*, pp.1–31; Martin, 'Origins'
2. Redlich, 'Science and charity'
3. McElroy, *Scotland's age of improvement*
4. Emerson, 'Science and the Scottish Enlightenment', p.348
5. Andrews, 'The acts of trade', p.279
6. Campbell, 'Scottish improvers', p.204
7. Lehmann, *Henry Home*, p.81

8. Ross, *Lord Kames*, p.315
9. Lehmann, *Henry Home*, p.115
10. Cloyd, *James Burnett, Lord Monboddo*, p.155
11. Wood, 'Science and the Aberdeen Enlightenment', p.53
12. Phillipson, 'Edinburgh and the Scottish Enlightenment', p.436; Fussell, 'Science and practice'
13. Henrey, *British botanical*, II, p.605; Emerson, 'The Edinburgh Society', p.81
14. Langford, *A polite and commercial people*, p.217
15. Withers, 'Improvement and enlightenment', p.111
16. Mitchison, *Agricultural Sir John*, p.85
17. Campbell, 'Scottish improvers', p.207
18. *DNB*, s.v.'George Dempster'
19. Mitchison, *Agricultural Sir John*, p.114
20. Anderson, *Observations*, pp.212-3
21. BL, Add. 56299:105, *Allan, 31 July 1819
22. BL, Add. 33978:30, Sinclair, 12 Sept. 1785
23. *ibid.*, pp.76-7, Sinclair, 24 July 1786
24. Sinclair, 'Preliminary observations', p.iv
25. Sinclair, *Account of the origin*, p.14
26. Sinclair, *Memoirs*, II, pp.48-9
27. Aspinall, *Later correspondence of George III*, II, p.91
28. Sinclair, *Address to the Board*, p.7
29. Ehrmann, *The Younger Pitt*, II, p.468; Mitchison, 'The old Board of Agriculture', p.42
30. Sinclair, *Essays*, p.293
31. Sinclair, *A plan*, p.1
32. Sinclair, *Memoirs*, II, p.49
33. Mitchison, 'The old Board of Agriculture', p.47
34. Sinclair, *Memoirs*, II, p.133
35. Mitchison, 'The old Board of Agriculture', p.59
36. Harrison, 'The Board of Agriculture', p.139
37. Sinclair, *A plan*, p.6
38. Aspinall, *The later correspondence of George III*, II, p.476
39. Roth., S 192.5: 125, Sinclair; *Sinclair, 23 April 1793
40. Sinclair, *Correspondence*, I, p.404
41. Smith E., *Banks*, p.101
42. DTC, 8.239, *Shepherd, 1 August 1793
43. Carter, *His Majesty's Spanish flock*, p.409
44. Y, Stephenson, 22 Feb. 1795
45. Roth., S192.5:57, Cragg, 16 April 1795
46. Aspinall, *Later Correspondence of George III*, II, p.405
47. House of Commons, *Reports from Committees . . .*, IX, p.135, *Lord Carrington, 3 Feb. 1801
48. Board of Agriculture, *Report 1795*, p.23
49. SL, Ag.2:86, *?, 13 August 1804
50. eg SL, Ag.3:59, n.d. 'Essay regarding experiments conducted to determine the amount of water needed to cultivate wheat, & the problem of mildew'
51. Carter, *Banks*, p.404
52. SL, Ag.2:97, March-April 1806
53. SL, Ag.3:40, n.d. 'Draft of an essay on methods of grinding wheat into flour, in relation to different sorts of wheat'
54. SL, Ag.2:95, October 1805
55. Banks, 'Communications', p.183
56. SL, Ag.3: 46, Pamphlet 1805
57. SL, Ag.3: 35, nd, 'A list of the names of some of the wheats of Sicily'
58. SL, Ag.3: 40, nd, 'Draft of an essay on methods of grinding wheat into flour'

59. Sinclair, *Observations*, p.6
60. SL, Ag.2: 80, Sinclair, 10 Nov. 1808
61. SL, Ag.2 : 69, Draft of letter or essay commenting on the possibility of using inferior grain as seed, 31 August 1809
62. BL, Add. 33980:163, *Tatham, 13 August 1798
63. SL, Ag. 3: 53, Sinclair, 4 Jan. 1800; Ag. 3:50, *Sinclair, 6 Jan. 1800;
64. Banks, *Some circumstances*
65. BL, Add. 33982: 73v, Sinclair, 18 Dec. 1814
66. Carter, *Sir Joseph Banks*, p.317
67. For a chronological listing see Hudson, *Patriotism*, pp.130–3
68. BL, Add. 33978:178, Shipley, 2 Feb. 1788
69. Ernle, *English farming*, p.209
70. Ragatz, *The fall*, pp.68–9
71. BL, Add. 33977:135, Steele, 14 July 1781
72. DTC, 14:88, Hinckes, 6 June 1803
73. Ashton, *The Industrial Revolution*, p.127
74. Carter, *Sir Joseph Banks*, p.586
75. Mylechreest, 'Thomas Andrew Knight', p.135
76. *Journal of the Royal Horticultural Society*, 79 (1954), figure 123, *Forsyth, 31 July 1801
77. Carter, *Sir Joseph Banks*, p.571
78. BL, Add. 33981:285, Brande, 22 Oct. 1808; Coley, 'The Animal Chemistry Club'
79. RS, CMO, VIII:313, 27 April 1809
80. Banks, 'Effect . . . upon drains', p.349
81. Berman, *Social Change*, p.40
82. DTC, 12:272, *Young, 30 October 1801
83. Peirson, 'On the connection', p.12
84. Home, *The gentleman farmer*, p.v
85. Curtis, *A catalogue*, p.9
86. Shapin, 'A gentleman', p.309
87. Jardine, 'Memoir', p.45
88. Lodge, *Portraits*, 'Sir Joseph Banks', XII, p.6
89. BAO: 44, *Boulton, 25 May 1795
90. Hunter, *Science and society*, p.92
91. Lennard, 'English agriculture', p.28
92. Vol.107, pp.36–7
93. Anon, 'The Right Honourable Sir Joseph Banks', p.97
94. Carter, *His Majesty's Spanish Flock*, p.409
95. On Banks's activities in promoting canals see Hunt, 'The role of Sir Joseph Banks'
96. Anon, 'The Right Honourable Sir Joseph Banks', p.106
97. RS, B:51, *Blagden, 16 Oct. 1814
98. Saunders, *The history . . . of Lincolnshire*, II, p.110
99. On which see the extensive correspondence with William Milnes, his steward at Overton, from 1793 to 1800 in ICL. Also SL, Coal 1:30 March and May 1793 notes headed 'Memorandums made at Overton record information from Messrs Nuttell & Fenton on coal in the environs'.
100. Y:OF, *Lord Palmerston, 28 March 1784
101. SL, Coal 1:20, 22 March 1797
102. *HRNSW*, III, p.649, Navy Board, 21 March 1799
103. Bodl., MS Montagu d.6: 87–8
104. DL, *?, 12 Jan. 1798; Banks, 'Communication on spring wheat', p.183
105. Kew, BC 1:48, Weston, 1 March 1775
106. Roth., S192.6:51–6, Minutes of a Board of Agriculture meeting (written by Banks), 5 March 1799, 12 March 1799
107. Roth., S192.6:61–6, *Lord Sommerville, 15 April 1799. This letter was later published in the *Communications to the Board of Agriculture* (Vol.2, pp.197–9) under the title, 'Account of experiments in cultivating rice, brought by Sir John Murray from India . . .'.

108. *ibid.*, pp.99–102, *[Lord Carrington], 15 May 1801
109. Roth., S192.5:62, Cragg, 25 August 1803
110. SL, Bo 1:59, *Board of Agriculture, 13 Feb. 1810
111. SL, Ag.3:65, 2 Dec. 1814
112. Board of Agriculture, *Report*, p.35
113. Roth., S192.5: 38, Campbell to Ld [Sommerville], 27 Dec. 1799
114. SL, SH1;16, Abstract of Banks's reply to the Court of Directors & their questions about St Helena, 8 Jan. 1791
115. SL, SH1:18, *East India Company, 27 August 1789
116. PRO, Cornwallis Papers, 30/11/13, *Yonge, 11 Jan. 1787
117. Carter, *Sir Joseph Banks*, p.232
118. See, for example, SL, SS 1:48, Banks, 'Scheme of plants for Botany Bay'. List of those plants which should do well in the NSW climate ... gooseberry, artichokes, peaches, apricots, etc, 1798
119. Banks, 'Some hints', pp.21, 24–5. (The original manuscript of this article is in the ANL, MS 202/10.)
120. SL, NF1:4, Banks, 'Crops & sowing methods best suited for Newfoundland & c', 1807 [?]
121. GM, 61 (1791), p.766, Extract of a letter from Joseph Banks, President of the Royal Society, to an Honourable Member of the Assembly at Kingston, in Jamaica, n.d.
122. Fortescue, *Correspondence of George III*, II, pp.466–7, Sir John Dalrymple to Lord Rochford, 26 March 1773
123. BL, Add. 33030: 464, Sheffield, 'Memorial regarding the West Indies'
124. Raffles, *History of Java*, I, p.151
125. Allan, *William Shipley*, p.192
126. Hudson and Luckhurst, *The Royal Society of Arts*, pp.576, 65 and Wood, *A history*, p.x
127. Gazley, *Life of Arthur Young*, pp.46, 130
128. Allan, *William Shipley*, p.16
129. Allan, 'Notions of economic policy', p.802
130. Allan, 'The Society for Arts ...', p.194
131. Ragatz, *The fall*, p.72
132. Guilding, *An account*, p.5
133. *Transactions of the Society of Arts*, 1 (1783), p.12
134. Rauschenberg, 'John Ellis', pp.153–4
135. CL, Shelburne 48:52, p.605
136. RSA, Collinson to the Society of Arts, 10 Nov. 1763
137. CL, Shelburne, 49:49, pp.747–8
138. BL, Add. 33977:18, V.Morris, 17 April 1772
139. Wood, *A history*, p.95
140. Ellis, *A description of the mangostan*, p.11. The project also had the support of Fothergill (see Savage, *Catalogue*, p.48, Fothergill to Ellis, [1776])
141. Mackay, *In the wake*, p.127
142. Hudson and Luckhurst, *The Royal Society of Arts*, p.57
143. RSA, E 1/12 f.1, Society of Arts, 19 May 1779
144. RSA, Red Book, 187, *Society of Arts, 29 July 1783
145. NLS, MS 3593: 10–12, *S. More, 17 April 1788
146. RSA, Red Book, 189, *S. More, 5 Aug. 1789
147. *ibid.*, p.39, *S. More, 9 April 1791
148. Anderson, *Observations on national industry*, p.66
149. Evans, 'The diffusion of science', p.290
150. LUL, AL 60/2C, Sheffield, 10 Jan. 1790
151. CUL, Add. 6294, 26 Dec. 1767
152. Schofield, *The Lunar Society*, p.351
153. Y, Wallace, 14 Dec. 1787
154. Mackay, *In the wake*, pp. 144–55

155. Y, *Blagden, 4 July 1783

156. Carter, *Sheep and wool correspondence*, ? to ?, [1787], p.100

157. eg SL, BL 1:5 Copy of a letter sent to Dr Blagden from Paris concerning acids used in bleaching &c 26 April 1788 and BL 1:3 Bleaching memo in French sent by Eden [Auckland] to Banks regarding a M.Devisne (?) who has found a method to bleach all sorts of material in just 24 hours, n.d.

158. Kew, BC1:304, G. Barton, 18 June 1788

159. BL, Add. 33982:75-80, A. Johnston, 12 Jan. 1815

160. Dickinson, *Matthew Boulton*, pp.122-3, PRO, BT5/9/197, Minutes, PC Comm. on Trade, 2 Feb.1795

161. BAO, 57, *Boulton, 12 Jan 1798

162. Kew, BC, 1:212, *Blagden, 23 Oct. 1785

163. PRO, BT, 5/11:12

164. SL, Alb 1:3, 17 July 1798

165. BAO, 1, *Boulton, [1778]

166. Carter, *Sir Joseph Banks*, p.344

167. BAO, 8,9, *Boulton, 9 Dec. 1783; Boulton, 11 Dec. 1783

168. CUL, Add. 6294, 9 Dec. 1767

169. Cited in Miller, 'Between hostile camps', p.8, M. Montagu to Mrs Montagu, 17 June 1794

170. *ibid.*, 12 Jan. 1768

171. BM (NH), L MSS BAN, Notes regarding Scottish visit, 31 Oct. 1772

172. BL, Add. 33272: 95-6, Blagden, 24 August 1791

173. Fitz. Memorial regarding the British Museum, [c.1801]

174. SL, Min 1.7, 26 Feb. 1798

175. KAO, U951/Z34: 6-7, 'Collections on the Subject of Old China', 1807

176. CUL, Add. 6294, 18 Dec. 1767

177. APS, *Fabroni, 22 July 1787

178. UKL, Etruria:30484-30, *Wedgwood, 12 August 1784. (I am grateful to the owners of these papers, Messrs Josiah Wedgwood and Sons Ltd, Barlaston, Stoke-on-Trent and the University of Keele, where they are deposited, for the opportunity to consult this material.)

179. Wedgwood, 'An attempt', p.306

180. UKL, Etruria: 30488-30, *Wedgwood, 3 April 1787; 30490-30, Wedgwood, 11 May 1787; *Wedgwood, 21 July 1791

181. Maiden, *Banks*, p.168

182. SL, C2: 45, *Wedgwood, 6 Feb. 1792

183. RS, B:52, *Blagden, 9 Nov. 1814

184. Rumford, *Works of Count Rumford*, IV, p.739

185. Berman, *Social change*, p.8

186. *ibid.*, p.41

187. Jones H.B., *The Royal Institution*, p.136

188. Martin, 'Origins', pp.50-2

189. Peacock, *Young*, p.135

190. Berman, *Social change*, p.55

191. Davy, *A discourse*, p.11

192. Berman, *Social change*, p.66

193. Davy, *A discourse*, pp.21-2

194. Berman, *Social change*, p.68

195. YB:OF, d.10:16, *Young, 27 May 1803

196. SL, Ag.2:46, H.Davy, 'Analysis of wheat', 26 April 1805

197. Berman, *Social change*, p.59

198. SL, Ag 3:71, 'Notes on Davy's experiments at the Royal Institution regarding the composition of wheat'

199. SL, Ag2:48, H.Davy, 'Commentary on the experiments regarding the composition of wheat and Banks's application of them'

200. Stern, 'Control v. freedom', p.442
201. Spiers, 'Sir Humphry Davy', p.104
202. SL, T1:23, Jenkinson, 14 March 1790
203. PRO, BT 5/11: 96, Minutes of 8 March 1798
204. DTC, 10(2):254, Jenkinson, 17 March 1798
205. SL, T1:17, 'Observations on the petition of the tanners, praying the repeal of the 1st of James 1st which prevent the using of elm bark in the tanning of leather'
206. Kew, 3:23, 'A proposal for establishing a society for the improving of naval architecture'
207. SL, T1:24, S. Purkis, 2 March 1798
208. SL, T1:22, S. Purkis, 21 March 1798
209. SL, T1:40, *Lord Glenbervie, 18 Feb. 1803; 'A brief abstract of the principal purport, of the old statutes relative to raw hides', 14 May 1803
210. SL, Ta1:10, Reeves, May 1806
211. SL, BA2:12, Purkis, 18 April 1810
212. SL, T1:44, Tanners' memorial [1801]
213. SL, T1:20, Jenkinson, 27 Nov. 1801
214. Spiers, 'Sir Humphry Davy', p.106
215. ibid., p.107
216. Berman, Social change, p.53
217. SL, Bo1:20
218. Berman, Social change, p.85
219. IO, Home Corr., Misc letters. 239:366, East India Company, 2 Jan. 1804
220. IO, Minutes of the Court of Directors, B/138, p.1252. 29 Feb.1804
221. IO, E/4/656:517-8
222. Berman, Social change, p.88
223. Spiers, 'Sir Humphry Davy', p.111
224. ibid., p.194
225. DTC, 14: 73-7, Blagden, 20 April 1803
226. Hatchett, 'On an artificial substance', pp.211, 126-7, 217, 224
227. Carter, Sir Joseph Banks, p.385
228. Farington, Diary, III, p.285
229. Cantor, 'Thomas Young's lectures', p.93
230. DTC, 14: 282-4, *Rumford, 6 June 1804
231. Caroe, The Royal Institution, p.34
232. ML, MSS 743/2, *Baring, 14 Oct. 1805
233. Bernard, 'Preliminary address', p.xii
234. Redlich, 'Science and charity'
235. Berman, Social change, p.8
236. LAO, Hill 22, 1/5, 'Sales of rice and herrings to the poor, 1800-1'
237. LAO, Hill Coll 5/8, *Roberts, 13 April 1801
238. BL, Add. 8099: 319-20, Cadet de Vaux, 12 Jan. 1803
239. YB:OF, d. 10/6, *Cadet de Vaux, Feb. 1803
240. Board of Agriculture, On the present scarcity, p.2
241. SL, RS 1:4, Call, 31 March 1800
242. Beastall, Agricultural revolution, p.127
243. Y, Gilbert, 3 July 1787
244. CLL, Lindsey, 11.3:12
245. Holroyd, Observations on . . . the Poor Law, pp.21-2, [3]
246. Holroyd, Remarks on the bill, p.63
247. Holroyd, Remarks on the deficiency, p.151
248. Rauschenberg, 'The journals of Joseph Banks', p.202
249. Farnsworth, 'A history of Revesby Abbey', p.238
250. Bayly, Imperial meridian, p.12
251. Barnes, A history of the English Corn Laws, pp.52-93
252. Wilson, 'Newspapers and industry'

253. [R.Mylne], *Reports*, pp.v, viii
254. CUL, Add. 6294. 21 Jan. 1768
255. BCL, 6, *Boulton and Watt, [16 Feb.1781]
256. BAO, 11, *Boulton, 17 July 1786
257. Dickinson, *Matthew Boulton*, pp.203, 206
258. DTC, 6:212, Boulton, 26 June 1789
259. BAO, 14, Boulton, 14 August 1789
260. BAO, 15, *Boulton, 21 August 1789
261. BAO, 23, Boulton, [3 July 1790]
262. Schofield, *Lunar society*, p.345
263. BAO, 53, *Boulton, 31 July 1797
264. BAO, 55, *Boulton, 11 August 1797
265. BL, Add. 38423:20-22, 26 August-3 Sept. 1797
266. BAO, 81, *Boulton, 2 August 1799
267. BCL, 83, Boulton, 29 Nov. 1799
268. BAO, 84, *Boulton, 2 Dec. 1799
269. BAO, 100, *Boulton, 6 Feb. 1804
270. BAO, 106, *Boulton, 6 March 1804
271. BAO, 109, *Boulton, 28 March 1804
272. BAO, 130, *Boulton, 15 Sept. 1804
273. Thomason, *Memoirs*, I, pp.144-5, *Thomason, 6 July 1817
274. BAO, 127, *Boulton, 31 August 1804
275. BAO, 141, *Boulton (son), 1 August 1806
276. Langford, *Polite and commercial people*, p.668
277. Schofield, *Lunar society*, pp.137-8
278. McKendrick, 'Josiah Wedgwood and factory discipline'
279. Jacob, *The cultural meaning*, p.136
280. *ibid.*
281. UKL, Etruria 30483-30, *Wedgwood, 6 April 1784
282. McNeil, *Under the banner ... Erasmus Darwin*, p.121
283. UKL, Etruria, 30491-30, *Wedgwood, 22 May 1787
284. Y, Holroyd, 8 Oct. 1786
285. Schofield, *Lunar Society*, pp.352-4
286. Bowden, 'The English manufacturers', p.21
287. *ibid.*, pp.22-3
288. SL, H. Butler to G. Savile, [c.1782]
289. Seymour, *A history of the Ordnance Survey*, p.1
290. Langford, *Public life*, pp.325-6
291. Staunton, *An historical account*, p.65
292. Langford, *Public life*, pp.139, 211
293. Bayly, *Imperial meridian*, p.80
294. DTC, 13:124, Marquis of Sligo, 23 May 1802
295. Banks, *Some circumstances*, pp.8-9

CHAPTER SIX   THE WANING OF THE ENGLISH ENLIGHTENMENT

1. BM(NH), Banksian MS 101:25, L'Héritier de Brutelle, 11 Oct. 1788 (author's translation from the French)
2. BL, Add. 8097:199, L'Héritier, 23 July 1789 (author's translation from the French)
3. *ibid.*: pp.200-1, 13 August 1789 (author's translation from the French)
4. LUL, AL 60/2 (i), Holroyd, Lord Sheffield, 10 Jan. 1790
5. Carter, *Sheep and wool*, p.211, Holroyd, 4 Sept. 1791
6. APS, *Fabroni, 22 Nov. 1790
7. BL, Add. 23669:179-80, *Rainsford, 17 August 1792
8. Aberconway, 'Two unpublished letters', p.344, Staunton, 24 Feb. 1793

9. Lonsdale, *Burney*, p.364, C. Burney to Mrs Crewe, 19 Sept. 1792
10. Uppsala, *Afzelius, 18 Jan. 1793
11. Eden, Lord Auckland, *Some remarks*, p.24
12. *ibid.*, p.23
13. BL, Egerton MS 2641: 147-8, * Hamilton, 20 Nov. 1792
14. RS, B:41, *Blagden, 19 Feb. 1793
15. NLW, MS 12415.E11, *Lloyd, 14 March 1793
16. CLL, Lindsey 11.1.6A: 3-4, 'My thoughts', 11 March [17]94
17. BL, Egerton 2641: 151-2, *Hamilton, 4 July 1794
18. LAO, Hawley 6/3/2, *Hawley, 17 Nov. 1794
19. APS, *Fabroni, 17 Nov. 1795
20. HIBD, *Koster, 19 Nov. 1795
21. Kew, 2:181, Hornemann to Edwards, 21 Sept. 1797
22. BL, Egerton 2641: 159, *Hamilton, 14 March 1798
23. For further detail on Banks's scientific relations with the French see De Beer, *The sciences were never at war*
24. APL, Grey MS 65, *William Wyndham, Baron Grenville, 20 July 1796
25. SL, France 1:1, *Charretié, 10 May [1797]
26. BM (NH), BC: 95v, *Manning, 20 April 1806
27. *HRNSW*, V, p.89. *Brown, 8 April 1803
28. BL, Add. 56302:22, Walls, 12 Nov. 1803
29. AAS, Dossier Banks, Banks to the National Institute, 21 Jan. 1802 (I am indebted to Dr G.Beales for a transcript of this document). Another copy of this letter is in NYPL, Joseph Banks miscellaneous file.
30. ML., A 80/4: 142, *[W. Aiton], 21 Dec. 1802
31. Misogallus, 'To Sir Joseph Banks', pp.328-9
32. Cobbett, 'Summary of politics', p.29
33. *HRNSW*, V,p.836, *King, 8 April 1803
34. MHSO, Gunther MS 14.17, *Gilbert, 16 Oct. 1816
35. De Beer, *The sciences*, p.103
36. BL, Add. 33272: 174-5, 181-2, Blagden, 12-3 April, 8 May, 1802
37. BL, Add. 33272: 187-8, Blagden, 25 May 1802
38. SL, France, 1:28, *Otto, 26 Jan. [1802]
39. Well., Banks outletter file, *[Delambre], 5 July 1806
40. The nearest Banks did come to such language was a congratulatory resolution of the Council of the Royal Society to the king 'on his providential Escape from the late atrocious attempt on his Life' which talks of the 'Importance of your Majesty's Sacred Life' and the role of 'the great Disposer of Events, for their evident Manifestation of Divine Mercy' RS, CMO, VIII: 169, 22 May 1800. We cannot know, however, how far the wording was drafted by others on the Council apart from Banks or how far such a formal and public address was being couched in terms which were thought to be particularly congenial to a devout king.
41. Horsley, *Sermons*, I, pp.141-2
42. Deane, *French Revolution*, p.32
43. RS, Misc MS 1.3, Horsley to Robison, 16 Nov. 1800
44. Jenkinson, *State of the country*, p.29
45. Jenkinson, *Speech*, p.5
46. NLW, MS 12415: 48, *Lloyd, 22 July 1800
47. BL, Add. 33980: 116, *Nylne, 3 Oct. 1797
48. SL, CRS: 52, *?, 21 April 1794
49. BL, Add. 5281: 14, Chislett, 13 Dec. 1792
50. LAO, Cragg 2/30: 25, Banks's notes on a letter by John Cartwright to JPs of Holland, 29 Oct. 1792
51. LAO, MCD 523, Cartwright, 19 Sept. 1799
52. SL, CR1:17, 'Plan of an Association . . . ', 5 Dec. 1792
53. Hampson, *The Enlightenment*, p.273

54. BL, Add.33979: 251, *Purkis, 2 March 1794
55. Jenkinson, *Speech*, pp.11-2
56. Thompson, *The making*, p.61
57. Carter, *Sir Joseph Banks*, p.573
58. Miller, 'Into the valley', pp.162-3
59. LPL, Roscoe MS 185, 23 Nov. 1819
60. DTC, 1:218, Manchester Lit. and Phil. Soc., 21 Dec. 1785
61. DTC, 4:201, *Manchester Lit. and Phil. Soc., [23 Dec. 1785]
62. Porter, *Doctor of Revolution*
63. DTC, 9:126-7, Georgina Cavendish (née Spencer), Duchess of Devonshire, 1 Dec. 1794
64. DTC, 9:125, *Cavendish, 30 Nov. 1794
65. Golinski, *Science*, p.163, James Watt to John Ferriar, 19 Dec. 1794
66. DTC, 7:104-5, Priestley, 25 April 1790
67. Kew, 2:9, *Priestley, 26 April 1790
68. RS, B41, *Blagden, 19 Feb. 1793
69. Aberconway, 'Two unpublished letters', p.344, *Staunton, 24 Feb. 1793
70. YB:OS, f.d.10/23, *Rumford, [April 1804]
71. Y, Banks Papers 58, Ser.I, Box 14, *Holroyd, 26 July [18]19
72. Miller, 'The Royal Society', p.6
73. *ibid.*, pp.75-143, Miller, 'Between hostile camps'
74. Carter, *Sir Joseph Banks*, p.572
75. Anon, 'Biographical sketch', p.339
76. RS, Misc. MSS 1:46a. Cited in Heilbron, 'A mathematicians' mutiny'
77. Miller, 'The revival'. p.132 and Smith C., 'Mechanical philosophy'
78. Lyons, *The Royal Society*, p.340
79. Miller, 'The Royal Society', p.60
80. Todd, *Beyond the blaze*, p.213
81. Miller, 'Sir Joseph Banks', p.290
82. YB:OS, *Thompson, [April 1804]
83. Coley, 'The Animal Chemistry Club', p.173
84. RS, CMO VIII: 314-5, 27 April 1809
85. Rudwick, 'The foundation of the Geological Society', p.331
86. Fitz., Laird, 4 March 1809
87. Weld, *A history of the Royal Society*, II, pp.247-9. Printed copies of these resolutions were sent to Banks by the Secretary of the Geological Society. Fitz., Laird, 13 March 1809
88. Rudwick, 'The foundation', p.351, NLS, MS 581, no.451, *Greville, 5 April [1809]
89. Rudwick, 'The foundation', p.351, Horner to Greenough, 4 [6] April 1809
90. *ibid.*, p.353, DTC, 18:10, *Greenough, 19 Feb. 1810
91. *ibid.*, p.345-6, Greville to Greenough, [Jan. 1809]
92. Weindling, 'Geological controversy', pp.253, 258. See also pp.261, 264
93. Miller, 'Between hostile camps', p.7, 'Sir Joseph Banks', p.240
94. Barrow, *Sketches*, p.10
95. [Gregory], 'A review', pp.255-6
96. *ibid.*, pp.252, 254
97. Hall, *All scientists now*, p.6
98. Weld, *A history*, II, p.299
99. Hall, *All scientists now*, p.6. For Banks's increasing disillusionment with the policies and direction of the Royal Institution after about 1804 see Chapter 5
100. Miller, 'Between hostile camps', p.30
101. Miller, 'The Royal Society', p.53
102. Foote, 'The place of science'
103. Clark, *A history of Australia*, I, p.70
104. Kippis, *A narrative*, p.364
105. Newbury, *The history*, p.18

List of Abbreviations

	Letter from Banks (name of correspondent without an asterisk or recipient signifies letter to Banks).
AAS	Archives de l'Académie des Sciences, Paris
ANL	Australian National Library, Canberra
APL	Auckland Public Library
APS	American Philosophical Society, Philadelphia
ATL	Alexander Turnbull Library, Wellington
BAO	Birmingham Assay Office MSS, Boulton Correspondence, Birmingham Central Library
BCL	Birmingham Central Library
BL Add.	British Library, Additional MSS
BM	British Museum Print Room
BM (NH)	British Museum of Natural History
Bodl.	Bodleian Library, Oxford
BRO	Buckinghamshire Record Office, Aylesbury
BrRO	Bristol Record Office
CL	William Clements Library, University of Michigan, Ann Arbor
CLL	Central Library, Lincoln
CUL	Cambridge University Library
DL	Dixson Library (State Library of New South Wales), Sydney
DNB	*Dictionary of National Biography* ed. S. Lee and L. Stephen, 22 vols. Smith Elder and Co., 1908-9
DRO	Derbyshire Record Office, Fitzherbert MSS
DSB	*Dictionary of Scientific Biography* ed. C. Gillispie, 16 vols. New York: Scribners, 1970-80
DTC	Dawson Turner Copies, Banks Correspondence (20 vols. in 21), Botany Library, British Museum of Natural History
ESRO	East Suffolk Record Office, Bury St Edmunds
ESusRO	East Sussex Record Office, Lewes
EUL	Edinburgh University Library
Fitz.	Fitzwilliam Museum, Cambridge, Perceval Collection MS 215
Gött	Niedersächssische Stadts und Universitätsbibliothek, Göttingen, Blumenbach MSS
GPL	Geneva Public Library
HC	Hawley Collection (transcripts by W. Dawson in BL. Add. 56301(7))
HIBD	Hunt Institute for Botanical Documentation, Carnegie-Mellon University, Pittsburgh
HRNSW	*Historical Records of New South Wales* ed. F. Bladen, 8 vols. Sydney, 1892-1901
HRO	Herefordshire Record Office, Thomas Andrew Knight Correspondence, Hereford
HSP	Historical Society of Pennsylvania, Philadelphia
ICL	Lyon-Playfair Library, Imperial College, University of London. Banks-William Milnes correspondence in the Robert Annan Mining Collection
IO	India Office, London
KAO	Kent Archives Office, Canterbury

Kew	Royal Botanic Gardens Library, Kew, Banks Correspondence
LAO	Lincolnshire Archives Office, Lincoln
LPL	Liverpool Public Library
LS	Linnean Society of London
LUL	London University Library
MHSO	Museum of the History of Science, Oxford, Gunther MSS
ML	Mitchell Library (State Library of New South Wales), Sydney
NLS	National Library of Scotland
NLW	National Library of Wales, John Lloyd Correspondence
NMM	National Maritime Museum, Greenwich
NRO	Northamptonshire Record Office, Northampton
NUL	Nottingham University Library
NYPL	New York Public Library
OED	*Oxford English Dictionary* ed. James Murray, 13 vols. Oxford: Oxford University Press 1933
PLS	Peabody Library, Salem
PML	Pierpont Morgan Library, New York
PRO	Public Records Office
PSLO	Plant Sciences Library, Oxford
RASA	Royal Anthropological Society Archives
RCS	Royal College of Surgeons
RHO	Rhodes House, Oxford
Roth.	Rothampstead Agricultural Research Station, Hertfordshire
RS	Royal Society
RSA	Royal Society of Arts
SD	Society of Dilettanti (archives held at the Society of Antiquaries)
SL	Sutro Library, San Francisco
SOAS	School of Oriental and African Studies, University of London
SPK	Staatsbibliothek Preussischer Kulturbesitz, Berlin, MS or oct.
SUL	Stockholm University Library
UKL	University of Keele Library
Uppsala	Carolina Library, University of Uppsala
Well.	Wellcome Institute for the History of Medicine, London
Wisc.	University of Wisconsin Library, Madison
Wor.	Worsley MSS (transcript in Banks Archive Office, BM (NH))
WSRO	West Sussex Record Office, Chichester
Y	Yale University, Sterling Memorial Library, Historical Manuscripts Collection, Banks Correspondence (arranged in chronological sequence)
YB: OF	Yale University, Beinecke Rare Book and Manuscript Library, Osborn Files
YB: OS	*ibid.*, Osborn Shelves

Bibliography

1. MANUSCRIPT SOURCES

The libraries which hold the MS sources on which this book is based are listed in the List of Abbreviations, above. For further details on these sources see Carter, H.B. *Sir Joseph Banks (1743-1820). A guide to biographical and bibliographical sources*, 1987.

2. PRINTED SOURCES

(**Note**: place of publication is London unless otherwise stated)

Aberconway, Lord 'Two unpublished letters written by Sir Joseph Banks', *Journal of the Royal Horticultural Society*, 99 (1974), 339-47.

Academicus, *An authentic narrative of the dissensions and debates in the Royal Society ...*, 1784.

Ackerknecht, E.H. 'George Forster, Alexander von Humboldt, and ethnology', *Isis*, 46 (1955), 83-95.

Adams, J. *Memoirs of the life and doctrines of ... John Hunter*, 1817.

Allan, D.G.C. 'Notions of economic policy expressed by the Society's correspondents and in its publications, 1754-1847; (i) Economic nationalism', *Journal of the Royal Society of Arts*, 106 (1958), 800-4.

——. 'The Society for the Encouragement of Arts, Manufactures and Commerce. Organization, membership and objectives in the first three decades (1755-84)', unpublished PhD thesis, University of London, 1979.

——. *William Shipley, Founder of the Royal Society of Arts*, Hutchinson, 1979.

Allen, D.E. *The naturalist in Britain. A social history*, Hutchinson, 1978.

Altick, R. *The shows of London*, Cambridge, Mass.: Harvard University Press, 1978.

Anderson, J. *Observations on national industry*, Edinburgh, [1777].

Andrews, C.M. 'The acts of trade' in J. Holland Rose, A.P. Newton and E.A. Benians (eds.), *The Cambridge History of the British Empire*, Vol. 1 *The Old Empire from the beginnings to 1783*, Cambridge: Cambridge University Press, 1960, 268-99.

Anon. 'An account of Lord Sandwich', *British Magazine and Review*, 1782, 327.

Anon. *An appeal to the present parliament of England, on the subject of the late Mr John Hunter's museum*, 1795?.

Anon. *An history of the instances of exclusion from the Royal Society ... with strictures on the formation of the Council, and other instances of the despotism of Sir J. Banks*, 1784.

Anon. 'Biographical memoir of the late Right Honourable Sir Joseph Banks, Bart, GCB, President of the Royal Society', *Philosophical Magazine and Journal*, 56 (1820), 40-46.

Anon. 'Biographical sketch of the life of Sir Joseph Banks ...', *Agricultural Magazine*, 9 (1811), 333-41.

Anon. 'Histories of the tête-à-tête annexed; or, Memoirs of the circumnavigator [i.e. Sir J. Banks] and Miss B---n', *Town and Country Magazine*, Sept. (1773), 457-8.

Anon. 'Introduction: containing an historical account of the origin and establishment of the Society of Antiquaries', *Archaeologia*, I (1772), i-iv.

Anon. 'Letters from Sir Charles Blagden to Sir Joseph Banks on American natural history and politics', *Bulletin of the New York Public Library*, 7 (1903), 407-446.

Anon. 'Memoir of Banks', *Asiatic Observer*, I (1823), 125-52.

Anon. *Memoirs, historical and illustrative, of the Botanical Garden at Chelsea; belonging to the Society of Apothecaries of London*, 1820.

Anon. *Mimosa, or the sensitive plant. A poem dedicated to Mr Banks . . .*, 1779.

Anon. 'Obituary. Sarah Sophia Banks', *Gentleman's Magazine*, 87 (1818), 472.

Anon. 'Obituary. Sir Joseph Banks', *Gentleman's Magazine*, 89 (1820), (1): 534, 637-8; (2): 86-9.

Anon. 'Review of *A new system of the natural history of quadrupeds . . .*', *Critical Review*, 3 (1791), 313-8.

Anon. 'Sir Joseph Banks' in *Public characters of 1800-01*, 1801, pp.370-401.

Anon. *The radical triumvirate, or, infidel Paine, Lord Byron, and Surgeon Lawrence, colleaguing with the patriotic radicals to emancipate mankind from all laws human and divine*, 1820.

Anon. 'The Right Honourable Sir Joseph Banks', *Annual Biography and Obituary*, 5 (1821), 97-120.

Arber, A. 'Sir Joseph Banks and botany', *Chronica Botanica*, 9 (1945), 94-106.

Ashton, T. *The Industrial Revolution 1760-1830*, Oxford: Oxford University Press, 1964.

Aspinall, A. (ed.) *The later correspondence of George III*, 5 vols., Cambridge: Cambridge University Press, 1962-70.

Banks, J. 'A report of the state of His Majesty's Flock of fine wooled Spanish sheep during the years 1800 and 1801 . . .', *Agricultural Magazine*, 9 (1803), 80-4.

——. *A short account of the disease in corn called by farmers the blight, the mildew and the rust, etc.*, 1812 (First published 1805).

——. 'Accounts of experiments in cultivating rice, brought by Sir John Murray from India: in a letter to Lord Somerville . . .', *Communications to the Board of Agriculture*, 2 (1800), 197-9.

——. 'An attempt to ascertain the time when the potato *Solanum tuberosum* was first introduced into the United Kingdom . . .', *Transactions of the Horticultural Society of London*, 1 (1807), 8-12.

——. 'Communication on spring wheat', *Agricultural Magazine*, 1 (1806), series 2, 340-3.

——. 'Communications on spring wheat', *Communications to the Board of Agriculture*, 5 (1806), 181-5.

——. 'Effect of the *Equistem palustre* upon drains: in a letter to Arthur Young from Woburn, 21 June 1798', *Communications to the Board of Agriculture*, 2 (1800), 349-50.

——. 'Instruction given to the council [= counsel], against the Wool Bill', *Annals of Agriculture*, 9 (1788), 479-506.

——. 'Some hints respecting the proper mode of inuring tender plants to our climate', *Transactions of the Horticultural Society of London*, 1 (1807), 21-5.

——. *Some circumstances relative to merino sheep . . .*, 1809.

Barnes, D.G. *A history of the English corn laws from 1660 to 1846*, New York: Kelley, 1961.

Barrett, C. and Dobson, A. (eds.) *Diary and letters of Madame d'Arblay*, 6 vols., Macmillan, 1904-5.

Barrington, D. *Miscellanies*, 1781.

——. *Observations on the statutes . . .*, 1766.

Barrow, J. *Sketches of the Royal Society and the Royal Society Club*, 1849.

——. *Travels in China*, 1804.

Bayly, C. *Imperial meridian. The British Empire and the world, 1780-1830*, Longman, 1989.

Beaglehole, J.C. (ed.) *Journals of Captain James Cook on his voyages of discovery*, 3 vols. in 4, Cambridge: Cambridge University Press (Hakluyt Society), 1955-74.

——. *The Endeavour Journal of Joseph Banks 1768-1771*, 2 vols., Sydney: the Trustees of the Public Library of New South Wales in association with Angus and Robertson, 1962.

Beaglehole, J.C. *The wandering scholars: address at the opening of an exhibition from the Alströmer Collection of the Ethnographical Museum of Sweden*, Wellington: Dominion Museum, 1966.

Beastall, J.W. *The agricultural revolution in Lincolnshire*, Lincoln: History of Lincolnshire Committee for the Society of Lincolnshire History and Archaeology, 1978.

Bendyshe, T. *The anthropological treatises of Johann Friedrich Blumenbach*, 1865.

——. 'The history of anthropology', *Memoirs read before the Anthropological Society of London*, I (1865), 335–458.

Berkenhout, J. *Outlines of the natural history of Great Britain and Ireland . . .*, 1769.

Berman, M. '"Hegemony" and the amateur tradition in British science', *Journal of Social History*, 8 (1974–5), 30–43.

——. *Social change and scientific organization. The Royal Institution 1799–1844*, Heinemann, 1978.

——. 'The early years of the Royal Institution 1799–1810', *Science Studies*, 2 (1972), 205–40.

Bernard, T. 'Preliminary address' in Society for Bettering the Condition . . . of the Poor, *Reports*, 1 (1978), xii.

Bewell, A. *Wordsworth and the Enlightenment: nature, man and society*, New Haven: Yale University Press, 1989.

Bickley, F. (ed.) *The diaries of Sylvester Douglas (Lord Glenbervie)*, 2 vols., Constable, 1928.

Bill, E.W. *Education at Christ Church Oxford 1660–1800*, Oxford: Clarendon Press, 1988.

Black, J. *The British and the Grand Tour*, Croom Helm, 1985.

Blumenbach, J.F. *A manual of the elements of natural history . . .*, translated from the German by R.T. Gore, 1825.

——. *An essay on generation*, translated from the German by A. Crichton, [1792].

——. *De generis humani varietate nativa . . .*, 3rd edn, Göttingen, 1795.

——. 'Observations on some Egyptian mummies opened in London. Addressed to Sir Joseph Banks', *Philosophical Transactions*, 84 (1794), 177–95.

——. 'Some anatomical remarks on the *Ornithorhynchus paradoxus*, from New South Wales', *Medical and Physical Journal*, 6 (1801), 73–5.

——. 'The human race compared with swine', *Philosophical Magazine*, 3 (1799), 284–90.

Board of Agriculture, *On the present scarcity of provisions*, [1795].

——. *Report of the committee, appointed by the Board of Agriculture, to take into consideration the state of the waste lands and common fields of this kingdom*, 1795.

Bovill, E.W. *Missions to the Niger*, Vol. 1, Cambridge: Cambridge University Press for the Hakluyt Society, 1964.

Bowden, J.K. *John Lightfoot. His work and travels*, Kew: Bentham-Moxon Trust Royal Botanic Gardens, 1989.

Bowden, W. 'The English manufacturers and the commercial treaty of 1786 with France', *American Historical Review*, 25 (1919–20), 18–35.

Braunholtz, H.J. *Sir Hans Sloane and ethnology*, British Museum, 1970.

Bretschneider, E. *History of European botanical discoveries in China*, 2 vols., 1898.

Brett-James, N.G. *The life of Peter Collinson*, Dunstan and Co., 1926.

Broberg, G. 'Homo sapiens. Linnaeus's classification of man' in T. Frängsmyr (ed.), *Linnaeus the man and his work*, Berkeley: University of California Press, 1983, pp. 156–94.

Brock, H. 'Dr Hunter's South Sea curiosities', *Scottish Art Review*, 14 (1973), 6–9, 37–8.

Brookes, R. *A new and accurate system of natural history*, 6 vols., 1763.

Brown, J. *The secular ark*, New Haven: Yale University Press, 1983.

Brown, R. *Prodromus florae Novae Hollandiae*, W.T. Stearn (ed.), New York, 1960.

Bruce-Mitford, R. *The Society of Antiquaries of London. Notes on its history and possessions*, Society of Antiquaries, 1951.

Buffon, G. *Natural history, general and particular . . .*, translated by William Smellie, 9 vols., 1791.

Burckhardt, J.L. *Travels in Nubia . . .*, 1822.

Burgess, T. *An essay on the study of antiquities*, Oxford, 1782.

Burke, J.G. 'The wild man's pedigree' in E. Dudley and M.E. Novak (eds.), *The wild man within. An image in Western thought from the Renaissance to Romanticism*, Pittsburgh: University of Pittsburgh, 1972, 259–80.

Burnett, J. *Of the origin and progress of language*, 6 vols., 1773–92.

Burrow, J. *Evolution and society. History in Victorian social theory*, Cambridge: Cambridge University Press, 1970.

Cameron, H.C. *Sir Joseph Banks*, Sydney: Angus and Robertson, 1966.

Campbell, R.H. 'Scottish improvers and the course of change in the eighteenth century', in L.M. Cullen and T.C. Smout (eds.), *Comparative aspects of Scottish and Irish economic history, 1600–1900*, Edinburgh: Donald, 1977, pp. 204–15.

Cannon, G. (ed.) *The letters of Sir William Jones*, 2 vols., Oxford: Clarendon Press, 1970.

Cantor, G.N. 'Thomas Young's lectures at the Royal Institution' *Notes and Records of the Royal Society of London*, 25 (1970), 87–112.

Caroe, G. *The Royal Institution. An informal history*, J. Murray, 1985.

Carter, H.B. *His Majesty's Spanish flock*, Sydney: Angus and Robertson, 1964.

———. *Sir Joseph Banks (1743-1820). A guide to biographical and bibliographical sources*, Winchester: St Pauls Bibliographies in assoc. with the British Museum (Natural History), 1987.

———. *Sir Joseph Banks 1743-1820*, British Museum (Natural History), 1988.

———. 'Sir Joseph Banks: the cryptic Georgian', *Lincolnshire History and Archaeology*, 16 (1981), 53–62.

———. 'Sir Joseph Banks the man and the myth', *Bulletin of Local History East Midland Region*, 24-5 (1989-90), 25-32.

———. *The sheep and wool correspondence of Sir Joseph Banks 1781-1820*: Sydney: Library Council of New South Wales, 1979.

Casson, S. *The discovery of man*, Readers Union, 1940.

Clark, C.M.H. *A history of Australia. Vol. I. From the earliest times to the Age of Macquarie*, Melbourne: Melbourne University Press, 1962.

Cloyd, E.L. *James Burnett, Lord Monboddo*, Oxford: Clarendon Press, 1972.

Cobban, A. and Smith, R.A. (eds.) *The correspondence of Edmund Burke*, Vol. VI, Chicago: University of Chicago Press, 1967.

Cobbett, W. 'Summary of politics', *Cobbett's Annual Register*, 3 (1803), 29.

Coke, M. *Journals*, 4 vols., Edinburgh, 1892.

Coley, N.G. 'The Animal Chemistry Club: assistant society to the Royal Society', *Notes and Records of the Royal Society*, 22 (1967), 173–85.

Colman, G. *Random recollections*, 2 vols., 1795.

Cornelius, P. 'Ellis and Solander's *zoophytes*, 1786: six unpublished plates and other aspects', *Bulletin of the British Museum (Natural History), (Historical Series)*, 16 (1988), 17–87.

Corner, B.C. and Booth, C.C. *Chain of friendship. Selected letters of Dr John Fothergill of London, 1735-1780*, Cambridge, Mass.: Harvard University Press, 1971.

Craig, J. *The Mint. A history of the London Mint from AD287 to 1948*, Cambridge: Cambridge University Press, 1953.

Cullum, J. *The history and antiquities of Hawsted, and Hardwick, in the County of Suffolk*, 1813.

Cunningham, J.D. 'Anthropology in the eighteenth century', *Journal of the Royal Anthropological Institute*, 39 (1908), 10–35.

Currey, J.E.B. (ed.) *George Caley's Reflections on the colony of New South Wales*, Melbourne: Lansdowne, 1966.

Curtin, P.D. *The image of Africa. British ideas and action, 1780-1850*, Madison, Wisc.: University of Wisconsin Press, 1965.

Curtis, W. *A catalogue of the British medicinal, culinary, and agricultural plants, cultivated in the London Botanic Garden*, 1783.

———. *Proposals for opening by subscription a botanic garden, to be called the London Botanic Garden*, 1778.

———. *William Curtis*, Winchester: Warren and Son, 1941.

Cust, L. *History of the Society of Dilettanti*, 1898.

Cuvier, G.L. *Recueil des éloges historiques*, 3 vols., Paris, 1827.

Da Costa, E.M. 'Notices and anecdotes of literati ...' *Gentleman's Magazine*, 82 (1812), 205-7, 513-7.

Dancer, T. *Some observations respecting the Botanical Garden*, Jamaica, 1804.

Daniel, G. *A hundred and fifty years of archaeology*, Duckworth, 1975.

Darlington, W. *Memorials of John Bartram and Humphrey Marshall*, New York, 1849.

Darnell, R. *Readings in the history of anthropology*, New York: Harper and Row, 1974.

Davies, J.D. 'The Banks family', *Notes and Records of the Royal Society*, 3 (1940), 85-7.

Davy, H. *A discourse, introductory to a course of lectures on chemistry, delivered in the theatre of the Royal Institution on the 21st of January 1802*, 1802.

Dawson, W.R. *The Banks letters. A calendar of the manuscript correspondence of Sir Joseph Banks preserved in the British Museum, The British Museum (Natural History) and other collections in Great Britain*, Trustees of the British Museum, 1958.

———. 'The first Egyptian society', *Journal of the Egyptian Archaeology*, 24 (1938), 259-60.

Deane, S. *The French Revolution and Enlightenment in England 1789-1832*, Cambridge, Mass.: Harvard University Press, 1988.

De Beer, G. *The sciences were never at war*, Edinburgh: Nelson, 1960.

Degérando, J-M. *The observation of savage peoples* translated by F.C.T. Moore, 1969.

Dickinson, H.W. *Matthew Boulton*, Cambridge: Cambridge University Press, 1936.

Dougherty, F.W.P. *Commercium epistolicum J.F. Blumenbachii. Aus einem Briefwechsel des klassischen Zeit alters der Naturgeschichte*, Göttingen: Niedersächssische Staats -und Universitäts Bibliothek, 1984.

Duchet, M. *Anthropologie et histoire au siècle des lumières. Buffon, Voltaire, Rousseau, Helvétius, Diderot*, Paris: Maspero, 1971.

Eden, W. *Some remarks on the apparent circumstances of the war in the fourth week of October 1795*, 1795.

Ehrman, J.P.W. *The younger Pitt*, 2 vols., Constable, 1969-83.

Ellis, H. *Original letters of eminent literary men the sixteenth, seventeenth and eighteenth centuries . . .*, 1843.

Ellis, J. *A description of the mangostan and the bread-fruit*, 1775.

Ellis, J. and Solander, D. *Natural history of many curious and uncommon zoophytes . . .*, 1786.

Emerson, R. 'Science and the Scottish Enlightenment', *History of Science*, 26 (1988), 333-66.

———. 'The Edinburgh Society for the Importation of Foreign Seeds and Plants, 1764-1773', *Eighteenth-Century Life*, 7 (1982), 73-95.

Engel, C.E. 'John Strange et la Suisse', *Gesnerus*, 6 (1949), 34-44.

Ernle, R. *English farming: past and present*, Heinemann, 1961.

Evans, J. *A history of the Society of Antiquaries*, Oxford: Oxford University Press, 1956.

Evans, R.J. 'The diffusion of science: the geographical transmission of natural philosophy in the English provinces, 1600-1760', unpublished PhD thesis, University of Cambridge, 1982.

Evans, R.P. 'Thomas Pennant (1726-98): "The father of Cambrian Tourists"', *Welsh Historical Review*, 13 (1987), 395-417.

Falconer, W. *Remarks on the influence of climate . . .*, 1781.

Farington, J. *The Farington diary*, ed. J. Greig, 7 vols., Hutchinson, 1923-8.

Farnsworth, J.R. 'A history of Revesby Abbey', unpublished PhD thesis, Yale University, 1955.

Ferguson, D. 'John Gideon Loten, FRS, the naturalist governor of Ceylon (1752-57), and the Sinhalese artist de Bevere', *Journal of the Royal Asiatic Society of Ceylon*, 19 (1907), 217-71.

Foner, P.S. (ed.) *The complete writings of Thomas Paine*, 2 vols., New York: Citadel Press, 1945.

Foote, G.A. 'The place of science in the British Reform Movement 1830-50', *Isis*, 42 (1951), 192-208.

Forster, G. *A voyage round the world . . .*, 2 vols., 1777.

Forster, J.R. *Observations made during a voyage around the world, on physical geography, natural history and ethic philosophy*, 1778.

Fortescue, J. (ed.) *The correspondence of King George the Third: from 1760 to December 1783 . . .*, 6 vols., Macmillan, 1927-8.

Foster, P.G.M. 'The honourable Daines Barrington, FRS - Annotations on two journals compiled by Gilbert White', *Notes and Records of the Royal Society*, 41 (1986), 77-93.

———. 'William Sheffield: four letters to Gilbert White', *Archives of Natural History*, 12 (1985), 1-21.

Fothergill, J. *The works*, 1784.

Freshfield, D.W. *The life of Horace Benedict de Saussure*, Edward Arnold, 1920.

Frost, A. *Arthur Phillip 1738-1814. His voyaging*, Melbourne: Oxford University Press, 1987.
——. 'The Pacific Ocean - the eighteenth century's new world' in W. Veit (ed.), *Captain James Cook: image and impact*, Vol. II, Melbourne: Hawthorn Press, 1979, pp.5-49.
Fry, H.T. *Alexander Dalrymple*, Cass, for the Royal Commonwealth Society, 1970.
Fussell, G.E. 'Science and practice in eighteenth century British agriculture', *Agricultural History*, 43 (1969), 7-18.

Garnier, R. *History of the English Landed Interest: its customs, laws and agriculture*, 2 vols., 1892-3.
Gascoigne, J. 'British anthropology in the Age of the Enlightenment' in M. Blackman (ed.), *Australian Aborigines and the French*, University of New South Wales, French-Australian Research Centre, Occasional Monographs No. 3, 1990, pp.15-24.
——. *Cambridge in the age of the Enlightenment. Science, religion and politics from the Restoration to the French Revolution*, Cambridge: Cambridge University Press, 1989.
——. 'The Wisdom of the Egyptians and the secularisation of history in the age of Newton' in S. Gaukroger (ed.), *The uses of antiquity. The Scientific Revolution and the classical tradition*, Dordrecht: Kluwer, 1991, pp. 171-212.
——. 'The scientist as patron and patriotic symbol: the changing reputation of Sir Joseph Banks', in M. Shortland and R. Yeo (eds.) *Telling lives: studies of scientific biography*, Cambridge: Cambridge University Press (forthcoming).
Gay, P. *The Enlightenment. An interpretation*, Wildwood House, 2 vols., 1970.
Gazley, J.F. *Life of Arthur Young, 1741-1820*, Philadelphia: American Philosophical Society, 1973.
Gillespie, N.C. 'Natural history, natural theology, and social order: John Ray and the "Newtonian ideology"', *Journal of the History of Biology*, 20 (1987), 1-50.
Glass, Dr. 'Letter to William Marsden, Esq. on the affinity of certain words in the language of the Sandwich and Friendly Isles in the Pacific Ocean, with the Hebrew', *Archaeologia*, 8 (1787), 81-4.
Golinski, J. *Science as public culture. Chemistry and Enlightenment in Britain, 1760-1820*, Cambridge: Cambridge University Press, 1992.
Goodfield Toulmin, J. 'Some aspects of English physiology: 1780-1840', *Journal of the History of Biology*, 2 (1969), 307-20.
Gordan, J.S. 'Reinhold and Georg Forster in England, 1766-1780', unpublished PhD thesis, Duke University, 1975.
Gorham, G.C. *Memoir of John Martyn and Thomas Martyn*, 1830.
Greene, J. 'The American debate on the Negro's place in nature, 1788-1815', *Journal of the History of Ideas*, 15 (1954), 384-96.
Gregory, G. 'An account of the caves of Cannara; in a letter from Hector Macneil, Esq. then at Bombay ...', *Archaeologia*, 8 (1787), 251-89.
[Gregory, O.] 'A review of some leading points in the official character and proceedings of the late President of the Royal Society', *London and Edinburgh Philosophical Magazine*, 56 (1820), 161-74, 241-57.
Griffiths, A. and Williams, R. *The Department of Prints and Drawings in the British Museum user's guide*, British Museum Publications, 1987.
Guilding, L. *An account of the botanic gardens in the island of St Vincent ...*, Glasgow, 1825.
Gunson, W. 'Co-operation without paradox: a reply to Dr Strauss', *Historical Studies Australia and New Zealand*, 2 (1965), 513-34.

Haddon, A.C. *History of anthropology*, Watts and Co., 1910.
Hahn, R. *Anatomy of a scientific institution. The Paris Academy of Sciences, 1666-1803*, Berkeley: University of California Press, 1971.
Hall, M.B. *All scientists now. The Royal Society in the nineteenth century*, Cambridge: Cambridge University Press, 1984.
Hallett, R. *The penetration of Africa: European enterprise and exploration principally in Northern and Western Africa up to 1830*, Vol. 1 to 1815, Routledge, 1965.
Hampson, N. *The Enlightenment*, Harmondsworth: Penguin, 1981.

Hankins, T.L. *Science and the Enlightenment*, Cambridge: Cambridge University Press, 1985.

Harlow, V. and Madden, F. (eds.) *British colonial developments 1774-1834*, Oxford: The Clarendon Press, 1953.

Harris, R.W. *Political ideas 1760-1792*, Gollancz, 1963.

Harrison, W. 'The Board of Agriculture, 1793-1822, with special reference to Sir John Sinclair', unpublished MA thesis, University of London, 1955.

Hatchett, C. 'A description of a process, by which corn tainted with must may be completely purified', *Philosophical Transactions*, 107 (1817), 36-7.

——. 'An analysis of the earthy substance from New South Wales, called *syneia*, or *Terra Australis* May 1798. Specimen supplied by Sir Joseph Banks', *Journal of Natural Philosophy, Chemistry and the Arts (Nicholson's)*, 2 (1799), 72-80.

——. 'On an artificial substance, which possesses the principal characteristic properties of tannin', *Philosophical Transactions of the Royal Society*, 95 (1805), 211-24, 285-315; 96 (1806), 109-46.

Hazard, P. *European thought in the eighteenth century*, Harmondsworth: Penguin, 1965.

——. *The European mind 1680-1715*, Cleveland: World Publications Co., 1969.

Heilbron, J. 'A mathematicians' mutiny with morals' to be published in a *Festschrift* for Thomas Kuhn (forthcoming).

Henrey, B. *British botanical and horticultural literature before 1800*, 3 vols., Oxford: Oxford University Press, 1975.

Herder, J.G. *Outlines of a philosophy of the history of man*, translated by T. Churchill, 1800.

Hill, F. *Georgian Lincoln*, Cambridge: Cambridge University Press, 1966.

Hill, J. *Fossils arranged according to their obvious characters*, 1771.

——. *The usefulness of a knowledge of plants . . .*, 1759.

Hingston-Fox, R. *Dr John Fothergill and his friends*, Macmillan, 1919.

Hoare, M.E. *The Resolution journal of Johann Reinhold Forster 1772-75*, 4 vols., Hakluyt Society, 1981.

——. *The tactless philosopher. Johann Reinhold Forster 1729-1798*, Melbourne: Hawthorn Press, 1976.

Hodgen, M.T. *Early anthropology in the sixteenth and seventeenth centuries*, Philadelphia: Pennsylvania University Press, 1964.

Hollman, A. 'The Chelsea Physic Garden', *Journal of the Royal College of Physicians*, 8 (1973), 87-94.

Holroyd, J.B. *Observations on the impolicy, abuses, false interpretation, and ruinous consequences of the poor law*, 2nd edn., 1818.

——. *Remarks on the bill of the last parliament for the amendment of the Poor Laws, with observations &c*, 1819.

——. *Remarks on the deficiency of grain . . .* 1801.

Holt-White, R. *The life and letters of Gilbert White*, 2 vols., J. Murray, 1901.

Home, H. *Sketches of the history of man*, 3 vols., Edinburgh, 1813.

——. *The gentleman farmer being an attempt to improve agriculture, by subjecting it to the test of rational principles*, Edinburgh, 1798.

——. *The Hunterian oration in honour of surgery*, 1822.

Hope, F.W. 'The autobiography of John C. Fabricius, translated from the Danish', *Transactions of the Entomological Society of London*, 4 (1845), i-xvi.

Horsley, S. *Sermons*, 3 vols., 1816.

Houghton, W.E. 'The English virtuoso in the seventeenth century', *Journal of the History of Ideas*, 3 (1942), 51-73, 190-219.

House of Commons, *Reports from Committees of the House of Commons 1715-1801 printed but not presented in the Journals of the House*, Vol. IX: *Corn, grain etc*, 1803.

Hudson, D. and Luckhurst, K.W. *The Royal Society of Arts 1754-1954*, 1954.

Hudson, K. *Patriotism with profit. British agricultural societies in the eighteenth and nineteenth centuries*, J. Murray, 1972.

Hunt, W.M. 'The role of Sir Joseph Banks, KB, PRS, in the promotion and development of Lincolnshire canals and navigations', unpublished PhD thesis, Open University, 1986.

Hunter, J. *Disputatio inauguralis . . . de hominum varietatibus*, Edinburgh, 1775.
Hunter, M. *Establishing the new science: the experience of the early Royal Society*, Woodbridge: Boydell Press, 1989.
——. *John Aubrey and the realm of learning*, Duckworth, 1975.
——. *Science and society in Restoration England*, Cambridge: Cambridge University Press, 1981.
——. 'The Royal Society and the origins of British archaeology', *Antiquity*, 65 (1971), 113-21, 187-92.

Jacob, M.C. *The cultural meaning of the Scientific Revolution*, New York: A.A. Knopf, 1988.
Jardine, W. 'Memoir of Sir Joseph Banks' in his *Naturalist's Library, Icthyology*, vol. 4, 1848, pp.17-48.
Jenkinson, C. *Speech . . . in the House of Lords . . . on the subject of the Catholic petition*, 1805.
——. *State of the country in the autumn of 1798*, 1798.
Jenkinson, R.B. *Speech of Lord Hawkesbury, in the House of Commons, Friday, 25 April, 1800*, 1800.
Jones, H.B. *The Royal Institution: its founder and its first professors*, 1871.
Jones, R. 'Images of natural man' in J. Bonnemains, *et al* (eds.), *Baudin in Australian waters*, Oxford: Oxford University Press, 1988, pp. 35-64.
Jones, W. *The religious use of botanical philosophy . . .* , 1784.
Jones, W.P. 'The vogue of natural history in England, 1750-1770', *Annals of Science*, 2 (1937), 345-52.

Kaeppler, A.L. *'Artificial curiosities'. An exposition of native manufactures collected on the three Pacific voyages of Captain James Cook RN*, Honolulu: Bishop Museum Press, 1978.
——. 'Tracing the history of Hawaiian Cook voyage artefacts in the Museum of Mankind' in T.C. Mitchell (ed.), *Captain Cook and the South Pacific*, British Museum Yearbook 3, 1979, pp.167-97.
Kalm, P. *Travels into North America*, translated by J.R. Forster, 2 vols., Warrington, 1770-1.
Kiernan, V.G. *The lords of humankind. European attitudes to the outside world in the imperial age*, Harmondsworth: Penguin, 1972.
Kippis, A. *A narrative of the voyages round the world performed by Captain James Cook*, 1883.
——. *Observations on the late contests in the Royal Society*, 1784.
Knight, D. *Ordering the world. A history of classifying man*, Burnett Books, 1981.
Knight, T.A. *A selection from the physiological and horticultural papers . . . to which is prefixed a sketch of his life*, 1841.

Labaree, L.W. *et al* (eds.) *The papers of Benjamin Franklin*, 26 vols. to date, New Haven: Yale University Press, 1959-.
Langford, P. *A polite and commercial people. England 1727-83*, Oxford: Clarendon Press, 1989.
——. *Public life and the propertied Englishman 1689-1798*, Oxford: Clarendon Press, 1991.
Lanyon-Orgill, P.A. *Captain Cook's South Sea Island vocabularies*, Byfleet, Surrey, privately published, 1979.
Lawrence, W. *Lectures on physiology, zoology, and the natural history of man delivered at the Royal College of Surgeons*, 1819.
Lee, J. *An introduction to botany extracted from the works of Dr Linnaeus*, 1794, 1810 (1st edn. 1760).
Lehmann, W.C. *Henry Home, Lord Kames, and the Scottish Enlightenment: a study in national character and in the history of ideas*, The Hague: Martinus Nijhoff, 1971.
Le Rougetel, H. 'Philip Miller/John Bartram botanical exchange', *Garden History*, 14 (1986), 32-9.
Lennard, R. 'English agriculture under Charles II: the evidence of the Royal Society Enquiries' *Economic History Review*, 4 (1932), 23-45.
Lettsom, John C. *Some account of the late John Fothergill*, 1783.
Levine, J.M. *Dr Woodward's shield. History, science, and satire in Augustan England*, Berkeley: California University Press, 1977.

——. *Humanism and history. Origins of modern English historiography*, Ithaca: Cornell University Press, 1987.

Levine, P. *The amateur and the professional. Antiquarians, historians and archaeologists in Victorian England*, Cambridge: Cambridge University Press, 1986.

Lightfoot, J. *A catalogue of the Portland Museum lately the property of the Duchess Dowager of Portland . . . which will be sold by auction*, [1786].

——. *Flora Scotica*, 1777.

Linnaeus, C. *A general system of nature, through the three grand kingdoms of animals, vegetables and minerals . . .* , 7 vols., 1802-6.

——. *Lachesis Lapponica: or, a tour in Lapland, now first published from the original manuscript journal of the celebrated Linnaeus*, 2 vols., 1811.

Lodge, E. *Portraits of illustrious personages of Great Britain*, 12 vols., 1835.

Long, E. *History of Jamaica . . .*, 3 vols., 1776.

Lonsdale, R. *Dr Charles Burney: a literary biography*, Oxford: Clarendon Press, 1965.

Lough, J. 'Reflections on "Enlightenment" and "Lumières"' in *L'età dei lumi. Studi storici sul settecento Europeo in Onore de Franco Venturi*, Vol. I, Napoli: Jovene, 1985, pp. 523-62.

Low, G. *Fauna Orcadensis*, W. Leach (ed.), 1813.

——. *Tour through Orkney and Shetland in 1776*, ed. by J. Anderson, Kirkwall, 1879.

Lyons, H. *The Royal Society 1660-1940. A history of its administration under its charters*, Cambridge: Cambridge University Press, 1944.

Lysaght, A.M. 'Banks's artists and his *Endeavour* collection' in T.C. Mitchell, (ed.), *Captain Cook and the South Pacific*, Canberra: Australian National University Press, 1979, pp.9-80.

——. 'Banksian reflections' in *The Journal of Joseph Banks in the Endeavour*, Guildford: Genesis Publications, 1980, pp. 13-28.

——. *Joseph Banks in Newfoundland and Labrador, 1766: His diary, manuscripts and collections*, Faber and Faber, 1971.

——. 'Some early letters from Joseph Banks to William Phelp Perrin', *Notes and Records of the Royal Society*, 29 (1974), 91-9.

——. 'Some eighteenth-century bird paintings in the library of Sir Joseph Banks (1743-1820)', *Bulletin of the British Museum (Natural History) (Historical Series)*, 1 (1959), 253-386.

MacGregor, A.G. and Turner, A.J. 'The Ashmolean Museum' in L. Sutherland and L. Mitchell (eds.), *The history of the University of Oxford. Vol. V: The eighteenth century*, Oxford: Clarendon Press, 1986, pp. 639-58.

Mackaness, G. *The life of Vice-Admiral William Bligh, RN, FRS*, Sydney: Angus and Robertson, 1951.

Mackay, D. *In the wake of Cook. Exploration, science and empire, 1780-1801*, Croom Helm, 1985.

Maddox, L. 'Gilbert White and the politics of natural history', *Eighteenth-century life*, 10 (1986), 45-57.

Maiden, J.H. *Sir Joseph Banks: The 'Father of Australia'*, Sydney: New South Wales Government Printer, 1909.

Mander Jones, P. 'History of the papers of Sir Joseph Banks', unpublished typescript, Mitchell Library (MS Ab 67-9/7), 1949 (with revisions in 1951 and 1953).

Marsden, E.W. *A brief memoir of the life and work of the late William Marsden by himself and edited by his widow, Mrs E.W. Marsden*, 1838.

Marsden, W. *A catalogue of dictionaries, vocabularies, grammars, and alphabets*, 1796.

——. *A dictionary of the Malayan language . . .*, 1812.

——. *Bibliotheca Marsdeniana philologica et orientalis . . .*, 1827.

——. *Miscellaneous works*, 1834.

——. *Numismata orientalia illustrata . . .*, 2 vols., 1823-5.

——. 'Observations on the language of Siwah in a letter to the Right Hon. Sir Joseph Banks' in *The Journal of Friederick Hornemann's Travels*, 1802, pp. 189-92.

——. 'Observations on the language of the people commonly called gypsies', *Archaeologia*, 7 (1785), 382-6.

——. 'Remarks on the Sumatran languages', *Archaeologia*, 6 (1782), 154-8.

——. *The history of Sumatra*, 1811, 3rd ed.

Marshall, J.B. 'Daniel Carl Solander, friend, librarian and assistant to Sir Joseph Banks', *Archives of Natural History*, 11 (1984), 451-6.

Marshall, P. and Williams, G. *The great map of mankind. British perceptions of the world in the age of Enlightenment*, Cambridge, Mass.: Harvard University Press, 1982.

Martin, T. 'Origins of the Royal Institution', *British Journal for the History of Science*, 1 (1962), 49-63.

Martyn, T. *Elements of natural history*, 1775.

——. *Heads of a course of lectures in botany, read at Cambridge*, 1764.

——. *Plantae Cantabrigienses . . .*, 1773.

Matthews, W. 'The Lincolnshire dialect in the eighteenth century', *Notes and Queries*, 169 (1935), 398-404.

Maugel, F-C. 'Une société de culture en Grande-Bretagne au XVIIIᵉ siècle La Société des Dilettanti (1734-1800)' *Revue historique*, 259 (1978), 389-414.

May, Henry F. *The Enlightenment in America*, New York: Oxford University Press, 1976.

McCormick, E.H. *Omai, Pacific envoy*, Auckland: Auckland University Press, 1977.

McCormmach, R. 'Henry Cavendish on the proper method of rectifying abuses' in E. Garber (ed.), *Beyond history of science. Essays in honor of Robert Schofield*, Bethlehem: Lehigh University Press, 1990, pp. 35-51.

McElroy, D.D. *Scotland's age of improvement. A survey of eighteenth-century literary clubs and societies*, Pullman, Washington: Washington State University Press, 1969.

McKendrick, N. 'Josiah Wedgwood and factory discipline', *Historical Journal*, 4 (1961), pp. 30-55.

McNeil, M. *Under the banner of science. Erasmus Darwin and his age*, Manchester: Manchester University Press, 1987.

Merrill, L. *The romance of Victorian natural history*, New York: Oxford University Press, 1989.

Miller, D.P. '"Into the valley of darkness": Reflections on the Royal Society in the eighteenth century', *History of Science*, 27 (1989), 155-66.

——. 'Between hostile camps: Sir Humphry Davy's Presidency of the Royal Society of London, 1820-1827', *British Journal for the History of Science*, 16 (1983), 1-47.

——. 'Method and the "micropolitics" of science: the early years of the Geological and Astronomical Societies of London' in J.A. Schuster and R. Yeo (eds.), *The Politics and rhetoric of scientific method. Historical Studies*, Dordrecht: Reidel, 1986, pp.227-58.

——. '"My favourite studdys": Lord Bute as naturalist' in K.W. Schweizer, (ed.), *Lord Bute: Essays in Reinterpretation*, Leicester: Leicester University Press, 1988, pp.213-39.

——. 'Sir Joseph Banks: An historiographical perspective', *History of Science*, 19 (1981), 284-92.

——. 'The revival of the physical sciences in Britain, 1815-50', *Osiris*, 2nd series, 2 (1986), 107-34.

——. 'The Royal Society of London 1800-1835: a study in the cultural politics of scientific organization', unpublished PhD thesis, University of Pennsylvania, 1981.

Misogallus, 'To Sir Joseph Banks, Bart., a letter dated 7 December 1802', *Cobbett's Annual Register*, 2 (1802), 743-5.

Mitchison, R. *Agricultural Sir John. The life of Sir John Sinclair of Ulbster 1754-1835*, Geoffrey Bles, 1962.

——. 'The old Board of Agriculture (1793-1822)', *English Historical Review*, 74 (1959), 41-69.

Montagu, J. *A voyage performed by the late Earl of Sandwich in the years 1728 and 1729*, 1799.

Moore, W. *The Gentlemen's Society at Spalding: Its origin and progress*, 1851.

Mudford, C.P. 'William Lawrence and the *Natural history of man*', *Journal of the History of Ideas*, 29 (1968), 430-6.

Mulvaney, D. 'The Australian aborigines 1606-1929: opinion and fieldwork, Part I: 1606-1859', *Historical Studies*, 8 (1958), 131-53.

Mylechreest, M. 'Thomas Andrew Knight and the founding of the Royal Horticultural Society', *Journal of the Garden History Society*, 12 (1984), 132-7.

[Mylne, R.] *Reports of the late Mr John Smeaton*, 1797.

Newbury, C.W. *The history of the Tahitian Mission 1799-1830 written by John Davies*, Cambridge University Press for the Hakluyt Society (2nd series, vol. 116), 1961.

Newcombe, C.F. and Forsyth, J. (eds.) *Menzies' Journal of Vancouver's Voyage, April to October, 1792* (British Columbia Archives Memoir 5), Victoria, B.C., 1923.

Nichols, J. *Illustrations of the literary history of the eighteenth century*, 8 vols., 1817-58.

———. *Literary anecdotes of the eighteenth century*, 9 vols., 1812-15.

Nicholson, W. 'Doubts concerning the existence of a new earth in the mineral from New South Wales examined by Wedgwood in the year 1790', *Journal of Natural Philosophy, Chemistry and the Arts (Nicholson's)*, 1 (1797), 404-11.

Norton, J.E. (ed.) *The letters of Edward Gibbon*, Cassell, 3 vols., 1945.

O'Brian, P. *Joseph Banks. A life*, Collins, Harvill, 1987.

O'Connor, R.D. *The weights and measures of England*, H.M.S.O., 1987.

Osbeck, P. *A voyage to China and the East Indies ...*, translated from the German by J.R. Forster, 2 vols., 1771.

Owen, D.M. (ed.) *The minute-books of the Spalding Gentlemen's Society 1712-1755*, Lincolnshire Records Society Publications, Vol. 73, Lincoln, 1981.

Palmer, J.F. *The works of John Hunter*, 4 vols., 1835.

Palmer, R.R. 'Turgot: paragon of the Continental Enlightenment', *Journal of Law and Economics*, 19 (1976), 607-19.

Parkinson, S. *A journal of a voyage on the South Seas, in His Majesty's ship, the Endeavour ...*, 1784.

Payne, H. *Philosophes and the people*, New Haven: Yale University Press, 1976.

Peacock, G. *Memoir of Dr Thomas Young*, 1855.

Pearson, G. 'Observations on some metallic arms and utensils; with some experiments to determine their composition', *Philosophical Transactions*, 86 (1796), 395-451.

Peirson, R. 'On the connection between botany and argriculture' in A. Hunter (ed.), *Georgical essays*, 2nd edn, 4 vols., 1773, pp.7-24

Pennant, T. 'An account of the turkey communicated by Joseph Banks' *Philosophical Transactions of the Royal Society of London*, 71 (1781), 67-81.

———. *Arctic zoology ...*, 3 vols., 1784-7.

———. *British zoology*, 4 vols., 1776 (4th edn.) (1st edn. 1766, Vol. I; 1768-70, Vols. II-IV.)

———. *Outlines of the Globe*, 4 vols., 1798.

———. *Synopsis of quadrupeds*, 1771.

———. *The literary life of the late Thomas Pennant, Esq. by himself*, 1793.

———. *Tour on the Continent 1765*, ed. by G.R. de Beer, Ray Society, 1948.

Perceval, S.G. 'Journal of an excursion to Eastbury and Bristol, etc. in May and June, 1767 by Sir Joseph Banks', *Proceedings of the Bristol Naturalists' Society*, n.s., 9 (1898), 6-37.

Phillipson, N. 'Culture and society in the eighteenth-century provinces: The case of Edinburgh and the Scottish Enlightenment' in L. Stone (ed.), *The University in Society*, Vol. 2, Princeton: Princeton University Press, 1974, pp. 407-48.

Piggott, S. *Ruins in a landscape. Essays in antiquarianism*, Edinburgh: Edinburgh University Press, 1976.

Pindar, P. *The poetical works*, 2 vols., 1833.

Pinkerton, J. *Literary correspondence*, 2 vols., 1830.

Plischke, H. 'Die malayische varietät Blumenbachs', *Zeitschrift für Rassenkunde*, 8 (1938), 225-31.

———. *Johann Friedrich Blumenbachs Einfluss auf der Entdeckungsreisenden seiner Zeit* (Abhandlungen der Gesellschaft der Wissenschaften zu Göttingen philologisch-historische Klasse, dritte Folge (Nr. 20), Göttingen, 1937.

Plumb, J.H. 'Reason and unreason in the eighteenth century: the English experience' in his *In the light of history*, Allen Lane, 1972, pp. 3-24.

——. 'The Grand Tour' in *Men and Places*, Cresset Press, 1963, pp.54–66.

Porter, R.S. *Doctor of society: Thomas Beddoes and the sick trade in late Enlightenment England*, Routledge for the Wellcome Institute series in the history of medicine, 1991.

——. 'Science, provincial culture and public opinion in Enlightenment England', *British Journal for Eighteenth-Century Studies*, 3 (1980), 20–46.

——. 'The enlightenment in England' in R.S. Porter and M. Teich (eds.), *The Enlightenment in national context*, Cambridge: Cambridge University Press, 1981, pp.1–18.

——. 'The exotic as erotic: Captain Cook at Tahiti' in G.S. Rousseau and R.Porter (eds.), *Exoticism in the Enlightenment*, Manchester: Manchester University Press, 1990, pp.117–144.

——. *The making of geology. Earth science in Britain 1660–1815*, Cambridge: Cambridge University Press, 1977.

Pownall, T. 'Description of the Carn Braich y Dinas . . .' *Archaeologia*, 3 (1774), 303–9.

——. 'Observations arising from an enquiry into the nature of the vases found on the Mosquito Shore in South America', *Archaeologia*, 5 (1779), 318–24.

Pulteney, R. *A general view of the writings of Linnaeus*, 1781.

——. *Historical and biographical sketches of the progress of botany in England*, 2 vols., 1790.

Raffles, T.S. *The history of Java*, 2 vols., Kuala Lumpur: Oxford University Press, 1978.

Ragatz, L.J. *The fall of the planter class in the British Caribbean 1763-1833*, New York: Octagon Books, 1971.

Raistrick, A. *The Hatchett diary*, Truro: D. Bradford, Barton, 1967.

Randall, J.H. *The making of the modern mind. A survey of the intellectual background of the present age*, Cambridge, Mass.: Harvard University Press, 1940.

Rauschenberg, R.A. 'A letter of Sir Joseph Banks describing the life of Daniel Solander', *Isis*, 55 (1964), 62–7.

——. 'Daniel Carl Solander, naturalist on the *Endeavour*', *Transactions of the American Philosophical Society*, n.s., 58 (1968), 1–66.

——. 'John Ellis, FRS: eighteenth-century naturalist and royal agent to West Florida' *Notes and Records of the Royal Society*, 32 (1978), 149–64.

——. 'The journals of Joseph Banks's voyage up Great Britain's West Coast to Iceland and to the Orkney Isles July to October, 1772', *Proceedings of the American Philosophical Society*, 117 (1973), 186–226.

Raven, C. *John Ray, naturalist*, Cambridge: Cambridge University Press, 1950.

Redlich, F. 'Science and charity: Count Rumford and his followers', *International Review of Social History*, 16 (1971), 184–216.

Riddelsdell, H.J. 'Journal of a botanical excursion to Wales', *Journal of Botany*, 43 (1978), 290–307.

Roderick, C. 'Sir Joseph Banks, Queen Oberea and the satirists' in W. Veit (ed.), *Captain James Cook: image and impact*, Vol. II, Melbourne: Hawthorn Press, 1972, pp.67–89.

Rolfe, W.D. 'William and John Hunter: breaking the Great Chain of Being' in W.F. Bynum and R. Porter (eds.), *William Hunter and the eighteenth-century medical world*, Cambridge: Cambridge University Press, 1985, pp.297–322.

Ross, I.S. *Lord Kames and the Scotland of his day*, Oxford: Clarendon Press, 1972.

Rudwick, M.J.S. 'The foundation of the Geological Society of London: its scheme for co-operative research and its struggle for independence', *British Journal for the History of Science*, 4 (1963), 325–55.

Rumford, B. *The complete works of Count Rumford*, 4 vols., Boston, 1870.

Russell, C. *Science and social change 1700-1900*, Macmillan, 1983.

Rutherford, H. 'Sir Joseph Banks and the exploration of Africa, 1788-1820', unpublished PhD thesis, University of California at Berkeley, 1952.

Ryden, S. *The Banks collection. An episode in eighteenth-century Anglo-Swedish relations*, Stockholm Almquisst and Wiksell, 1963.

Saine, Thomas P. *Georg Forster*, New York: Twayne Publishers, 1972.

Saunders, J. *The history of the County of Lincolnshire*, 2 vols., 1833.

Savage, S. *Catalogue of the manuscripts in the library of the Linnean Society of London*, Part IV: *Calendar of the Ellis Manuscripts*, Linnean Society, 1948.

Schneer, C. 'The rise of historical geology in the seventeenth century', *Isis*, 45 (1954), 256–68.

Schofield, R.E. *The Lunar Society of Birmingham*, Oxford: Clarendon Press, 1963.

Schuyler, R.L. *The fall of the old colonial system. A study in British free trade 1770–1870*, New York: Oxford University Press, 1945.

Seymour, W.A. (ed.) *A history of the Ordnance Survey*, Folkestone: Dawson, 1980.

Shackleton, R. *Montesquieu. A critical biography*, Oxford: Oxford University Press, 1961.

Shapin, S. '"A scholar and a gentleman": The problematic identity of the scientific practitioner in Early Modern England', *History of Science*, 29 (1991), 279–327.

Shapiro, B. 'History and natural history in sixteenth- and seventeenth-century England: An essay on the relationship between humanism and science' in *English scientific virtuosi in the sixteenth and seventeenth centuries*, Los Angeles: University of California Press, 1979, pp. 3–55.

Shaw, G. *Zoological lectures delivered at the Royal Institution in the years 1806 and 1807*, 2 vols., 1809.

Shawcross, W. 'The Cambridge University collection of Maori artefacts, made on Captain Cook's first voyage', *Journal of the Polynesian Society*, 17 (1970), 305–48.

Sherborn, C.D. 'The earliest known geological section across England', *Naturalist*, 29 (1928–9), 393–4.

Sim, K. *Desert traveller. The life of Jean Louis Burckhardt*, Gollancz, 1969.

Sinclair, J. *A plan for establishing a Board of Agriculture and Internal Improvement*, 1793.

——. *Account of the origin of the Board of Agriculture, and its progress for three years after its establishment*, 1796.

——. *Address to the Board of Agriculture stating the progress that has been made by the Board, during the fourth session since its establishment*, [1797].

——. *Essays on miscellaneous subjects*, 1802.

——. *Memoirs of the life and works of the late Right Honourable Sir John Sinclair*, 2 vols., 1837.

——. *Observations on the nature and advantages of spring or summer wheat*, [1805?].

——. 'Preliminary observations on the origin of the Board of Agriculture', *Communications to the Board of Agriculture*, 1 (1797), i–xv.

——. *The correspondence of the Right Honourable Sir John Sinclair*, 2 vols., 1831.

Slotkin, J.S. *Readings in early anthropology*, Methuen, 1965.

Smith, B. *European vision and the South Pacific*, Sydney: Harper and Row, 1985.

Smith, C. '"Mechanical philosophy" and the emergence of physics in Britain: 1800–50', *Annals of Science*, 33 (1976), 21–9.

Smith, E. *The life of Sir Joseph Banks, President of the Royal Society with some notices of his friends and contemporaries*, Bodley Head, 1911.

Smith, J.E. *A review of the modern state of botany . . .*, 1817.

——. *A selection from the correspondence of Linnaeus and other naturalists*, 2 vols., 1821.

Smith, J.E. and Sowerby, J. *English botany*, 16 vols., 1790–1803.

Smith, J.T. *A book for a rainy day: or, recollections of the events of the last sixty-six years*, Methuen, 1905.

Smith, P. *Memoir and correspondence of the late Sir James Edward Smith*, 2 vols., 1832.

Smith, S.S. *An essay on the causes of the variety of complexion and figure in the human species. To which are added, strictures on Lord Kames's Discourse on the original diversity of mankind*, Edinburgh, 1788.

Snip, Simon *The philosophical puppet show . . .*, [1785].

Sotheby's, *[Sale of] English literature and history . . .*, 14–5 Dec., 1992.

Spadafora, D.L. *The idea of progress in eighteenth-century Britain*, New Haven: Yale University Press, 1990.

Spiers, C.H. 'Sir Humphry Davy and the leather industry' *Annals of Science*, 24 (1968), 99–113.

——. 'William Thomas Brande, leather expert', *Annals of Science*, 25 (1969), 179–201.

Sprigge, T.L.S. *The correspondence of Jeremy Bentham*, Athlone Press, Vol. 2, 1968.

Stafleu, F.A. *Linnaeus and the Linnaeans. The spreading of their ideas in systematic botany, 1735-1789*, Utrecht: Oosthoek, 1971.

Staunton, G.L. *An historical account of the embassy to the Emperor of China*, 1797.

Stearn, W.T. 'Introduction to Carl Linnaeus', *Species plantarum. A facsimile of the first edition* 1753, 1957-9.

Stephen, L. *History of English thought in the eighteenth century*, 2 vols., Hart-Davis 1962.

Stephens, P.G. and George, M.D. *Catalogue of political and personal satires*, 11 vols., 1870-1954.

Stern, W.M. 'Control v. freedom in leather production from the early seventeenth to the early nineteenth century', *Guildhall Miscellany*, 2 (1968), 438-58.

Stieber, M.T. and Karg, A.L. 'Guide to the botanical records and papers in the archives of the Hunt Institute', *Huntia: A Journal of Botanical History*, 4 (1981), 1-89.

Stillingfleet, B. *Literary life and select works*, W. Coxe (ed.), 2 vols., 1811.

Stoever, D.H. *The life of Sir Charles Linnaeus . . .*, translated by Joseph Trapp, 1794.

Stone, L. *The crisis of the aristocracy*, Oxford: Clarendon Press, 1971.

Strauss, W.P. 'Paradoxical co-operation: Sir Joseph Banks and the London Missionary Society', *Historical Studies Australia and New Zealand*, 2 (1965), 246-52.

Stuart, J. *Botanical tables . . .*, [1785?]

Suttor, G. *Memoirs historical and scientific of the Right Hon. Sir Joseph Banks*, Parramatta, 1855.

Thiselton-Dyer, W.T. 'Historical account of Kew to 1841', *Bulletin of Miscellaneous Information, Royal Botanic Gardens, Kew*, 60 (1891), 279-327.

Thomason, E. *Memoirs during half a century*, 2 vols., 1845.

Thompson, E.P. *The making of the English working class*, Harmondsworth: Penguin, 1977.

Thomson, T. *History of the Royal Society, from its institution to the end of the eighteenth century*, 1812.

Thornton, R.J. 'Sketch of the life and writings of the late James Lee' in J. Lee, *An introduction to the science of botany*, 4th edn., 1810, pp.v-xix.

Thunberg, C. *Travels in Europe, Africa and Asia performed between the years 1770 and 1779*, 3 vols., n.d.

Todd, A.C. *Beyond the blaze. A biography of Davies Gilbert*, Truro: D. Bradford Barton, 1967.

Tuckey, J.K. *Narrative of an expedition to explore the River Zaire . . .*, 1818.

Tuke, J.H. *A sketch of the life of John Fothergill*, n.d.

Urness, C. (ed.) *A naturalist in Russia. Letters from Peter Simon Pallas to Thomas Pennant*, Minneapolis: University of Minnesota Press, 1967.

Venturi, F. *Utopia and reform in the Enlightenment*, Cambridge: Cambridge University Press, 1971.

Voget, F.W. 'Progress, science, history and evolution in eighteenth- and nineteenth-century anthropology', *Journal of the History of the Behavioural Sciences*, 3 (1967), 132-55.

Wall, C., Cameron H.S., and Ashworth Underwood, E. *A history of the Worshipful Society of Apothecaries of London*, Vol. 1, 1617-1815, Oxford University Press for the Wellcome Medical Historical Museum, 1963.

Watson, R.S. *The history of the Literary and Philosophical Society of Newcastle-upon-Tyne (1793-1896)*, 1897.

Watson, W. 'An account of a treatise in Latin intitled *Caroli Linnaei . . . Species plantarum . . .*', *Gentleman's Magazine*, 24 (1754), 553-8.

Webster, C. 'The medical faculty and the physic garden' in L. Sutherland and L.G. Mitchell, (eds.), *The history of the University of Oxford*, Vol. V: *The eighteenth century*, Oxford: Clarendon Press, 1986, pp. 683-724.

Wedgwood, J. 'An attempt to make a thermometer for measuring the higher degrees of heat, from a red heat up to the strongest that vessels made of clay can support', *Philosophical Transactions of the Royal Society of London*, 72 (1783), 305-26.

——. 'On the analysis of a mineral substance from New South Wales. In a letter to Sir Joseph Banks', *Philosophical Transactions*, 80 (1791), 306–20.

Weindling, P.J. 'Geological controversy and its historiography: the prehistory of the Geological Society of London' in L.F. Jordanova and R. Porter (eds.), *Images of the earth. Essays in the history of environmental sciences*, Chalfont St Giles: British Society for the History of Science, 1979.

Weld, C.R. *A history of the Royal Society, with memoirs of the presidents*, 2 vols., 1848

West, H. 'The limits of enlightenment anthropology: Georg Forster and the Tahitians', *History of European Ideas*, 10 (1989), 147–60.

Whewell, W. *History of the inductive sciences*, 3 vols., 1837.

White, C. *An account of the regular gradation in man . . .*, 1799.

White, G. *The natural history and antiquities of Selborne*, Oxford: Oxford University Press, 1951.

Wilberforce, W. *A practical view . . .*, SCM 1958 edn.

Williams, G. 'Reactions on Cook's voyages' in I. and T. Donaldson (eds.), *Seeing the first Australians*, Sydney: George Allen and Unwin, 1985, pp. 35–50.

——. *The British search for the Northwest Passage in the eighteenth century*, Longman, 1962.

Willson E.J. *James Lee and the Vineyard Nursery*, Hammersmith Local History Group, 1961.

Wilson, R. 'Newspapers and industry: the export of wool controversy in the 1780s' in M. Harris and A. Lee (eds.), *The press in English society from the seventeenth to the nineteenth centuries*, Associated University Presses 1986, pp.80–104.

Withers, C.W.J. 'Improvement and Enlightenment: Agriculture and natural history in the work of the Rev Dr John Walker (1731–1803)' in P. Jones (ed.), *Philosophy and Science in the Scottish Enlightenment*, Edinburgh: Donald 1988, pp.102–16.

Wood, H.T. *A history of the Royal Society of Arts*, John Murray, 1913.

Wood, P. 'Science and the Aberdeen Enlightenment' in P. Jones (ed.), *Philosophy and Science in the Scottish Enlightenment*, Edinburgh: Donald, 1988, pp. 39–66.

Wood, P.B. 'The natural history of man in the Scottish Enlightenment' *History of Science*, 27 (1989), 89–123.

Wortham, J.D. *British Egyptology 1549–1906*, Newton Abbot: David and Charles, 1971.

Index

Printed in the United Kingdom
by Lightning Source UK Ltd.
130985UK00001BB/191-198/A